PHILIP'S

MODERN SCHOOL ATLAS

94TH EDITION

IN ASSOCIATION WITH
THE ROYAL GEOGRAPHICAL SOCIETY
WITH THE INSTITUTE OF BRITISH GEOGRAPHERS

Published in Great Britain in 2003
by Philip's,
a division of Octopus Publishing Group Limited,
2–4 Heron Quays, London E14 4JP

Cartography by Philip's

Ninety-fourth edition
Copyright © 2003 Philip's

ISBN 0–540–08088–8 Paperback edition
ISBN 0–540–08087–X Hardback edition

Printed in Hong Kong

Details of other Philip's titles and services
can be found on our website at:
www.philips-maps.co.uk

Philip's World Atlases are published in association with The Royal Geographical
Society (with The Institute of British Geographers).

The Society was founded in 1830 and given a Royal Charter in 1859 for
'the advancement of geographical science'. Today it is a leading world centre
for geographical learning – supporting education, teaching, research and
expeditions, and promoting public understanding of the subject.

Further information about the Society and how to join may be found on its
website at: **www.rgs.org**

PHOTOGRAPHIC ACKNOWLEDGEMENTS
All satellite images in the atlas are courtesy of NPA Group Ltd, Edenbridge, Kent,
with the exception of the following: p. 17 M-SAT Ltd/Science Photo Library;
p. 49 PLI/Science Photo Library; p. 134 NASA/GSFC.

SUBJECT LIST

MAP SYMBOLS

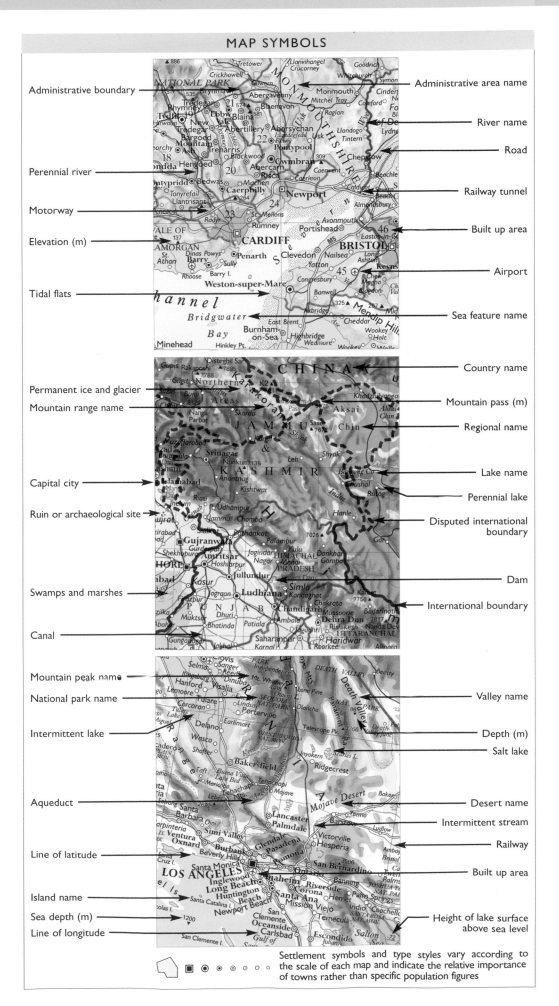

SCALE

The scale of a map is the relationship of the distance between two points shown on the map and the distance between the same two points on the Earth's surface. For instance, 1 inch on the map represents 1 mile on the ground, or 10 kilometres on the ground is represented by 1 centimetre on the map.

Instead of saying 1 centimetre represents 10 kilometres, we could say that 1 centimetre represents 1 000 000 centimetres on the map. If the scale is stated so that the same unit of measurement is used on both the map and the ground, then the proportion will hold for any unit of measurement. Therefore, the scale is usually written 1:1 000 000. This is called a 'representative fraction' and usually appears at the top of the map page, above the scale bar.

Calculations can easily be made in centimetres and kilometres by dividing the second figure in the representative fraction by 100 000 (i.e. by deleting the last five zeros). Thus at a scale of 1:5 000 000, 1 cm on the map represents 50 km on the ground. This is called a 'scale statement'. The calculation for inches and miles is more laborious, but 1 000 000 divided by 63 360 (the number of inches in a mile) shows that 1:1 000 000 can be stated as 1 inch on the map represents approximately 16 miles on the ground.

Many of the maps in this atlas feature a scale bar. This is a bar divided into the units of the map – miles and kilometres – so that a map distance can be measured with a ruler, dividers or a piece of paper, then placed along the scale bar, and the distance read off. To the left of the zero on the scale bar there are usually more divisions. By placing the ruler or dividers on the nearest rounded figure to the right of the zero, the smaller units can be counted off to the left.

The map extracts to the right show Los Angeles and its surrounding area at six different scales. The representative fraction, scale statement and scale bar are positioned above each map. Map 1 is at 1:27 000 and is the largest scale extract shown. Many of the individual buildings are identified and most of the streets are named, but at this scale only part of central Los Angeles can be shown within the given area. Map 2 is much smaller in scale at 1:250 000. Only a few important buildings and streets can be named, but the whole of central Los Angeles is shown. Maps 3, 4 and 5 show how greater areas can be depicted as the map scale decreases, down to Map 6 at 1:35 000 000. At this small scale, the entire Los Angeles conurbation is depicted by a single town symbol and a large part of the south-western USA and part of Mexico is shown.

The scales of maps must be used with care since large distances on small-scale maps can be represented by one or two centimetres. On certain projections scale is only correct along certain lines, parallels or meridians. As a general rule, the larger the map scale, the more accurate and reliable will be the distance measured.

LATITUDE AND LONGITUDE

Accurate positioning of individual points on the Earth's surface is made possible by reference to the geometric system of latitude and longitude.

Latitude is the distance of a point north or south of the Equator measured at an angle with the centre of the Earth, whereby the Equator is latitude 0 degrees,

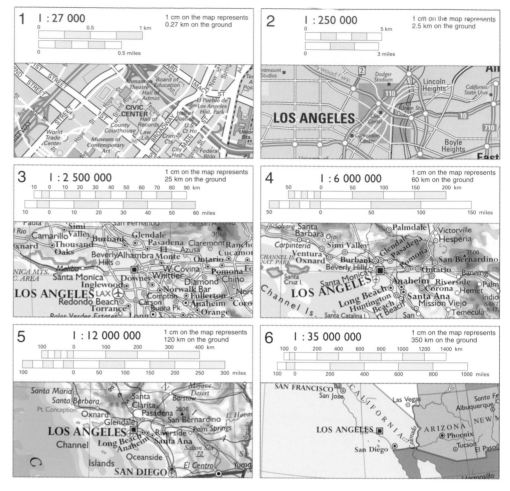

the North Pole is 90 degrees north and the South Pole 90 degrees south. Latitude parallels are drawn west–east around the Earth, parallel to the Equator, decreasing in diameter from the Equator until they become a point at the poles. On the maps in this atlas the lines of latitude are represented by blue lines running across the map in smooth curves, with the degree figures in blue at the sides of the maps. The degree interval depends on the scale of the map.

Lines of longitude are meridians drawn north–south, cutting the lines of latitude at right angles on the Earth's surface and intersecting with one another at the poles. Longitude is measured by an angle at the centre of the Earth from the prime meridian (0 degrees), which passes through Greenwich in London. It is given as a measurement east or west of the Greenwich Meridian from 0 to 180 degrees. The meridians are normally drawn north–south vertically down the map, with the degree figures

in blue in the top and bottom margins of the map.

In the index each place name is followed by its map page number, its letter-figure grid reference, and then its latitude and longitude. The unit of measurement is the degree, which is subdivided into 60 minutes. An index entry states the position of a place in degrees and minutes. The latitude is followed by N(orth) or S(outh) and the longitude E(ast) or W(est).

For example:

Helston, U.K.   27 G3   50 7N   5 17W
Helston is on map page 27, in grid square G3, and is 50 degrees 7 minutes north of the Equator and 5 degrees 17 minutes west of Greenwich.

McKinley, Mt., U.S.A.   108 B4   63 4N   151 0W
Mount McKinley is on map page 108, in grid square B4, and is 63 degrees 4 minutes north of the Equator and 151 degrees west of Greenwich.

How to locate a place or feature

The two diagrams (left) show how to estimate the required distance from the nearest line of latitude or longitude on the map page, in order to locate a place or feature listed in the index (such as Helston in the UK and Mount McKinley in the USA, as detailed in the above example).

In the left-hand diagram there are 30 minutes between the lines and so to find the position of Helston an estimate has to be made: 7 parts of the 30 degrees north of the 50 0N latitude line, and 17 parts of the 30 degrees west of the 5 0W longitude line.

In the right-hand diagram it is more difficult to estimate because there is an interval of 10 degrees between the lines. In the example of Mount McKinley, the reader has to estimate 3 degrees 4 minutes north of 60 0N and 1 degree west of 150 0W.

MAP PROJECTIONS

A map projection is the systematic depiction of the imaginary grid of lines of latitude and longitude from a globe on to a flat surface. The grid of lines is called the 'graticule' and it can be constructed either by graphical means or by mathematical formulae to form the basis of a map. As a globe is three dimensional, it is not possible to depict its surface on a flat map without some form of distortion. Preservation of one of the basic properties listed below can only be secured at the expense of the others and thus the choice of projection is often a compromise solution.

Correct area

In these projections the areas from the globe are to scale on the map. This is particularly useful in the mapping of densities and distributions. Projections with this property are termed 'equal area', 'equivalent' or 'homolographic'.

Correct distance

In these projections the scale is correct along the meridians, or, in the case of the 'azimuthal equidistant', scale is true along any line drawn from the centre of the projection. They are called 'equidistant'.

Correct shape

This property can only be true within small areas as it is achieved only by having a uniform scale distortion along both the 'x' and 'y' axes of the projection. The projections are called 'conformal' or 'orthomorphic'.

Map projections can be divided into three broad categories – **'azimuthal'**, **'conic'** and **'cylindrical'**. Cartographers use different projections from these categories depending on the map scale, the size of the area to be mapped, and what they want the map to show.

AZIMUTHAL OR ZENITHAL PROJECTIONS

These are constructed by the projection of part of the graticule from the globe on to a plane tangential to any single point on it. This plane may be tangential to the equator (equatorial case), the poles (polar case) or any other point (oblique case). Any straight line drawn from the point at which the plane touches the globe is the shortest distance from that point and is known as a 'great circle'. In its 'gnomonic' construction any straight line on the map is a great circle, but there is great exaggeration towards the edges and this reduces its general uses. There are five different ways of transferring the graticule on to the plane and these are shown below. The diagrams below also show how the graticules vary, using the polar case as the example.

| Equidistant | Equal Area | Orthographic | Gnomonic | Stereographic (conformal) |

Polar case

The polar case is the simplest to construct and the diagram on the right shows the differing effects of all five methods of construction, comparing their coverage, distortion, etc, using North America as the example.

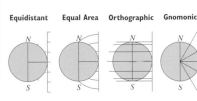

Equidistant
Equal Area
Stereographic
Gnomonic
Orthographic

Oblique case

The plane touches the globe at any point between the Equator and poles. The oblique orthographic uses the distortion in azimuthal projections away from the centre to give a graphic depiction of the Earth as seen from any desired point in space.

Equatorial case

The example shown here is Lambert's Equivalent Azimuthal. It is the only projection which is both equal area and where bearing is true from the centre.

CONICAL PROJECTIONS

These use the projection of the graticule from the globe on to a cone which is tangential to a line of latitude (termed the 'standard parallel'). This line is always an arc and scale is always true along it. Because of its method of construction, it is used mainly for depicting the temperate latitudes around the standard parallel, i.e. where there is least distortion. To reduce the distortion and include a larger range of latitudes, the projection may be constructed with the cone bisecting the surface of the globe so that there are two standard parallels, each of which is true to scale. The distortion is thus spread more evenly between the two chosen parallels.

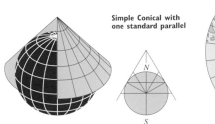

Simple Conical with one standard parallel

Bonne

This is a modification of the simple conic, whereby the true scale along the meridians is sacrificed to enable the accurate representation of areas. However, scale is true along each parallel but shapes are distorted at the edges.

Albers Conical Equal Area

This projection uses two standard parallels. The selection of these relative to the land area to be mapped is very important. It is equal area and is especially useful for large land masses oriented east–west, such as the USA.

CYLINDRICAL AND OTHER WORLD PROJECTIONS

This group of projections are those which permit the whole of the Earth's surface to be depicted on one map. They are a very large group of projections and the following are only a few of them. Cylindrical projections are constructed by the projection of the graticule from the globe on to a cylinder tangential to the globe. Although cylindrical projections can depict all the main land masses, there is considerable distortion of shape and area towards the poles. One cylindrical projection, Mercator, overcomes this shortcoming by possessing the unique navigational property that any straight line drawn on it is a line of constant bearing ('loxodrome'). It is used for maps and charts between 15° either side of the Equator. Beyond this, enlargement of area is a serious drawback, although it is used for navigational charts at all latitudes.

Simple Cylindrical

Cylindrical with two standard parallels

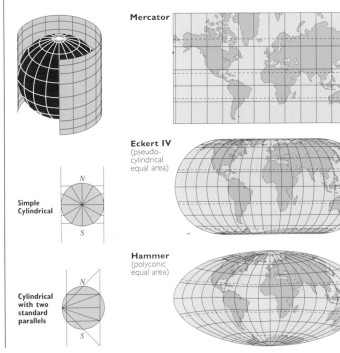

Mercator

Eckert IV (pseudo-cylindrical equal area)

Hammer (polyconic equal area)

The first satellite to monitor our environment systematically was launched as long ago as April 1961. It was called TIROS-1 and was designed specifically to record atmospheric change. The first of the generation of Earth resources satellites was Landsat-1, launched in July 1972.

The succeeding decades have seen a revolution in our ability to survey and map our global environment. Digital sensors mounted on satellites now scan vast areas of the Earth's surface day and night. They collect and relay back to Earth huge volumes of geographical data which is processed and stored by computers.

Satellite imagery and remote sensing

Continuous development and refinement, and freedom from national access restrictions, have meant that sensors on these satellite platforms are increasingly replacing surface and airborne data-gathering techniques. Twenty-four hours a day, satellites are scanning and measuring the Earth's surface and atmosphere, adding to an ever-expanding range of geographic and geophysical data available to help us identify and manage the problems of our human and physical environments. Remote sensing is the science of extracting information from such images.

Satellite orbits

Most Earth-observation satellites (such as the Landsat, SPOT and IRS series) are in a near-polar, Sun-synchronous orbit (*see diagram opposite*). At altitudes of around 700–900 km the satellites revolve around the Earth approximately every 100 minutes and on each orbit cross a particular line of latitude at the same local (solar) time. This ensures that the satellite can obtain coverage of most of the globe, replicating the coverage typically within 2–3 weeks. In more recent satellites, sensors can be pointed sideways from the orbital path, and 'revisit' times with high-resolution frames can thus be reduced to a few days.

Exceptions to these Sun-synchronous orbits include the geostationary meteorological satellites, such as Meteosat. These have a 36,000 km high orbit and rotate around the Earth every 24 hours, thus remaining above the same point on the Equator.

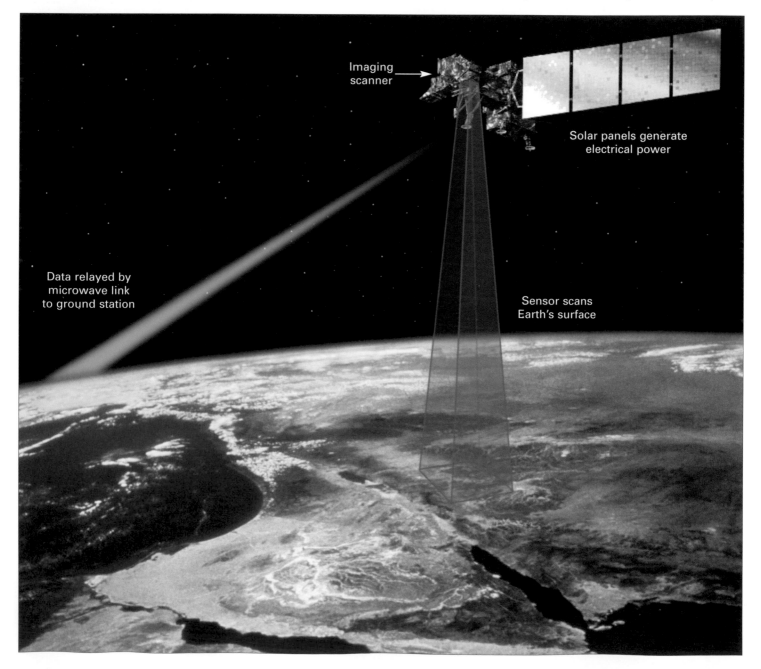

Imaging scanner

Solar panels generate electrical power

Data relayed by microwave link to ground station

Sensor scans Earth's surface

Landsat-7
This is the latest addition to the Landsat Earth-observation satellite programme, orbiting at 705 km above the Earth. With onboard recorders, the satellite can store data until it passes within range of a ground station. Basic geometric and radiometric corrections are then applied before distribution of the imagery to users.

These satellites acquire frequent images showing cloud and atmospheric moisture movements for almost a full hemisphere.

In addition, there is the Global Positioning System (GPS) satellite 'constellation', which orbits at a height of 20,200 km, consisting of 24 satellites. These circle the Earth in six different orbital planes, enabling us to fix our position on the Earth's surface to an accuracy of a few centimetres. Although developed for military use, this system is now available to individuals through hand-held receivers and in-car navigation systems. The other principal commercial uses are for surveying and air and sea navigation.

Digital sensors
Early satellite designs involved images being exposed to photographic film and returned to Earth by capsule for processing, a technique still sometimes used today. However, even the first commercial satellite imagery, from Landsat-1, used digital imaging sensors and transmitted the data back to ground stations (*see diagram opposite*).

Passive, or optical, sensors record the radiation reflected from the Earth for specific wavebands. Active sensors transmit their own microwave radiation, which is reflected from the Earth's surface back to the satellite and recorded. The SAR (Synthetic Aperture Radar) Radarsat images on page 15 are examples of the latter.

Whichever scanning method is used, each satellite records image data of constant width but potentially several thousand kilometres in length. Once the data has been received on Earth, it is usually split into approximately square sections or 'scenes' for distribution.

Spectral resolution, wavebands and false-colour composites
Satellites can record data from many sections of the electromagnetic spectrum (wavebands) simultaneously. Since we can only see images made from the three primary colours (red, green and blue), a selection of any three wavebands needs to be made in order to form a picture that will enable visual interpretation of the scene to be made. When any combination other than the visible bands are used, such as near or middle infrared, the resulting image is termed a 'false-colour composite'. An example of this is shown on page 8.

The selection of these wavebands depends on the purpose of the final image – geology, hydrology, agronomy and environmental requirements each have their own optimum waveband combinations.

GEOGRAPHIC INFORMATION SYSTEMS

A Geographic Information System (GIS) enables any available geospatial data to be compiled, presented and analysed using specialized computer software.

Many aspects of our lives now benefit from the use of GIS – from the management and maintenance of the networks of pipelines and cables that supply our homes, to the exploitation or protection of the natural resources that we use. Much of this is at a regional or national scale and the data collected from satellites form an important part of our interpretation and understanding of the world around us.

GIS systems are used for many aspects of central planning and modern life, such as defence, land use, reclamation, telecommunications and the deployment of emergency services. Commercial companies can use demographic and infrastructure data within a GIS to plan marketing strategies, identifying where their services would be most needed, and thus decide where best to locate their businesses. Insurance companies use GIS to determine premiums based on population distribution, crime figures and the likelihood of natural disasters, such as flooding or subsidence.

Whatever the application, all the geographically related information that is available can be input and prepared in a GIS, so that a user can display the specific information of interest, or combine data to produce further information which might answer or help resolve a specific problem. From analysis of the data that has been acquired, it is often possible to use a GIS to generate a 'model' of possible future situations and to see what impact might result from decisions and actions taken. A GIS can also monitor change over time, to aid the observation and interpretation of long-term change.

A GIS can utilize a satellite image to extract useful information and map large areas, which would otherwise take many man-years of labour to achieve on the ground. For industrial applications, including hydrocarbon and mineral exploration, forestry, agriculture, environmental monitoring and urban development, such dramatic and beneficial increases in efficiency have made it possible to evaluate and undertake projects and studies in parts of the world that were previously considered inaccessible, and on a scale that would not have been possible before.

SELECTED REMOTE SENSING SATELLITES			
Year Launched	Satellite	Country	Pixel Size (Resolution)
Passive Sensors (Optical)			
1972	Landsat-1 MSS	USA	80 m
1975	Landsat-2 MSS	USA	80 m
1978	Landsat-3 MSS	USA	80 m
1978	NOAA AVHRR	USA	1.1 km
1981	Cosmos TK-350	Russia	10 m
1982	Landsat-4 TM	USA	30 m
1984	Landsat-5 TM	USA	30 m
1986	SPOT-1	France	10 / 20 m
1988	IRS-1A	India	36 / 72 m
1988	SPOT-2	France	10 / 20 m
1989	Cosmos KVR-1000	Russia	2 m
1991	IRS-1B	India	36 / 72 m
1992	SPOT-3	France	10 / 20 m
1995	IRS-1C	India	5.8 / 23.5 m
1997	IRS-1D	India	5.8 / 23.5 m
1998	SPOT-4	France	10 / 20 m
1999	Landsat-7 ETM	USA	15 / 30 m
1999	UoSAT-12	UK	10 / 32 m
1999	IKONOS-2	USA	1.0 / 4 m
1999	ASTER	USA	15 m
2000	Hyperion	USA	30 m
2000	EROS-A1	International	1.8 m
2001	Quickbird	USA	0.61 / 2.4 m
2002	SPOT-5	France	2.5 / 5 / 10 m
Active Sensors (Synthetic Aperture Radar)			
1991	ERS-1	Europe	25 m
1992	JERS-1	Japan	18 m
1995	ERS-2	Europe	25 m
1995	Radarsat	Canada	8–100 m
2002	ENVISAT	Europe	25 m

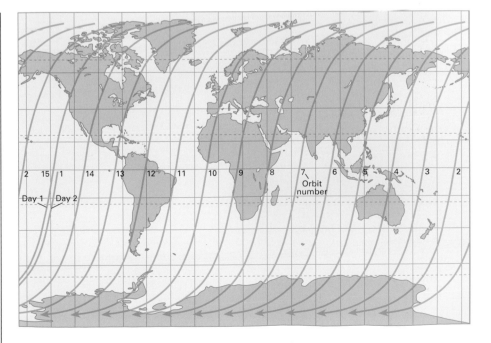

Satellite orbits
Landsat-7 makes over 14 orbits per day in its Sun-synchronous orbit. During the full 16 days of a repeat cycle, coverage of the areas between those shown is achieved.

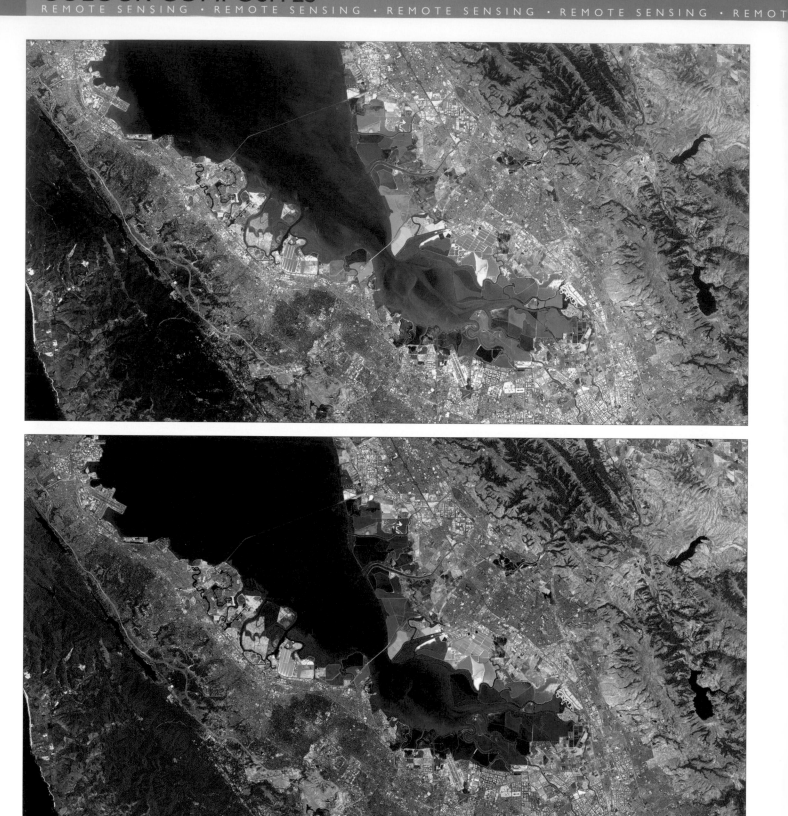

Natural-colour and false-colour composites
These images show the salt ponds at the southern end of San Francisco Bay, which now form the San Francisco Bay National Wildlife Refuge. They demonstrate the difference between 'natural colour' (*top*) and 'false colour' (*bottom*) composites.

The top image is made from visible red, green and blue wavelengths. The colours correspond closely to those one would observe from an aircraft. The salt ponds appear green or orange-red due to the colour of the sediments they contain. The urban areas appear grey and vegetation is either dark green (trees) or light brown (dry grass).

The bottom image is made up of near-infrared, visible red and visible green wavelengths. These wavebands are represented here in red, green and blue, respectively. Since chlorophyll in healthy vegetation strongly reflects near-infrared light, this is clearly visible as red in the image.

False-colour composite imagery is therefore very sensitive to the presence of healthy vegetation. The bottom image thus shows better discrimination between the 'leafy' residential urban areas, such as Palo Alto (south-west of the Bay) from other urban areas by the 'redness' of the trees. The high chlorophyll content of watered urban grass areas shows as bright red, contrasting with the dark red of trees and the brown of natural, dry grass. *(EROS)*

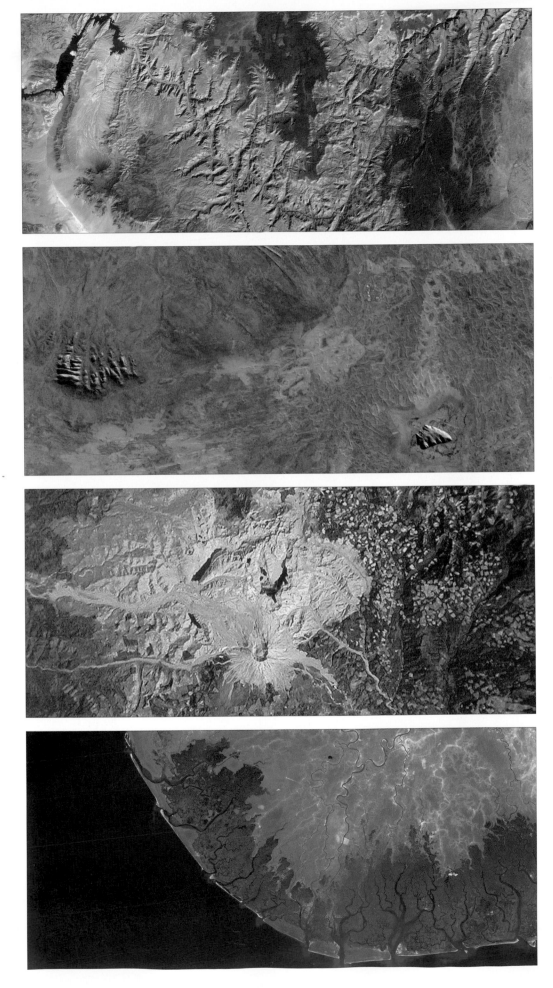

Western Grand Canyon, Arizona, USA
This false-colour image shows in bright red the sparse vegetation on the limestone plateau, including sage, mesquite and grasses. Imagery such as this is used to monitor this and similar fragile environments. The sediment-laden river, shown as blue-green, can be seen dispersing into Lake Mead to the north-west. Side canyons cross the main canyon in straight lines, showing where erosion along weakened fault lines has occurred. *(EROS)*

Ayers Rock and Mt Olga, Northern Territory, Australia
These two huge outliers are the remnants of Precambrian mountain ranges created some 500 million years ago and then eroded away. Ayers Rock (*seen at right*) rises 345 m above the surrounding land and has been a part of Aboriginal life for over 10,000 years. Their dramatic coloration, caused by oxidized iron in the sandstone, attracts visitors from around the world. *(EROS)*

Mount St Helens, Washington, USA
A massive volcanic eruption on 18 May 1980 killed 60 people and devastated around 400 sq km of forest within minutes. The blast reduced the mountain peak by 400 m to its current height of 2,550 m, and volcanic ash rose some 25 km into the atmosphere. The image shows Mount St Helens eight years after the eruption in 1988. The characteristic volcanic cone has collapsed in the north, resulting in the devastating 'liquid' flow of mud and rock. *(EROS)*

Niger Delta, West Africa
The River Niger is the third longest river in Africa after the Nile and Congo. Deltas are by nature constantly evolving sedimentary features and often contain many ecosystems within them. In the case of the Niger Delta, there are also vast hydrocarbon reserves beneath it with associated wells and pipelines. Satellite imagery helps to plan activity and monitor this fragile and changing environment. *(EROS)*

Europe at night

This image was derived as part of the Defense Meteorological Satellite Program. The sensor recorded all the emissions of near-infrared radiation at night, mainly the lights from cities, towns and villages. Note also the 'lights' in the North Sea from the flares of the oil production platforms. This project was the first systematic attempt to record human settlement on a global scale using remote sensing. *(NOAA)*

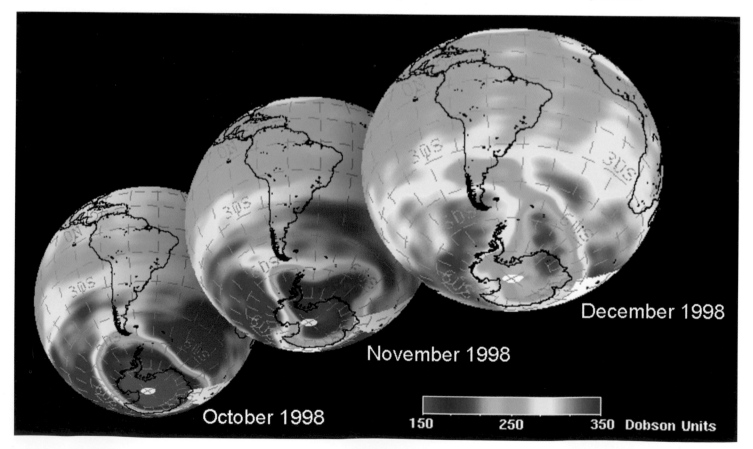

December 1998

November 1998

October 1998

150   250   350 Dobson Units

Ozone distribution

The Global Ozone Monitoring Experiment (GOME) sensor was launched in April 1995. This instrument can measure a range of atmospheric trace constituents, in particular global ozone distributions. Environmental and public health authorities need this up-to-date information to alert people to health risks. Low ozone levels result in increased UV-B radiation, which is harmful and can cause cancers, cataracts and impact the human immune system. 'Dobson Units' indicate the level of ozone depletion (normal levels are around 280DU). *(DLR)*

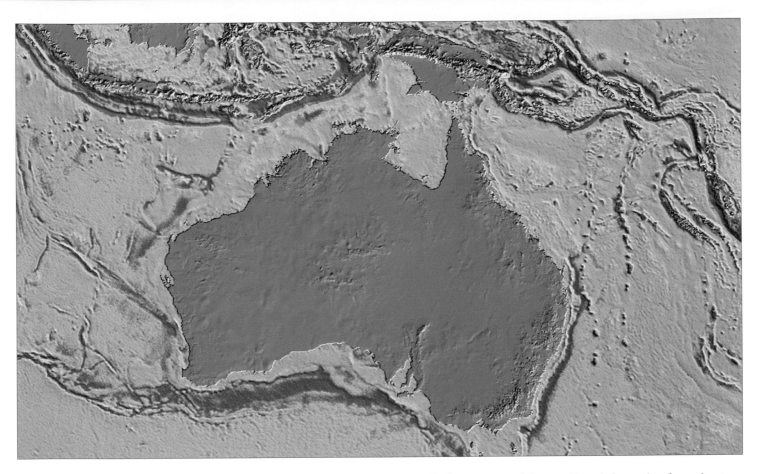

Gravitational fields

The strength of the Earth's gravitational field at its surface varies according to the ocean depth and the density of local rocks. This causes local variations in the sea level. Satellites orbiting in precisely determined orbits are able to measure the sea level to an accuracy of a few centimetres. These variations give us a better understanding of the geological structure of the sea floor. Information from these sensors can also be used to determine ocean wave heights, which relate to surface wind speed, and are therefore useful in meteorological forecasting. *(NPA)*

Weather monitoring

Geostationary and polar orbiting satellites monitor the Earth's cloud and atmospheric moisture movements, giving us an insight into the global workings of the atmosphere and permitting us to predict weather change. *(J-2)*

Hurricane Andrew

Although Hurricane Andrew, which hit Florida on 23 August 1992, was the most expensive natural disaster ever to strike the USA, its effects would have been even worse had its path not been tracked by images such as this from the AVHRR sensor. *(NOAA)*

Kuwait City, Kuwait

This image (*right*) shows Kuwait after the 1991 war with Iraq. During this conflict, more than 600 oil wells were set on fire and over 300 oil lakes were formed (visible as dark areas to the south). Satellite imagery helped reduce the costs of mapping these oil spills and enabled the level of damage to be determined prior to clean-up operations. (*Space Imaging*)

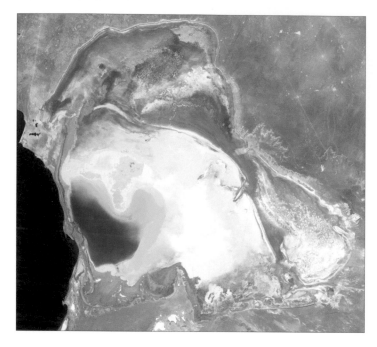

Kara-Bogaz-Gol, Turkmenistan

The Kara-Bogaz-Gol (*above and below*) is a large, shallow lagoon joined by a narrow, steep-sided strait to the Caspian Sea. Evaporation makes it one of the most saline bodies of water in the world. Believing the Caspian sea level was falling, the straight was dammed by the USSR in 1980 with the intention of conserving the water to sustain the salt industry. However, by 1983 it had dried up completely (*above*), leading to widespread wind-blown salt, soil poisoning and health problems downwind to the east. In 1992 the Turkmenistan government began to demolish the dam to re-establish the flow of water from the Caspian Sea (*below*). Satellite imagery has helped to monitor and map the Kara-Bogaz-Gol as it has fluctuated in size. (*EROS*)

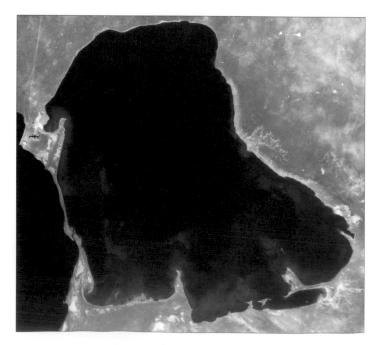

Lake Amadeus, Northern Territory, Australia

This saline lake system (*below*) is an important wetland environment at the heart of one of the most arid areas in Australia. It supports a wide range of complex habitats and exists due to seepage from the central groundwater system. Changes in its extent in an otherwise remote site can be monitored using satellite imagery such as this Landsat ETM scene. (*EROS*)

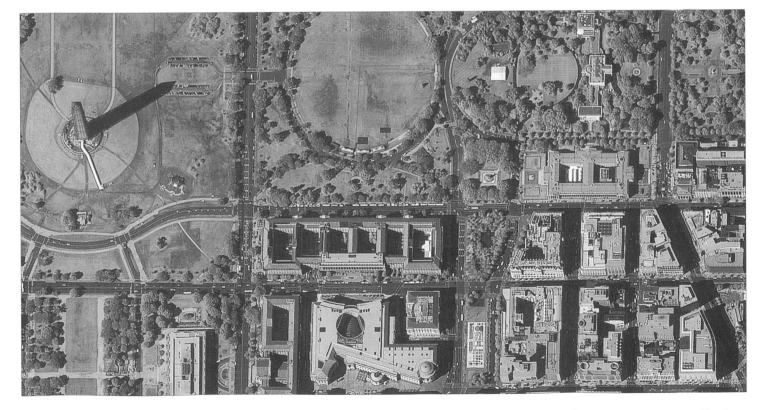

Gulf of Izmit, north-west Turkey
An earthquake measuring 7.4 on the Richter scale caused extensive damage and loss of life around Izmit on 17 August 1999. The image above is a composite of two black-and-white images, one recorded on 7 August 1999 and the other on 24 September 1999. The colours indicate change: orange highlights damaged buildings and areas where debris has been deposited during the rescue operation; blue indicates areas submerged beneath sea level as a result of the Earth's movement during the earthquake and fire-damaged oil tanks in the north-west. *(NPA)*

Washington, DC, USA
This image, with the White House seen at top right and the Washington Monument to the left, was recorded on 30 September 1999 by Space Imaging's IKONOS-2 satellite. It was the first satellite image to be commercially available with a ground-sampling interval (pixel size) of 1 m. With a directional sensor, image acquisition attempts can be made in as little as 1–3 days (cloud cover permitting). This level of resolution enables satellite imagery to be used as a data source for many applications that otherwise require expensive aerial surveys to be flown. In addition, data can be readily acquired for projects in remote regions of the world or areas where access is restricted. *(Space Imaging)*

Sichuan Basin, China

The north-east/south-west trending ridges in this image are anticlinal folds developed in the Earth's crust as a result of plate collision and compression. Geologists map these folds and the lowlands between them formed by synclinal folds, as they are often the areas where oil or gas are found in commercial quantities. The river shown in this image is the Yangtze, near Chongqing. *(China RSGS)*

North Anatolian Fault, Turkey

The east–west trending valley running through the centre of this image is formed by the North Anatolian wrench fault. It is the result of Arabia colliding with southern Eurasia, forcing most of Turkey westwards towards Greece. The valley was created by the Kelkit river removing the loosened rock formed by the two tectonic plates grinding together. This active fault has also caused considerable damage further east in the Gulf of Izmit *(see page 13)*. *(EROS)*

Wadi Hadhramaut, Yemen

Yemen is extremely arid – however, in the past it was more humid and wet, enabling large river systems to carve out the deep and spectacular gorges and dried-out river beds (*wadis*) seen in this image. The erosion has revealed many contrasting rock types. The image has been processed to exaggerate this effect, producing many shades of red, pink and purple, which make geological mapping easier and more cost-effective. *(EROS)*

Zagros Mountains, Iran

These mountains were formed as Arabia collided with Southern Eurasia. The upper half of this colour-enhanced image shows an anticline that runs east–west. The dark grey features are called *diapirs*, which are bodies of viscous rock salt that are very buoyant and sometimes rise to the surface, spilling and spreading out like a glacier. The presence of salt in the region is important as it stops oil escaping to the surface. *(EROS)*

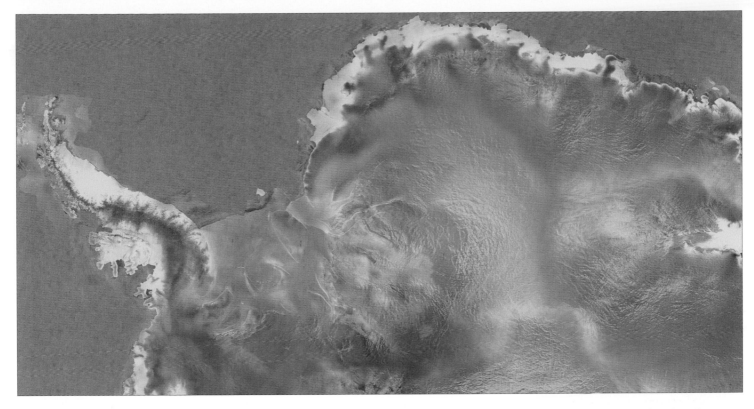

Antarctic Peninsula
Synthetic Aperture Radar (SAR) image brightness is dependent on surface texture. This image of part of Antarctica clearly shows the ice tongues projecting from the Wilkins and George VI Ice Shelves at the south-west end of the peninsula, as well as other coastal ice features. Images can be received, even during the winter 'night', and over a period of time form a valuable resource in our ability to monitor the recession of the ice. *(Radarsat)*

Montserrat, Caribbean Sea
SAR sensors send out a microwave signal and create an image from the radiation reflected back. The signal penetrates cloud cover and does not need any solar illumination. This image of Montserrat shows how the island can still be seen, despite clouds and the continuing eruption of the Soufrière volcano in the south. The delta visible in the sea to the east is being formed by lava flows pouring down the Tar River Valley. *(Radarsat)*

Las Vegas, Nevada, USA

Two satellite images viewing the same area of ground from different orbits can be used to compile a Digital Elevation Model (DEM) of the Earth's surface. A computer compares the images and calculates the ground surface elevation to a vertical precision of 8–15 m, preparing this for thousands of square kilometres in just a few minutes. Overlaying a colour satellite image on to a DEM produced the picture of Las Vegas shown here. (NPA)

Urban (tall)
Urban dense
Urban
Industrial
Paved
Urban / Tree mix
Trees (coniferous)
Trees (deciduous)
Forest clearing
Grass or crops
Open
Water

Seattle, Washington, USA

Image-processing software can use the differing spectral properties of land cover to 'classify' a multispectral satellite image. This classification of the area around Seattle was used together with elevation data to model the transmission of mobile phone signals before installation of the network. Microwave signals are affected by the absorption, reflection and scattering of the signal from vegetation and urban structures as well as the topography. (NPA)

BRITISH ISLES

SHETLAND ISLANDS
on same scale

Projection : Conical with two standard parallels

West from Greenwich

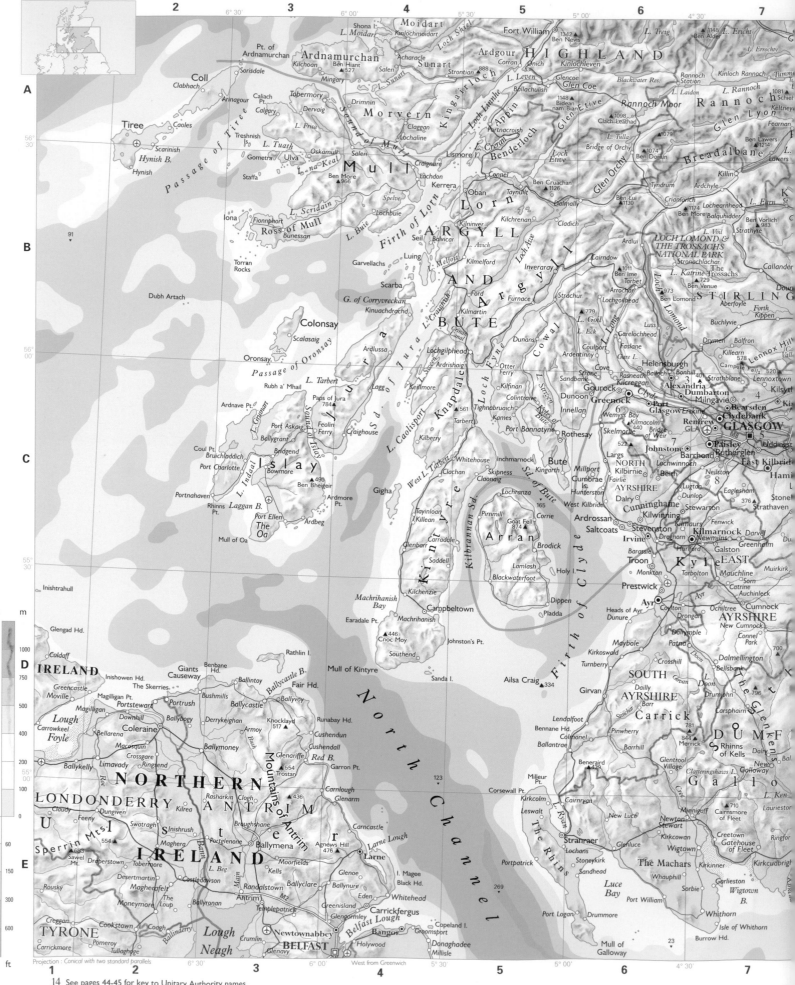

NORTH

SEA

ANGUS

Montrose

Arbroath

Dundee

Perth

St. Andrews

FIFE

Firth of Forth

EDINBURGH

Berwick-upon-Tweed

LOTHIAN

SCOTTISH
BORDERS

Holy I.

NORTHUMBERLAND
NATIONAL PARK

NORTHUMBERLAND

DUMFRIES
& GALLOWAY

Cheviot Hills

Carlisle

NEWCASTLE-UPON-TYNE

TYNE
& WEAR

Sunderland

CUMBRIA

Pennines

DURHAM

Hartlepool

Tees Bay
Redcar

Teesside
Middlesbrough

1:1 000 000

10   5   0   10   20   30   40   50 km

5   0   5   10   15   20   25   30   35 miles

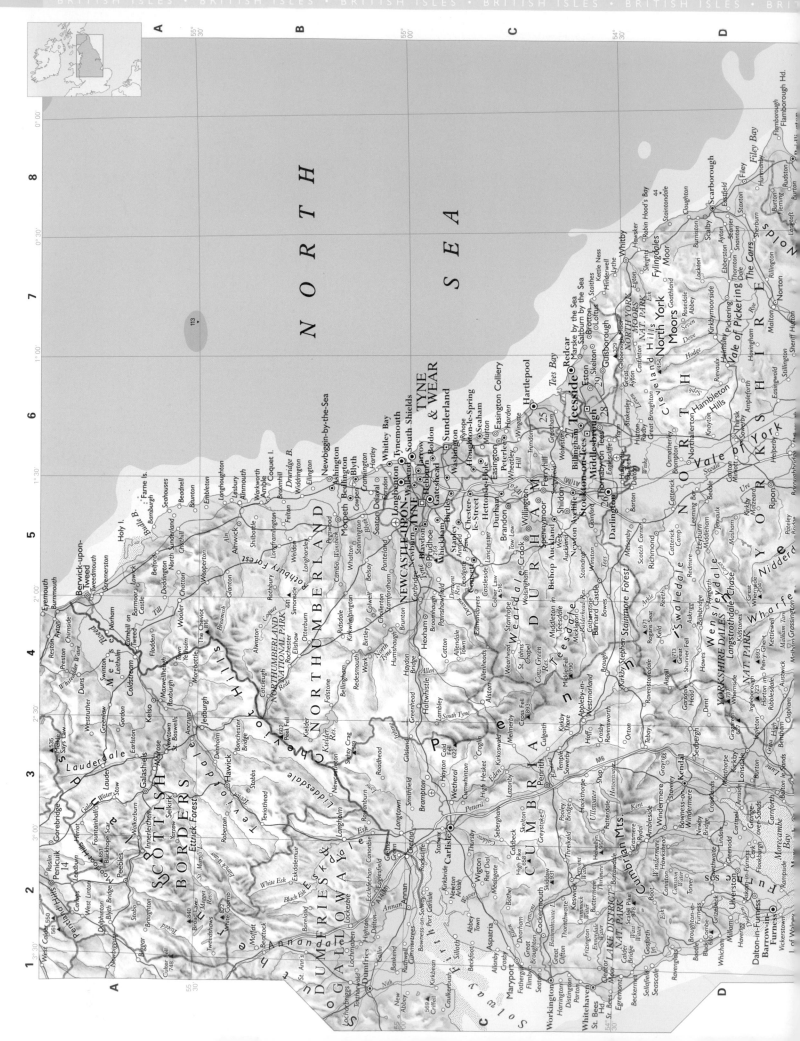

See pages 44–45 for key to Unitary Authority names.

1:1 000 000

COPYRIGHT PHILIP'S

Projection: Conical with two standard parallels

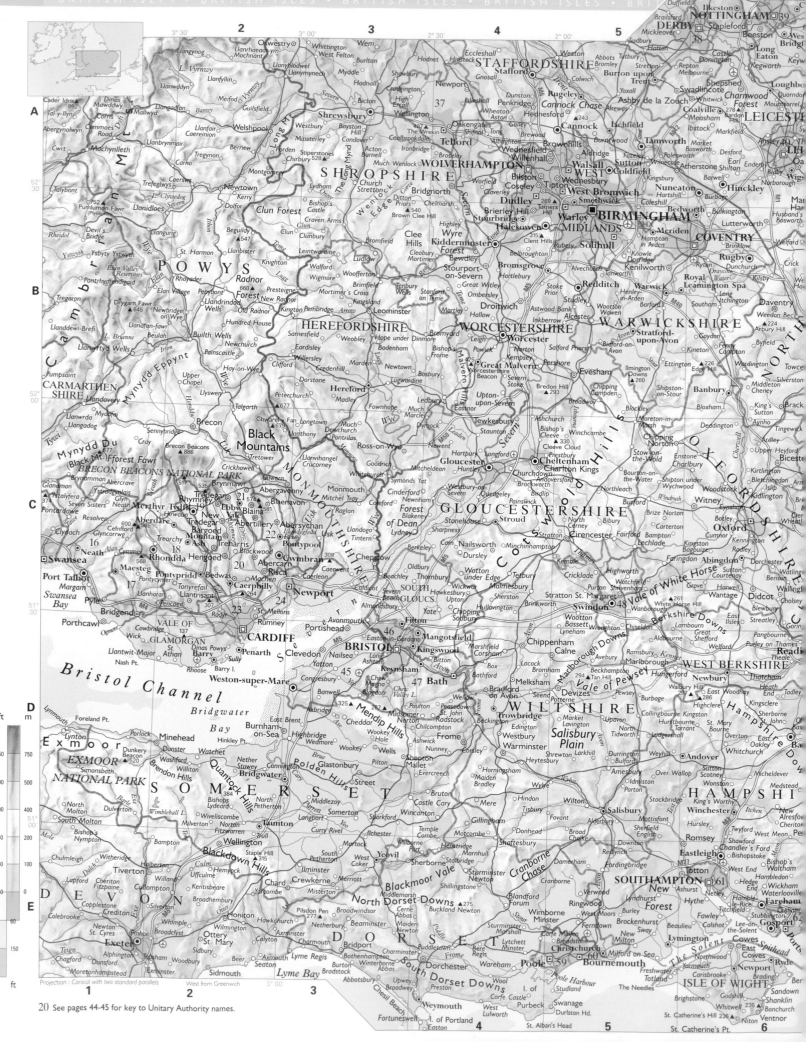

Projection : Conical with two standard parallels
West from Greenwich
20 See pages 44–45 for key to Unitary Authority names.

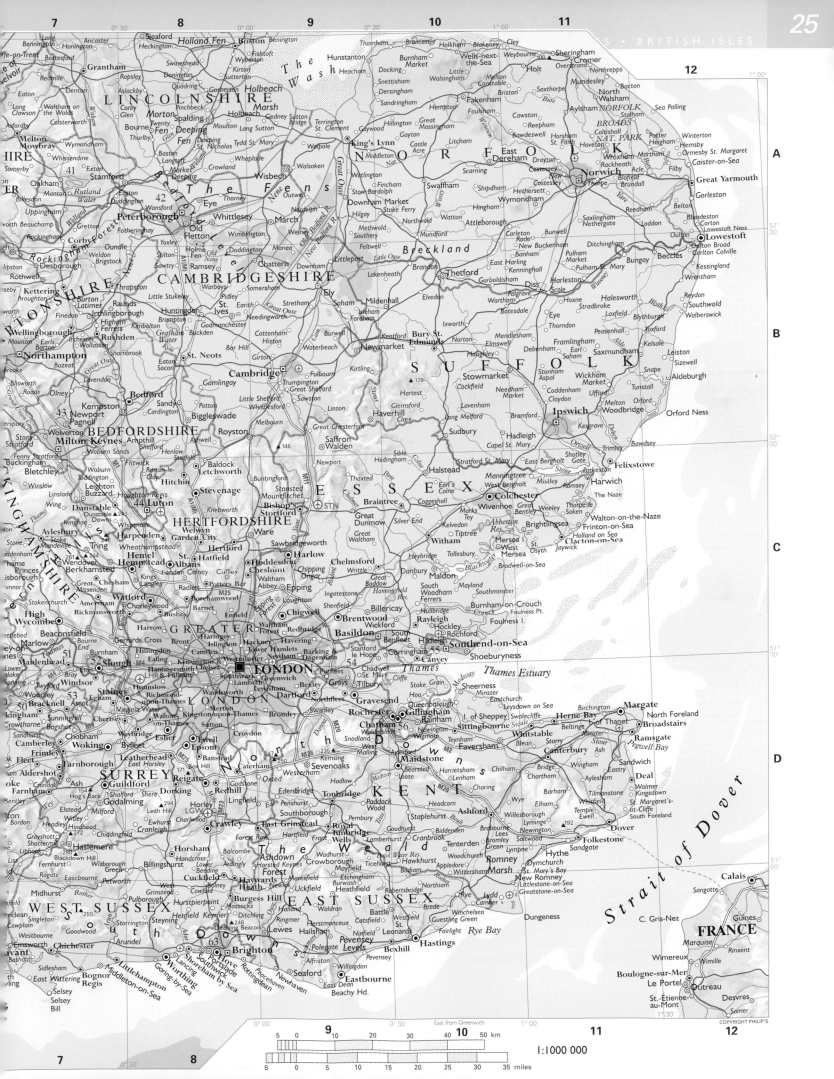

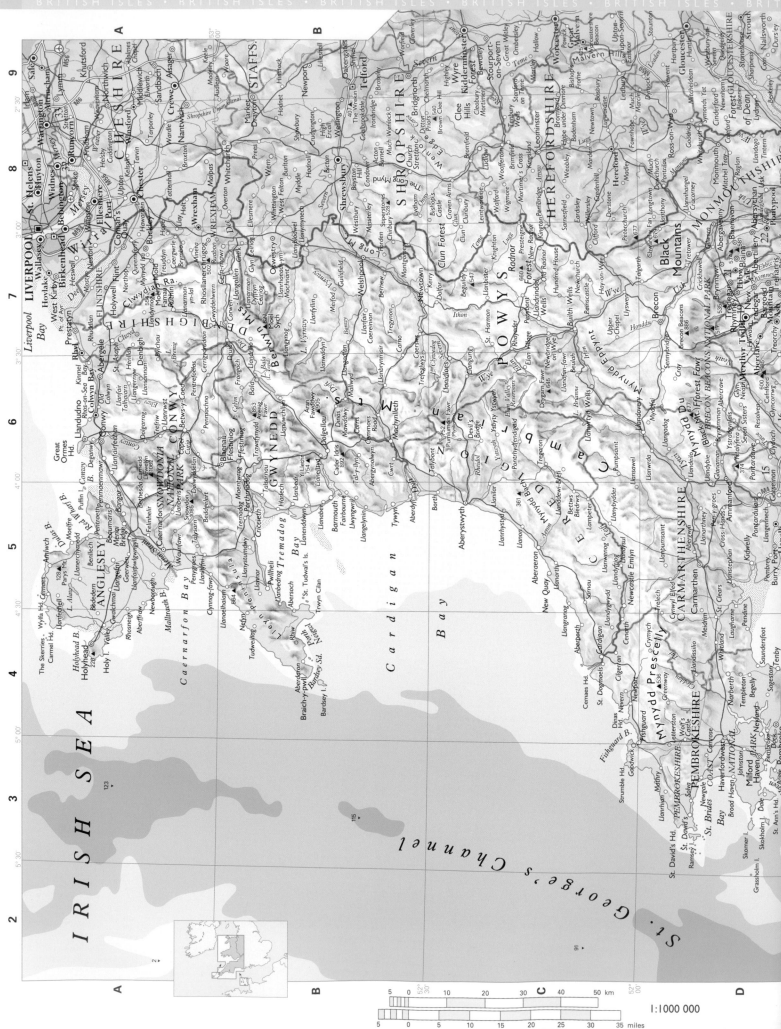

1:1 000 000

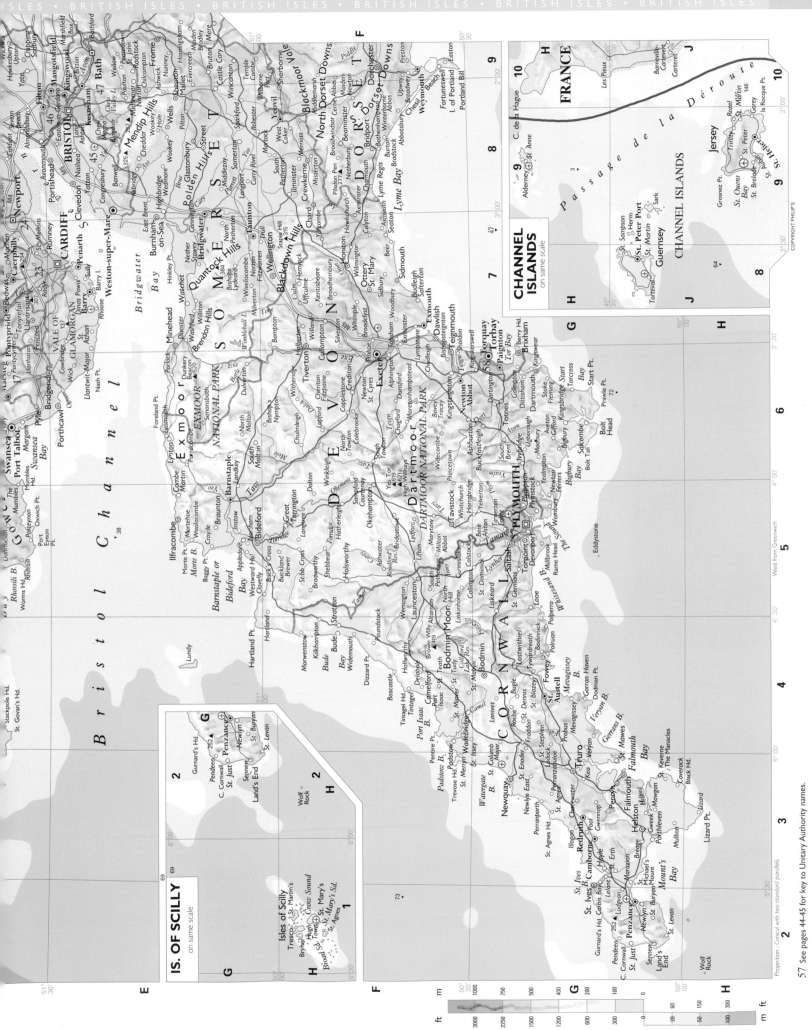

CHANNEL ISLANDS
on same scale

FRANCE

C. de la Hague
St. Anne
Alderney
Les Pieux
Barneville-Carteret
Carteret
Passage de la Déroute
Grosnez Pt.
Trinity
Rozel
St. Ouens Bay
St. Peter
St. Martin
Gorey
la Rocque Pt.
Jersey
St. Helier
St. Brelade
CHANNEL ISLANDS
Sampson
St. Peter Port
St. Martin
Herm
Sark
Guernsey
Torteval

COPYRIGHT PHILIP'S

SOMERSET
DORSET
DEVON
CORNWALL
DARTMOOR NATIONAL PARK
EXMOOR NATIONAL PARK

Bristol Channel

Bridgwater Bay

Barnstaple or Bideford Bay

Lyme Bay

Falmouth Bay

Mount's Bay

BRISTOL
CARDIFF
Newport
Swansea
Plymouth
Exeter
Torquay
Torbay
Paignton

IS. OF SCILLY
on same scale

Isles of Scilly
Tresco
St. Martin's
Hugh Town
St. Mary's
St. Agnes
Bryher

Lundy

Wolf Rock

Land's End
Penzance
St. Just
Newlyn
St. Buryan
St. Levan
Sennen
C. Cornwall
Pendeen
Gurnard's Hd.

Projection : Conical with two standard parallels

57 See pages 44-45 for key to Unitary Authority names.

West from Greenwich

m
ft
3000
2250
1500
1200
600
300
0
1000
750
500
400
200
100
0
-20 -50
-100 -300
ft
m

A T L A N T I C

O C E A N

Projection : Conical with two standard parallels

West from Greenwich

COPYRIGHT PHILIP'S

1:1 000 000

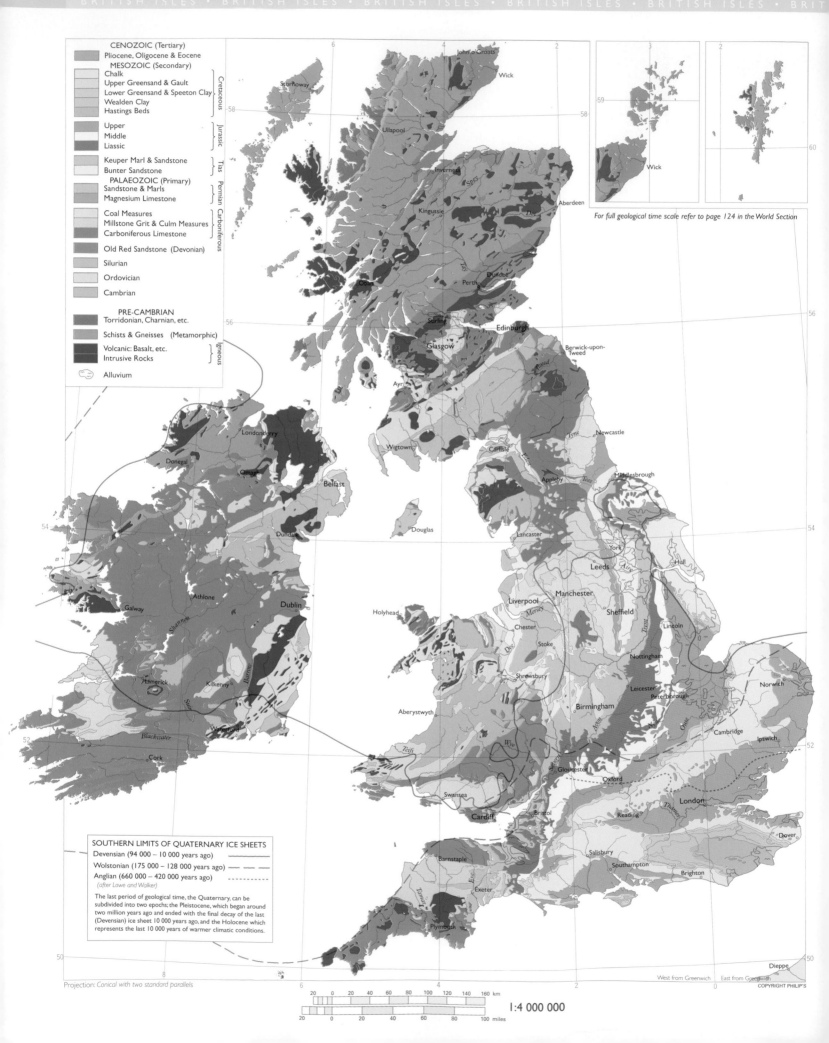

CENOZOIC (Tertiary)
Pliocene, Oligocene & Eocene
MESOZOIC (Secondary)
Chalk
Upper Greensand & Gault
Lower Greensand & Speeton Clay — *Cretaceous*
Wealden Clay
Hastings Beds

Upper
Middle — *Jurassic*
Liassic

Keuper Marl & Sandstone — *Trias*
Bunter Sandstone

PALAEOZOIC (Primary)
Sandstone & Marls — *Permian*
Magnesium Limestone

Coal Measures
Millstone Grit & Culm Measures — *Carboniferous*
Carboniferous Limestone

Old Red Sandstone (Devonian)

Silurian

Ordovician

Cambrian

PRE-CAMBRIAN
Torridonian, Charnian, etc.

Schists & Gneisses (Metamorphic)

Volcanic: Basalt, etc. — *Igneous*
Intrusive Rocks

Alluvium

For full geological time scale refer to page 124 in the World Section

SOUTHERN LIMITS OF QUATERNARY ICE SHEETS
Devensian (94 000 – 10 000 years ago)
Wolstonian (175 000 – 128 000 years ago)
Anglian (660 000 – 420 000 years ago)
(after Lowe and Walker)

The last period of geological time, the Quaternary, can be subdivided into two epochs; the Pleistocene, which began around two million years ago and ended with the final decay of the last (Devensian) ice sheet 10 000 years ago, and the Holocene which represents the last 10 000 years of warmer climatic conditions.

Projection: *Conical with two standard parallels*

1:4 000 000

COPYRIGHT PHILIP'S

West from Greenwich   East from Greenwich

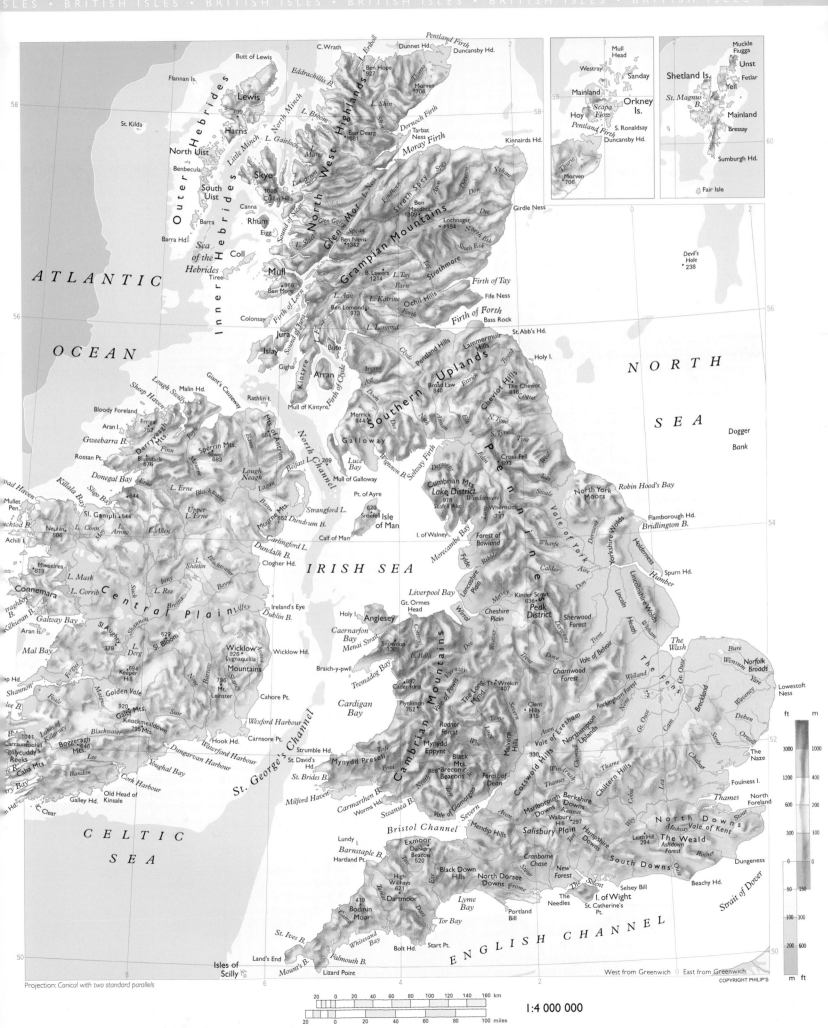

Projection: Conical with two standard parallels

1:4 000 000

COPYRIGHT PHILIP'S

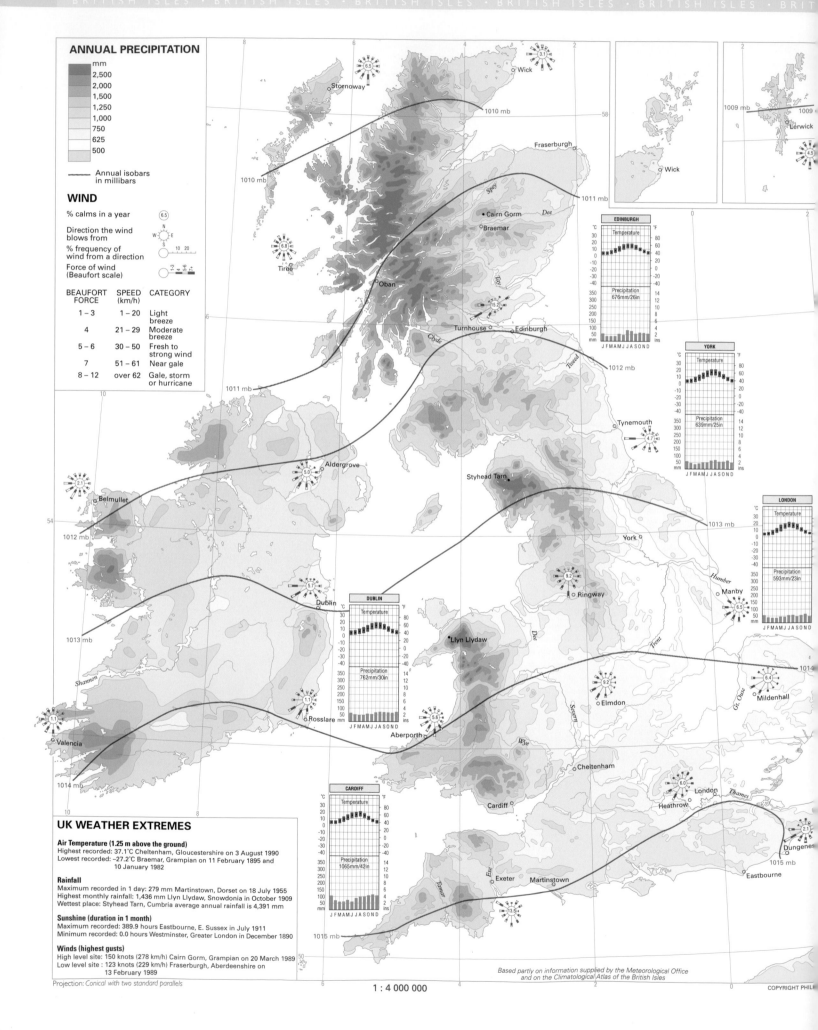

ANNUAL PRECIPITATION

mm
2,500
2,000
1,500
1,250
1,000
750
625
500

—— Annual isobars in millibars

WIND

% calms in a year

Direction the wind blows from

% frequency of wind from a direction

Force of wind (Beaufort scale)

BEAUFORT FORCE	SPEED (km/h)	CATEGORY
1 – 3	1 – 20	Light breeze
4	21 – 29	Moderate breeze
5 – 6	30 – 50	Fresh to strong wind
7	51 – 61	Near gale
8 – 12	over 62	Gale, storm or hurricane

UK WEATHER EXTREMES

Air Temperature (1.25 m above the ground)
Highest recorded: 37.1°C Cheltenham, Gloucestershire on 3 August 1990
Lowest recorded: –27.2°C Braemar, Grampian on 11 February 1895 and 10 January 1982

Rainfall
Maximum recorded in 1 day: 279 mm Martinstown, Dorset on 18 July 1955
Highest monthly rainfall: 1,436 mm Llyn Llydaw, Snowdonia in October 1909
Wettest place: Styhead Tarn, Cumbria average annual rainfall is 4,391 mm

Sunshine (duration in 1 month)
Maximum recorded: 389.9 hours Eastbourne, E. Sussex in July 1911
Minimum recorded: 0.0 hours Westminster, Greater London in December 1890

Winds (highest gusts)
High level site: 150 knots (278 km/h) Cairn Gorm, Grampian on 20 March 1989
Low level site : 123 knots (229 km/h) Fraserburgh, Aberdeenshire on 13 February 1989

Projection: Conical with two standard parallels

1 : 4 000 000

Based partly on information supplied by the Meteorological Office and on the Climatological Atlas of the British Isles

COPYRIGHT PHIL

CLIMATE GRAPHS

Average monthly minimum temperature in degrees Celsius

Average monthly maximum temperature in degrees Celsius

Height of meteorological station above sea level in metres

		Jan
Ambleside	46 m	
Temperature	Daily max. °C	6
	Daily min. °C	0
	Average monthly °C	3
Rainfall	Monthly total mm	214
	No. of days	20
Sunshine	Hours per day	1.1

Average daily duration of bright sunshine per month in hours

Number of days per month with over 0.1 mm precipitation

Average monthly precipitation in millimetres

Average monthly temperature in degrees Celsius

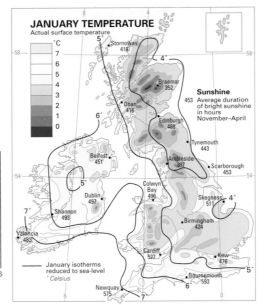

JANUARY TEMPERATURE
Actual surface temperature

°C
7
6
5
4
3
2
1
0

Sunshine
453 Average duration
of bright sunshine
in hours
November–April

— January isotherms
reduced to sea-level
° Celsius

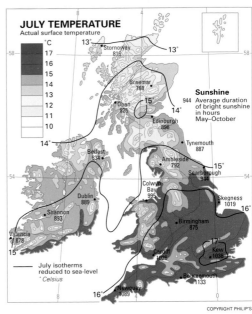

JULY TEMPERATURE
Actual surface temperature

°C
17
16
15
14
13
12
11
10

Sunshine
944 Average duration
of bright sunshine
in hours
May–October

— July isotherms
reduced to sea-level
° Celsius

COPYRIGHT PHILIP'S

		Jan	Feb	Mar	Apr	May	June	July	Aug	Sept	Oct	Nov	Dec	Year
Ambleside	**46 m**													
Temperature	Daily max. °C	6	7	9	12	16	19	20	19	17	13	9	7	13
	Daily min. °C	0	0	2	4	6	9	11	11	9	6	3	1	5
	Average monthly °C	3	4	6	8	11	14	15	15	13	10	6	4	9
Rainfall	Monthly total mm	214	146	112	101	90	111	134	139	184	196	209	215	1,851
	No. of days	20	17	15	15	14	15	14	17	18	19	19	21	208
Sunshine	Hours per day	1.1	2	3.2	4.5	6	5.7	4.5	4.2	3.3	2.2	1.4	1	3.3
Belfast	**4 m**													
Temperature	Daily max. °C	6	7	9	12	15	18	18	18	16	13	9	7	12
	Daily min. °C	2	2	3	4	6	9	11	11	9	7	4	3	6
	Average monthly °C	4	4	6	8	11	13	15	15	13	10	7	5	9
Rainfall	Monthly total mm	80	52	50	48	52	68	94	77	80	83	72	90	845
	No. of days	20	17	16	16	15	16	19	17	18	19	19	21	213
Sunshine	Hours per day	1.5	2.3	3.4	5	6.3	6	4.4	4.4	3.6	2.6	1.8	1.1	3.5
Birkenhead	**60 m**													
Temperature	Daily max. °C	6	6	9	11	15	17	19	19	16	13	9	7	12
	Daily min. °C	2	2	3	5	8	11	13	13	11	8	5	3	7
	Average monthly °C	4	4	6	8	11	14	16	16	14	10	7	5	10
Rainfall	Monthly total mm	64	46	40	41	55	55	67	80	66	71	76	65	726
	No. of days	18	13	13	13	13	13	15	15	14	17	17	19	181
Sunshine	Hours per day	1.6	2.4	3.5	5.3	6.3	6.7	5.7	5.4	4.2	2.9	1.8	1.3	3.9
Birmingham	**163 m**													
Temperature	Daily max. °C	5	6	9	12	16	19	20	20	17	13	9	6	13
	Daily min. °C	2	2	3	5	7	10	12	12	10	7	5	3	7
	Average monthly °C	3	4	6	8	11	15	16	16	14	10	7	5	10
Rainfall	Monthly total mm	74	54	50	53	64	50	69	69	61	69	84	67	764
	No. of days	17	15	13	13	14	13	15	14	14	15	17	18	178
Sunshine	Hours per day	1.4	2.1	3.2	4.6	5.4	6	5.4	5.1	3.9	2.8	1.6	1.2	3.6
Cambridge	**12 m**													
Temperature	Daily max. °C	6	7	11	14	17	21	22	22	19	15	10	7	14
	Daily min. °C	1	1	2	4	7	10	12	12	10	6	4	2	6
	Average monthly °C	3	4	6	9	12	15	17	17	14	10	7	5	10
Rainfall	Monthly total mm	49	35	36	37	45	45	58	55	51	51	54	41	558
	No. of days	15	13	10	11	11	11	12	11	11	13	14	14	147
Sunshine	Hours per day	1.7	2.5	3.8	5.1	6.2	6.7	6	5.7	4.6	3.4	1.9	1.4	4.1
Craibstone	**91 m**													
Temperature	Daily max. °C	5	6	8	10	13	16	18	17	15	12	8	6	11
	Daily min. °C	0	0	2	3	5	8	10	10	8	6	3	1	5
	Average monthly °C	3	3	5	7	9	12	14	13	12	9	6	4	8
Rainfall	Monthly total mm	78	55	53	51	63	54	95	75	67	92	93	80	856
	No. of days	19	16	15	15	14	14	18	15	16	18	19	18	197
Sunshine	Hours per day	1.8	2.9	3.5	4.9	5.9	6.1	5.1	4.8	4.3	3.1	2	1.5	3.8
Durham	**102 m**													
Temperature	Daily max. °C	6	6	9	12	15	18	20	19	17	13	9	7	13
	Daily min. °C	0	0	1	3	6	9	11	10	9	6	3	2	5
	Average monthly °C	3	3	5	7	10	13	15	15	13	9	6	4	9
Rainfall	Monthly total mm	59	51	38	38	51	49	61	67	60	63	66	55	658
	No. of days	17	15	14	13	13	14	15	14	14	16	17	17	179
Sunshine	Hours per day	1.7	2.5	3.3	4.6	5.4	6	5.1	4.8	4.1	3	1.9	1.4	3.6
Lerwick	**82 m**													
Temperature	Daily max. °C	5	5	6	8	11	13	14	14	13	10	8	6	9
	Daily min. °C	1	1	2	3	5	7	10	10	8	6	4	3	5
	Average monthly °C	3	3	4	5	8	10	12	12	11	8	6	4	7
Rainfall	Monthly total mm	109	87	69	68	52	55	72	71	87	104	111	118	1,003
	No. of days	25	22	20	21	15	15	17	17	19	23	24	25	243
Sunshine	Hours per day	0.8	1.8	2.9	4.4	5.3	5.3	4	3.8	3.5	2.2	2.2	0.5	3
Plymouth	**27 m**													
Temperature	Daily max. °C	8	8	10	12	15	18	19	19	18	15	11	9	14
	Daily min. °C	4	4	5	6	8	11	13	13	12	9	7	5	8
	Average monthly °C	6	6	7	9	12	15	16	16	15	12	9	7	11
Rainfall	Monthly total mm	99	74	69	53	63	53	70	77	78	91	113	110	950
	No. of days	19	15	14	12	12	12	14	14	15	16	17	18	178
Sunshine	Hours per day	1.9	2.9	4.3	6.1	7.1	7.4	6.4	6.4	5.1	3.7	2.2	1.7	4.6
Renfrew	**6 m**													
Temperature	Daily max. °C	5	7	9	12	15	18	19	19	16	13	9	7	12
	Daily min. °C	1	1	2	4	6	9	11	11	9	6	4	2	6
	Average monthly °C	3	4	6	8	11	14	15	15	13	9	7	4	9
Rainfall	Monthly total mm	111	85	69	67	63	70	97	93	102	119	106	127	1,109
	No. of days	19	16	15	15	14	15	17	17	18	18	18	20	201
Sunshine	Hours per day	1.1	2.1	2.9	4.7	6	6.1	5.1	4.4	3.7	2.3	1.4	0.8	3.4
St Mary's	**50 m**													
Temperature	Daily max. °C	9	9	11	12	14	17	19	19	18	15	12	10	14
	Daily min. °C	6	6	7	7	9	12	13	14	13	11	9	7	9
	Average monthly °C	8	7	9	10	12	14	16	16	15	13	10	9	12
Rainfall	Monthly total mm	91	71	69	46	56	49	61	64	67	80	96	94	844
	No. of days	22	17	16	13	14	14	15	14	16	17	19	21	200
Sunshine	Hours per day	2	2.9	4.2	6.4	7.6	7.6	6.7	6.7	5.2	3.9	2.5	1.8	4.8
Southampton	**20 m**													
Temperature	Daily max. °C	7	8	11	14	17	20	22	22	19	15	11	8	15
	Daily min. °C	2	2	3	5	8	11	13	13	11	7	5	3	7
	Average monthly °C	5	5	7	10	13	16	17	17	15	11	8	6	11
Rainfall	Monthly total mm	83	56	52	45	56	49	60	69	70	86	94	84	804
	No. of days	17	13	13	12	12	12	13	13	14	14	16	17	166
Sunshine	Hours per day	1.8	2.6	4	5.7	6.7	7.2	6.5	6.4	4.9	3.6	2.2	1.6	4.5
Tiree	**9 m**													
Temperature	Daily Max. °C	7	7	9	10	13	15	16	16	15	12	10	8	12
	Daily Min. °C	4	3	4	5	7	10	11	11	10	8	6	5	7
	Average Monthly °C	5	5	6	8	10	12	14	14	13	10	8	6	9
Rainfall	Monthly Total mm	117	77	67	64	55	70	91	90	118	129	122	128	1,128
	No. of Days	23	19	17	17	15	16	20	18	20	23	22	24	234
Sunshine	Hours per Day	1.3	2.6	3.7	5.7	7.5	6.8	5.2	5.3	4.2	2.6	1.6	0.9	4
Valencia	**9 m**													
Temperature	Daily max. °C	9	9	11	13	15	17	18	18	17	14	12	10	14
	Daily min. °C	5	4	5	6	8	11	12	13	11	9	7	6	8
	Average monthly °C	7	7	8	9	11	14	15	15	14	12	9	8	11
Rainfall	Monthly total mm	165	107	103	75	86	81	107	95	122	140	151	168	1,400
	No. of days	20	15	14	13	13	13	15	15	16	17	18	21	190
Sunshine	Hours per day	1.6	2.5	3.5	5.2	6.5	5.9	4.7	4.9	3.8	2.8	2	1.3	3.7

WATER SUPPLY

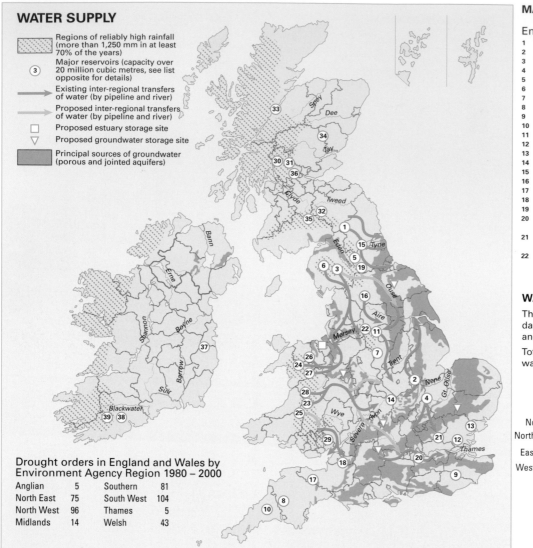

Regions of reliably high rainfall (more than 1,250 mm in at least 70% of the years)

③ Major reservoirs (capacity over 20 million cubic metres, see list opposite for details)

→ Existing inter-regional transfers of water (by pipeline and river)

→ Proposed inter-regional transfers of water (by pipeline and river)

☐ Proposed estuary storage site

▽ Proposed groundwater storage site

Principal sources of groundwater (porous and jointed aquifers)

Drought orders in England and Wales by Environment Agency Region 1980 – 2000

Anglian	5	Southern	81
North East	75	South West	104
North West	96	Thames	5
Midlands	14	Welsh	43

MAJOR RESERVOIRS (with capacity in million

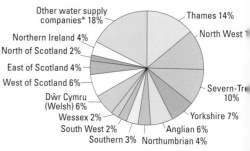

England

1	Kielder Res.	198
2	Rutland Water	123
3	Haweswater	85
4	Grafham Water	59
5	Cow Green Res.	41
6	Thirlmere	41
7	Carsington Res.	36
8	Roadford Res.	35
9	Bewl Water Res.	31
10	Colliford Lake	29
11	Ladybower Res.	28
12	Hanningfield Res.	27
13	Abberton Res.	25
14	Draycote Water	23
15	Derwent Res.	22
16	Grimwith Res.	22
17	Wimbleball Lake	21
18	Chew Valley Lake	20
19	Balderhead Res.	20
20	Thames Valley (linked reservoirs)	
21	Lea Valley (linked reservoirs)	
22	Longendale (linked reservoirs)	

Wales

23	Elan Valley	99
24	Llyn Celyn	74
25	Llyn Brianne	62
26	Llyn Brenig	60
27	Llyn Vyrnwy	60
28	Llyn Clywedog	48
29	Llandegfedd Res.	22

Scotland

30	Loch Lomond	86
31	Loch Katrine	64
32	Megget Res.	64
33	Loch Ness	26
34	Blackwater Res.	25
35	Daer Res.	23
36	Carron Valley Res.	21

Ireland

37	Poulaphouca Res.	168
38	Inishcarra Res.	57
39	Carrigadrohid Res.	33

WATER SUPPLY IN THE UK

The pie graph represents the 18,002 million litres a day that were supplied by the public water authority and services companies in the UK in 1999.

Total water abstraction in England and Wales in 1999 was approximately 37,000 million litres a day.

Other water supply companies* 18%
Thames 14%
North West 1
Northern Ireland 4%
North of Scotland 2%
East of Scotland 4%
West of Scotland 6%
Dŵr Cymru (Welsh) 6%
Wessex 2%
South West 2%
Southern 3%
Severn-Tre 10%
Yorkshire 7%
Anglian 6%
Northumbrian 4%

*This is a group of 17 privately-owned companies who are not connected with the other water authorities

WATER ABSTRACTIONS

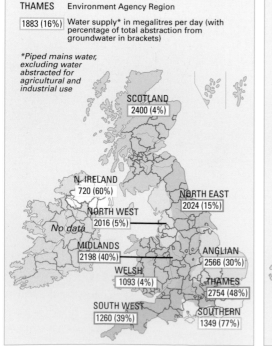

THAMES Environment Agency Region

1883 (16%) Water supply* in megalitres per day (with percentage of total abstraction from groundwater in brackets)

*Piped mains water, excluding water abstracted for agricultural and industrial use

SCOTLAND 2400 (4%)

N. IRELAND 720 (60%)

NORTH EAST 2024 (15%)

NORTH WEST 2016 (5%)

No data

MIDLANDS 2198 (40%)

ANGLIAN 2566 (30%)

WELSH 1093 (4%)

THAMES 2754 (48%)

SOUTH WEST 1260 (39%)

SOUTHERN 1349 (77%)

WATER QUALITY

The percentage of all rivers and canals of very good quality within each Environment Agency Region 2000

Under 15%
15% – 30%
30% – 60%
Over 60%

The percentage of bathing beaches complying with EC standards in 2001

100%
90% – 99%
80% – 89%

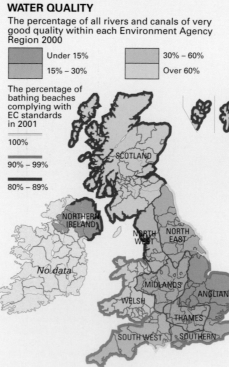

SCOTLAND

NORTHERN IRELAND

No data

NORTH WEST

NORTH EAST

MIDLANDS

WELSH

ANGLIAN

THAMES

SOUTH WEST

SOUTHERN

FLOOD RISK IN ENGLAND AND WALES

Areas at greatest risk from flooding (as designated by the Environment Agency in 2002)

Settlements with over 100 properties flooded in 2001

Ponteland
Skinningrove
Malton and Norton
Stockbridge
York
Barlby
Gowdall
Catcliffe
Ruthin
Mold
Shrewsbury
Hatton
Bewdley
Waltham Abbey
Newport
Wanstead
Woking
Uckfield
Portsmouth
Lewes

COPYRIGHT PHI

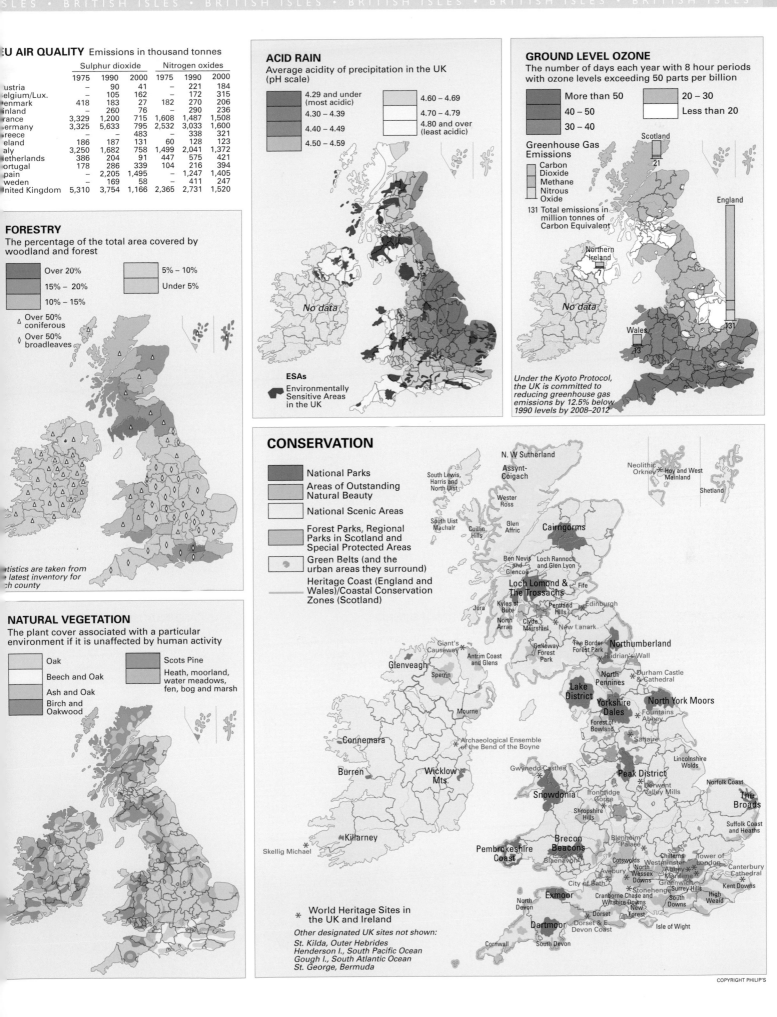

EU AIR QUALITY
Emissions in thousand tonnes

	Sulphur dioxide			Nitrogen oxides		
	1975	1990	2000	1975	1990	2000
Austria	–	90	41	–	221	184
Belgium/Lux.	–	105	162	–	172	315
Denmark	418	183	27	182	270	206
Finland	–	260	76	–	290	236
France	3,329	1,200	715	1,608	1,487	1,508
Germany	3,325	5,633	795	2,532	3,033	1,600
Greece	–	–	483	–	338	321
Ireland	186	187	131	60	128	123
Italy	3,250	1,682	758	1,499	2,041	1,372
Netherlands	386	204	91	447	575	421
Portugal	178	286	339	104	216	394
Spain	–	2,205	1,495	–	1,247	1,405
Sweden	–	169	58	–	411	247
United Kingdom	5,310	3,754	1,166	2,365	2,731	1,520

FORESTRY
The percentage of the total area covered by woodland and forest

- Over 20%
- 15% – 20%
- 10% – 15%
- 5% – 10%
- Under 5%
- △ Over 50% coniferous
- ◇ Over 50% broadleaves

...tistics are taken from ...e latest inventory for ...ch county

NATURAL VEGETATION
The plant cover associated with a particular environment if it is unaffected by human activity

- Oak
- Beech and Oak
- Ash and Oak
- Birch and Oakwood
- Scots Pine
- Heath, moorland, water meadows, fen, bog and marsh

ACID RAIN
Average acidity of precipitation in the UK (pH scale)

- 4.29 and under (most acidic)
- 4.30 – 4.39
- 4.40 – 4.49
- 4.50 – 4.59
- 4.60 – 4.69
- 4.70 – 4.79
- 4.80 and over (least acidic)

No data

ESAs
Environmentally Sensitive Areas in the UK

GROUND LEVEL OZONE
The number of days each year with 8 hour periods with ozone levels exceeding 50 parts per billion

- More than 50
- 40 – 50
- 30 – 40
- 20 – 30
- Less than 20

Greenhouse Gas Emissions
- Carbon Dioxide
- Methane
- Nitrous Oxide

131 Total emissions in million tonnes of Carbon Equivalent

Scotland 21
Northern Ireland 7
England 131
Wales 13

No data

Under the Kyoto Protocol, the UK is committed to reducing greenhouse gas emissions by 12.5% below 1990 levels by 2008–2012

CONSERVATION

- National Parks
- Areas of Outstanding Natural Beauty
- National Scenic Areas
- Forest Parks, Regional Parks in Scotland and Special Protected Areas
- Green Belts (and the urban areas they surround)
- Heritage Coast (England and Wales)/Coastal Conservation Zones (Scotland)

✳ World Heritage Sites in the UK and Ireland

Other designated UK sites not shown:
St. Kilda, Outer Hebrides
Henderson I., South Pacific Ocean
Gough I., South Atlantic Ocean
St. George, Bermuda

Map labels: N.W Sutherland, Assynt-Coigach, South Lewis, Harris and North Uist, Neolithic Orkney, Hoy and West Mainland, Shetland, Wester Ross, Scotland, South Uist Machair, Glen Affric, Cairngorms, Cuillin Hills, Ben Nevis and Glencoe, Loch Rannoch and Glen Lyon, Loch Lomond & The Trossachs, Fife, Jura, Kyles of Bute, Pentland Hills, Edinburgh, North Arran, Clyde Muirshiel, New Lanark, Giant's Causeway, Antrim Coast and Glens, Galloway Forest Park, The Border Forest Park, Northumberland, Glenveagh, Sperrin, Hadrian's Wall, Durham Castle & Cathedral, North Pennines, Lake District, Yorkshire Dales, North York Moors, Mourne, Fountains Abbey, Forest of Bowland, Saltaire, Connemara, Archaeological Ensemble of the Bend of the Boyne, Lincolnshire Wolds, Burren, Wicklow Mts., Gwynedd Castles, Peak District, Norfolk Coast, Snowdonia, Ironbridge Gorge, Derwent Valley Mills, Shropshire Hills, The Broads, Killarney, Suffolk Coast and Heaths, Skellig Michael, Brecon Beacons, Blenheim Palace, Chilterns, Tower of London, Pembrokeshire Coast, Blaenavon, Cotswolds, Westminster Abbey, North Wessex Downs, Avebury, Maritime Greenwich, Surrey Hills, Canterbury Cathedral, City of Bath, Stonehenge, South Downs, Kent Downs, Exmoor, Cranborne Chase and Wiltshire Downs, New Forest, High Weald, North Devon, Dorset, Dorset & E. Devon Coast, Isle of Wight, Dartmoor, Cornwall, South Devon

COPYRIGHT PHILIP'S

TYPES OF FARM

- Dairy cattle
- Beef cattle
- Sheep
- ● Pigs and/or Poultry
- Mixed farming
- Market gardening (fruit and vegetables)
- Cereals
- Other crops (mainly potatoes, sugar beet)
- ⌒ Northern limit of 9 month growing season
- Forests
- Built-up areas

Areas with over 1,000 mm rainfall per year

CEREAL FARMING

The percentage of the total farmland used for growing cereals in 2000 (Ireland 1999)

- Over 40%
- 30 – 40%
- 20 – 30%
- 10 – 20%
- 0 – 10%
- No data

Cereal Production (2000)
UK 24 million tonnes
Ireland 2 million tonnes

AGRICULTURAL LAND USE IN THE UK

- Other agricultural land 18.0%
- Wheat 8.8%
- Barley 6.7%
- Oats 0.6%
- Potatoes 0.9%
- Sugar beet 1.
- Rapeseed 2.2
- Horticultural 1.8%
- Rough grazing 23.9%
- Pasture 36.6%

Total agricultural land area (2001) 18.5 million hectares

DAIRY FARMING

The number of dairy cows per 100 hectares of farmland in 2000 (Ireland 1999)

- Over 40
- 30 – 40
- 20 – 30
- 10 – 20
- 0 – 10
- No data

Milk Production (2000)
UK 14,071 million litres
Ireland 530 million litres

LIVESTOCK FARMING

The number of cattle, sheep and pigs per 100 hectares of farmland in 2000 (Ireland 1999)

- Over 400
- 300 – 400
- 200 – 300
- 100 – 200
- 0 – 100
- No data

FOOT-AND-MOUTH DISEASE

The number of confirmed cases of foot-and-mouth disease in 2001

- Over 200
- 100 – 200
- 50 – 100
- 25 – 50
- 0 – 25
- Unaffected areas

Total number of slaughtered animals: 4,059,039

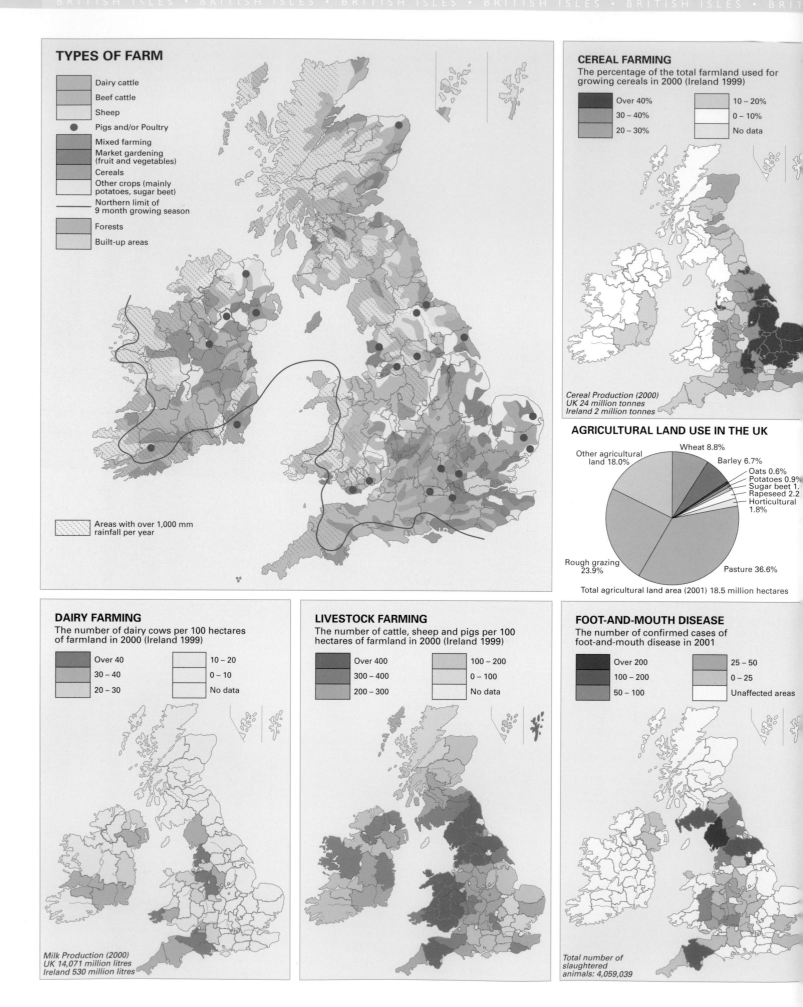

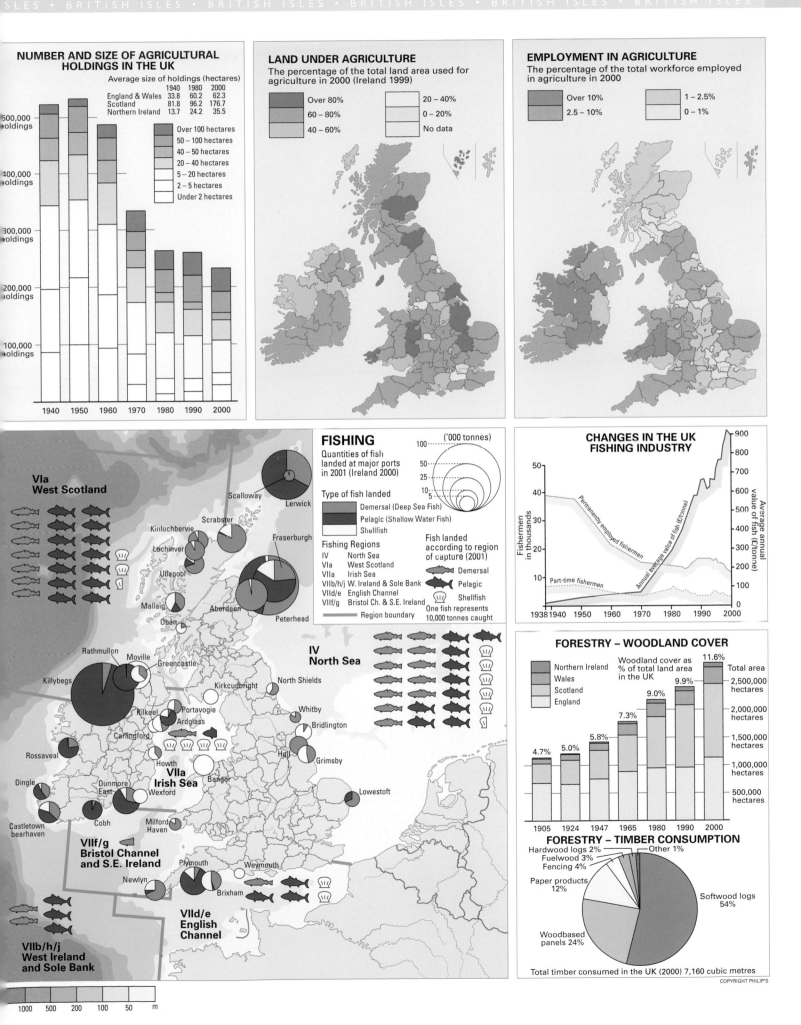

NUMBER AND SIZE OF AGRICULTURAL HOLDINGS IN THE UK

Average size of holdings (hectares)

	1940	1980	2000
England & Wales	33.8	60.2	62.3
Scotland	81.8	96.2	176.7
Northern Ireland	13.7	24.2	35.5

- Over 100 hectares
- 50 – 100 hectares
- 40 – 50 hectares
- 20 – 40 hectares
- 5 – 20 hectares
- 2 – 5 hectares
- Under 2 hectares

500,000 holdings
400,000 holdings
300,000 holdings
200,000 holdings
100,000 holdings

1940 1950 1960 1970 1980 1990 2000

LAND UNDER AGRICULTURE
The percentage of the total land area used for agriculture in 2000 (Ireland 1999)

- Over 80%
- 60 – 80%
- 40 – 60%
- 20 – 40%
- 0 – 20%
- No data

EMPLOYMENT IN AGRICULTURE
The percentage of the total workforce employed in agriculture in 2000

- Over 10%
- 2.5 – 10%
- 1 – 2.5%
- 0 – 1%

FISHING
Quantities of fish landed at major ports in 2001 (Ireland 2000)

('000 tonnes)
100
50
25
10
5

Type of fish landed
- Demersal (Deep Sea Fish)
- Pelagic (Shallow Water Fish)
- Shellfish

Fishing Regions
- IV — North Sea
- VIa — West Scotland
- VIIa — Irish Sea
- VIIb/h/j — W. Ireland & Sole Bank
- VIId/e — English Channel
- VIIf/g — Bristol Ch. & S.E. Ireland

Fish landed according to region of capture (2001)
- Demersal
- Pelagic
- Shellfish

One fish represents 10,000 tonnes caught

— Region boundary

VIa West Scotland

Scalloway
Lerwick
Scrabster
Kinlochbervie
Fraserburgh
Lochinver
Ullapool
Mallaig
Aberdeen
Oban
Peterhead

IV North Sea

Rathmullan
Moville
Greencastle
Killybegs
Kirkcudbright
North Shields
Portavogie
Kilkeel
Whitby
Ardglass
Bridlington
Carlingford
Hull
Rossaveal
Grimsby
Howth
Bangor
Wexford
VIIa Irish Sea
Dingle
Dunmore East
Castletown bearhaven
Cobh
Milford Haven
Lowestoft

VIIf/g Bristol Channel and S.E. Ireland

Plymouth
Weymouth
Newlyn
Brixham

VIId/e English Channel

VIIb/h/j West Ireland and Sole Bank

1000 500 200 100 50 m

CHANGES IN THE UK FISHING INDUSTRY

900
800
700
600
500
400
300
200
100
0

50
40
30
20
10

Fishermen in thousands
Average annual value of fish (£/tonne)

Permanently employed fishermen
Annual average value of fish (£/tonne)
Part-time fishermen

1938 1940 1950 1960 1970 1980 1990 2000

FORESTRY – WOODLAND COVER

- Northern Ireland
- Wales
- Scotland
- England

Woodland cover as % of total land area in the UK

Total area
2,500,000 hectares
2,000,000 hectares
1,500,000 hectares
1,000,000 hectares
500,000 hectares

4.7% 5.0% 5.8% 7.3% 9.0% 9.9% 11.6%

1905 1924 1947 1965 1980 1990 2000

FORESTRY – TIMBER CONSUMPTION

Hardwood logs 2%
Fuelwood 3%
Fencing 4%
Paper products 12%
Other 1%
Softwood logs 54%
Woodbased panels 24%

Total timber consumed in the UK (2000) 7,160 cubic metres

COPYRIGHT PHILIP'S

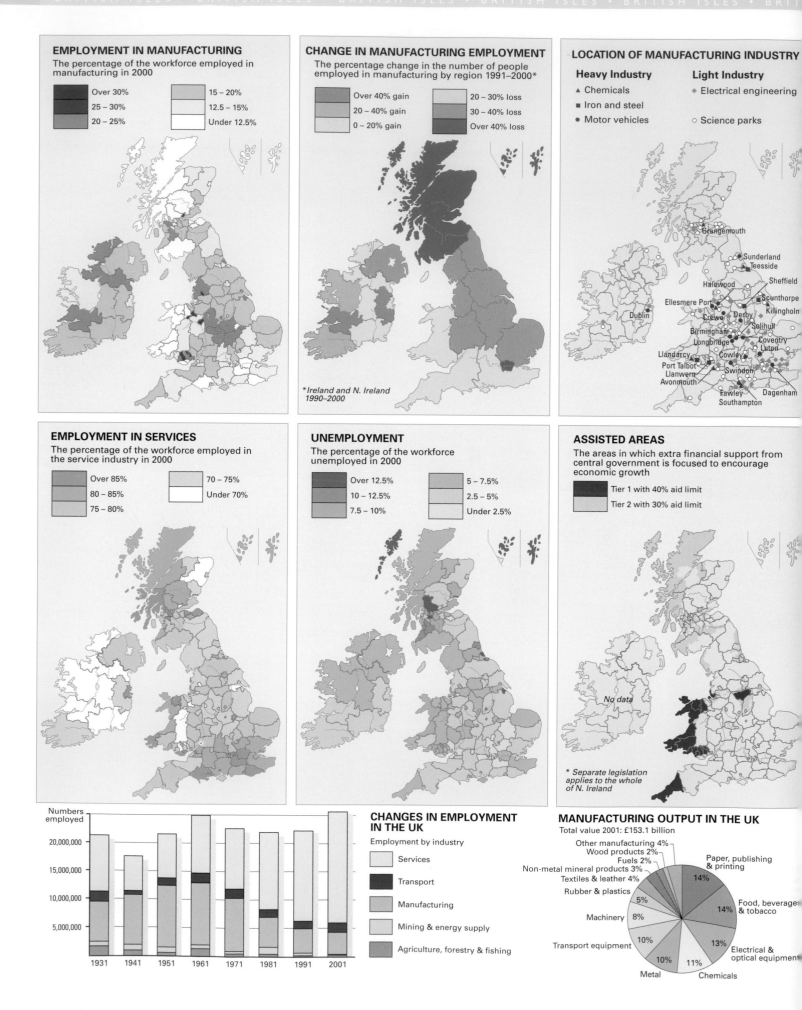

EMPLOYMENT IN MANUFACTURING

The percentage of the workforce employed in manufacturing in 2000

- Over 30%
- 25 – 30%
- 20 – 25%
- 15 – 20%
- 12.5 – 15%
- Under 12.5%

CHANGE IN MANUFACTURING EMPLOYMENT

The percentage change in the number of people employed in manufacturing by region 1991–2000*

- Over 40% gain
- 20 – 40% gain
- 0 – 20% gain
- 20 – 30% loss
- 30 – 40% loss
- Over 40% loss

Ireland and N. Ireland 1990–2000

LOCATION OF MANUFACTURING INDUSTRY

Heavy Industry
- ▲ Chemicals
- ■ Iron and steel
- ● Motor vehicles

Light Industry
- ◆ Electrical engineering
- ○ Science parks

Grangemouth
Sunderland
Teesside
Sheffield
Halewood
Ellesmere Port
Scunthorpe
Killingholm
Dublin
Crewe
Derby
Birmingham
Solihull
Longbridge
Coventry
Luton
Llandarcy
Cowley
Port Talbot
Llanwern
Swindon
Avonmouth
Fawley
Dagenham
Southampton

EMPLOYMENT IN SERVICES

The percentage of the workforce employed in the service industry in 2000

- Over 85%
- 80 – 85%
- 75 – 80%
- 70 – 75%
- Under 70%

UNEMPLOYMENT

The percentage of the workforce unemployed in 2000

- Over 12.5%
- 10 – 12.5%
- 7.5 – 10%
- 5 – 7.5%
- 2.5 – 5%
- Under 2.5%

ASSISTED AREAS

The areas in which extra financial support from central government is focused to encourage economic growth

- Tier 1 with 40% aid limit
- Tier 2 with 30% aid limit

No data

* Separate legislation applies to the whole of N. Ireland

Numbers employed

20,000,000

15,000,000

10,000,000

5,000,000

1931 1941 1951 1961 1971 1981 1991 2001

CHANGES IN EMPLOYMENT IN THE UK

Employment by industry

- Services
- Transport
- Manufacturing
- Mining & energy supply
- Agriculture, forestry & fishing

MANUFACTURING OUTPUT IN THE UK

Total value 2001: £153.1 billion

- Other manufacturing 4%
- Wood products 2%
- Fuels 2%
- Non-metal mineral products 3%
- Textiles & leather 4%
- Rubber & plastics 5%
- Machinery 8%
- Transport equipment 10%
- Metal 10%
- Chemicals 11%
- Electrical & optical equipment 13%
- Food, beverage & tobacco 14%
- Paper, publishing & printing 14%

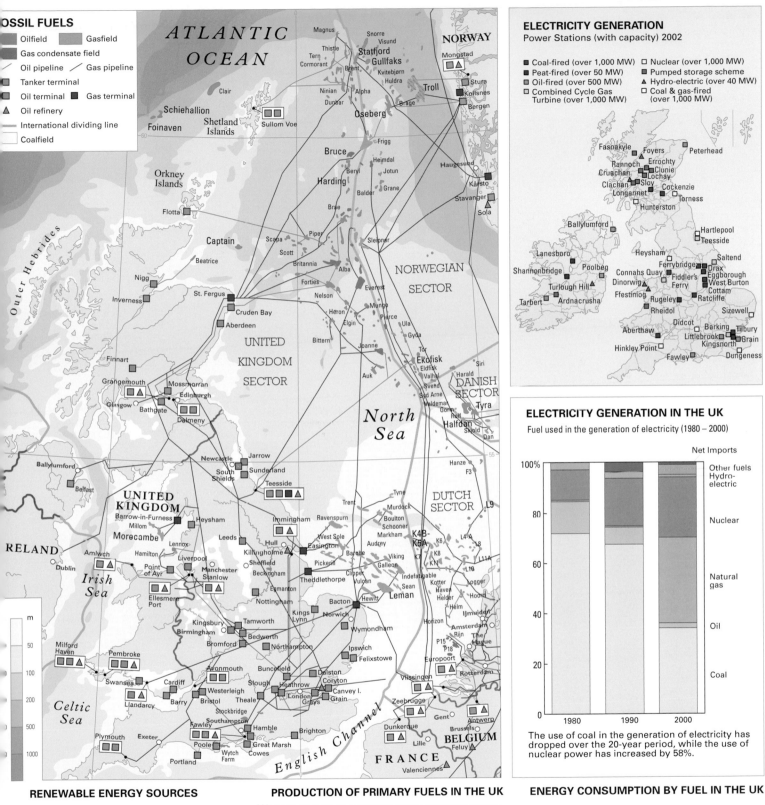

...OSSIL FUELS

- Oilfield
- Gasfield
- Gas condensate field
- / Oil pipeline / Gas pipeline
- ■ Tanker terminal
- ■ Oil terminal ■ Gas terminal
- ▲ Oil refinery
- International dividing line
- Coalfield

ATLANTIC OCEAN

NORWAY

Magnus
Snorre
Visund
Tern Thistle
Cormorant
Brent
Statfjord
Gullfaks
Mongstad
Kvitebjørn
Stura
Kollsnes
Clair
Troll
Bergen
Schiehallion
Ninian
Alpha
Dunbar
Oseberg
Brage
Foinaven
Shetland
Islands
Sullom Voe
Frigg
Haugesund
Bruce
Heimdal
Kårstø
Beryl
Jotun
Harding
Balder
Grane
Stavanger
Sola
Brae
Orkney
Islands
Scapa
Piper
Britannia
Flotta
Scott
Sleipner
Captain
Beatrice
Forties
NORWEGIAN SECTOR
Alba
Nelson
Everest
Nigg
St. Fergus
Mungo
Inverness
Heron
Cruden Bay
Elgin
Aberdeen
Bittern
Ula
Gyda
UNITED KINGDOM SECTOR
Joanne
Tor
Ekofisk
Eldfisk
Valhal
Siri
Auk
Harald
Svend
DANISH SECTOR
Finnart
Gorm Tyra
Halfdan
Grangemouth
Dan
Mossmorran
Edinburgh
Glasgow
Bathgate
Dalmeny
North Sea
Hanze
F3
Newcastle
Jarrow
South Shields
Sunderland
Teesside
DUTCH SECTOR
L9
Tyne
Murdock
Trent
Ravenspurn
Boulton
Schooner
Markham
L4-A
L8
Immingham
West Sole
Barque
K4B-K5A
K6
Heysham
Leeds
Hull
Killingholme
Easington
Audrey
Viking
Galleon
K7 K8 KN
L11A
Barrow-in-Furness
Millom
Sheffield
Pickerill
Clipper
Vulcan
Indefatigable
Logger
L10
Morecambe
Lennox
Beckingham
Theddlethorpe
Sean
Kotter
Helder
Hoord
Amlwch
Hamilton
Liverpool
Point of Ayr
Manchester
Stanlow
Egmanton
Leman
Helm
Ijmuiden
Dublin
Nottingham
Bacton
Hewett
Horizon
Amsterdam
Ellesmere
Port
Kings Lynn
Norwich
Wymondham
Rijn
P15
The Hague
Kingsbury
Tamworth
Ipswich
P18
Birmingham
Bedworth
Northampton
Felixstowe
Europoort
Bromford
Rotterdam
Milford Haven
Avonmouth
Buncefield
Dalston
Pembroke
Swansea
Cardiff
Slough
Heathrow
Coryton
Vissingen
Llandarcy
Barry
Westerleigh
Theale
London
Canvey I.
Zeebrugge
Bristol
Grays
Grain
Stockbridge
Southampton
Hamble
Brighton
Dunkerque
Gent
Antwerp
Fawley
Poole
Great Marsh
Cowes
Lille
BELGIUM
Plymouth
Exeter
Wytch Farm
English Channel
Brussels
Feluy
Portland
FRANCE
Valenciennes

Outer Hebrides
IRELAND
Ballylumford
Belfast
UNITED KINGDOM
Irish Sea
Celtic Sea

m
50
100
200
500
1000

ELECTRICITY GENERATION
Power Stations (with capacity) 2002

- ■ Coal-fired (over 1,000 MW)
- ■ Peat-fired (over 50 MW)
- ■ Oil-fired (over 500 MW)
- □ Combined Cycle Gas Turbine (over 1,000 MW)
- □ Nuclear (over 1,000 MW)
- □ Pumped storage scheme
- ▲ Hydro-electric (over 40 MW)
- □ Coal & gas-fired (over 1,000 MW)

Fasnakyle
Foyers
Peterhead
Rannoch
Errochty
Cruachan
Clunie
Lochay
Clachan
Sloy
Cockenzie
Longannet
Torness
Hunterston
Ballylumford
Hartlepool
Teesside
Lanesboro
Heysham
Shannonbridge
Poolbeg
Ferrybridge
Saltend
Connahs Quay
Drax
Turlough Hill
Dinorwig
Fiddler's Ferry
Eggborough
West Burton
Tarbert
Ardnacrusha
Ffestiniog
Rugeley
Cottam
Ratcliffe
Rheidol
Didcot
Sizewell
Aberthaw
Barking
Tilbury
Hinkley Point
Littlebrook
Grain
Kingsnorth
Fawley
Dungeness

ELECTRICITY GENERATION IN THE UK
Fuel used in the generation of electricity (1980 – 2000)

Net Imports

Other fuels
Hydro-electric
Nuclear
Natural gas
Oil
Coal

100%
80
60
40
20
0
1980 1990 2000

The use of coal in the generation of electricity has dropped over the 20-year period, while the use of nuclear power has increased by 58%.

RENEWABLE ENERGY SOURCES

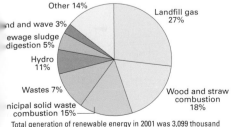

- Other 14%
- Landfill gas 27%
- ...nd and wave 3%
- ...ewage sludge digestion 5%
- Hydro 11%
- Wood and straw combustion 18%
- Wastes 7%
- ...nicipal solid waste combustion 15%

Total generation of renewable energy in 2001 was 3,099 thousand tonnes of oil equivalent, 1% of total energy production in the UK

PRODUCTION OF PRIMARY FUELS IN THE UK

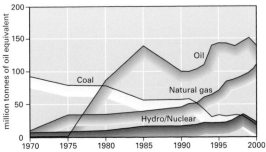

million tonnes of oil equivalent

200
150
100
50
0

Oil
Coal
Natural gas
Hydro/Nuclear

1970 1975 1980 1985 1990 1995 2000

ENERGY CONSUMPTION BY FUEL IN THE UK

Hydro 0.2%
Other 1.6%
Nuclear 9%
Coal 17.5%
Natural gas 40%
Oil 32%

Total consumption in 2001: 237.7 million tonnes of oil equivalent

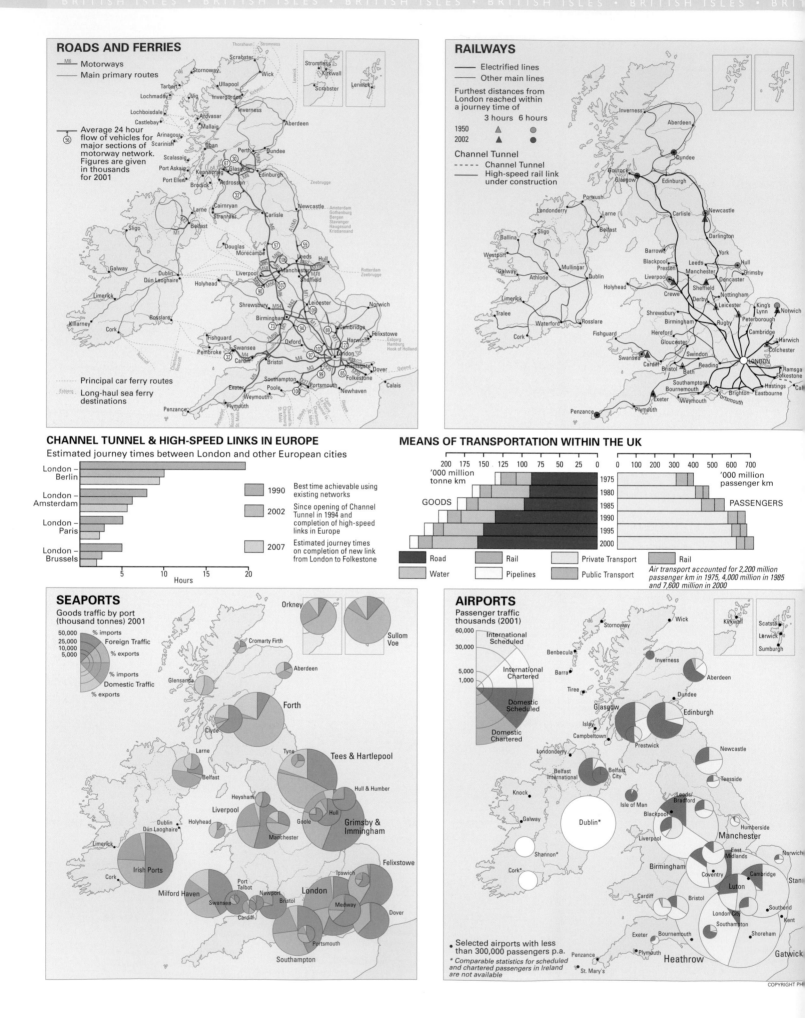

ROADS AND FERRIES

— M8 Motorways
— Main primary routes

(56) Average 24 hour flow of vehicles for major sections of motorway network. Figures are given in thousands for 2001

---- Principal car ferry routes

Esbjerg Long-haul sea ferry destinations

RAILWAYS

— Electrified lines
— Other main lines

Furthest distances from London reached within a journey time of
            3 hours   6 hours
1950   ▲   ●
2002   ▲   ●

Channel Tunnel
- - - - Channel Tunnel
— High-speed rail link under construction

CHANNEL TUNNEL & HIGH-SPEED LINKS IN EUROPE

Estimated journey times between London and other European cities

London – Berlin
London – Amsterdam
London – Paris
London – Brussels

1990 Best time achievable using existing networks
2002 Since opening of Channel Tunnel in 1994 and completion of high-speed links in Europe
2007 Estimated journey times on completion of new link from London to Folkestone

Hours: 5 10 15 20

MEANS OF TRANSPORTATION WITHIN THE UK

GOODS
'000 million tonne km
200 175 150 125 100 75 50 25 0
1975
1980
1985
1990
1995
2000

PASSENGERS
'000 million passenger km
0 100 200 300 400 500 600 700
1975
1980
1985
1990
1995
2000

Road
Water
Rail
Pipelines
Private Transport
Public Transport
Rail

Air transport accounted for 2,200 million passenger km in 1975, 4,000 million in 1985 and 7,600 million in 2000

SEAPORTS

Goods traffic by port (thousand tonnes) 2001

50,000
25,000
10,000
5,000

% imports Foreign Traffic
% exports
% imports Domestic Traffic
% exports

AIRPORTS

Passenger traffic thousands (2001)

60,000 International Scheduled
30,000
5,000
1,000 International Chartered
Domestic Scheduled
Domestic Chartered

• Selected airports with less than 300,000 passengers p.a.

* Comparable statistics for scheduled and chartered passengers in Ireland are not available

COPYRIGHT PH

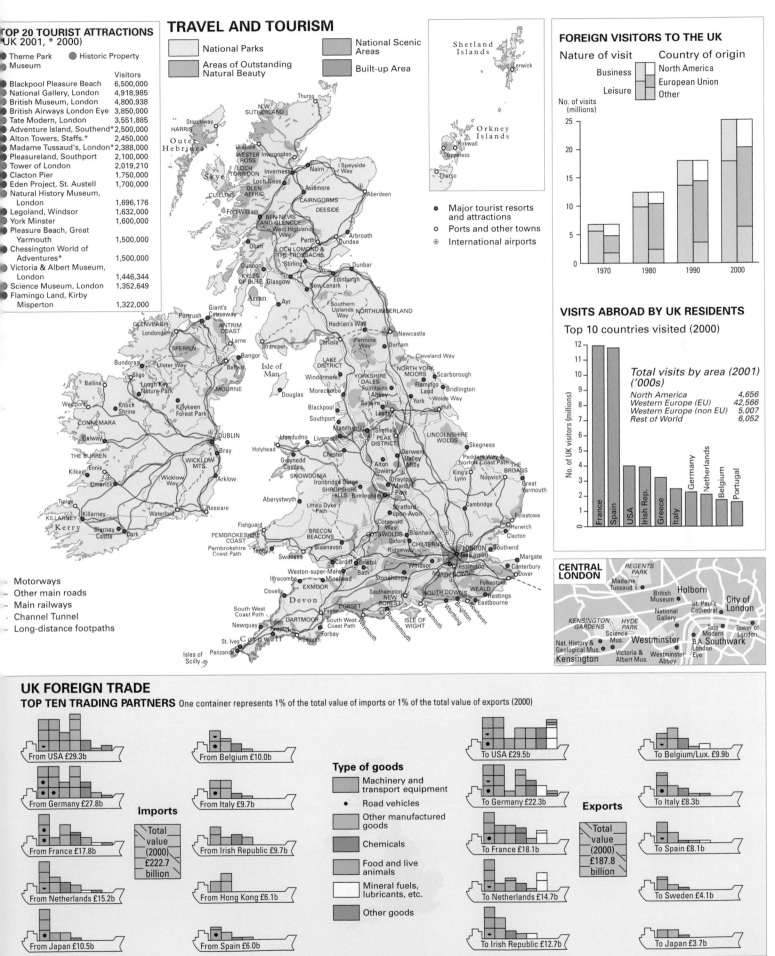

TRAVEL AND TOURISM

National Parks

Areas of Outstanding Natural Beauty

National Scenic Areas

Built-up Area

• Major tourist resorts and attractions
○ Ports and other towns
⊕ International airports

TOP 20 TOURIST ATTRACTIONS
UK 2001, * 2000

● Theme Park   ● Historic Property
● Museum

	Visitors
● Blackpool Pleasure Beach	6,500,000
● National Gallery, London	4,918,985
● British Museum, London	4,800,938
● British Airways London Eye	3,850,000
● Tate Modern, London	3,551,885
● Adventure Island, Southend*	2,500,000
● Alton Towers, Staffs.*	2,450,000
● Madame Tussaud's, London*	2,388,000
● Pleasureland, Southport	2,100,000
● Tower of London	2,019,210
● Clacton Pier	1,750,000
● Eden Project, St. Austell	1,700,000
● Natural History Museum, London	1,696,176
● Legoland, Windsor	1,632,000
● York Minster	1,600,000
● Pleasure Beach, Great Yarmouth	1,500,000
● Chessington World of Adventures*	1,500,000
● Victoria & Albert Museum, London	1,446,344
● Science Museum, London	1,352,649
● Flamingo Land, Kirby Misperton	1,322,000

═ Motorways
─ Other main roads
─ Main railways
─ Channel Tunnel
─ Long-distance footpaths

FOREIGN VISITORS TO THE UK

Nature of visit
- Business
- Leisure

Country of origin
- North America
- European Union
- Other

No. of visits (millions) — 1970, 1980, 1990, 2000

VISITS ABROAD BY UK RESIDENTS

Top 10 countries visited (2000)

No. of UK visitors (millions): France, Spain, USA, Irish Rep., Greece, Italy, Germany, Netherlands, Belgium, Portugal

Total visits by area (2001) ('000s)	
North America	4,656
Western Europe (EU)	42,566
Western Europe (non EU)	5,007
Rest of World	6,052

CENTRAL LONDON

UK FOREIGN TRADE

TOP TEN TRADING PARTNERS One container represents 1% of the total value of imports or 1% of the total value of exports (2000)

Type of goods
- Machinery and transport equipment
- • Road vehicles
- Other manufactured goods
- Chemicals
- Food and live animals
- Mineral fuels, lubricants, etc.
- Other goods

Imports
- From USA £29.3b
- From Germany £27.8b
- From France £17.8b
- From Netherlands £15.2b
- From Japan £10.5b
- From Belgium £10.0b
- From Italy £9.7b
- From Irish Republic £9.7b
- From Hong Kong £6.1b
- From Spain £6.0b

Total value (2000) £222.7 billion

Exports
- To USA £29.5b
- To Germany £22.3b
- To France £18.1b
- To Netherlands £14.7b
- To Irish Republic £12.7b
- To Belgium/Lux. £9.9b
- To Italy £8.3b
- To Spain £8.1b
- To Sweden £4.1b
- To Japan £3.7b

Total value (2000) £187.8 billion

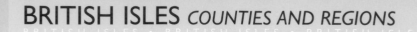

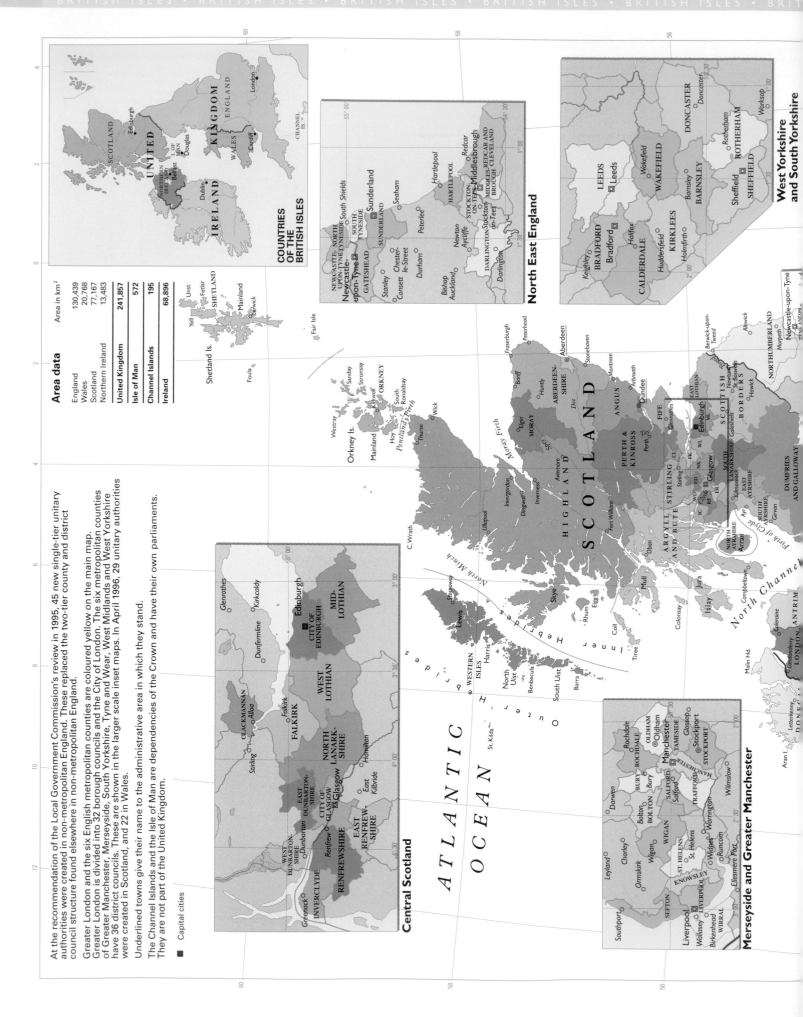

At the recommendation of the Local Government Commission's review in 1995, 45 new single-tier unitary authorities were created in non-metropolitan England. These replaced the two-tier county and district council structure found elsewhere in non-metropolitan England.

Greater London and the six English metropolitan counties are coloured yellow on the main map. Greater London is divided into 32 borough councils and the City of London. The six metropolitan counties of Greater Manchester, Merseyside, South Yorkshire, Tyne and Wear, West Midlands and West Yorkshire have 36 district councils. These are shown in the larger scale inset maps. In April 1996, 29 unitary authorities were created in Scotland, and 22 in Wales.

Underlined towns give their name to the administrative area in which they stand.

The Channel Islands and the Isle of Man are dependencies of the Crown and have their own parliaments. They are not part of the United Kingdom.

■ Capital cities

Area data

	Area in km²
England	130,439
Wales	20,768
Scotland	77,167
Northern Ireland	13,483
United Kingdom	**241,857**
Isle of Man	572
Channel Islands	195
Ireland	**68,896**

COUNTRIES OF THE BRITISH ISLES

North East England

West Yorkshire and South Yorkshire

Central Scotland

Merseyside and Greater Manchester

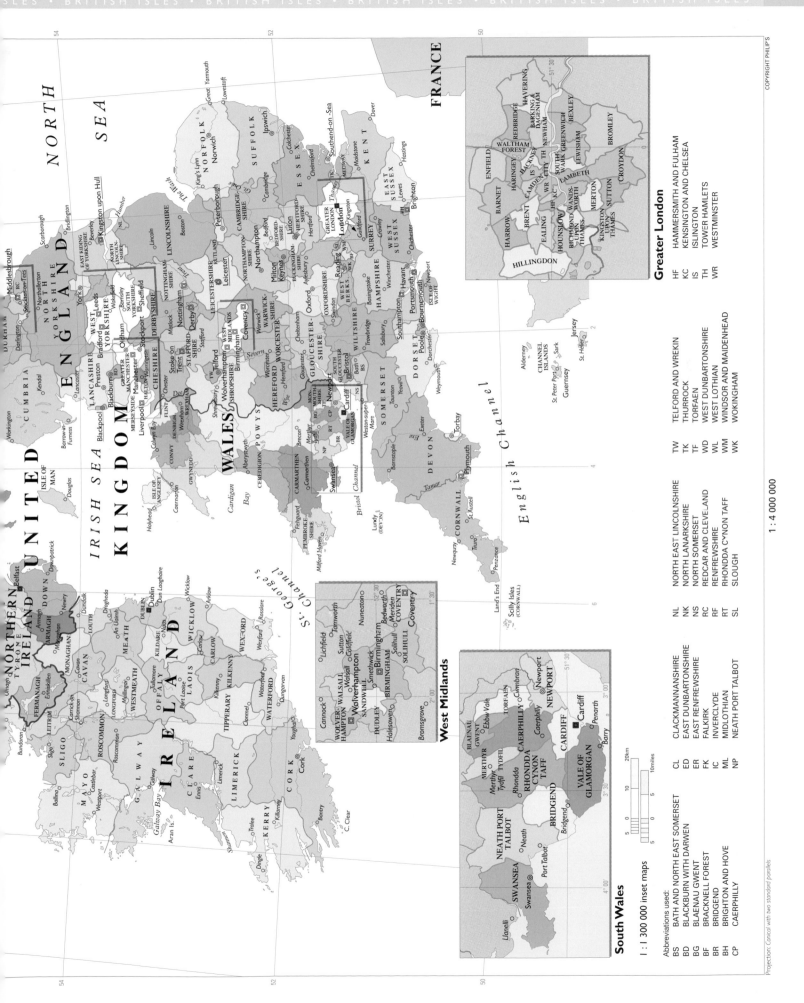

POPULATION DENSITY

Persons per sq km (2001)

- Over 5,000
- 2,000 – 5,000
- 1,000 – 2,000
- 500 – 1,000
- 200 – 500
- 100 – 200
- 20 – 100
- Under 20

POPULATION CHANGE 1981–2001

The percentage change in the number of people between 1981 and 2001

△ Over 20% increase   ▽ Over 5% decrease

POPULATION DATA

	% Change 1981–2001	Population 2001 ('000s)	Density (persons per sq km)
England	5.0	49,181	378
Wales	3.2	2,903	140
Scotland	-2.2	5,064	65
Northern Ireland	9.5	1,689	124
United Kingdom	4.4	58,837	243
Ireland	13.0	3,897	57

Projection: Conical with two standard parallels

1 : 4 000 000

COPYRIGHT PHI

POPULATION DENSITY IN 1891

Persons per sq km

- Over 1,000
- 500 – 1,000
- 200 – 500
- 100 – 200
- 50 – 100
- 25 – 50
- Under 25

*K 142 people
er sq km, Ireland 49
eople per sq km

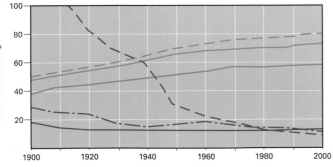

ETHNIC GROUPS

Ethnic minorities as a % of total population in 2000–1

- Over 6%
- 4 – 6%
- 2 – 4%
- 0 – 2%

Ethnic minority groups

- Indian/ Pakistani/ Bangladeshi
- W. Indian/ African
- Other

77 000 Total number of ethnic minority people in each region

No available data

SCOTLAND 77 000

NORTH EAST 41 000

YORKSHIRE & THE HUMBER 290 000

NORTH WEST & MERSEYSIDE 282 000

EAST MIDLANDS 204 000

WEST MIDLANDS 525 000

EASTERN 216 000

WALES 50 000

SOUTH WEST 91 000

SOUTH EAST 282 000

LONDON 1 982 000

% foreign born by country
UK (excl. N.Ireland) 8.4%
Ireland 7.0%

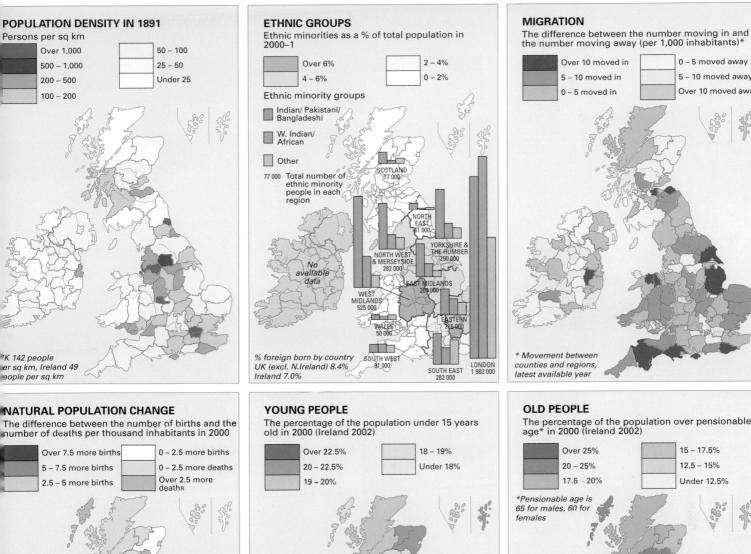

MIGRATION

The difference between the number moving in and the number moving away (per 1,000 inhabitants)*

- Over 10 moved in
- 5 – 10 moved in
- 0 – 5 moved in
- 0 – 5 moved away
- 5 – 10 moved away
- Over 10 moved away

* Movement between counties and regions, latest available year

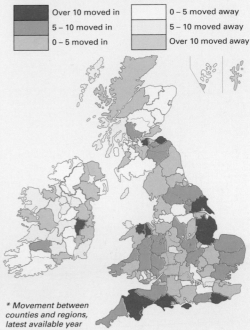

NATURAL POPULATION CHANGE

The difference between the number of births and the number of deaths per thousand inhabitants in 2000

- Over 7.5 more births
- 5 – 7.5 more births
- 2.5 – 5 more births
- 0 – 2.5 more births
- 0 – 2.5 more deaths
- Over 2.5 more deaths

*K 1.2 more
rths than deaths
land 6.1 more
rths than deaths

YOUNG PEOPLE

The percentage of the population under 15 years old in 2000 (Ireland 2002)

- Over 22.5%
- 20 – 22.5%
- 19 – 20%
- 18 – 19%
- Under 18%

% young by country
UK 20.1%
Ireland 21.1%

OLD PEOPLE

The percentage of the population over pensionable age* in 2000 (Ireland 2002)

- Over 25%
- 20 – 25%
- 17.5 – 20%
- 15 – 17.5%
- 12.5 – 15%
- Under 12.5%

*Pensionable age is 65 for males, 60 for females

% old by country
UK 18.4%
Ireland 11.2%

K VITAL STATISTICS (1900–2000)

- Total population (in millions)
- Infant mortality (deaths per 1,000 live births)
- Birth rate (births per 1,000 of the population)
- Death rate (deaths per 1,000 of the population)
- Male life expectancy (in years)
- Female life expectancy (in years)

COPYRIGHT PHILIP'S

AGE STRUCTURE OF THE UK

- 1901
- 2001
- Projected 2150

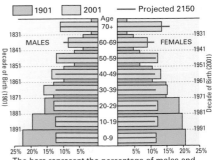

Age
70+
60-69
50-59
40-49
30-39
20-29
10-19
0-9

MALES   FEMALES

Decade of Birth (1901)
1831, 1841, 1851, 1861, 1871, 1881, 1891

Decade of Birth (2001)
1931, 1941, 1951, 1961, 1971, 1981, 1991

25% 20% 15% 10% 5%   5% 10% 15% 20% 25%

The bars represent the percentage of males and females in the age group shown

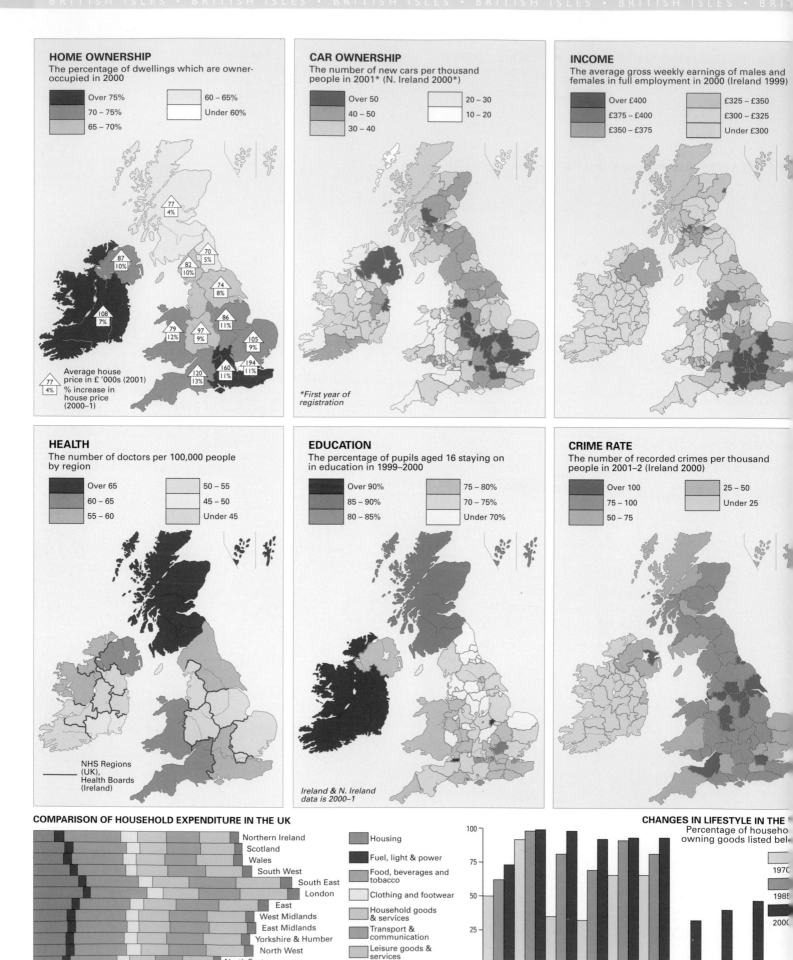

HOME OWNERSHIP
The percentage of dwellings which are owner-occupied in 2000

- Over 75%
- 70 – 75%
- 65 – 70%
- 60 – 65%
- Under 60%

77
4%
Average house price in £ '000s (2001)
% increase in house price (2000–1)

CAR OWNERSHIP
The number of new cars per thousand people in 2001* (N. Ireland 2000*)

- Over 50
- 40 – 50
- 30 – 40
- 20 – 30
- 10 – 20

*First year of registration

INCOME
The average gross weekly earnings of males and females in full employment in 2000 (Ireland 1999)

- Over £400
- £375 – £400
- £350 – £375
- £325 – £350
- £300 – £325
- Under £300

HEALTH
The number of doctors per 100,000 people by region

- Over 65
- 60 – 65
- 55 – 60
- 50 – 55
- 45 – 50
- Under 45

NHS Regions (UK), Health Boards (Ireland)

EDUCATION
The percentage of pupils aged 16 staying on in education in 1999–2000

- Over 90%
- 85 – 90%
- 80 – 85%
- 75 – 80%
- 70 – 75%
- Under 70%

Ireland & N. Ireland data is 2000–1

CRIME RATE
The number of recorded crimes per thousand people in 2001–2 (Ireland 2000)

- Over 100
- 75 – 100
- 50 – 75
- 25 – 50
- Under 25

COMPARISON OF HOUSEHOLD EXPENDITURE IN THE UK

Northern Ireland
Scotland
Wales
South West
South East
London
East
West Midlands
East Midlands
Yorkshire & Humber
North West
North East

0   £100   £200   £300   £400 per week
Average household expenditure per week in UK in 2000: £348.20

- Housing
- Fuel, light & power
- Food, beverages and tobacco
- Clothing and footwear
- Household goods & services
- Transport & communication
- Leisure goods & services
- Miscellaneous goods

COPYRIGHT PHILIP'S

CHANGES IN LIFESTYLE IN THE
Percentage of househo owning goods listed bel

100
75
50
25

Car   TV   Phone   Central heating   Fridge   Washing machine   PC with internet   Satellite or cable TV   Mobile phone

1970
1985
2000

Equatorial Scale 1:89 000 000

Projection: Hammer Equal Area

Projection : Hammer Equal Area

Hanoi ● Capital Cities

Equatorial Scale 1:95 000 000

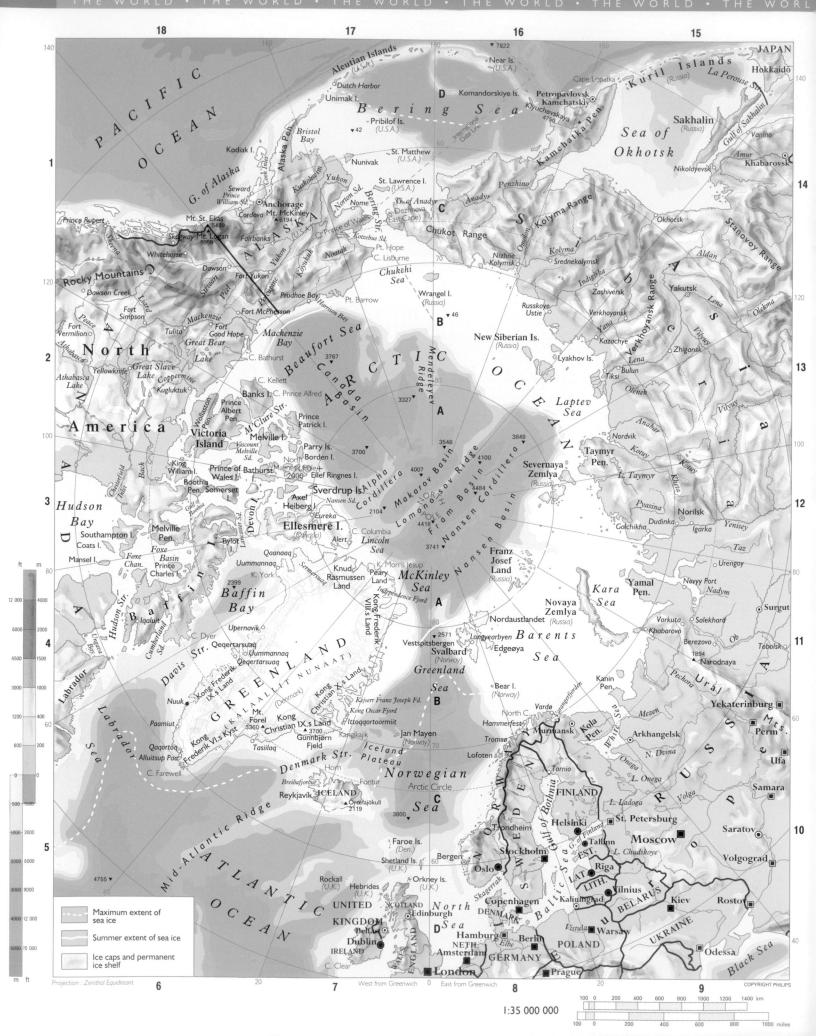

Maximum extent of sea ice

Summer extent of sea ice

Ice caps and permanent ice shelf

Projection : Zenithal Equidistant

1:35 000 000

COPYRIGHT PHILIPS

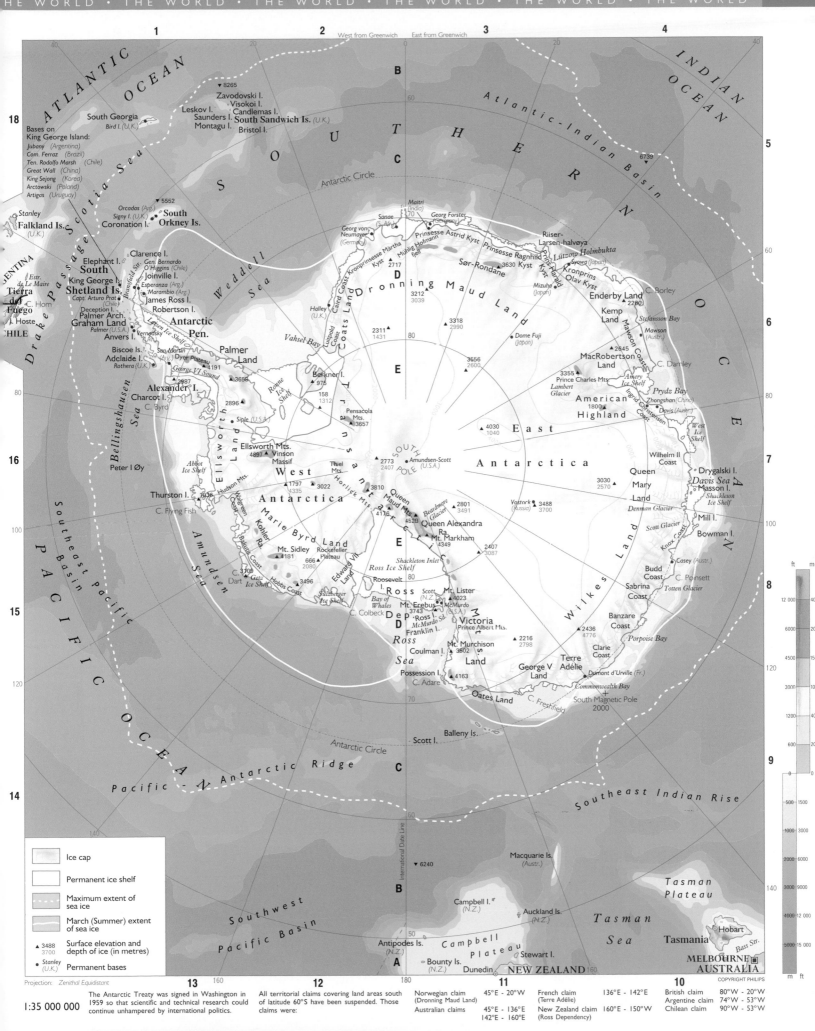

Bases on
King George Island:
Jubany (Argentina)
Com. Ferraz (Brazil)
Ten. Rodolfo Marsh (Chile)
Great Wall (China)
King Sejong (Korea)
Arctowski (Poland)
Artigas (Uruguay)

Legend:

- Ice cap
- Permanent ice shelf
- Maximum extent of sea ice
- March (Summer) extent of sea ice
- ▲ 3488 / 3700   Surface elevation and depth of ice (in metres)
- • Stanley (U.K.)   Permanent bases

Projection: Zenithal Equidistant

1:35 000 000

The Antarctic Treaty was signed in Washington in 1959 so that scientific and technical research could continue unhampered by international politics.

All territorial claims covering land areas south of latitude 60°S have been suspended. Those claims were:

Norwegian claim (Dronning Maud Land)   45°E – 20°W
Australian claims   45°E – 136°E / 142°E – 160°E
French claim (Terre Adélie)   136°E – 142°E
New Zealand claim (Ross Dependency)   160°E – 150°W
British claim   80°W – 20°W
Argentine claim   74°W – 53°W
Chilean claim   90°W – 53°W

COPYRIGHT PHILIPS

ROCKALL Sea areas named in weather forecasts

100 0 100 200 300 400 500 600 700 800 km
100 0 100 200 300 400 500 miles

1:20 000 000

Projection: Bonne

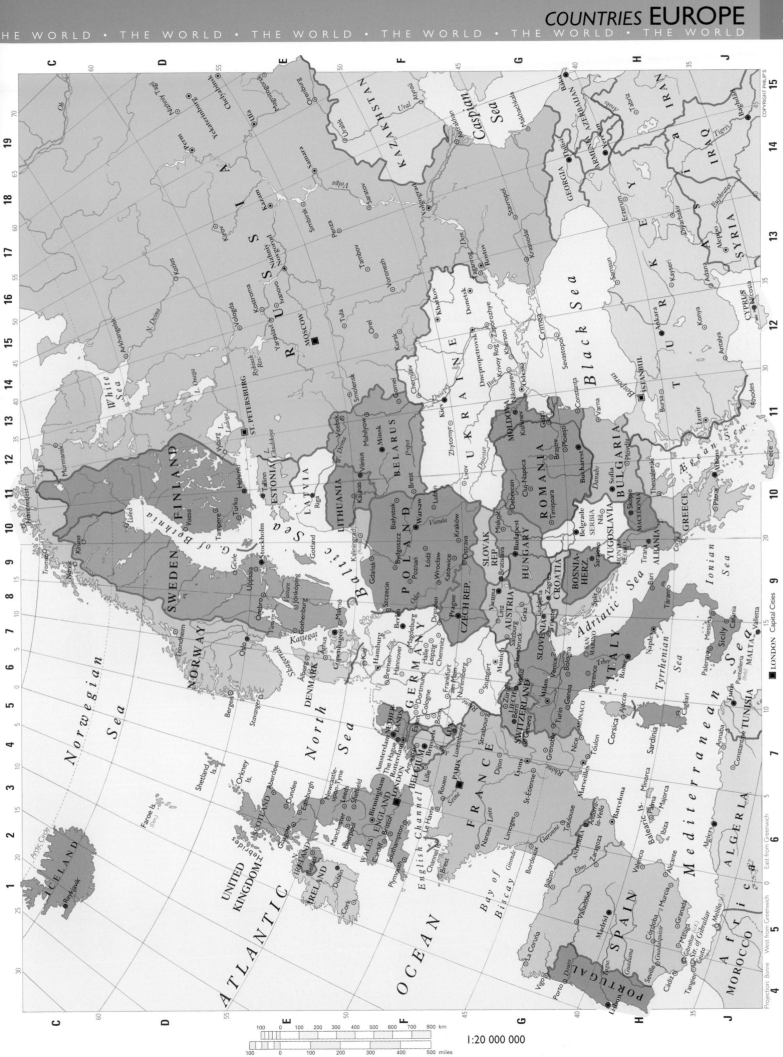

1:20 000 000

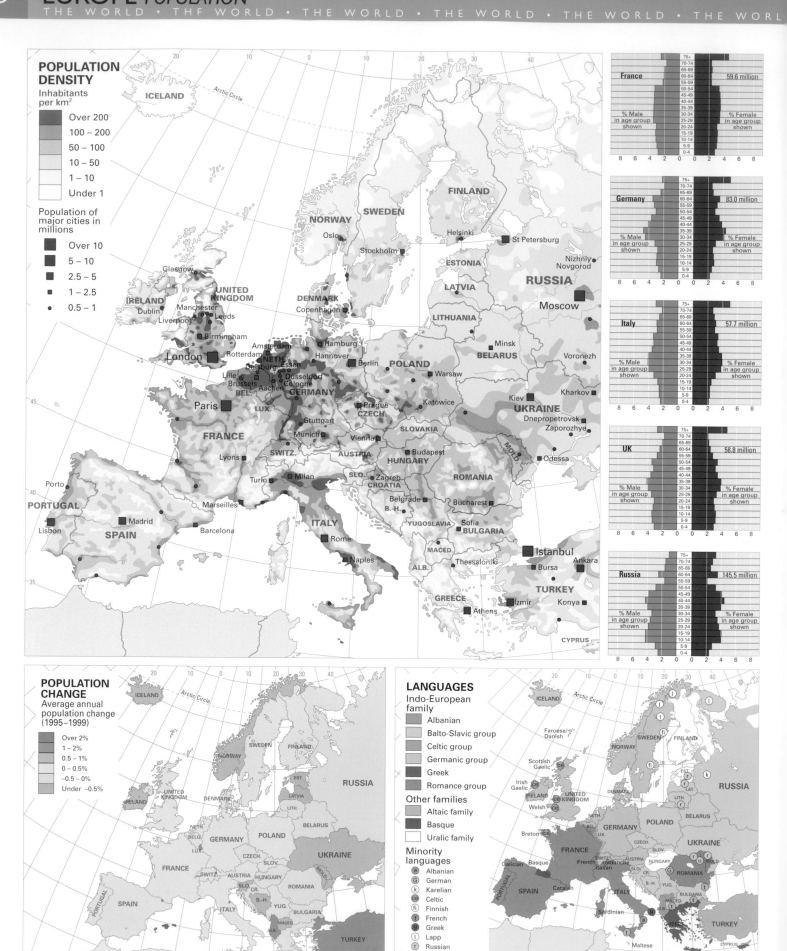

POPULATION DENSITY
Inhabitants per km²

- Over 200
- 100 – 200
- 50 – 100
- 10 – 50
- 1 – 10
- Under 1

Population of major cities in millions

- Over 10
- 5 – 10
- 2.5 – 5
- 1 – 2.5
- 0.5 – 1

Age-sex pyramids:

- France — 59.6 million — % Male in age group shown / % Female in age group shown
- Germany — 83.0 million — % Male in age group shown / % Female in age group shown
- Italy — 57.7 million — % Male in age group shown / % Female in age group shown
- UK — 58.8 million — % Male in age group shown / % Female in age group shown
- Russia — 145.5 million — % Male in age group shown / % Female in age group shown

POPULATION CHANGE
Average annual population change (1995–1999)

- Over 2%
- 1 – 2%
- 0.5 – 1%
- 0 – 0.5%
- -0.5 – 0%
- Under -0.5%

Projection: Bonne

LANGUAGES
Indo-European family

- Albanian
- Balto-Slavic group
- Celtic group
- Germanic group
- Greek
- Romance group

Other families

- Altaic family
- Basque
- Uralic family

Minority languages

- a Albanian
- G German
- k Karelian
- ce Celtic
- fi Finnish
- f French
- g Greek
- l Lapp
- r Russian
- t Turkish
- u Ukrainian

COPYRIGHT PHILIP'S

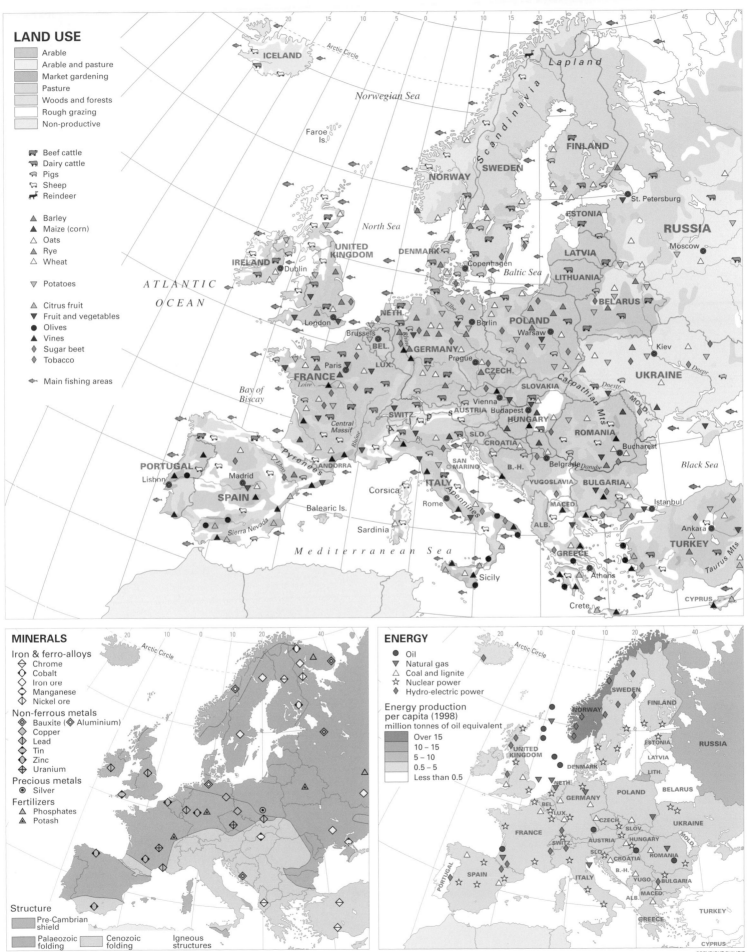

LAND USE

Arable
Arable and pasture
Market gardening
Pasture
Woods and forests
Rough grazing
Non-productive

Beef cattle
Dairy cattle
Pigs
Sheep
Reindeer

Barley
Maize (corn)
Oats
Rye
Wheat

Potatoes

Citrus fruit
Fruit and vegetables
Olives
Vines
Sugar beet
Tobacco

Main fishing areas

MINERALS

Iron & ferro-alloys
Chrome
Cobalt
Iron ore
Manganese
Nickel ore

Non-ferrous metals
Bauxite (Aluminium)
Copper
Lead
Tin
Zinc
Uranium

Precious metals
Silver

Fertilizers
Phosphates
Potash

Structure
Pre-Cambrian shield
Palaeozoic folding
Cenozoic folding
Igneous structures

ENERGY

Oil
Natural gas
Coal and lignite
Nuclear power
Hydro-electric power

Energy production
per capita (1998)
million tonnes of oil equivalent

Over 15
10 – 15
5 – 10
0.5 – 5
Less than 0.5

Projection: Bonne

COPYRIGHT PHILIP'S

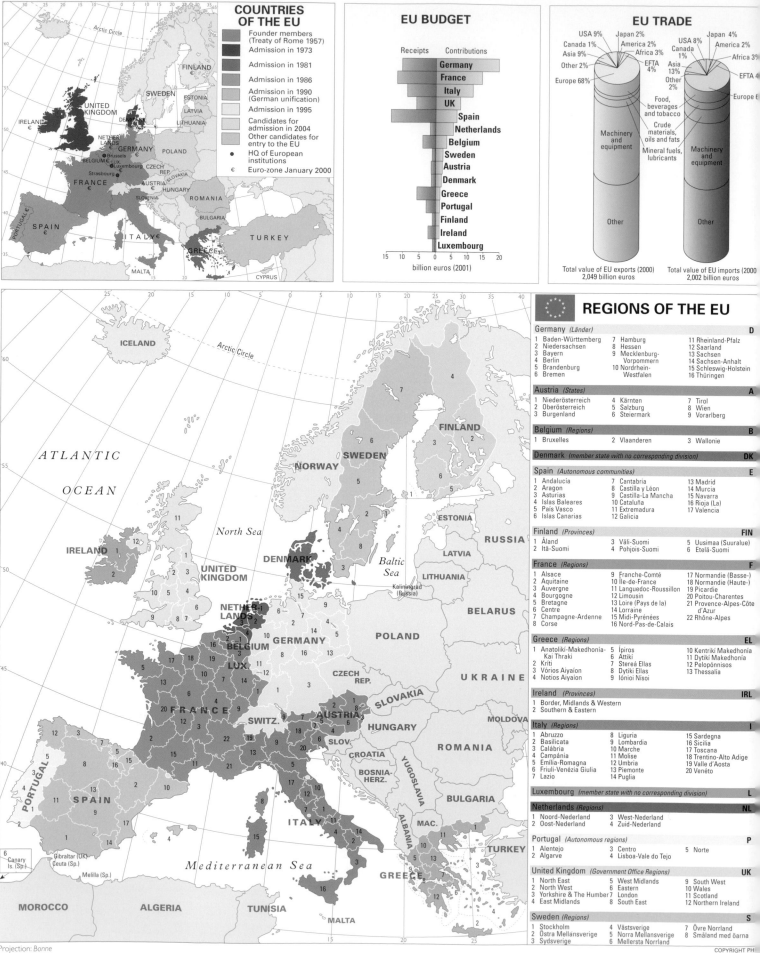

COUNTRIES OF THE EU

- Founder members (Treaty of Rome 1957)
- Admission in 1973
- Admission in 1981
- Admission in 1986
- Admission in 1990 (German unification)
- Admission in 1995
- Candidates for admission in 2004
- Other candidates for entry to the EU
- • HQ of European institutions
- € Euro-zone January 2000

EU BUDGET

Receipts   Contributions

Germany
France
Italy
UK
Spain
Netherlands
Belgium
Sweden
Austria
Denmark
Greece
Portugal
Finland
Ireland
Luxembourg

15 10 5 0 5 10 15 20
billion euros (2001)

EU TRADE

Exports:
- USA 9%
- Canada 1%
- Japan 2%
- America 2%
- Asia 9%
- Africa 3%
- Other 2%
- EFTA 4%
- Europe 68%
- Machinery and equipment
- Food, beverages and tobacco
- Crude materials, oils and fats
- Mineral fuels, lubricants
- Other

Imports:
- USA 8%
- Canada 1%
- Japan 4%
- America 2%
- Asia 13%
- Africa 3%
- Other 2%
- EFTA 4%
- Europe 6
- Machinery and equipment
- Other

Total value of EU exports (2000) 2,049 billion euros
Total value of EU imports (2000) 2,002 billion euros

REGIONS OF THE EU

Germany (Länder) D
1 Baden-Württemberg	7 Hamburg	11 Rheinland-Pfalz
2 Niedersachsen	8 Hessen	12 Saarland
3 Bayern	9 Mecklenburg-Vorpommern	13 Sachsen
4 Berlin	10 Nordrhein-Westfalen	14 Sachsen-Anhalt
5 Brandenburg		15 Schleswig-Holstein
6 Bremen		16 Thüringen

Austria (States) A
1 Niederösterreich	4 Kärnten	7 Tirol
2 Oberösterreich	5 Salzburg	8 Wien
3 Burgenland	6 Steiermark	9 Vorarlberg

Belgium (Regions) B
1 Bruxelles	2 Vlaanderen	3 Wallonie

Denmark (member state with no corresponding division) DK

Spain (Autonomous communities) E
1 Andalucía	7 Cantabria	13 Madrid
2 Aragon	8 Castilla y Léon	14 Murcia
3 Asturias	9 Castilla-La Mancha	15 Navarra
4 Islas Baleares	10 Cataluña	16 Rioja (La)
5 País Vasco	11 Extremadura	17 Valencia
6 Islas Canarias	12 Galicia	

Finland (Provinces) FIN
1 Åland	3 Väli-Suomi	5 Uusimaa (Suuralue)
2 Itä-Suomi	4 Pohjois-Suomi	6 Etelä-Suomi

France (Regions) F
1 Alsace	9 Franche-Comté	17 Normandie (Basse-)
2 Aquitaine	10 Ile-de-France	18 Normandie (Haute-)
3 Auvergne	11 Languedoc-Roussillon	19 Picardie
4 Bourgogne	12 Limousin	20 Poitou-Charentes
5 Bretagne	13 Loire (Pays de la)	21 Provence-Alpes-Côte d'Azur
6 Centre	14 Lorraine	22 Rhône-Alpes
7 Champagne-Ardenne	15 Midi-Pyrénées	
8 Corse	16 Nord-Pas-de-Calais	

Greece (Regions) EL
1 Anatoliki-Makedhonía-Kai Thraki	5 Ípiros	10 Kentrikí Makedhonía
2 Kríti	6 Attikí	11 Dytikí Makedhonía
3 Vórios Aiyaíon	7 Stereá Ellas	12 Pelopónnisos
4 Notios Aiyaíon	8 Dytiki Ellas	13 Thessalía
	9 Iónioi Nísoi	

Ireland (Provinces) IRL
1 Border, Midlands & Western
2 Southern & Eastern

Italy (Regions) I
1 Abruzzo	8 Liguria	15 Sardegna
2 Basilicata	9 Lombardia	16 Sicilia
3 Calàbria	10 Marche	17 Toscana
4 Campánia	11 Molise	18 Trentino-Alto Adige
5 Emília-Romagna	12 Umbria	19 Valle d'Aosta
6 Friuli-Venézia Giulia	13 Piemonte	20 Véneto
7 Lazio	14 Puglia	

Luxembourg (member state with no corresponding division) L

Netherlands (Regions) NL
1 Noord-Nederland	3 West-Nederland
2 Oost-Nederland	4 Zuid-Nederland

Portugal (Autonomous regions) P
1 Alentejo	3 Centro	5 Norte
2 Algarve	4 Lisboa-Vale do Tejo	

United Kingdom (Government Office Regions) UK
1 North East	5 West Midlands	9 South West
2 North West	6 Eastern	10 Wales
3 Yorkshire & The Humber	7 London	11 Scotland
4 East Midlands	8 South East	12 Northern Ireland

Sweden (Regions) S
1 Stockholm	4 Västsverige	7 Övre Norrland
2 Östra Mellansverige	5 Norra Mellansverige	8 Småland med öarna
3 Sydsverige	6 Mellersta Norrland	

Projection: Bonne

WEALTH

Gross Domestic Product expressed as Purchasing Power Parity in Euros per capita (2000)

- Over 35,000
- 30,000 – 35,000
- 25,000 – 30,000
- 20,000 – 25,000
- 15,000 – 20,000
- Under 15,000

Government debt as percentage of GDP (2001)

Italy	109.8%
Belgium	107.6%
Greece	107.0%
Austria	63.2%
Germany	59.5%
UK	39.0%

HEALTH

Number of doctors per thousand inhabitants (2000)

- Over 7
- 6 – 7
- 5 – 6
- 4 – 5
- 3 – 4
- 2 – 3
- Under 2

Deaths by circulatory causes, deaths per 100,000 by country (1999)

- □ Over 500
- ○ 400 – 500
- □ 300 – 400
- ○ Under 300

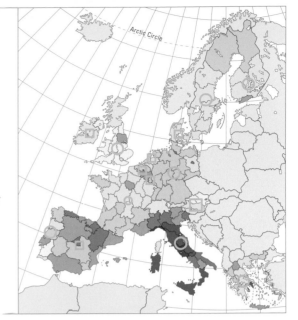

OUT OF WORK

The percentage of the workforce unemployed (2001)

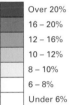

- Over 20%
- 16 – 20%
- 12 – 16%
- 10 – 12%
- 8 – 10%
- 6 – 8%
- Under 6%

Unemployment rate for people under 25 years old (2001)

- ■ Over 30%
- ■ 20 – 30%
- • Under 20%

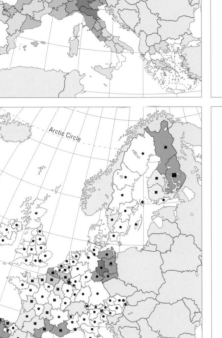

EDUCATION

The percentage of people aged 15 – 24 in education (2000)

- Over 70%
- 60 – 70%
- 50 – 60%
- 40 – 50%
- 30 – 40%
- Under 30%

Expenditure on education as percentage of GDP by country (1995–97)

- □ Over 7%
- □ 5% – 7%
- ○ Under 5%

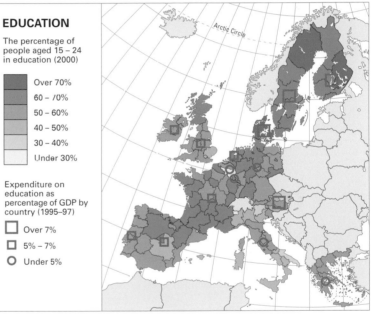

TRANSPORT

Airports with over 10 million passengers a year (2000)

- 50 million
- 25 million
- 10 million

— European high-speed rail network built or planned for 2010

Planned journey times by rail from London

	1990	2010
Amsterdam	7 h 38	3 h 45
Barcelona	20 h 00	6 h 40
Berlin	16 h 35	8 h 25
Brussels	4 h 55	2 h 05
Bordeaux	9 h 48	4 h 45
Frankfurt	11 h 26	5 h 00
Lyons	9 h 04	4 h 00
Madrid	21 h 32	9 h 20
Paris	5 h 15	2 h 10
Venice	20 h 45	7 h 45

INDUSTRY

The percentage of the workforce employed in industry (2001)

- Over 40%
- 35 – 40%
- 30 – 35%
- 25 – 30%
- 20 – 25%
- Under 20%

SERVICES

Percentage of total employment in services by country (2001)

- □ Over 75%
- □ 65 – 75%
- ○ Under 65%

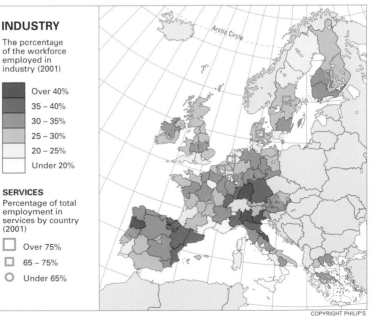

ion: Bonne

Data Source: Eurostat 2000–1

COPYRIGHT PHILIP'S

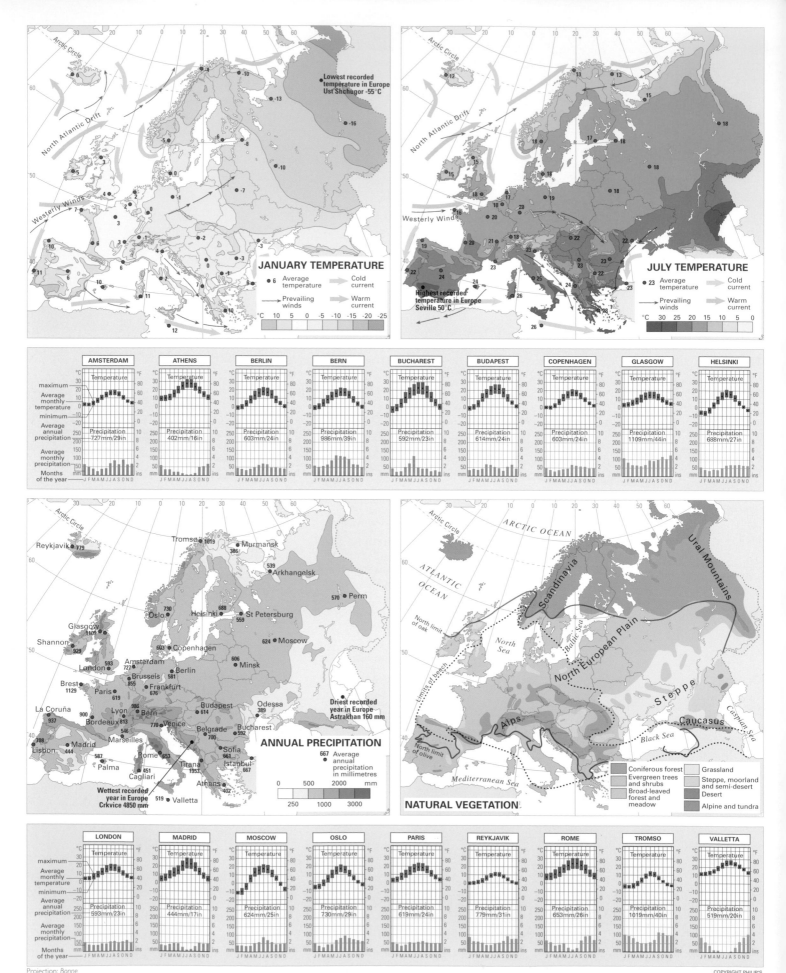

JANUARY TEMPERATURE

Lowest recorded temperature in Europe Ust'Shchugor -55°C

- 6 Average temperature
→ Prevailing winds
⇒ Cold current
⇒ Warm current

°C 10 5 0 -5 -10 -15 -20 -25

JULY TEMPERATURE

Highest recorded temperature in Europe Seville 50°C

- 23 Average temperature
→ Prevailing winds
⇒ Cold current
⇒ Warm current

°C 30 25 20 15 10 5 0

Climate graphs (top row)

AMSTERDAM — Temperature — Precipitation 727mm/29in
ATHENS — Temperature — Precipitation 402mm/16in
BERLIN — Temperature — Precipitation 603mm/24in
BERN — Temperature — Precipitation 986mm/39in
BUCHAREST — Temperature — Precipitation 592mm/23in
BUDAPEST — Temperature — Precipitation 614mm/24in
COPENHAGEN — Temperature — Precipitation 603mm/24in
GLASGOW — Temperature — Precipitation 1109mm/44in
HELSINKI — Temperature — Precipitation 688mm/27in

Labels (left column):
maximum
Average monthly temperature
minimum
Average annual precipitation
Average monthly precipitation
Months of the year

ANNUAL PRECIPITATION

Reykjavik 779
Tromso 1019
Murmansk 386
Arkhangelsk 539
Perm 570
Oslo 730
Helsinki 688
St Petersburg 559
Moscow 624
Glasgow 1109
Shannon 929
Copenhagen 603
Amsterdam 727
Berlin 581
Minsk 606
London 593
Brussels 855
Frankfurt 676
Brest 1129
Paris 619
Lyon 813
Bern 986
Budapest 614
Odessa 389
La Coruña 937
Bordeaux 770
Venice 900
Belgrade 700
Bucharest 592
Madrid 444
Marseilles 546
Sofia 661
Istanbul 667
Lisbon 708
Rome 653
Titana 1353
Palma 587
Cagliari 451
Athens 402
Valletta 519

Driest recorded year in Europe Astrakhan 160 mm
Wettest recorded year in Europe Crkvice 4850 mm

- 667 Average annual precipitation in millimetres

0 250 500 1000 2000 3000 mm

NATURAL VEGETATION

ARCTIC OCEAN
ATLANTIC OCEAN
North limit of oak
Limits of beech
North limit of olive
Scandinavia
Ural Mountains
North European Plain
Alps
Steppe
Caucasus
North Sea
Baltic Sea
Black Sea
Caspian Sea
Mediterranean Sea

Legend:
- Coniferous forest
- Evergreen trees and shrubs
- Broad-leaved forest and meadow
- Grassland
- Steppe, moorland and semi-desert
- Desert
- Alpine and tundra

Climate graphs (bottom row)

LONDON — Temperature — Precipitation 593mm/23in
MADRID — Temperature — Precipitation 444mm/17in
MOSCOW — Temperature — Precipitation 624mm/25in
OSLO — Temperature — Precipitation 730mm/29in
PARIS — Temperature — Precipitation 619mm/24in
REYKJAVIK — Temperature — Precipitation 779mm/31in
ROME — Temperature — Precipitation 653mm/26in
TROMSO — Temperature — Precipitation 1019mm/40in
VALLETTA — Temperature — Precipitation 519mm/20in

Labels (left column):
maximum
Average monthly temperature
minimum
Average annual precipitation
Average monthly precipitation
Months of the year

Projection: Bonne

COPYRIGHT PHILIP'S

West from Greenwich

ICELAND

ICELAND
on same scale

Ísafjörður · Húnaflói · Siglufjörður · Húsavik · Sauðárkrókur · Akureyri · Seyðisfjörður · Breiðafjörður · 1765 · 2000 · Vatnajökull · Akranes · Reykjavik · Keflavík · Hjörtur · Grænafjökull 2119 · Helmaey · Surtsey

NORWEGIAN SEA

Arctic Circle

BARENTS SEA

Nordkapp · Sørøya · Hammerfest · Varanger-halvøya · Vardø · Vadsø · Varangerfjorden · Rybachi Pen. · Pechenga · Zapolyarnyy · Port Vladimir · Polyarny · Severomorsk · Kola · Murmansk · Gremikha

Tromsø · Senja · Vesterålen · Lofoten · Narvik · Inarijärvi · Inari · Olenegorsk · Monchegorsk · 1191 · Kirovsk · Apatity · Kovdor · Kandalaksha · Kola Peninsula · Ponoy · Kuzomen · Umba · G. of Kandalaksha · White Sea

Bodø · Tornetträsk · 2117 · Kebnekaise · Kiruna · Porttipahtan tekojärvi · Lokkan tekojärvi · Alakurtti · Kestenga

Mo i Rana · 1913 · Stora Lulevatten · Gällivare · Rovaniemi · Kemijärvi · Kemijoki · Kem · Belomorsk · Segezha · Nadvoitsy · Onega

Vega · Horna-van · Storavan · Haparanda · Tornio · Kuusamo · Kemijoki · KARELIA

Vikna · Folda · Storuman · Skellefte älv · Boden · Kemi · Kuopio · Kajaani · Medvezhyegorsk · Povenets

Trondheimsfjorden · Hitra · Vilhelmina · Piteå · Luleå · Hailuoto · Oulu · Oulujärvi · Suoyarvi · Kondopoga · Konevo

Kristiansund · Steinkjer · Ume älv · Skellefteå · Raahe · Ouluujoki · Sortavala · Petrozavodsk · L. Onega · Kargopol

Molde · Levanger · Storuman · Umeå · Kokkola · Iisalmi · Pielinen · Joensuu · 330 · Pudozh

Ålesund · Trondheim · Östersund · Örnsköldsvik · Vaasa · Jyväskylä · Kuopio · Priozersk · Olonets · Lodeynoye Pole · Vytegra

Flora · Dovrefjell · Bräcke · Härnösand · Seinäjoki · Saimaa · Imatra · L. Ladoga · Podporozhye · Voznesenye

Snøhetta 2286 · Storsjön · Sundsvall · Pori · Tampere · Hämeenlinna · Vyborg · Navaya Ladoga · Belozersk

Galdhøpiggen 2469 · Hitra · Östersund · Hudiksvall · Rauma · Lahti · Kouvola · Priozersk · Tikhvin · Cherepovets

Høyanger · Sognefjorden · Flåm · Lillehammer · Gilma · Mora · Uusikaupunki · Turku · Vantaa · Helsinki · Kotka · Kronstadt · ST. PETERSBURG · Kolpino · Tikhvin

Bergen · Hardangerfjorden · 1719 · Hamar · Mjøsa · Falun · Gävle · Åland · Hanko · Gulf of Finland · Tallinn · Narva · Borovichi · Rybinsk Res.

Hønefoss · OSLO · Svealand · Avesta · Sala · Uppsala · Gdov · Luga · Novgorod · L. Ilmen · Bologoye · Vyshniy Volochek

Haugesund · Drammen · Dalälven · Hiiumaa (Dagö) · Kohtla-Järve · L. Chudskoye · Pskov · Dno · Staraya Russa · Tver

Stavanger · Skien · Karlstad · Västerås · Eskilstuna · STOCKHOLM · Saaremaa (Ösel) · Pärnu · Tartu · Valga · Kholm · Valdai Hills · Volga · Rzhev

Kristiansand · Arendal · Fredrikstad · Halden · Hjälmaren · Mälaren · Norrköping · ESTONIA · L. Võrtsjärv · Valga · Velikiye Luki · Staritsa · Zelenograd

Mandal · Lindesnes · Vänern · Vättern · Linköping · Gotland · Gulf of Riga · Ventspils · RĪGA · LATVIA · Veliky · Nevel · Toropets · MOSCOW · Odintsovo

Skagerrak · Göteborg · Göta älv · Götaland · Västervik · Visby · Saaremaa · Jelgava · Rēzekne · Daugava · Vitebsk · Vyazma · Kaluga · Oka

Frederikshavn · Skagen · Borås · Jönköping · Öland · Liepāja · Daugavpils · Polatsk · Smolensk · Roslavl · Belev

Holstebro · Ålborg · Kattegat · Varberg · Oskarshamn · Klaipėda · Šiauliai · Panevėžys · Lyepyel · Orsha · Mahilyow · Seltso

DENMARK · Randers · Jutland · Århus · Halmstad · Helsingborg · Kalmar · Karlskrona · LITHUANIA · Neman · Baryzaw · Dnieper · Bryansk

Esbjerg · Odense · COPENHAGEN · Lund · Malmö · Bornholm · Sovetsk · Kaliningrad (Russia) · Kaunas · Vilnius · MINSK · Babruysk · Zhlobin · Orel

Helgoland · Flensburg · Kiel · Gedser · Rügen · Sassnitz · Gdynia · Gdańsk · Elbląg · Suwałki · Hrodna · BELARUS · Baranavichy · Slutsk · Gomel

Emden · HAMBURG · Bremen · Lübeck · Stralsund · Rostock · Świnoujście · Koszalin · Olsztyn · Łomża · Białystok · Pinsk · Pripet Marshes · Chernihiv

Osnabrück · Hannover · Potsdam · BERLIN · Braunschweig · Magdeburg · Szczecin · Bydgoszcz · Toruń · Płock · Brest · Mazyr · Novhorod-Siverskyy

Münster · Dortmund · Kassel · Halle · Leipzig · Dresden · Frankfurt · Poznań · POLAND · Warta · Vistula · WARSAW · Radom · Lublin · Kovel · Pripet · UKRAINE · Konotop

GERMANY · Erfurt · Chemnitz · Plauen · Legnica · Wrocław · Kalisz · Łódź · Kielce · Lutsk · Rivne · KIEV · Pryluky · Okhtyrka

Frankfurt · Darmstadt · Würzburg · Fulda · 1602 · Śnieżka · Opole · Częstochowa · Chorzów · Kraków · Chervonohrad · Zhytomyr · Korosten · Kiev Res. · Chernobyl · Nizhyn · Sumy

Heidelberg · Nürnberg · PRAGUE · Plzeň · Hradec Králové · Ostrava · Tychy · Katowice · Rzeszów · Przemyśl · Ternopil · Bila Tserkva · Cherkasy

CZECH REP. · 2655 · Žilina · Cieszyn · Tarnów · Lviv · Berdychiv · Pereyaslav-Khmelnytskyy · Poltava

NORWEGIAN SEA · SWEDEN · NORWAY · Norrland · Gulf of Bothnia · FINLAND · Lapland · RUSSIA · BALTIC SEA

Projection: Conical with two standard parallels

East from Greenwich

COPYRIGHT PHILIP'S

50 0 100 200 300 400 km
50 0 50 100 150 200 250 miles

1:10 000 000

ft m
6000 2000
4500 1500
3000 1000
1500 500
600 200
0 0
200 600
1500 5000
2000 6000
4000 12 000
m ft

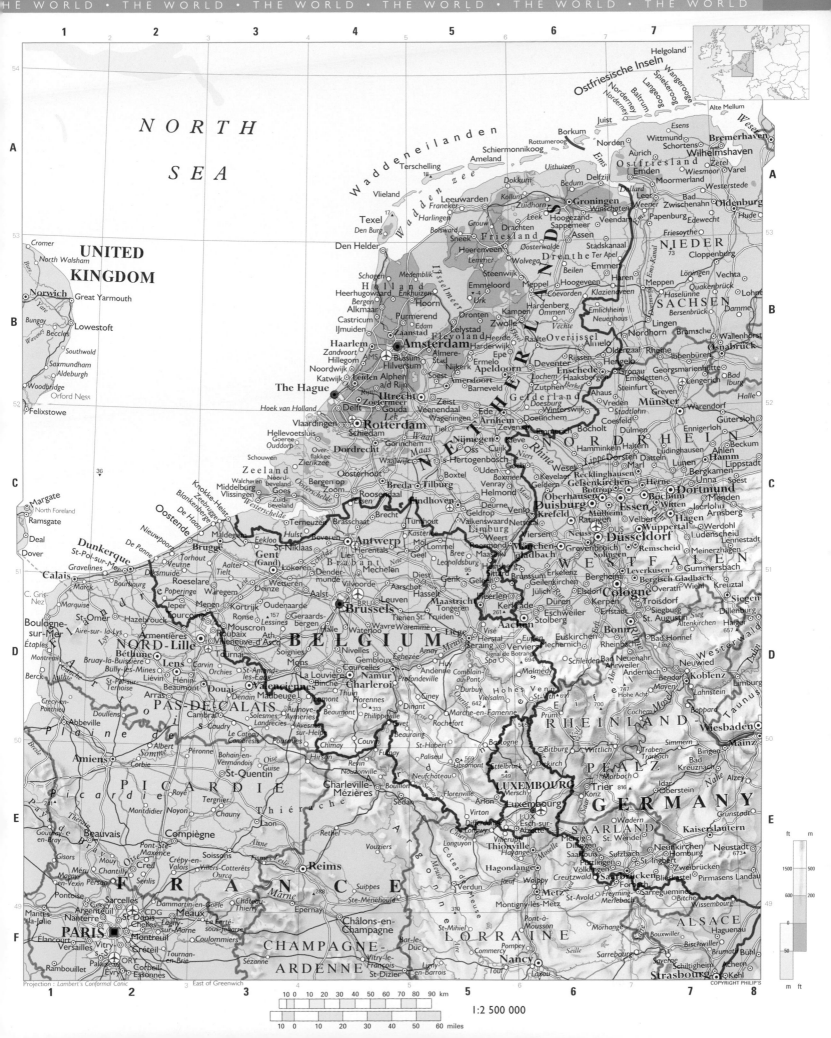

NORTH SEA

UNITED KINGDOM

NETHERLANDS

BELGIUM

LUXEMBOURG

GERMANY

FRANCE

Projection : Lambert's Conformal Conic

1:2 500 000

COPYRIGHT PHILIP'S

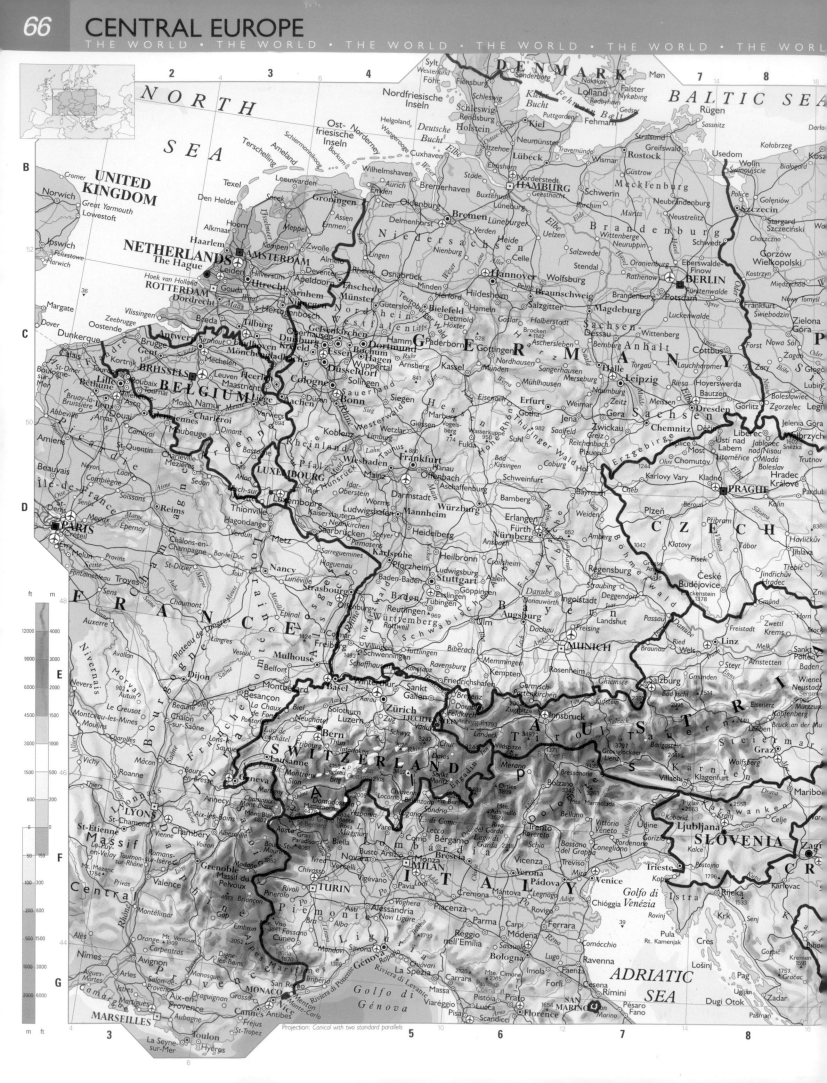

1:5 000 000

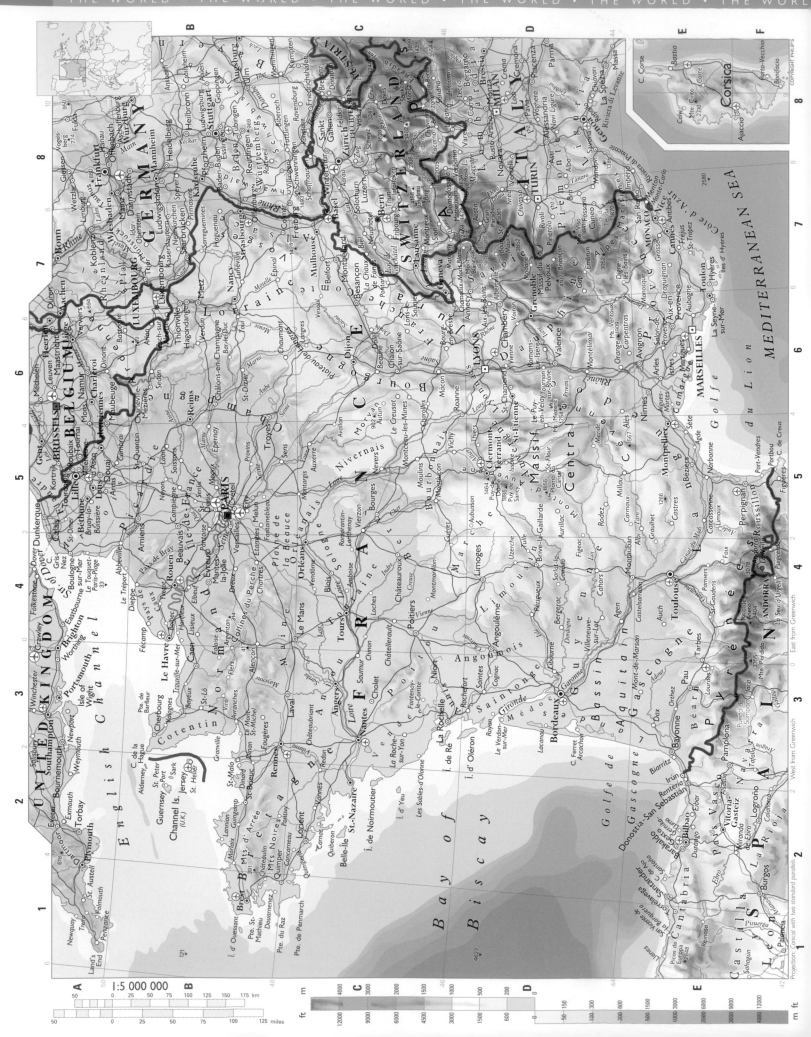

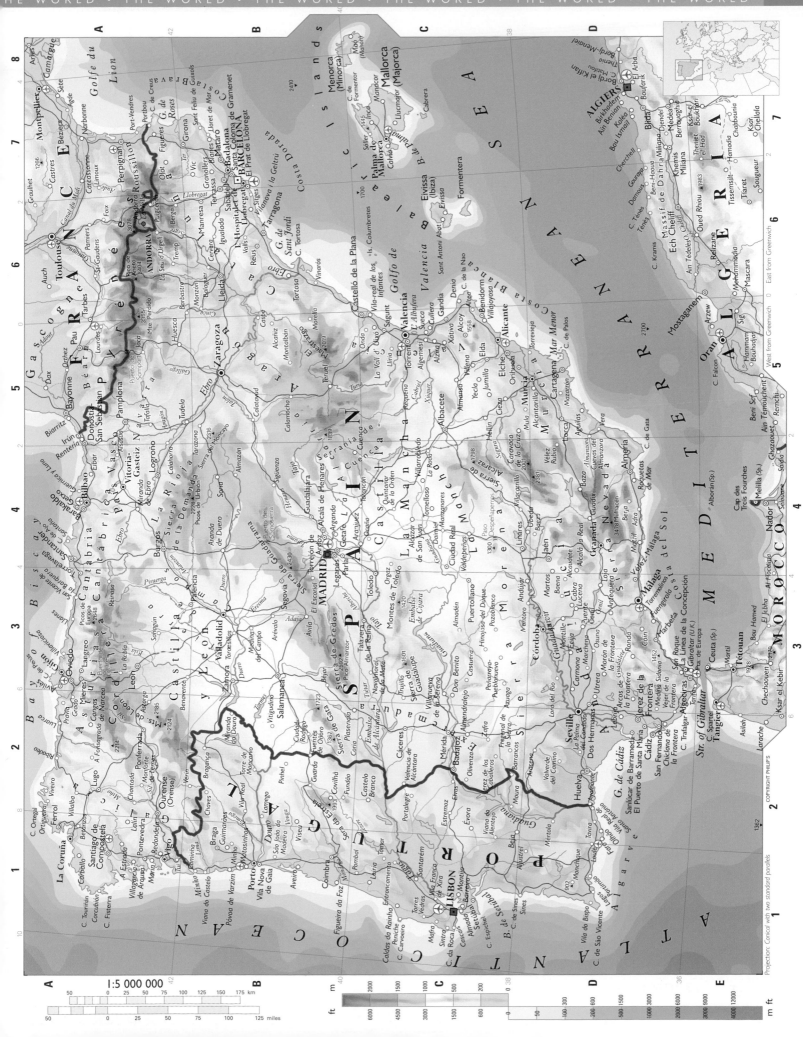

1:5 000 000

East from Greenwich

1:5 000 000

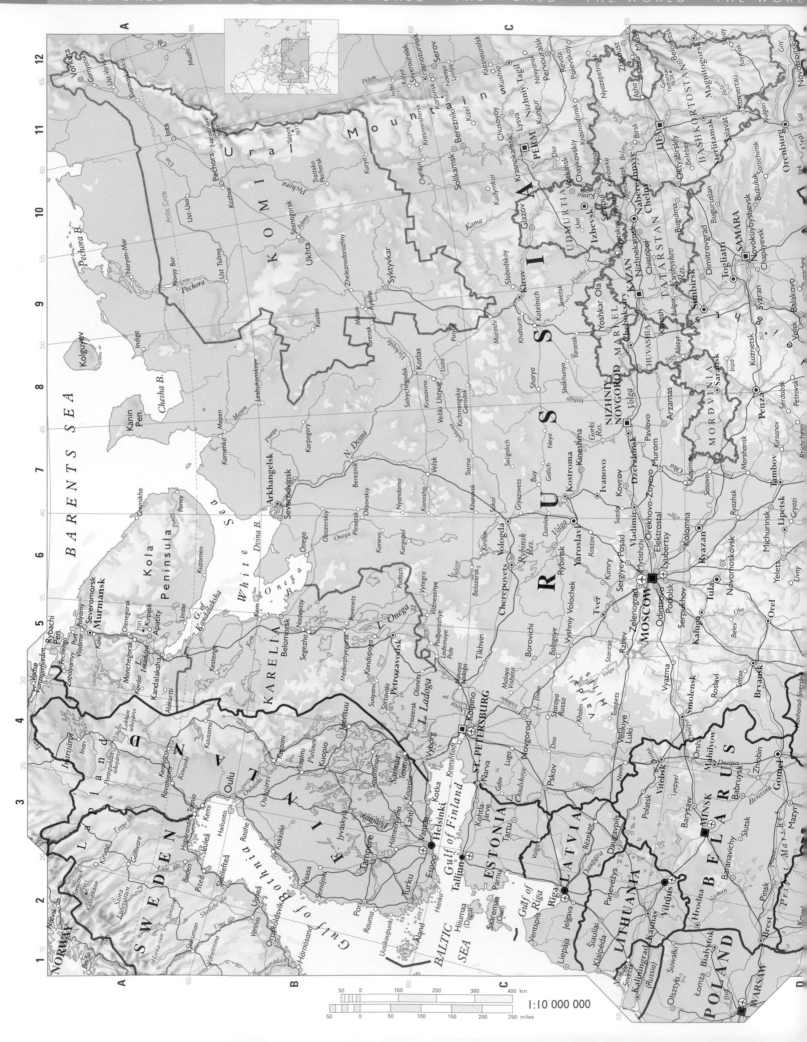

1:10 000 000

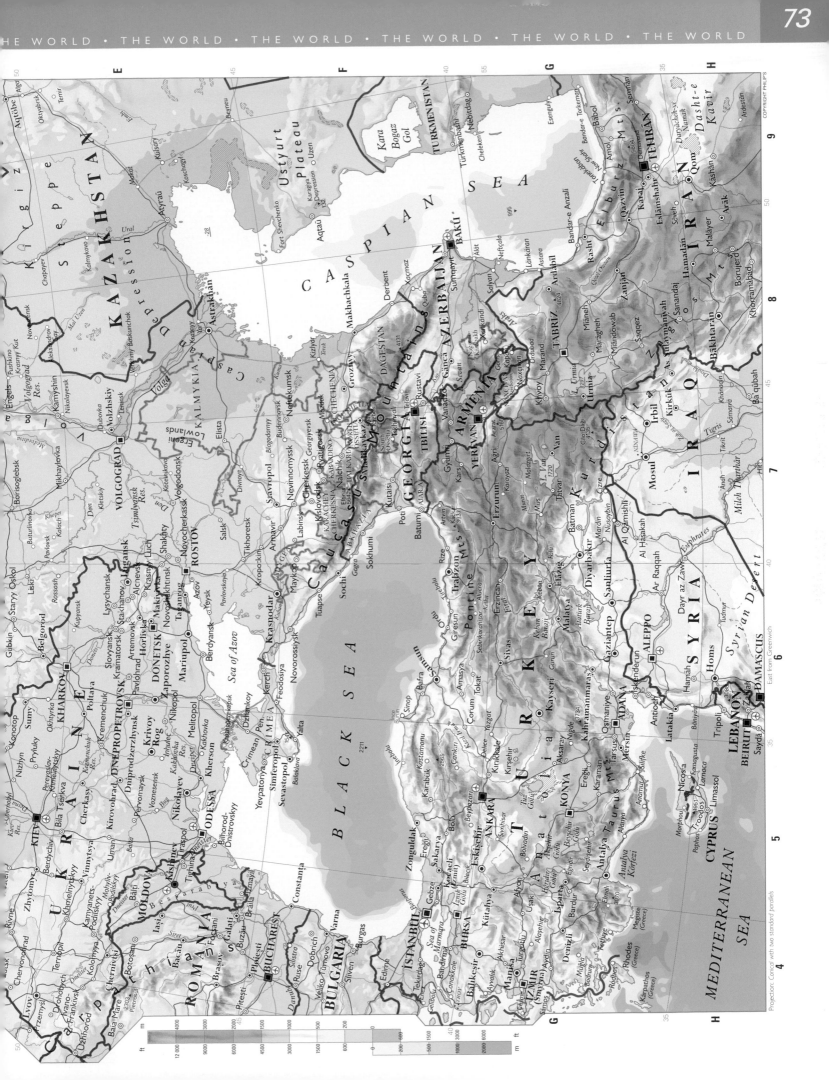

COPYRIGHT PHILIP'S

East from Greenwich

Projection: Conical with two standard parallels

CASPIAN SEA

BLACK SEA

MEDITERRANEAN SEA

KAZAKHSTAN

TURKMENISTAN

IRAN

IRAQ

SYRIA

TURKEY

GEORGIA

AZERBAIJAN

ARMENIA

UKRAINE

ROMANIA

BULGARIA

MOLDOVA

CYPRUS

LEBANON

TEHRĀN

BAKÜ

TBILISI

YEREVAN

ANKARA

ISTANBUL

IZMIR

BUCHAREST

KISHINEV

ODESA

KIEV

KHARKOV

VOLGOGRAD

DONETSK

ROSTOV

DAMASCUS

BEIRUT

ALEPPO

ADANA

KONYA

BURSA

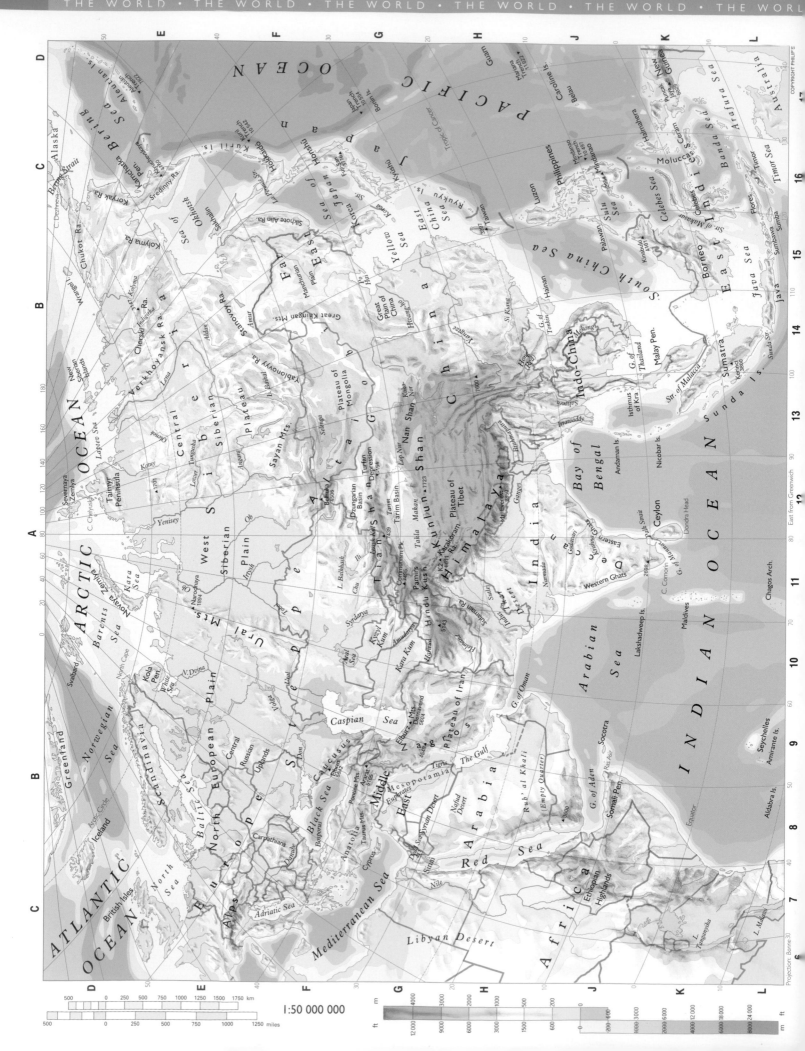

500 0 250 500 750 1000 1250 1500 1750 km

500 0 250 500 750 1000 1250 miles

1:50 000 000

Projection: Bonne

East from Greenwich

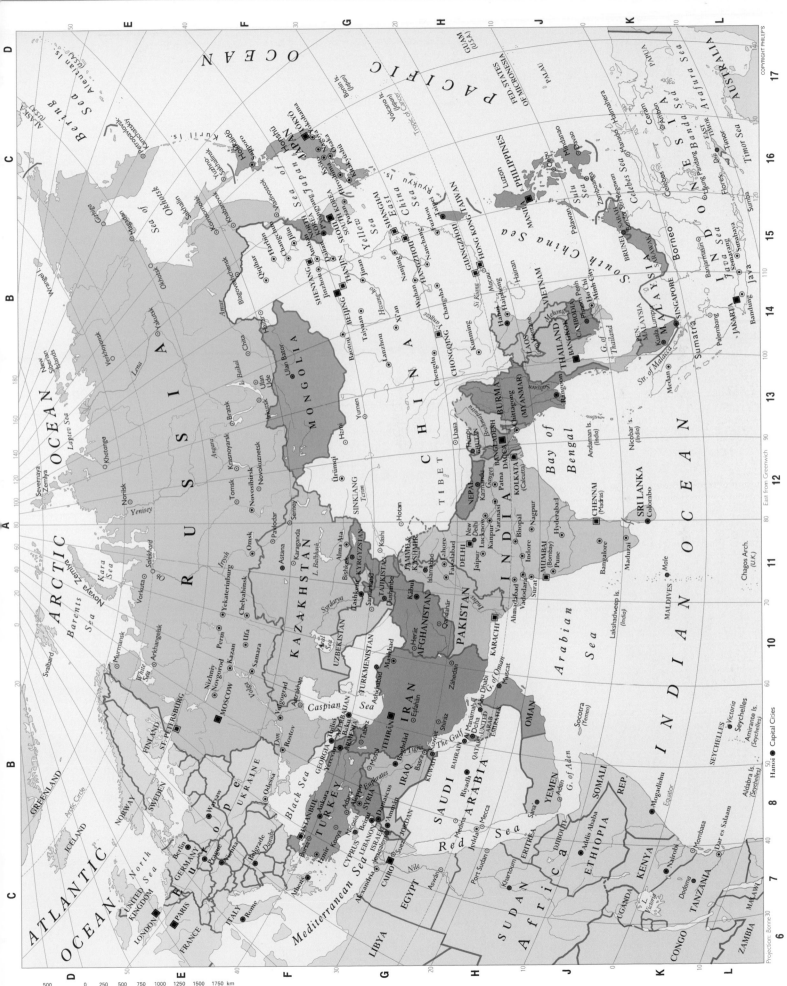

1:50 000 000

500   250 0   250 500 750 1000 1250 1500 1750 km

500   0   250   500   750   1000   1250 miles

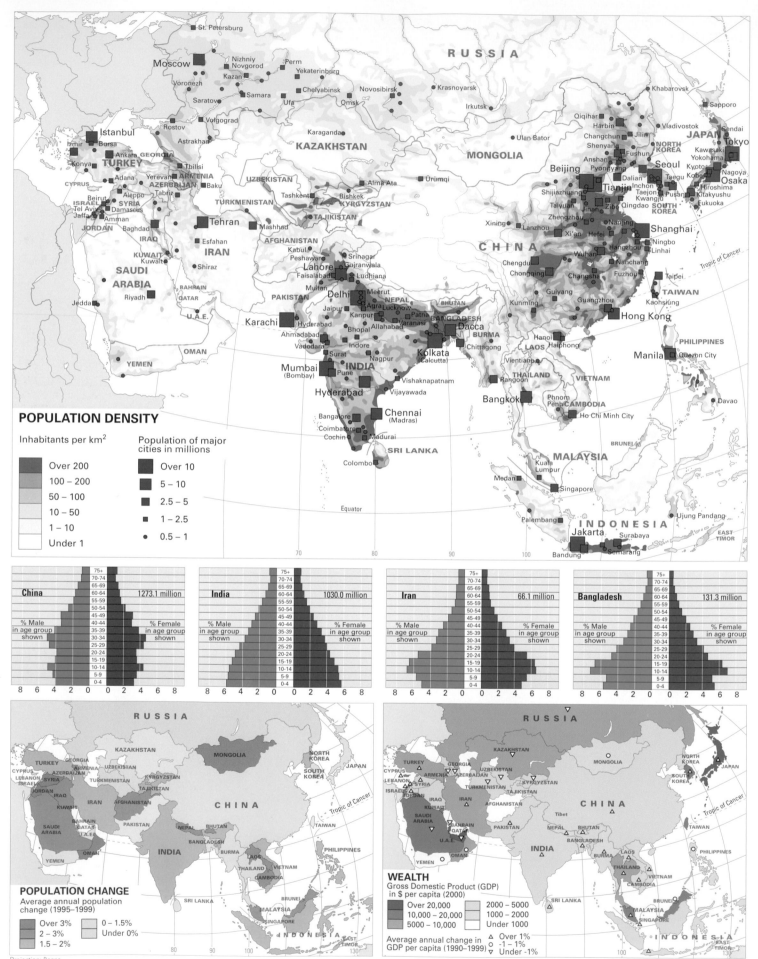

POPULATION DENSITY

Inhabitants per km²

- Over 200
- 100 – 200
- 50 – 100
- 10 – 50
- 1 – 10
- Under 1

Population of major cities in millions

- Over 10
- 5 – 10
- 2.5 – 5
- 1 – 2.5
- 0.5 – 1

China 1273.1 million
% Male in age group shown | % Female in age group shown
8 6 4 2 0 0 2 4 6 8

India 1030.0 million
% Male in age group shown | % Female in age group shown
8 6 4 2 0 0 2 4 6 8

Iran 66.1 million
% Male in age group shown | % Female in age group shown
8 6 4 2 0 0 2 4 6 8

Bangladesh 131.3 million
% Male in age group shown | % Female in age group shown
8 6 4 2 0 0 2 4 6 8

POPULATION CHANGE

Average annual population change (1995–1999)

- Over 3%
- 2 – 3%
- 1.5 – 2%
- 0 – 1.5%
- Under 0%

WEALTH

Gross Domestic Product (GDP) in $ per capita (2000)

- Over 20,000
- 10,000 – 20,000
- 5000 – 10,000
- 2000 – 5000
- 1000 – 2000
- Under 1000

Average annual change in GDP per capita (1990–1999)
- △ Over 1%
- ○ -1 – 1%
- ▽ Under -1%

Projection: Bonne

COPYRIGHT PHILIP'S

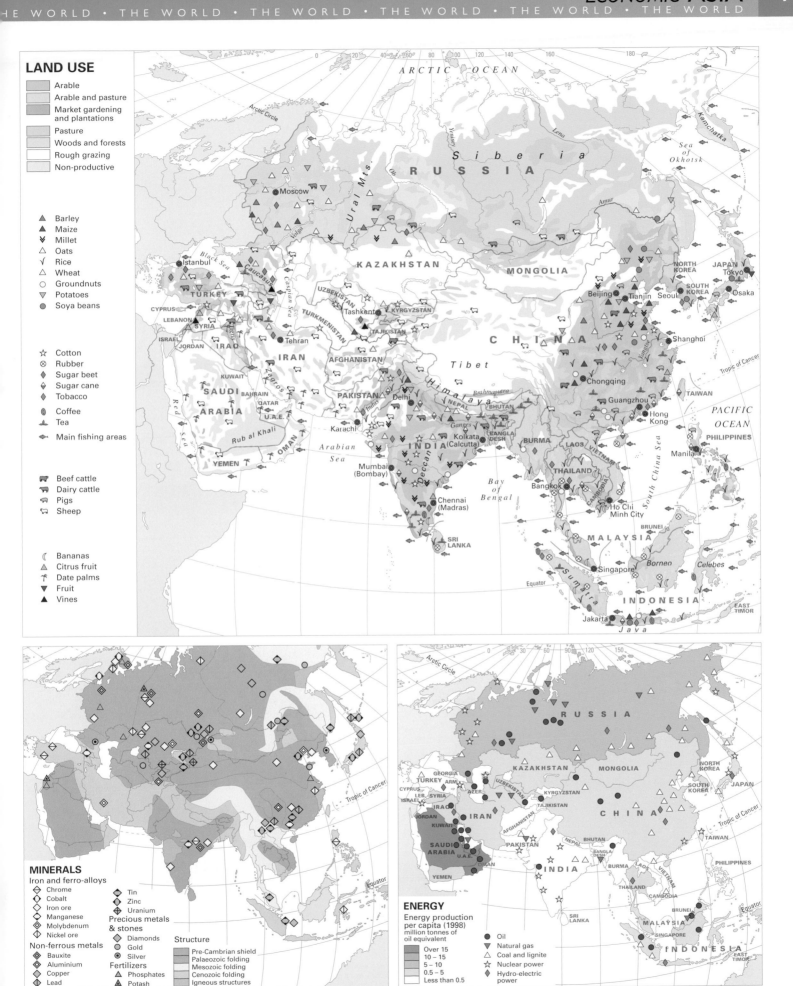

LAND USE

- Arable
- Arable and pasture
- Market gardening and plantations
- Pasture
- Woods and forests
- Rough grazing
- Non-productive

- ▲ Barley
- ▲ Maize
- ⩔ Millet
- △ Oats
- √ Rice
- △ Wheat
- ○ Groundnuts
- ▽ Potatoes
- ● Soya beans

- ☆ Cotton
- ⊗ Rubber
- ◇ Sugar beet
- ◇ Sugar cane
- ◇ Tobacco
- ◖ Coffee
- ⚓ Tea

- ⬱ Main fishing areas

- Beef cattle
- Dairy cattle
- Pigs
- Sheep

- ☾ Bananas
- △ Citrus fruit
- ⚑ Date palms
- ▼ Fruit
- ▲ Vines

MINERALS

Iron and ferro-alloys
- ◇ Chrome
- ◇ Cobalt
- ◇ Iron ore
- ◇ Manganese
- ◈ Molybdenum
- ◈ Nickel ore

Non-ferrous metals
- ◇ Bauxite
- ◇ Aluminium
- ◇ Copper
- ◈ Lead
- ◇ Tin
- ◇ Zinc
- ◇ Uranium

Precious metals & stones
- ◇ Diamonds
- ○ Gold
- ⊙ Silver

Fertilizers
- △ Phosphates
- ▲ Potash

Structure
- Pre-Cambrian shield
- Palaeozoic folding
- Mesozoic folding
- Cenozoic folding
- Igneous structures

Projection: *Bonne*

ENERGY

Energy production per capita (1998)
million tonnes of oil equivalent

- Over 15
- 10 – 15
- 5 – 10
- 0.5 – 5
- Less than 0.5

- ● Oil
- ▼ Natural gas
- △ Coal and lignite
- ☆ Nuclear power
- ◆ Hydro-electric power

COPYRIGHT PHILIP'S

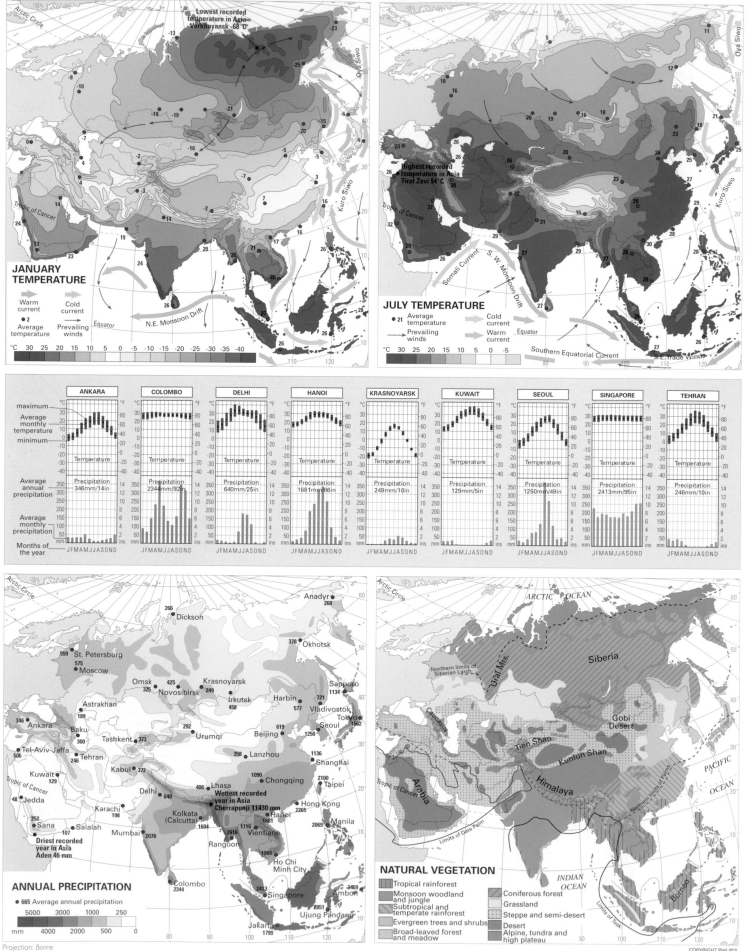

Projection: Bonne

COPYRIGHT PHILIP'S

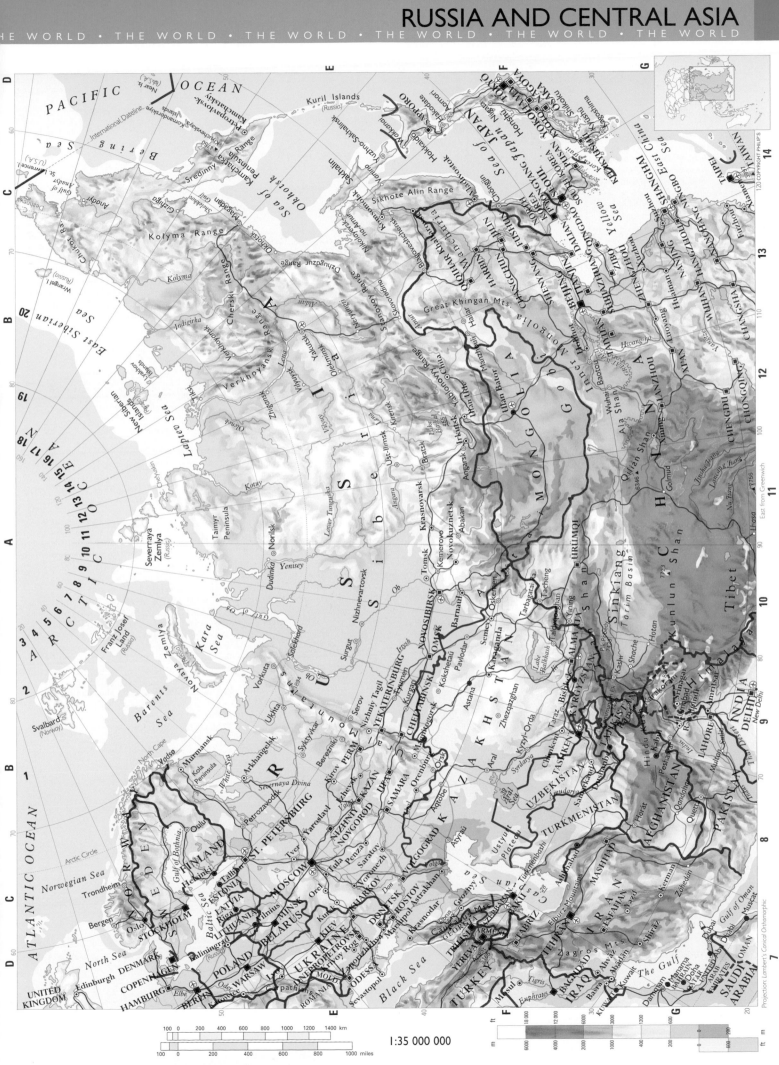

1:35 000 000

Projection: Lambert's Conical Orthomorphic

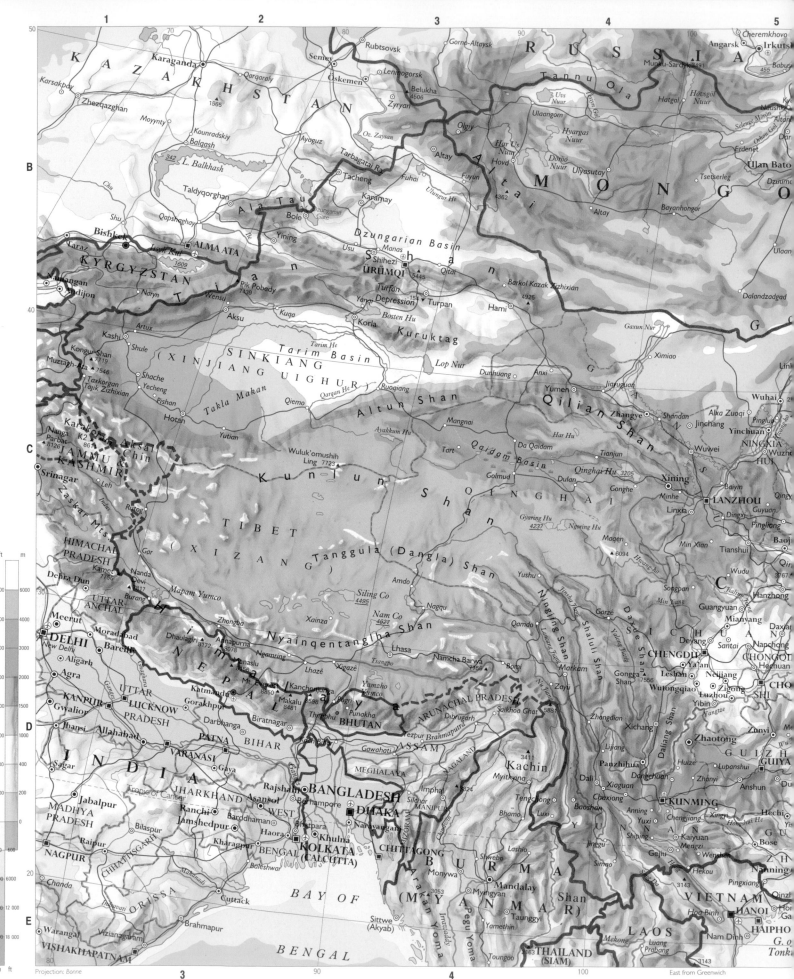

Projection: Bonne

East from Greenwich

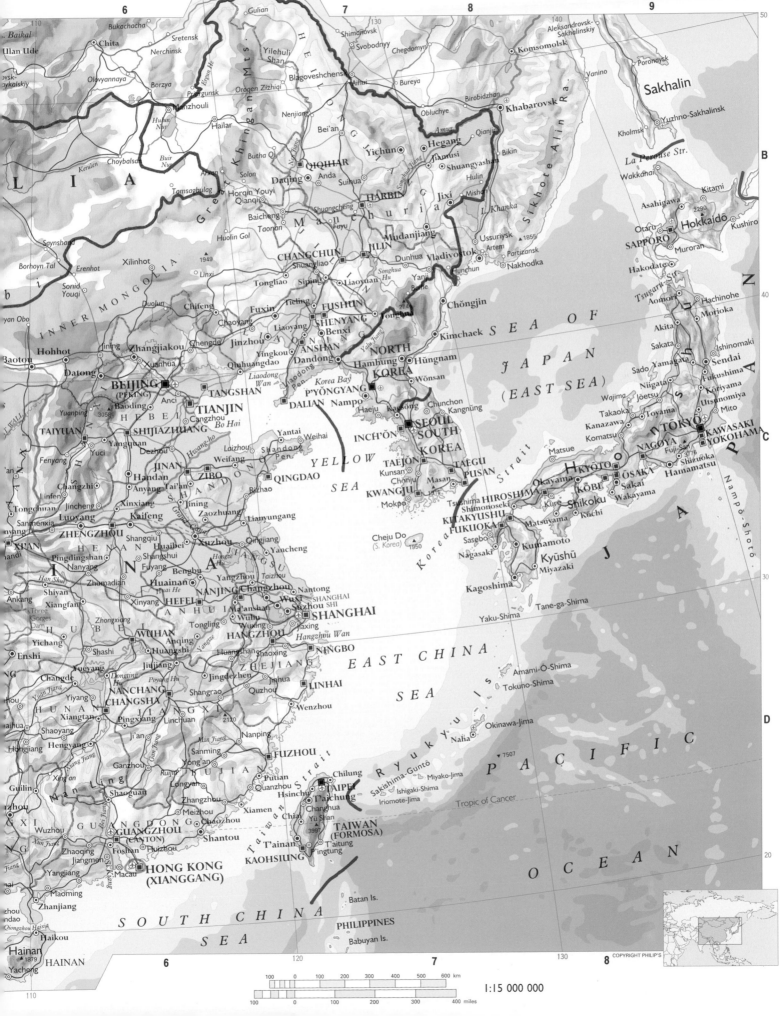

COPYRIGHT PHILIP'S

1:15 000 000

CHINA

RUSSIA

Linkou
Novokachalinsk
Kamen-
Rybolov
L. Khanka
Spassk Dalniy
Lipovcy
Manzovka
Suifenhe
Ussuriysk
Trudovoye
Vladivostok
Slavyanka
Nakhodka
Khasan
Najin
Chŏngjin

NORTH
KOREA

Iesozavodsk
Kirovskiy
Ariadnoye
Yakovleyka
Gornyy
Dalnegorsk
Arsenev
Kavalerovo
Margaritovo
Lazo
Plastun
Terney
Preobrazheniye

Sikhote Alin

1855
1498

SOUTH
KOREA

Ullŭng-do
(S. Korea)
Tok-do

Pohang

SEA OF

JAPAN

(EAST SEA)

JAPAN

Korea

Strait

Wakkanai
Rebun-Tō
Rishiri-Tō
Teshio
Embetsu
Haboro
Rumoi
Otaru
SAPPORO
Iwanai
Suttsu
Setana
Okushiri-Tō
Esashi
Matsumae
Shiragami-Misaki

Esashi
Ōmu
Mombetsu
Otoineppu
Nayoro
Engaru
Shibetsu
Asahigawa
2290
Daisetsu-Zan
2077
Kitami
Bibai
Iwamizawa
Ebetsu
Atsuta
Ishikari-Wan
Kamui-Misaki
Shikotu-Ko
Toya-Ko
Tomakomai
Uchiura-
Wan
Muroran
Yakumo
Hakodate
Esan-Misaki
Tsugaru
Strait
Ohato
Kanagi
Mutsu
Shiriya-Zaki

Yūbetsu
Abashiri
Abashiri-
Wan
Shari
Rausu-
Dake
1661
Nakashibetsu
Shibecha
Akkeshi
Kushiro
Hiroo
Samani
Erimo-misaki

Hokkaidō

Obihiro
Poroshiri-
Dake
2052
Tokachi

Mutsu-
Wan
Aomori
Goshogawara
Hirosaki
Henashi-Misaki
Noshiro
Oga-Hantō
Oga
Akita
Honjō
Sakata
Tsuruoka
Yamagata

Towada
Towada-
Ko
Odate
Iwate-San
2041
Omagari
Hanamaki
2230
1980
Mogami-Gawa

Hachinohe
Kuji
Iwaizumi
Miyako
Morioka
Kamaishi
Ichinoseki
Kesennuma
Ishinomaki
Furukawa
Sendai
Sendai-Wan

Honshū

Sado
Ryōtsu
Aikawa
Niigata
Niitsu
Sanjo
Nagaoka
Wajima
Nanao
Suzu-
Misaki
Suzu-
Toyama-Wan
Himi
Takada
Toyama
Takaoka
Kanazawa
Komatsu
Fukui
Takefu
Tsuruga

Shibata
Fukushima
Higashiagatsuma-Sam
2024
Aizuwakamatsu
Kōriyama
Sukagawa
Tajima
Tanakura
2578
Takayama
3063
Takayama
2782

Sōma
Haranomachi
Iwaki
Kitaibaraki
Hitachi
Nagano
Matsubashi
Kiryū
Utsunomiya
Oyama
Takasaki
Maebashi
Hodaka-
Dake
3190
Matsumoto
Kumagaya
Kawagoe
Mito
Tsuchiura
8412
Kawaguchi
Kawagoe
Ina
Kōfu
TOKYO
KAWASAKI
YOKOHAMA
Funabashi
Chiba
Ichihara
Yokosuka

Nii-Jima
9076
Miyake-Jima

Matsue
Yonago
Izumo
Ōda
Hamada
Masuda
Hagi
Yamaguchi
Ube
Shimonoseki
Nōgata
KITAKYŪSHŪ
Buzen
FUKUOKA
Karatsu
Imari
Saga
Kurume
Ōmuta
Isahaya
Sasebo
Nagasaki
Yatsushiro
Iki
Tsushima
(Japan)
Goto-
Retto
Fukue-Shima

Oki-Shoto
(Japan)
Kyō-ga-Saki
Wakasa-
Wan
Maizuru
Toyooka
Fukuchiyama
Tottori
Tsuyama
Sanchi
1712
Himeji
KYŌTO
Ōtsu
Amagasaki
KOBE
OSAKA
Okayama
Fuchū
Fukuyama
Kure
Imabari
Tokuyama
Hofu
Marugame
Takamatsu
Naruto
Awaji
Tokushima
Yawatahama
Uwajima
Matsuyama
Kōchi
Anan
Mugi
Nakamura
Sukumo
Ashizuri-Zaki
HIROSHIMA
Iwakuni
Chūgoku

Ōgaki
Ichinomiya
Gifu
NAGOYA
Yokkaichi
Toyota
Okazaki
Toyohashi
Iwata
Hamamatsu
Higashiosaka
Izumi-Sano
Matsusaka
Wakayama
Tanabe
Shingū
Kushimoto
Shio-no-
Misaki
Owase
Daiō-Misaki
1915
Ikeda
1955
Tosa-Wan
Muroto
Muroto-Misaki
Biwa-Ko
Kiso-Gawa

Shizuoka
3192
Fuji
Fuji-San
3776
Numazu
Itō
Ō-Shima
Suruga-Wan
Irō-Zaki
Nojima-Zaki
Tateyama
Odawara
Ina
Iida
Kōfu

Izu-Shoto

Nampo-Shoto

Hachijō-Jima
Aoga-Shima

PACIFIC OCEAN

Shikoku

Kumamoto
1787
Ōita
Saiki
Beppu
Bungo Channel
Nichinan
Miyazaki
Miyakonojō
Kagoshima
Kanoya
Makurazaki
Ibusuki
Koshikijima-
Retto
Sendai
Sata-Misaki
Amakusa-Shoto
Ushibuka
Minamata
Hyūga
Nobeoka

Kyūshū

Kō-Kumagun

Inland Sea

Ku Channel

ft   m
9000   3000
6000   2000
4500   1500
3000   1000
1200   400
600   200
0   0
600   200
6000   2000
12 000   4000
18 000   6000
24 000   8000
ft   m

50   0   25   50   75   100   125   150   175 km
50   0   25   50   75   100   125 miles

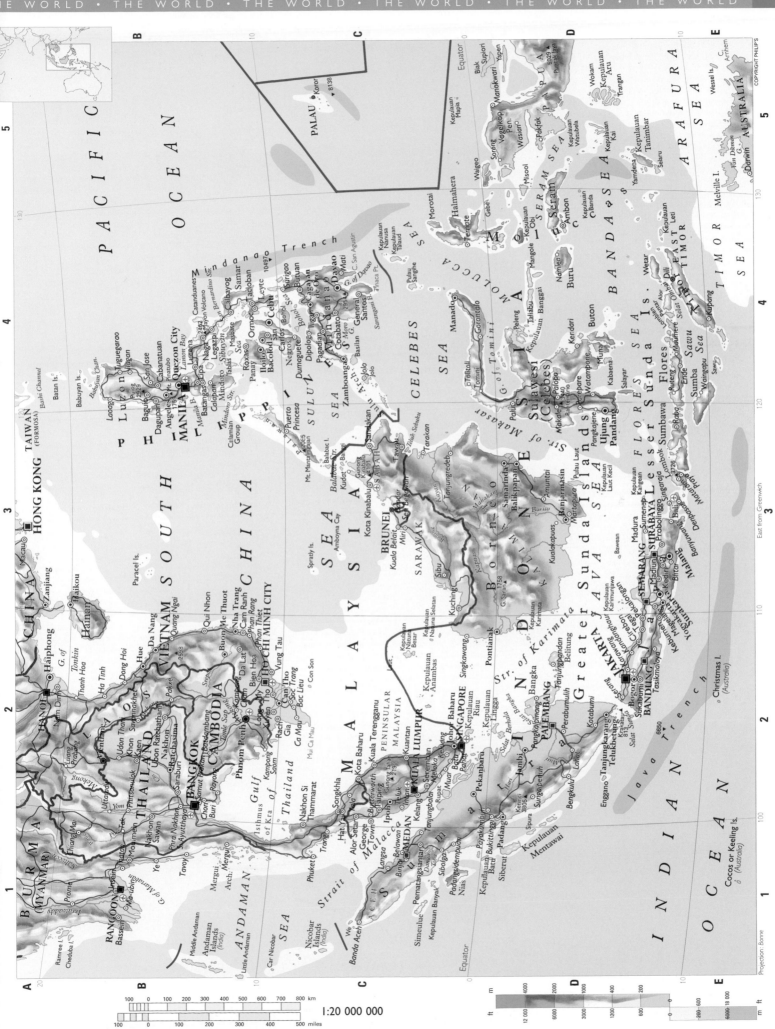

1:20 000 000

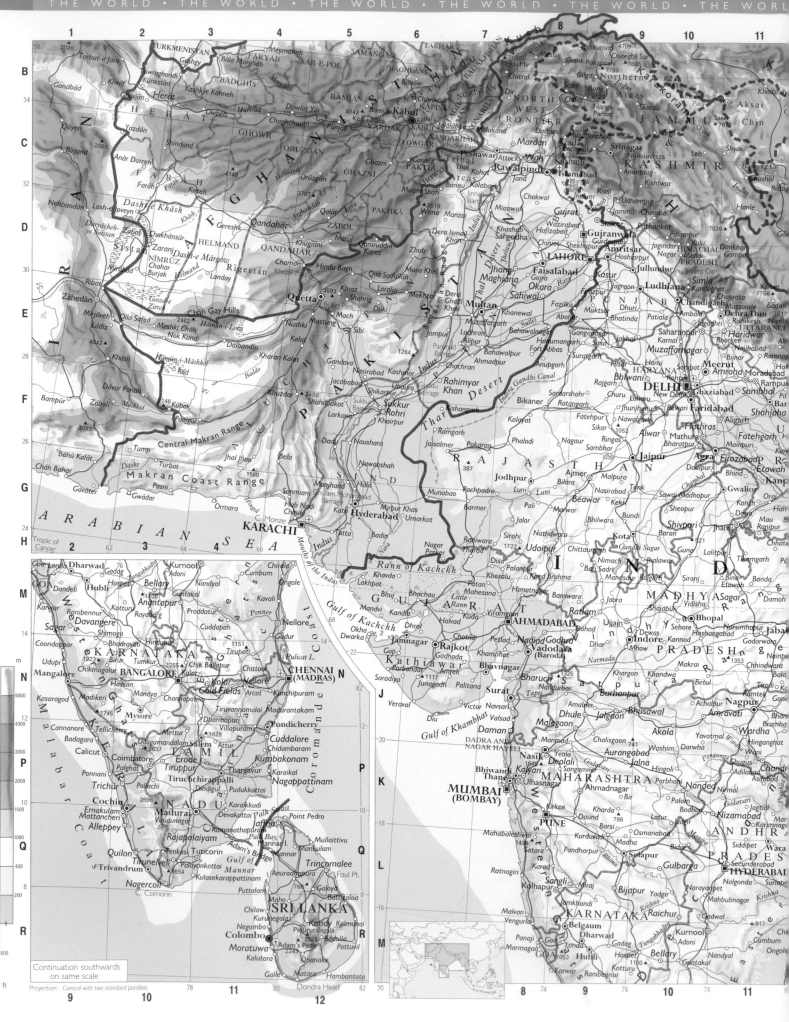

Continuation southwards on same scale

Projection: Conical with two standard parallels

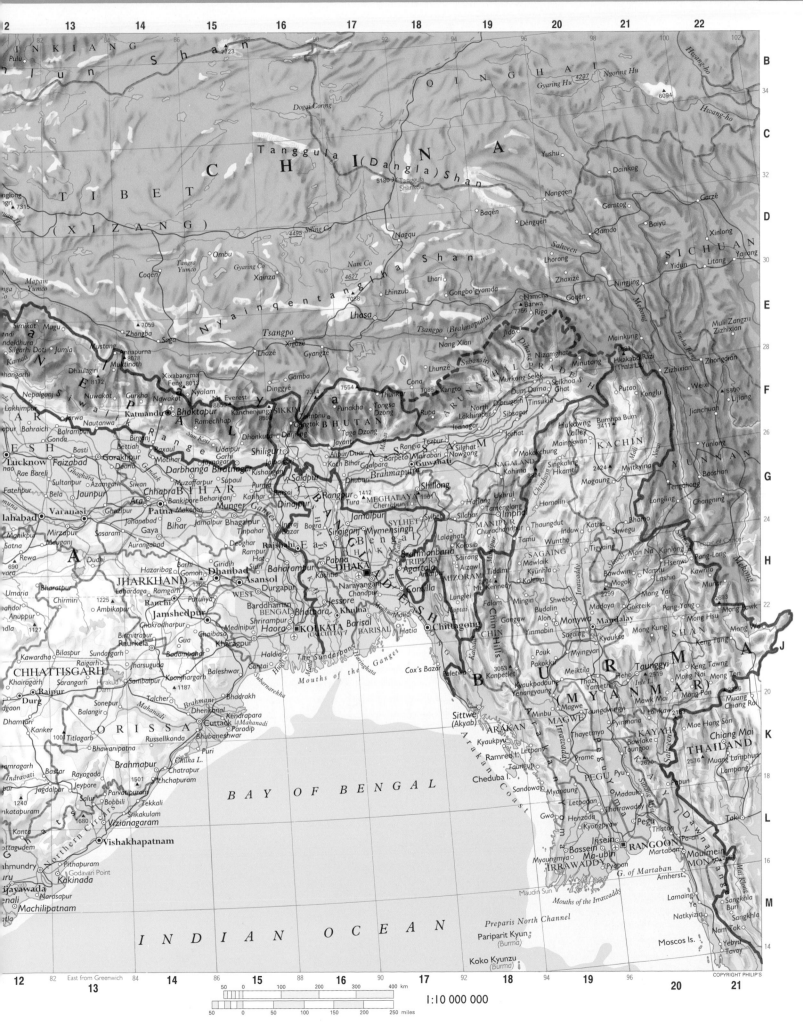

BAY OF BENGAL

INDIAN OCEAN

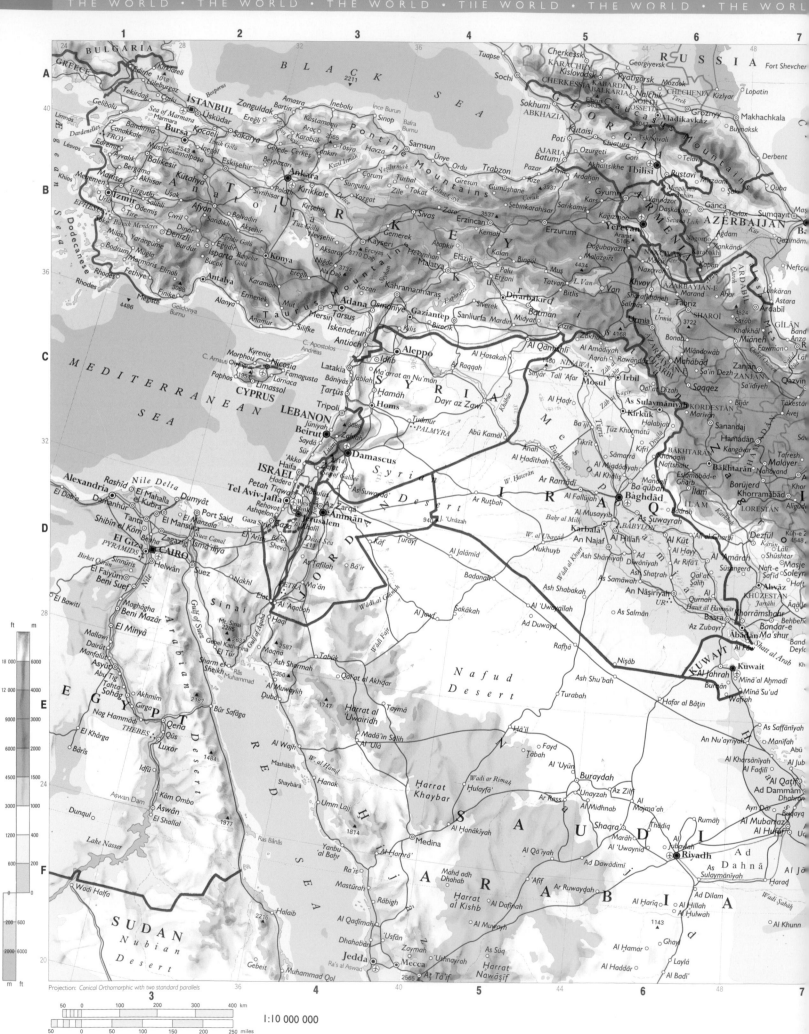

Projection: Conical Orthomorphic with two standard parallels

1:10 000 000

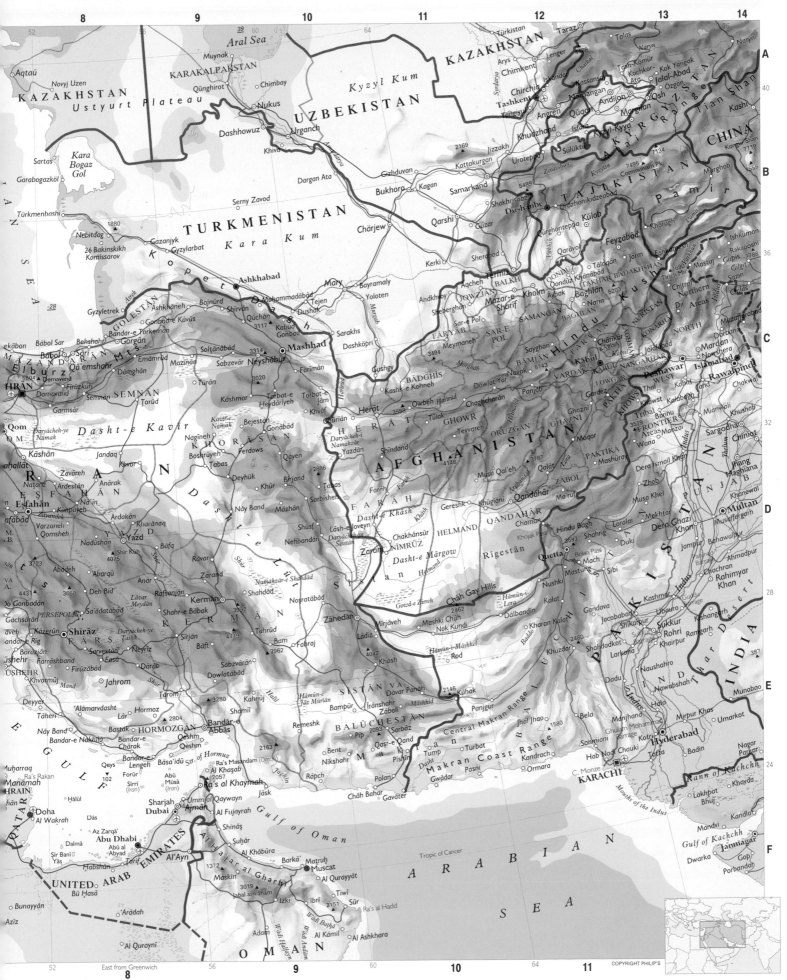

1. VA B. = CHAHĀR MAHĀLL VA BAKHTĪARĪ
Á B. A. = KOHKĪLŪYEH VA BŪYER AHMADĪ

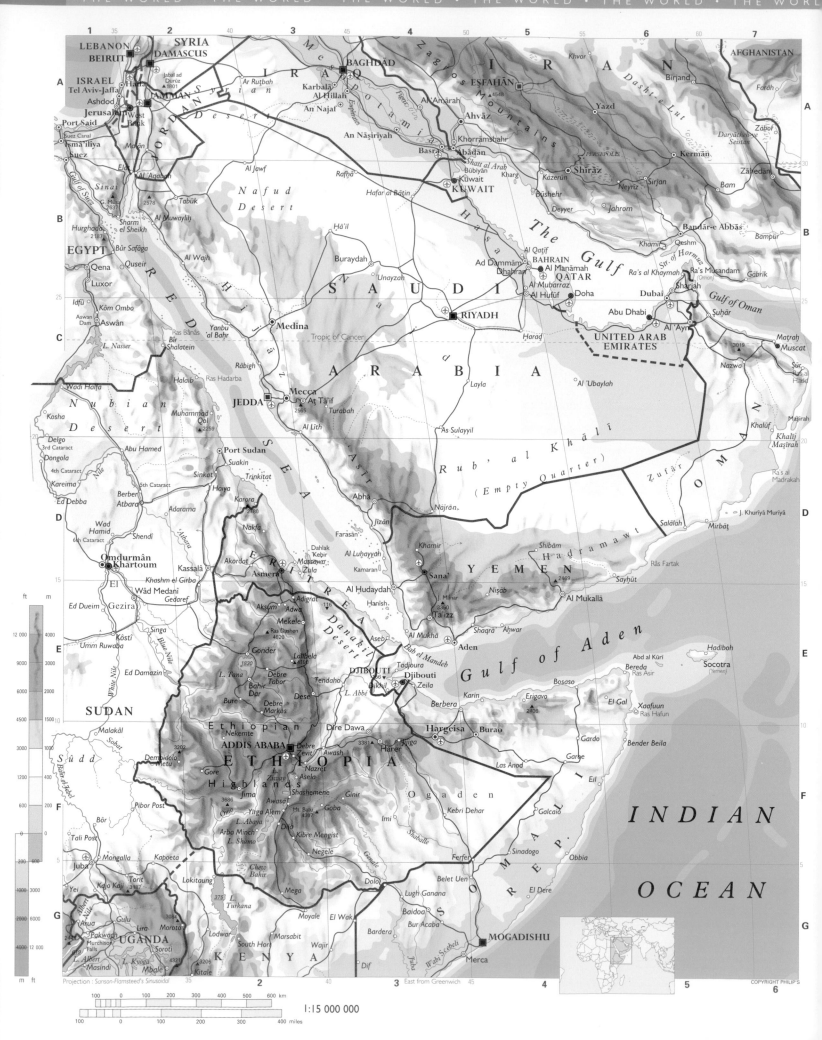

Projection : Sanson-Flamsteed's Sinusoidal

1:15 000 000

East from Greenwich

COPYRIGHT PHILIP'S

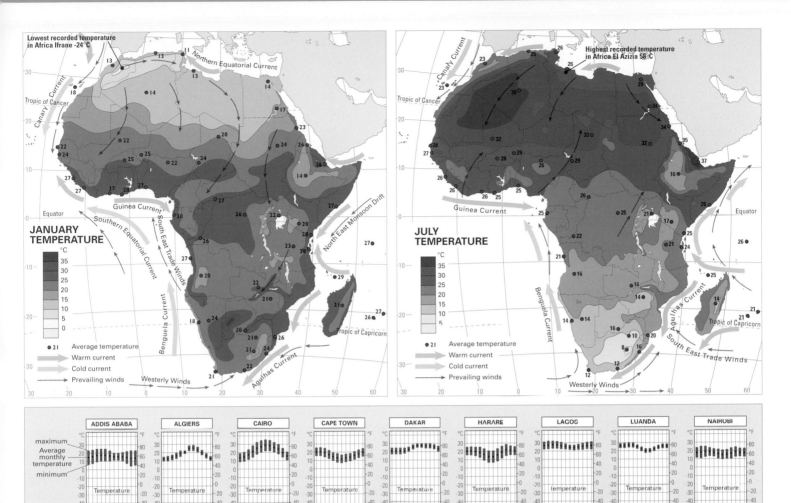

Lowest recorded temperature in Africa Ifrane -24 °C

Northern Equatorial Current
Canary Current
Tropic of Cancer
Guinea Current
Southern Equatorial Current
South East Trade Winds
Equator
Benguela Current
North East Monsoon Drift
Westerly Winds
Agulhas Current

JANUARY TEMPERATURE

°C
35
30
25
20
15
10
5
0

• 21   Average temperature
→ Warm current
→ Cold current
→ Prevailing winds

Highest recorded temperature in Africa El Azizia 58 °C
Canary Current
Tropic of Cancer
Guinea Current
Benguela Current
Agulhas Current
South East Trade Winds
Tropic of Capricorn
Westerly Winds

JULY TEMPERATURE

°C
35
30
25
20
15
10
5

• 21   Average temperature
→ Warm current
→ Cold current
→ Prevailing winds

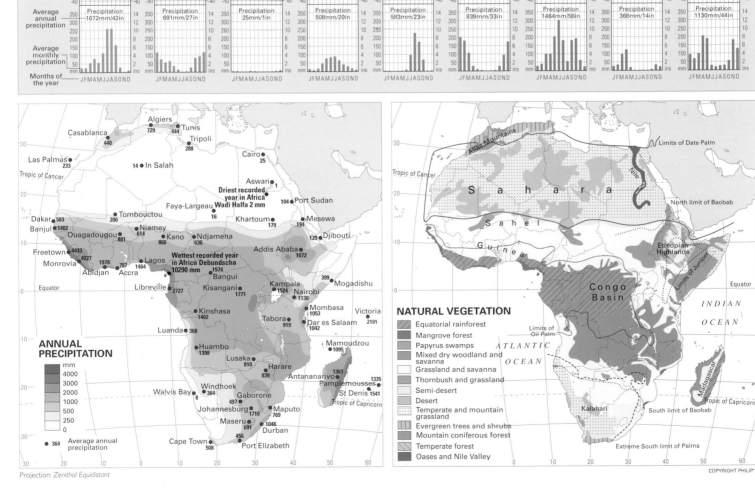

Climate graphs: ADDIS ABABA, ALGIERS, CAIRO, CAPE TOWN, DAKAR, HARARE, LAGOS, LUANDA, NAIROBI

maximum
Average monthly temperature
minimum

Average annual precipitation

Average monthly precipitation

Months of the year

ADDIS ABABA — Precipitation 1072mm/42in
ALGIERS — Precipitation 691mm/27in
CAIRO — Precipitation 25mm/1in
CAPE TOWN — Precipitation 508mm/20in
DAKAR — Precipitation 583mm/23in
HARARE — Precipitation 839mm/33in
LAGOS — Precipitation 1464mm/58in
LUANDA — Precipitation 368mm/14in
NAIROBI — Precipitation 1130mm/44in

ANNUAL PRECIPITATION

Algiers 729
Tunis 444
Tripoli 288
Casablanca 440
Las Palmas 233
Tropic of Cancer
Cairo 25
Aswan 1
Driest recorded year in Africa Wadi Halfa 2 mm
14 • In Salah
Faya-Largeau 16
Port Sudan 104
Dakar 583
Tombouctou 206
Khartoum 179
Mesewa 194
Banjul 1402
Niamey 614
Kano 866
Ndjamena 636
Djibouti 129
Ouagadougou 881
Addis Ababa 1072
Freetown 4433
Monrovia 4227
Abidjan 1978
Accra 787
Lagos 1464
Wettest recorded year in Africa Debundscha 10290 mm
Bangui 1574
Mogadishu 399
Libreville 2727
Kisangani 1771
Kampala 1524
Nairobi 1130
Kinshasa 1402
Mombasa 1053
Tabora 919
Dar es Salaam 1042
Victoria 2191
Luanda 368
Huambo 1398
Mamoudzou 1095
Lusaka 810
Harare 1361
Antananarivo 839
Pamplemousses 1335
Windhoek 364
St Denis 1541
Walvis Bay 8
Gaborone 497
Johannesburg 769
Maseru 691
Maputo 1046
Durban 456
Cape Town 508
Port Elizabeth 839

mm
4000
3000
2000
1000
500
250
0

• 364   Average annual precipitation

Projection: Zenithal Equidistant

NATURAL VEGETATION

Atlas Mountains
Limits of Date Palm
Sahara
Nile
North limit of Baobab
Sahel
Guinea
Ethiopian Highlands
Limits of Juniper
Limits of Oil Palm
Congo Basin
Equator
ATLANTIC OCEAN
INDIAN OCEAN
Kalahari
South limit of Baobab
Tropic of Capricorn
Extreme South limit of Palms
Madagascar

Equatorial rainforest
Mangrove forest
Papyrus swamps
Mixed dry woodland and savanna
Grassland and savanna
Thornbush and grassland
Semi-desert
Desert
Temperate and mountain grassland
Evergreen trees and shrubs
Mountain coniferous forest
Temperate forest
Oases and Nile Valley

COPYRIGHT PHILIP'S

AFRICA RELIEF OF LAND

NORTH ATLANTIC OCEAN

Azores

Madeira

Canary Is.
Tenerife

Cape Verde Is.
C. Vert

B. of Biscay

British Isles

Europe

Mont Blanc 4807

Pyrénées

Iberian Peninsula

Corsica

Sardinia

Str. of Gibraltar

6578

Alps

Apennines

Adriatic Sea

Dinaric Alps

Carpathians

Black Sea

Elbrus 5633

Caucasus

Caspian Sea

Aral Sea

Mediterranean Sea

Sicily

Bon

Malta

5121

Crete

Cyprus

Anatolia

Asia

Levant

Syrian Desert

Mesopotamia

Euphrates

Tigris

The Gulf

High Plateaux

Saharan Atlas

Middle Atlas 4165

High Atlas

Anti Atlas

Toubkal

Maghreb

Chott Djerid

G. of Gabès

Tripolitania

G. of Sidra

Cyrenaica

Libyan Desert

Egypt

Al Kufrah

El Khârga

Mt Sinai 2285

Arabian Desert

R. Nile

Red Sea

Hejaz

Arabia

Tropic of Cancer

Tasili Plateau

Hoggar

Sahara

Adrar

Aïr

Tibesti

Bilma

Bahr el Ghazal

Nubian Desert

Nubia

Kordofân

'Atbara

Ras Dashen 4620

116

Barim

66

Bab el Mandeb

G. of Aden

Ras Asir

Ras Nouâdhibou

Senegal

Senegambia

Gambia

Fouta Djalon

Niger

Volta

Niger

Sahel

Chari

L. Chad

Benue

White Nile

Blue Nile

L. Tana

Ethiopian Highlands

Somali Peninsula

Guinea

Grain Coast

Ivory Coast

C. Palmas

Gold Coast

Slave Coast

Bight of Benin

Mt Cameroon 4070

Bioko

Adamawa Highlands

Dar Banda

Bahr el Ghazâl

Uele

Shabelle

Juba

Bight of Bonny

I. de Principe

Gulf of Guinea

São Tomé

C. Lopez

Annobón

Equator

Ogooué

Oubangi

Congo

Congo

Chutes Boyoma

Rift Valley

L. Albert

Ruwenzori 5109

Mt Elgon

L. Edward

4321

Mt Kenya 5199

Lualaba

L. Victoria

Kilimanjaro 5895

L. Kivu

L. Turkana

Tana

Congo Basin

Kasai

Sankuru

Kasai

Cuango

Lukuga

L. Tanganyika

L. Mweru

Rungwe 2961

Pemba I.

INDIAN OCEAN

Seychelle

Cuanza

Katanga

Bangweulu Swamp

L. Nyasa (L. Malawi)

C. Delgado

Comoros

Aldabra Is.

Ascension I.

SOUTH ATLANTIC OCEAN

St. Helena

Bié Plateau

Cuando

Cubango

Zambezi

Zambezi

Lungula

Mozambique Channel

Madagascar

2643

Maurit

Réunion

C. Fria

Cunene

Okavango Delta

Victoria Falls

Limpopo

Tropic of Capricorn

Walvis Bay

Namib Desert

Kalahari

Orange

Vaal

High Veld

Delagoa B.

Drakensberg

Algoa B.

Compass Mt 2505

Niewveldberge

Great Karoo

Swartberge

3482

C. of Good Hope

C. Agulhas

ft   m
12000 4000
9000   3000
6000   2000
3000   1000
1500   500
600   200
0   0
200   600
1000   3000
2000   6000
4000   12000
m   ft

200   200 400 600 800 1000 1200 1400 1600 1800 km

200   200 400 600 800 1000 1200 miles

1 : 42 000 000

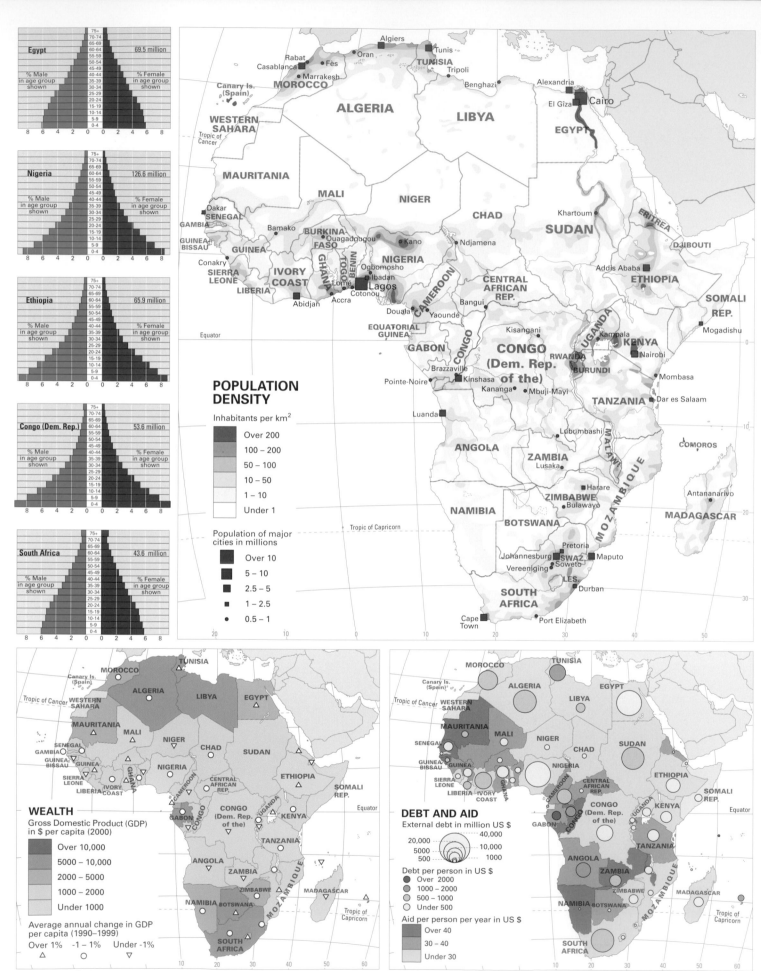

Egypt   69.5 million

% Male in age group shown   % Female in age group shown

Nigeria   126.6 million

% Male in age group shown   % Female in age group shown

Ethiopia   65.9 million

% Male in age group shown   % Female in age group shown

Congo (Dem. Rep.)   53.6 million

% Male in age group shown   % Female in age group shown

South Africa   43.6 million

% Male in age group shown   % Female in age group shown

POPULATION DENSITY

Inhabitants per km²

- Over 200
- 100 – 200
- 50 – 100
- 10 – 50
- 1 – 10
- Under 1

Population of major cities in millions

- Over 10
- 5 – 10
- 2.5 – 5
- 1 – 2.5
- 0.5 – 1

WEALTH

Gross Domestic Product (GDP) in $ per capita (2000)

- Over 10,000
- 5000 – 10,000
- 2000 – 5000
- 1000 – 2000
- Under 1000

Average annual change in GDP per capita (1990–1999)

Over 1%   –1 – 1%   Under -1%

△   ○   ▽

DEBT AND AID

External debt in million US $

40,000
20,000
10,000
5000
500   1000

Debt per person in US $

- Over 2000
- 1000 – 2000
- 500 – 1000
- Under 500

Aid per person per year in US $

- Over 40
- 30 – 40
- Under 30

Projection: Zenithal Equidistant

COPYRIGHT PHILIP'S

LAND USE

- Arable
- Plantations and intensive cultivation
- Woods and forests
- Rough grazing
- Rough grazing with trees (savanna)
- Non-productive

- Camels
- Cattle
- Sheep
- Millet and sorghum
- Rice
- Wheat
- Maize
- Groundnuts
- Yams
- Bananas and plantains
- Citrus fruit
- Date Palms
- Olives
- Vines
- Cacao
- Cloves
- Cotton
- Palm oil
- Rubber
- Sisal
- Sugar cane
- Tobacco
- Coffee
- Tea
- Main fishing areas

MINERALS

Iron & ferro-alloys
- Chrome
- Cobalt
- Iron ore
- Manganese
- Nickel ore

Non-ferrous metals
- Bauxite
- Copper
- Uranium

Precious metals & stones
- Diamonds
- Gold

Fertilizers
- Phosphates

Structure
- Pre-Cambrian shield
- Palaeozoic folding
- Cenozoic folding
- Igneous structures

ENERGY

- Oil
- Natural gas
- Coal and lignite
- Nuclear power
- Hydro-electric power

Energy production per capita (1998)
million tonnes of oil equivalent
- Over 15
- 10 – 15
- 5 – 10
- 0.5 – 5
- Less than 0.5

Projection: Zenithal Equidistant

COPYRIGHT PHILIP'S

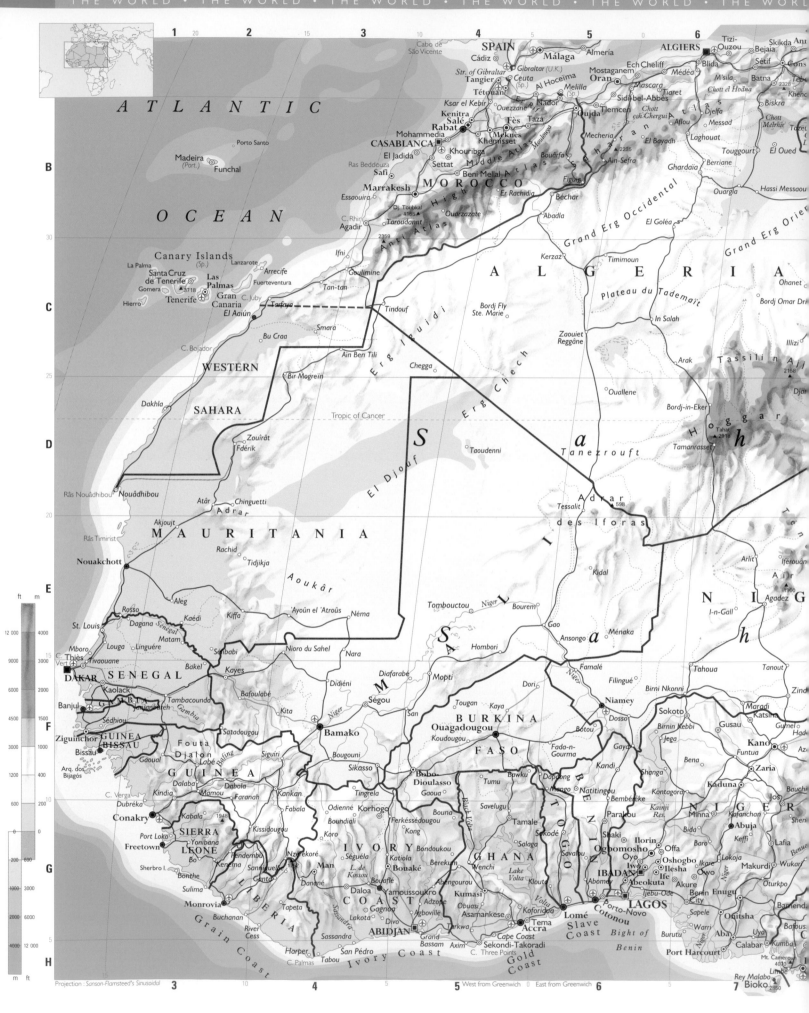

ATLANTIC

OCEAN

SPAIN
Cabo de
São Vicente
Cádiz   Málaga Almería
Str. of Gibraltar Gibraltar (U.K.)
Tangier Ceuta (Sp.) Al Hoceima
Tétouan Melilla (Sp.)
Ksar el Kebir Nador
Ouezzane Taza
Kenitra Fès
Salé Meknès
Rabat Khemisset
Mohammedia Khouribga
CASABLANCA El Jadida Settat
Ras Beddouza Beni Mellal
Safi
Marrakesh MOROCCO Middle Atlas
Essaouira
C. Rhir Taroudannt Ouarzazate
Agadir Dj. Toubkal 4165
Ifni Anti Atlas
2359
Goulimine
Tan-tan
Tindouf

ALGIERS Tizi-Ouzou Skikda
Bejaia Setif
Ech Cheliff Blida 2328
Mostaganem Médéa M'sila Batna
Oran Mascara Biskra
Sidi-bel-Abbes Tiaret Chott el Hodna
Tlemcen Djelfa
Chott ech Chergui Aflou
Mecheria El Bayadh Laghouat
Bouarfa Messad Chott
Ain-Sefra Melrhir
Figuig Ghardaïa Berriane El Oued
Er Rachidia Béchar Touggourt
Abadla Ouargla Hassi Messaoul
Grand Erg Occidental El Goléa Grand Erg Orient

ALGERIA
Kerzaz
Timimoun
Bordj Fly Plateau du Tademaït Ohanet
Ste. Marie In Salah Bordj Omar Dri
Zaouiet Illizi
Reggane Ouallene Arak Tassili n Ajjer 2158
Bordj-in-Eker Tahat Hoggar
Tamanrasset 2918

WESTERN

SAHARA
Dakhla
Bu Craa
C. Bojador
Tropic of Cancer
Zouîrat
Fdérik

Madeira
(Port.) Funchal
Porto Santo

Canary Islands (Sp.)
La Palma Lanzarote
Santa Cruz Arrecife
de Tenerife Fuerteventura
Gomera 3718 Las Palmas
Hierro Tenerife Gran Canaria
C. Juby
El Aaiún Tarfaya

Ras Nouâdhibou Nouâdhibou
Atâr Chinguetti
Akjoujt Adrar
Ras Timirist
Rachid
MAURITANIA Tidjikja
Nouakchott
Taoudenni
El Djouf
Aoukâr
Tessalit Adrar 598
des Iforas
Kidal
Arlit Iférouan
Aïr 1900
NIGER
Agadez

St. Louis Rosso
Dagana Sénégal Kaédi
Louga Matam
C. Thiès Tivaouane Linguère
Vert SENEGAL
DAKAR Kaolack
Banjul GAMBIA Tambacounda
Ziguinchor GUINEA Janjanbureh
Bissau BISSAU Sédhiou
Arq. dos Fouta
Bijagós Djalon Labé Gaoual
GUINEA Dalaba Mamou
Conakry Kindia 1948 Faranah
Dubréka Kabala
Port Loko SIERRA Kissidougou
Freetown Yonibana Koro
LEONE Bo Kenema N'zérékoré
Sherbro I. Bonthe Sulima Ganta
LIBERIA
Monrovia Tapeta
Buchanan
River Cess
Grain Coast Harper San Pédro
C. Palmas Tabou Ivory Coast

Kiffa 'Ayoûn el 'Atroûs Néma
Aleg
Bakel Nioro du Sahel
Kayes Nara
Séibabi Diafarabé Mopti
Kita Bafoulabé Ségou
Bamako San
Siguiri Bougouni
Kankan Sikasso Bobo
Kabala Dioulasso Tumu
Odienné Korhogo
Dabola Fabala Tingrela Gaoua
Boundiali Ferkéssédougou Kong
SIERRA Koro Bouna
Séguéla Katiola
Man IVORY Bouaké
Danané L. de Bouaflé
Kossou Yamoussoukro Bondoukou
Daloa Gagnoa Divo Abengourou Kumasi
COAST Agboville Obuasi
Sassandra Lakota Adzopé Asamankese
Sassandra ABIDJAN Grand
Bassam Axim Sekondi-Takoradi
C. Three Points Gold
Coast

Tombouctou Niger Bourem
Gao
Hombori Ménaka
Ansongo
SAHEL I-n-Gall
Famalé
Mopti Dori Tahoua Tanout
Diafarabé
Douentza Filingué Birni Nkonni
Tougan Kaya Niamey Sokoto Maradi
BURKINA Dosso Gusau
Ouagadougou Botou Birnin Kebbi Katsina
Koudougou FASO Gaya Jega Gumel
Fada-n- Kandi Funtua Kano
Gourma Bawku Dapaong Kontagora Bena Zaria
Mango Natitingou Kaduna
Savelugu Bembéréke Kainji Jos Bauchi
Tamale Parakou Res. Minna
Salaga Kafanchan
Sekodé Savalou Shaki Bida Abuja
Wenchi Ilorin Keffi
GHANA Ogbomosho Offa Lokoja Lafia
Lake Iwo Oshogbo Ikare Makurdi
Volta Iseyin Oyo Ilesha Ife Owo
Klouto IBADAN Ijebu-Ode Enugu
Cape Coast Accra Abeokuta Benin City Onitsha
Tema Porto-Novo LAGOS Sapele
Lomé Cotonou Warri Aba
Slave Coast Bight of Calabar
Benin Port Harcourt
NIGER Mt. Cameroun 4010
Rey Malabo Limbe
Bioko 2850

GUINEA
Kindia
Freetown
LIBERIA

ft m
12 000 4000
9000 3000
6000 2000
4500 1500
3000 1000
1200 400
600 200
0
200 600
1000 3000
2000 6000
4000 12 000
m ft

1:15 000 000

100   0   100   200   300   400   500   600 km

100   0   100   200   300   400 miles

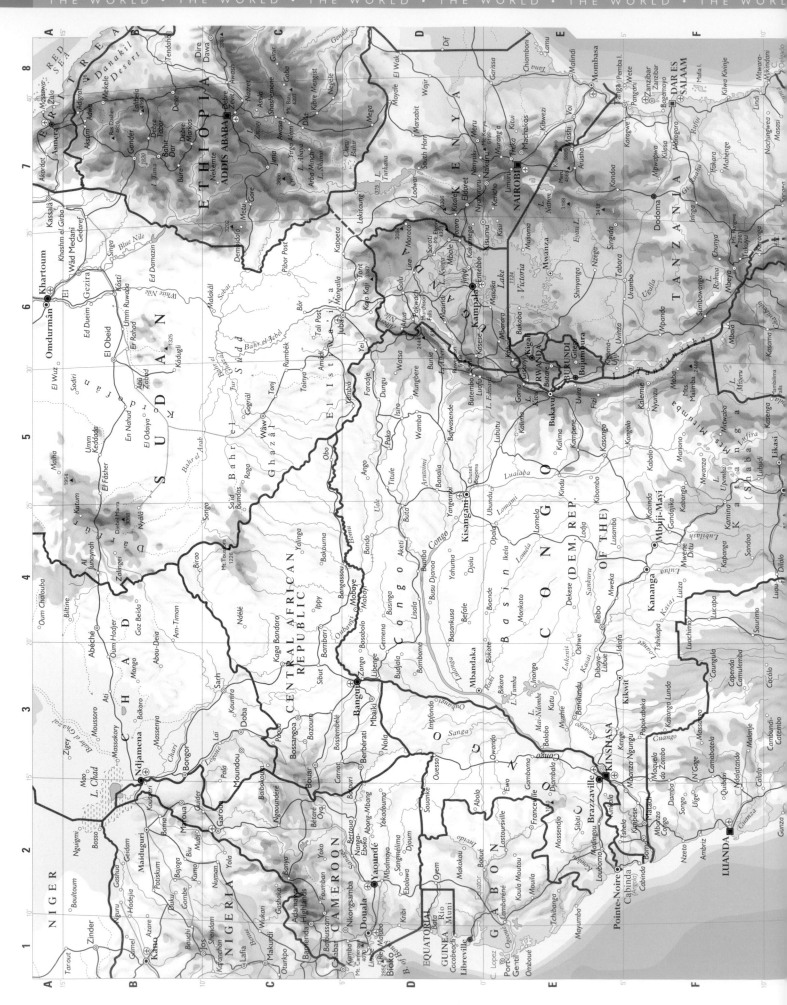

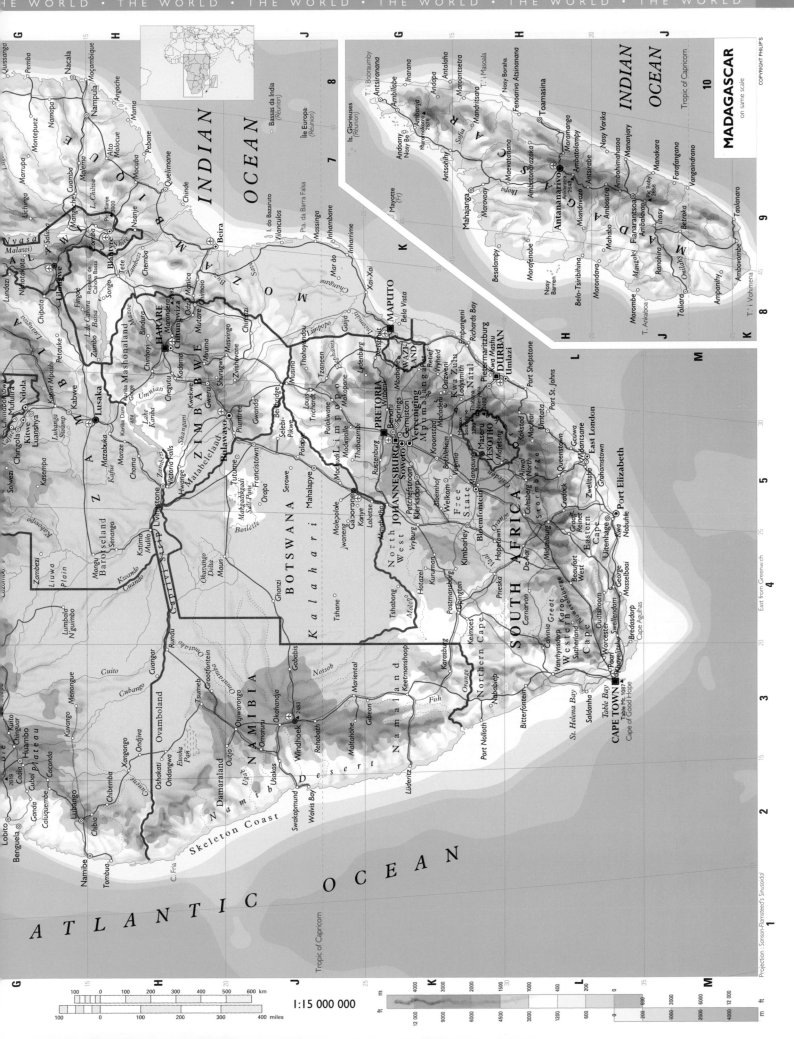

MADAGASCAR
on same scale

INDIAN OCEAN

INDIAN OCEAN

ATLANTIC OCEAN

Projection : Sanson-Flamsteed's Sinusoidal

1:15 000 000

100   0   100   200   300   400   500   600 km
100   0   100   200   300   400 miles

Projection: Lambert's Equivalent Azimuthal

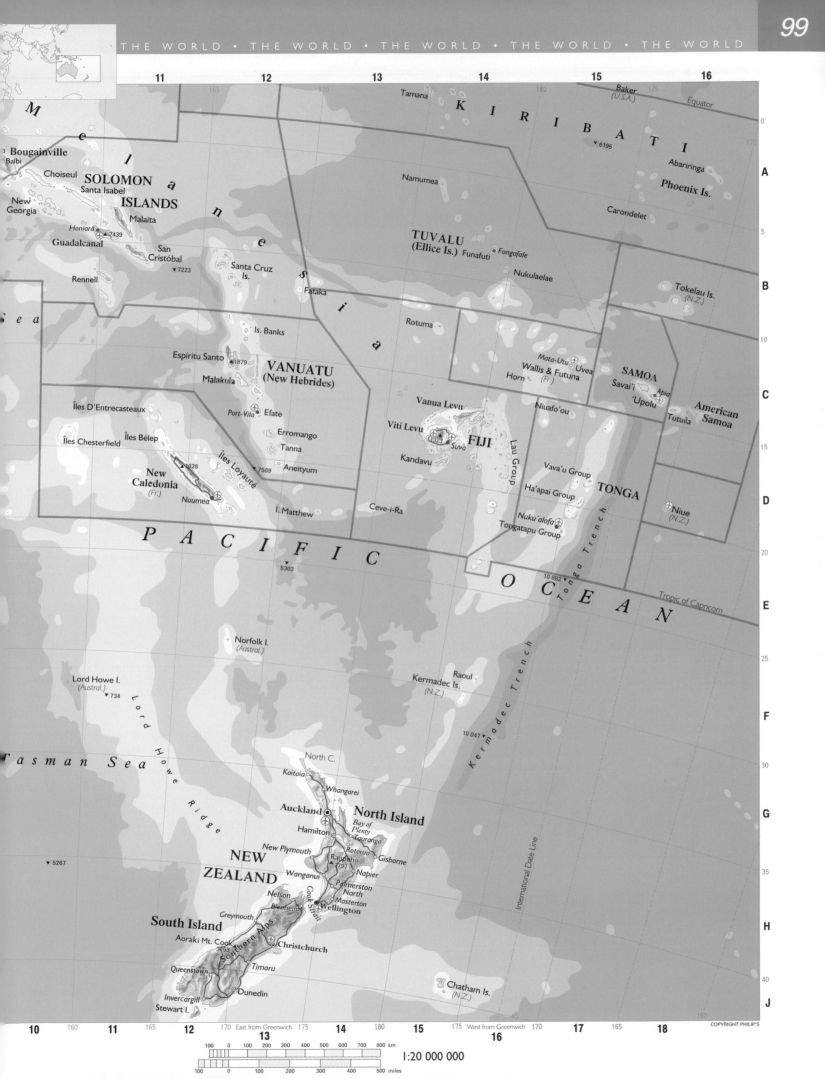

11   12   13   14   15   16

Melanesia

KIRIBATI

Tamana

▾6195

Equator

³Bougainville
Balbi

Choiseul

SOLOMON
Santa Isabel
ISLANDS

New
Georgia

Malaita

Honiará ▲2439

Guadalcanal

San
Cristóbal

▾7223

Rennell

Santa Cruz
Is.

Fataka

Namumea

Abariringa

Phoenix Is.

Carondelet

TUVALU
(Ellice Is.) Funafuti •Fongafale

Nukulaelae

Tokelau Is.
(N.Z.)

A

5

B

Sea

Is. Banks

Rotuma

10

Espíritu Santo ▲1879

VANUATU
(New Hebrides)

Malakula

Mata-Utu⊕ Uvea
Wallis & Futuna
Horn⊕   (Fr.)

SAMOA
Savai'i
'Upolu Apia⊕

American
Samoa

Tutuila

C

Îles D'Entrecasteaux

Port-Vila⊕ Efate

Vanua Levu

Niuafo'ou

Îles Chesterfield Îles Bélep

Erromango

Tanna

Viti Levu
⊕
1323
Suva

FIJI

15

Kandavu

New
Caledonia
(Fr.)
▲1628

Îles Loyauté

Noumea⊕

▾7569 Aneityum

I. Matthew

Ceve-i-Ra

Lau Group

Vava'u Group

Ha'apai Group

TONGA

Niue
(N.Z.)

D

Nuku'alofa⊕
Tongatapu Group

PACIFIC

▾5303

10 882

Tonga Trench

OCEAN

Tropic of Capricorn

20

E

Norfolk I.
(Austral.)

25

Lord Howe I.
(Austral.) ▾734

Raoul

Kermadec Is.
(N.Z.)

Kermadec Trench

F

Tasman Sea

North C.

Kaitaia

10 047

30

Lord Howe Ridge

Whangarei

Auckland⊙ North Island

Hamilton

Bay of
Plenty
Tauranga

▾5267

New Plymouth

Rotorua

Gisborne

G

NEW
ZEALAND

Wanganui

Raupahu
▲
2797

Napier

35

International Date Line

Nelson

Palmerston
North
Masterton

Greymouth

Blenheim

Cook Strait

Wellington⊛

H

South Island

Southern Alps

Aoraki Mt. Cook
3753

Christchurch

Queenstown

Timaru

40

Invercargill

Chatham Is.
(N.Z.)

Stewart I.

Dunedin

J

10   160   11   165   12   170 East from Greenwich 175   14   180   15   175 West from Greenwich 170   17   165   18

13   16

100 0 100 200 300 400 500 600 700 800 km

1:20 000 000

100 0 100 200 300 400 500 miles

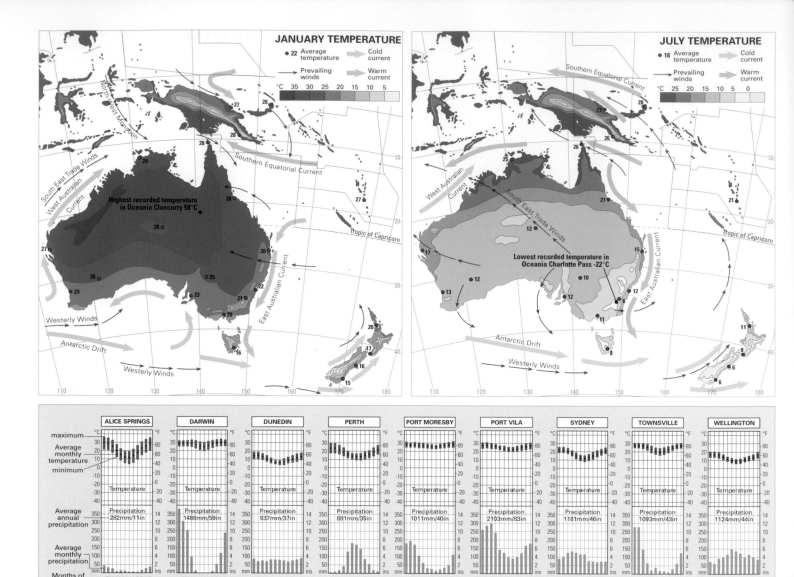

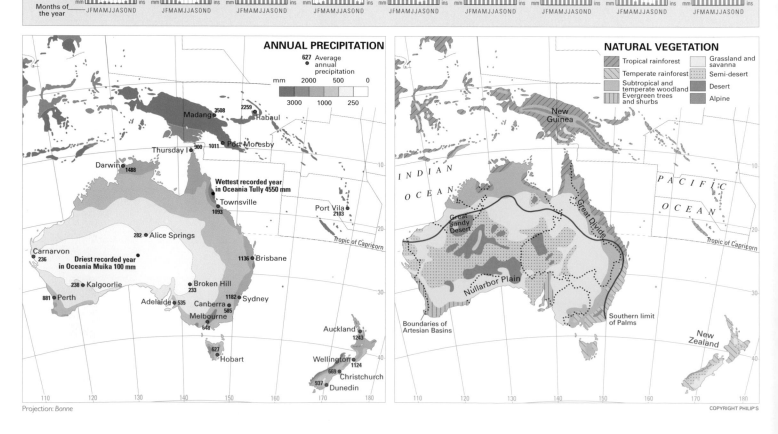

Projection: Bonne

COPYRIGHT PHILIP'S

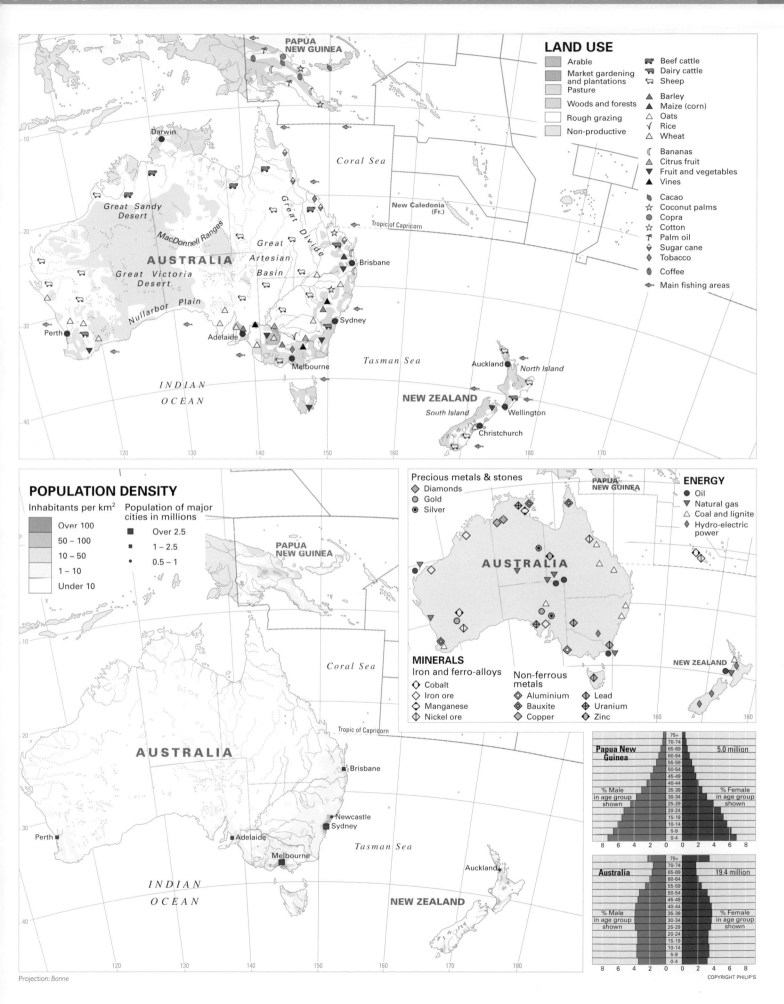

LAND USE

Arable	Beef cattle
Market gardening and plantations	Dairy cattle
Pasture	Sheep
Woods and forests	Barley
Rough grazing	Maize (corn)
Non-productive	Oats

- Rice
- Wheat
- Bananas
- Citrus fruit
- Fruit and vegetables
- Vines
- Cacao
- Coconut palms
- Copra
- Cotton
- Palm oil
- Sugar cane
- Tobacco
- Coffee
- Main fishing areas

PAPUA NEW GUINEA

Darwin

Coral Sea

New Caledonia (Fr.)

Tropic of Capricorn

Great Sandy Desert

MacDonnell Ranges

Great Victoria Desert

AUSTRALIA

Great Artesian Basin

Great Divide

Brisbane

Nullarbor Plain

Perth

Adelaide

Sydney

Melbourne

INDIAN OCEAN

Tasman Sea

Auckland

North Island

NEW ZEALAND

South Island

Wellington

Christchurch

POPULATION DENSITY

Inhabitants per km²

Over 100	
50 – 100	
10 – 50	
1 – 10	
Under 10	

Population of major cities in millions

- Over 2.5
- 1 – 2.5
- 0.5 – 1

PAPUA NEW GUINEA

Coral Sea

AUSTRALIA

Tropic of Capricorn

Brisbane

Newcastle
Sydney

Perth

Adelaide

Melbourne

Tasman Sea

Auckland

INDIAN OCEAN

NEW ZEALAND

Precious metals & stones

- Diamonds
- Gold
- Silver

PAPUA NEW GUINEA

AUSTRALIA

NEW ZEALAND

MINERALS

Iron and ferro-alloys
- Cobalt
- Iron ore
- Manganese
- Nickel ore

Non-ferrous metals
- Aluminium
- Bauxite
- Copper
- Lead
- Uranium
- Zinc

ENERGY

- Oil
- Natural gas
- Coal and lignite
- Hydro-electric power

Papua New Guinea — 5.0 million

	% Male in age group shown	% Female in age group shown
75+		
70-74		
65-69		
60-64		
55-59		
50-54		
45-49		
40-44		
35-39		
30-34		
25-29		
20-24		
15-19		
10-14		
5-9		
0-4		

8 6 4 2 0 0 2 4 6 8

Australia — 19.4 million

	% Male in age group shown	% Female in age group shown
75+		
70-74		
65-69		
60-64		
55-59		
50-54		
45-49		
40-44		
35-39		
30-34		
25-29		
20-24		
15-19		
10-14		
5-9		
0-4		

8 6 4 2 0 0 2 4 6 8

Projection: Bonne

COPYRIGHT PHILIP'S

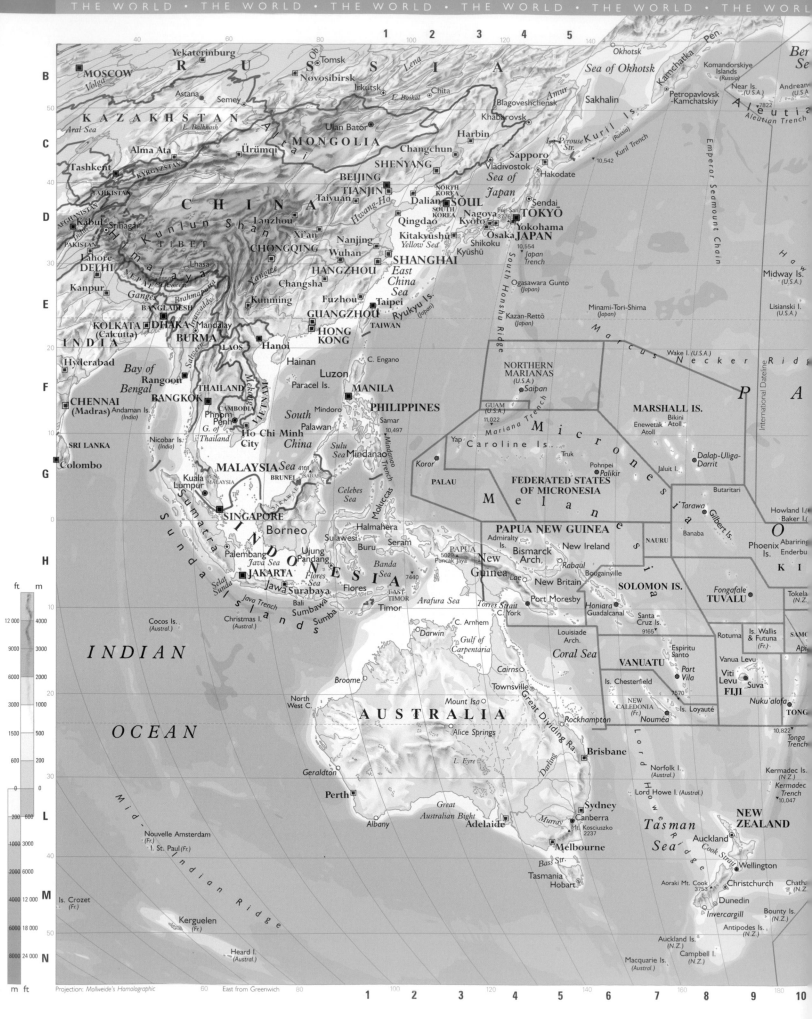

1:54 000 000

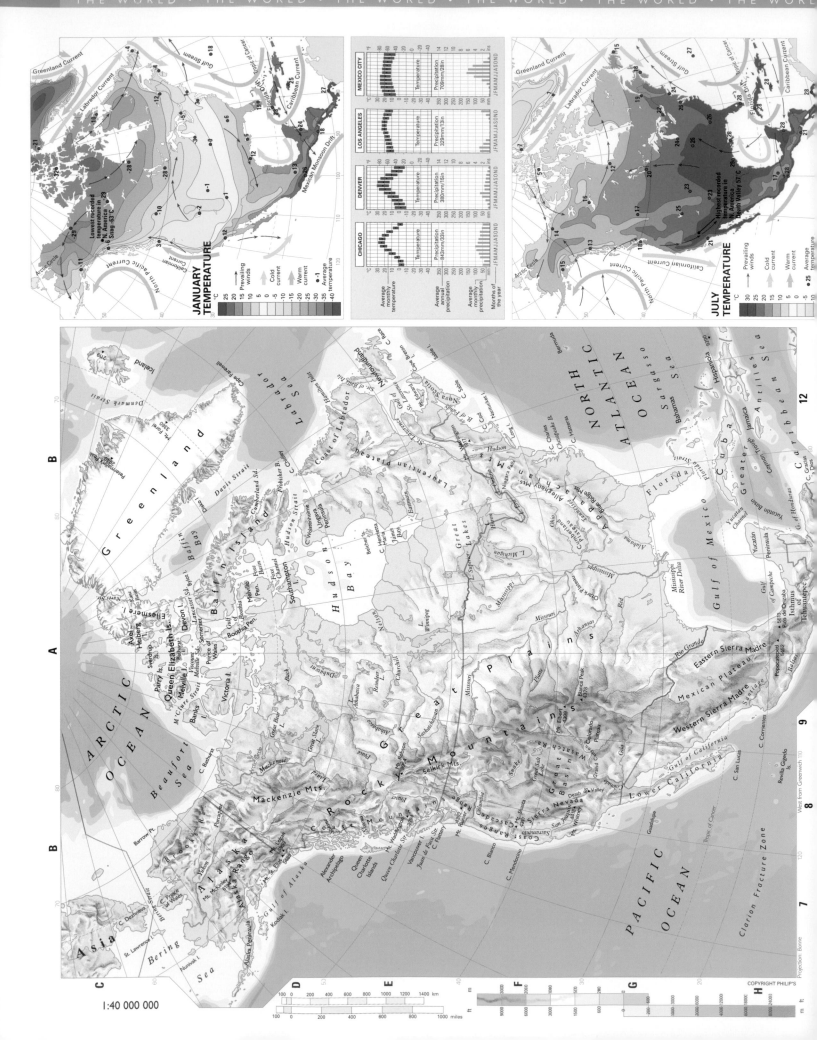

ANNUAL PRECIPITATION

Wettest recorded in N. America
Henderson Lake 6,500 mm

Driest recorded
year in N. America
Bataque 30 mm

mm
4000
3000
2000
1000
500
250
0

709 Average annual
precipitation

VANCOUVER — Temperature — Precipitation 1529mm/60in
SAN SALVADOR — Temperature — Precipitation 1778mm/70in
NUUK — Temperature — Precipitation 599mm/24in
NEW YORK — Temperature — Precipitation 1100mm/43in
MIAMI — Temperature — Precipitation 1516mm/60in

NATURAL VEGETATION

- Sub-tropical rainforest
- Tropical rainforest
- Tropical thorn forest
- Evergreen trees and shrubs
- Broad-leaved forest and meadow
- Coniferous forest
- Grassland
- Scrub and semi-desert
- Desert
- Tundra and alpine

1:40 000 000

Projection: Bonne

COPYRIGHT PHILIP'S

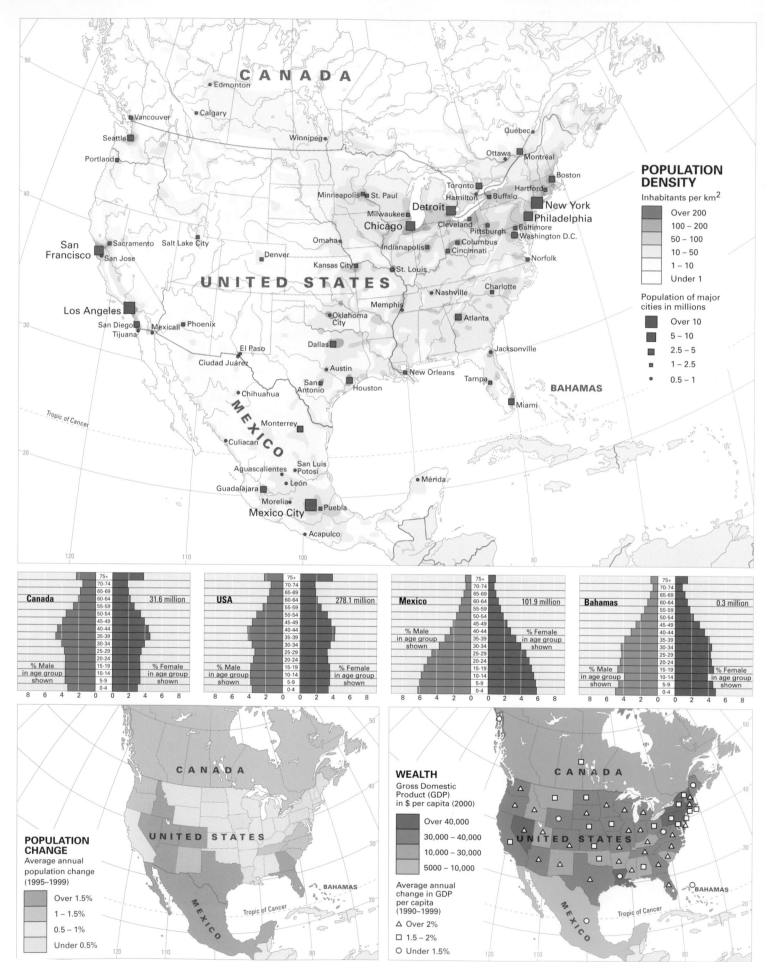

POPULATION DENSITY

Inhabitants per km²

- Over 200
- 100 – 200
- 50 – 100
- 10 – 50
- 1 – 10
- Under 1

Population of major cities in millions

- Over 10
- 5 – 10
- 2.5 – 5
- 1 – 2.5
- 0.5 – 1

Canada 31.6 million
USA 278.1 million
Mexico 101.9 million
Bahamas 0.3 million

POPULATION CHANGE

Average annual population change (1995–1999)

- Over 1.5%
- 1 – 1.5%
- 0.5 – 1%
- Under 0.5%

WEALTH

Gross Domestic Product (GDP) in $ per capita (2000)

- Over 40,000
- 30,000 – 40,000
- 10,000 – 30,000
- 5000 – 10,000

Average annual change in GDP per capita (1990–1999)

- △ Over 2%
- ☐ 1.5 – 2%
- ○ Under 1.5%

Projection: Bonne

COPYRIGHT PHILIP'S

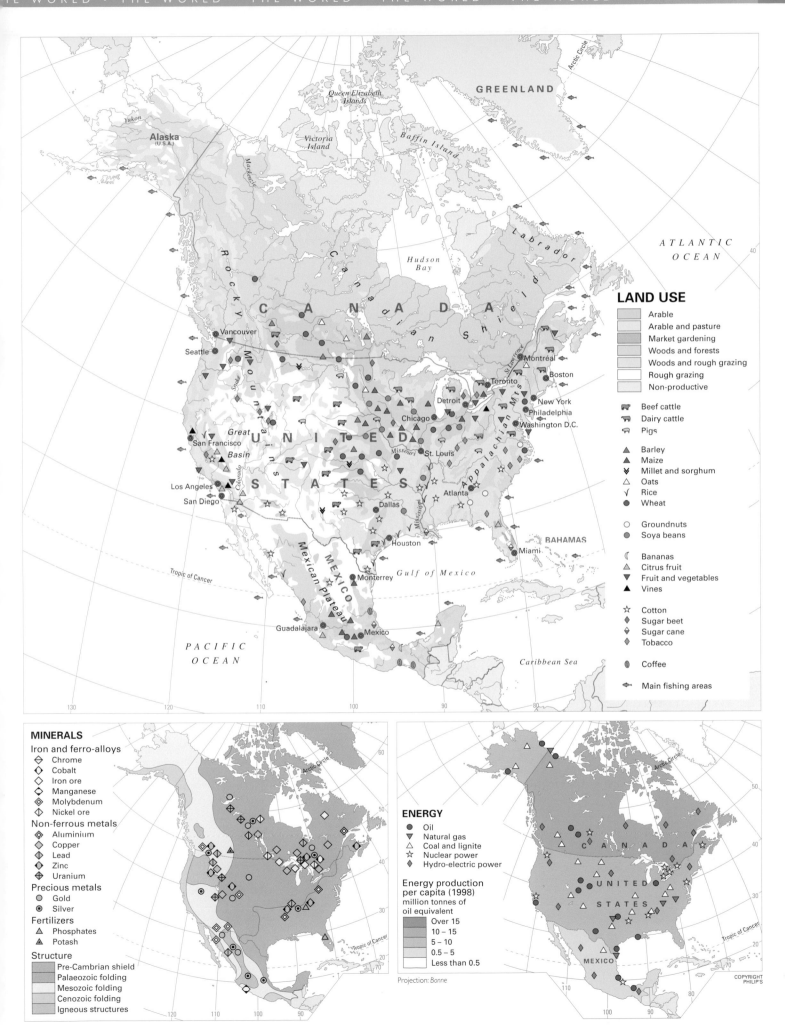

GREENLAND

Queen Elizabeth
Islands

Alaska
(U.S.A.)

Victoria
Island

Baffin Island

Yukon

Mackenzie

ATLANTIC
OCEAN

Labrador

Hudson
Bay

C A N A D A

Canadian Shield

Rocky   Mountains

Vancouver

Seattle

St Lawrence
Montréal
Boston

Toronto
Detroit
New York
Philadelphia
Washington D.C.

Chicago

Great
Basin
San Francisco

U N I T E D

Missouri
St. Louis

Appalachian Mts

Los Angeles

Colorado

S T A T E S

Atlanta

San Diego

Dallas

Mississippi

BAHAMAS

MEXICO
Mexican Plateau

Houston

Gulf of Mexico

Miami

Tropic of Cancer

Monterrey

Guadalajara
Mexico

PACIFIC
OCEAN

Caribbean Sea

LAND USE

	Arable
	Arable and pasture
	Market gardening
	Woods and forests
	Woods and rough grazing
	Rough grazing
	Non-productive

- Beef cattle
- Dairy cattle
- Pigs

- ▲ Barley
- ▲ Maize
- Millet and sorghum
- △ Oats
- Rice
- ● Wheat

- ○ Groundnuts
- ● Soya beans

- ☾ Bananas
- △ Citrus fruit
- ▼ Fruit and vegetables
- ▲ Vines

- ☆ Cotton
- ◆ Sugar beet
- ◇ Sugar cane
- ◈ Tobacco

- ● Coffee

- Main fishing areas

MINERALS

Iron and ferro-alloys
- ◇ Chrome
- ◇ Cobalt
- ◇ Iron ore
- ◇ Manganese
- ◈ Molybdenum
- ◈ Nickel ore

Non-ferrous metals
- ◈ Aluminium
- ◈ Copper
- ◆ Lead
- ◆ Zinc
- ✛ Uranium

Precious metals
- ● Gold
- ◉ Silver

Fertilizers
- △ Phosphates
- ▲ Potash

Structure
	Pre-Cambrian shield
	Palaeozoic folding
	Mesozoic folding
	Cenozoic folding
	Igneous structures

Arctic Circle

Tropic of Cancer

ENERGY
- ● Oil
- ▼ Natural gas
- △ Coal and lignite
- ☆ Nuclear power
- ◆ Hydro-electric power

Energy production per capita (1998)
million tonnes of oil equivalent
	Over 15
	10 – 15
	5 – 10
	0.5 – 5
	Less than 0.5

C A N A D A

U N I T E D

S T A T E S

MEXICO

Arctic Circle

Tropic of Cancer

Projection: Bonne

COPYRIGHT
PHILIP'S

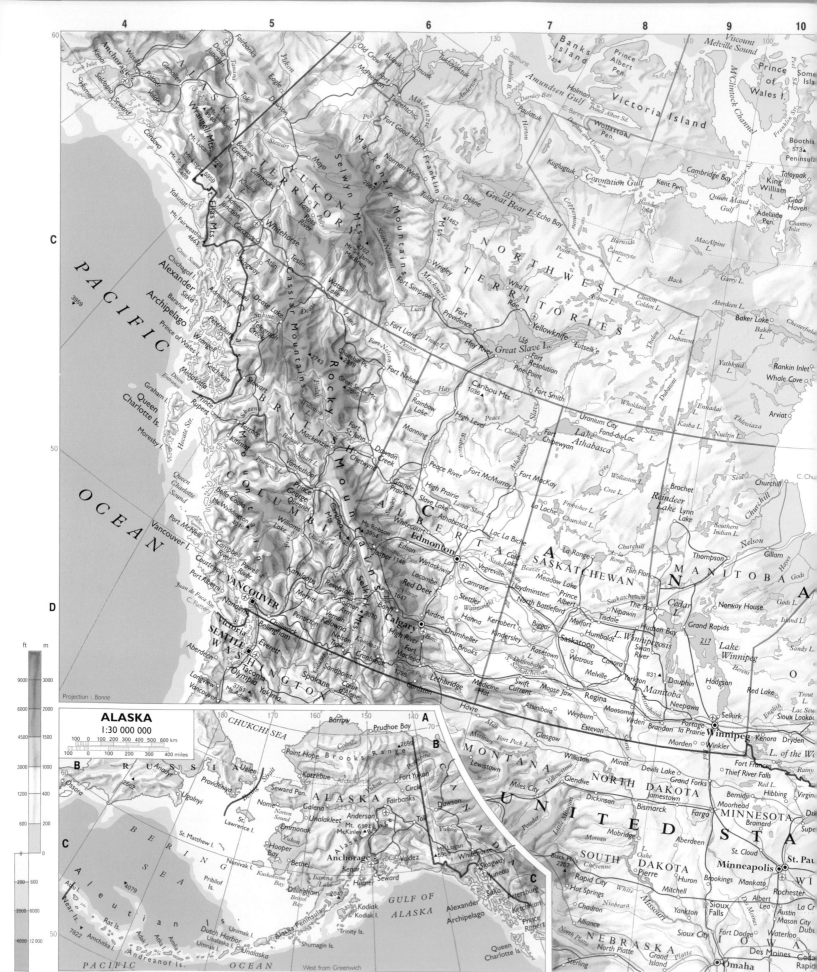

ALASKA
1:30 000 000

Projection : Bonne

West from Greenwich

1:15 000 000

COPYRIGHT PHILIP'S

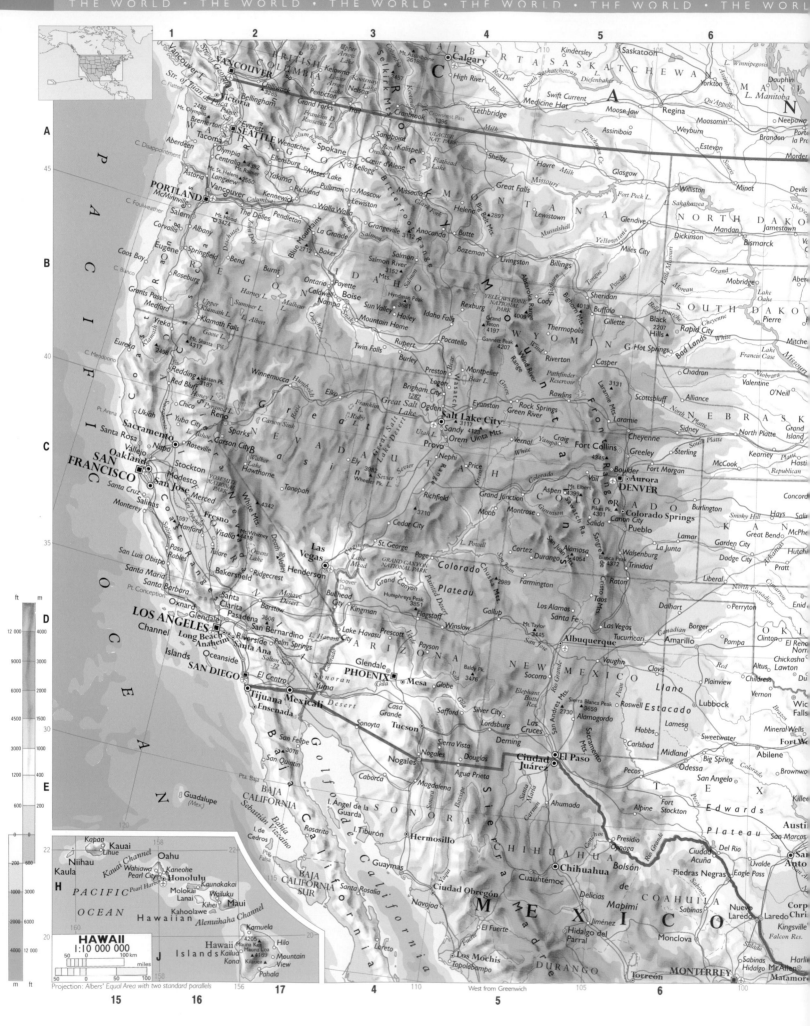

Projection: Albers' Equal Area with two standard parallels

HAWAII 1:10 000 000
West from Greenwich

1:12 000 000

COPYRIGHT PHILIP'S

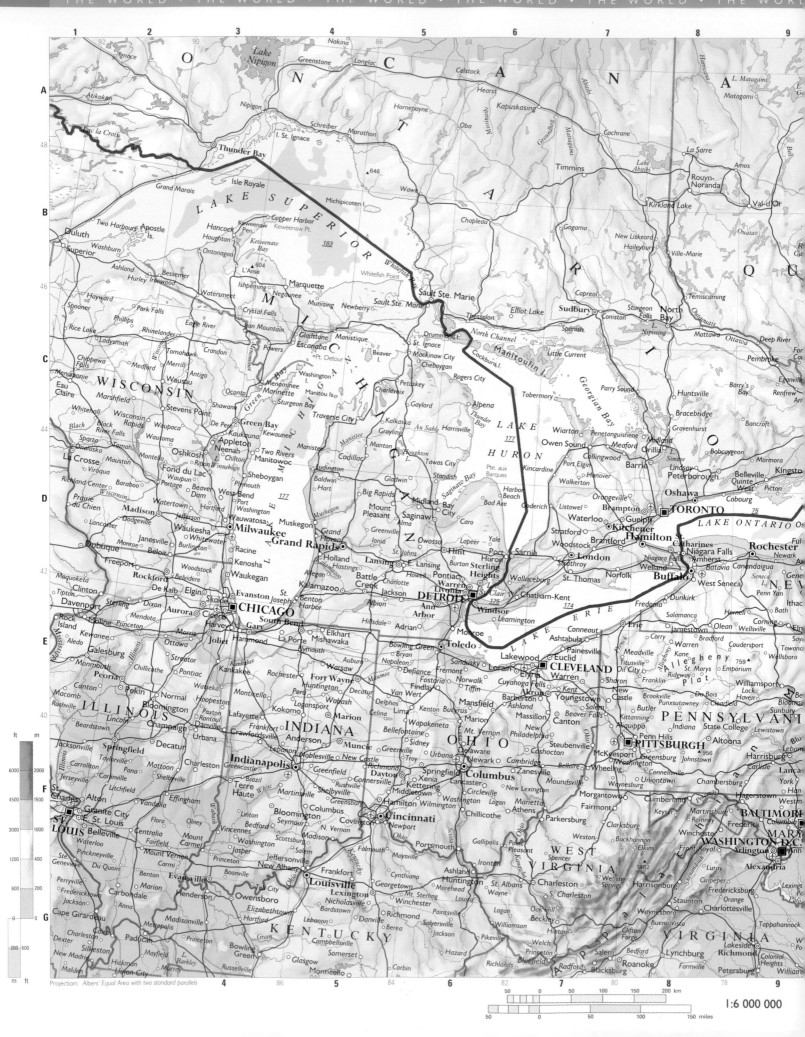

Projection: Albers' Equal Area with two standard parallels

1:6 000 000

10   11   12   13   14   15   16   17

D

A

Chibougamau
L. Chibougamau
556

Rés.
Gouin

Dolbeau-
Mistassini

Port-Cartier
Port-Menier

Î. d'Anticosti
Pte.
Heath

Baie Comeau
Cap-Chat
Matane
Mts. Chic-Chocs   Gaspé
1310   C. Gaspé

Rés. Pipmuacan

St.-Félicien
St.-Jean
Roberval
Chicoutimi
Jonquière

Pén. de la Gaspésie

GULF OF
ST. LAWRENCE

48

B

E
C

L. Kempt
La Tuque

Rimouski

Rivière-du-Loup

Dalhousie
Chaleur Bay
Bathurst

Campbellton

Miramichi Bay
North C.   Tignish
Miramichi
Newcastle

Îs. de la
Madeleine
(Quebec)

C. North

532   Cape Breton
Island
Glace Bay
Sydney

Rés.
Baskatong

La Malbaie

Bnie-St-Paul

Edmundston

Fort
Kent
Eagle
Lake
Van
Buren
Caribou

Grand
Falls

N E W

B R U N S W I C K

819

PRINCE EDWARD
ISLAND

Summerside

Northumberland Str.

East Pt.
Souris

Charlottetown

New Glasgow
Springhill   Stellarton
Chipman   Moncton   Cape Tormentine   Truro   Chedabucto B.
Canso

L'Annonciation   968   Grand-Mère
Shawinigan
Cap-de-la-Madeleine
Trois-Rivières   Québec   Î. d'Orléans
Lévis

Presque Isle

Chamberlain
L.
Houlton
Patten

Grand L.
Fredericton

Sussex

Bras d'Or

N
O
V
A

S
C
O
T
I
A

Laurier
St-Jérôme

Joliette

Plessisville
Ste-Marie
St-Georges

Eagle L.
1605   Chesuncook L.
Mt. Katahdin

Kentville

44

ingham   Hawkesbury
Victoriaville   Thetford
Mines
Drummondville   Asbestos
Lac-
Mégantic

Mooseheaf
L.
Millinocket

Saint
John

Bay of Fundy

Dartmouth

Halifax

Ottawa
Cornwall
Beauharnois

MONTRÉAL
Granby
Magog
Sherbrooke

Coaticook
Colebrook
Richardson
Lakes

Greenville

Lincoln
Dover
Foxcroft

Calais
Eastport

Digby

Bridgewater
L. Rossignol
Liverpool

Ottawa
St-Hyacinthe
Cowansville
Newport
Island Pond

M
A
I
N
E

Old Town
Brewer
Bangor

St. Stephen

Yarmouth

Shelburne
C. Sable

44

Falls
Massena
Ogdensburg
Potsdam
Canton
Gouverneur
Saranac Lakes

Malone
St. Albans
Plattsburgh
Lake
Champlain
Burlington
Winooski
St. Johnsbury

Newport
Lancaster
Berlin
Mt. Washington
1917
Rumford
Farmington
Augusta
Waterville

Skowhegan

Machias
Grand
Manan I.

D

Watertown
Lowville
Lake Pleasant
Rome
Utica
syracuse

Adirondack Mts.
1629
Ticonderoga
Lake
George
Middlebury
Barre
Montpelier

VERMONT

Conway

Belfast

Bar
Harbor
Mt. Desert
I.

Penobscot Bay

Ellsworth

42

YORK

and
Norwich

Schenectady
Albany
Troy

Greenville
Rutland
Claremont
Lebanon
Franklin
Concord

Dover
Rochester
Portsmouth

Lewiston
Auburn
Gardiner
Bath
Brunswick
Westbrook
Saco
Biddeford

Portland

Rockland

Binghamton Mts.
1281
Pittsfield
Catskill
Catskill
Hudson

Glens
Falls
Saratoga Springs
Amsterdam

Keene
Brattleboro

NEW HAMPSHIRE
Laconia
Manchester
Haverhill
Nashua
Lawrence
Lowell
Salem
Newburyport

C. Ann

42

Oneonta

Kingston
Northampton
Chicopee
Springfield
Woonsocket

Fitchburg
Leominster

MASS
Cambridge
BOSTON
Quincy

Poughkeepsie
Hartford
Pawtucket
Worcester
Taunton
Brockton
Cape Cod

Carbondale
Dunmore
Scranton
Wilkes-Barre
Hazleton

Newburgh
Middletown

New Britain
Waterbury
Beacon

Meriden

CONN
New

Providence
Warwick
Fall River
New Bedford
Hyannis

R.I.
Newport

Martha's
Vineyard

E

Delaware

Easton
Allentown
Reading
Pottstown

Bethlehem

Danbury
Bridgeport
Haven
New
London

Stamford
Mount Vernon
Yonkers
Paterson
Newark
Elizabeth
Jersey City
Long Island

Long Island
Riverhead

Block I.

Nantucket I.

ville

Chester
PHILADELPHIA
Camden

Trenton
New Brunswick

NEW YORK
Long Branch
Asbury Park

40

rristown

Wilmington
Vineland
Hammonton

Bridgeton
Millville
DELAMARE
Seaford

ambridge
bury

Milford

Dover
Ocean City

Snow Hill

Cape May

Atlantic City
Ocean City

NEW
JERSEY

Henlopen

Delaware Bay

A T L A N T I C

O C E A N

38

Accomac

pe Charles

C. Charles

G

10   74   11   West from Greenwich   72   12   70   13

TOURISM IN THE USA

Olympic N.P.
North Cascades N.P.
Seattle
Mt. Rainier N.P.
Glacier N.P.
Acadia N.P.

Theodore
Roosevelt N.P.
Voyageurs N.P.
Isle Royale N.P.
Boston

Redwood
N.P.
Crater Lake N.P.
Yellowstone
N.P.
Badlands N.P.
Niagara
Falls
New York

Lassen Volcanic
N.P.
Grand
Teton N.P.
Wind Cave N.P.
Minneapolis
Detroit
Philadelphia
Atlantic City

San
Francisco
Great Basin
N.P.
Capitol Reef
N.P.
Rocky Mt. N.P.
Chicago
Washington

Yosemite
N.P.
Arches
N.P.
Denver
Kansas City
St. Louis
Shenandoah N.P.
Great Smoky Mountains N.P.
Mammoth Cave N.P.

Kings Canyon N.P.
Bryce
Canyon N.P.
Zion N.P.
Mesa Verde N.P.

Sequoia N.P.
Death Valley N.P.
Grand Canyon N.P.
Petrified Forest N.P.

Channel
Islands N.P.
Las Vegas
Phoenix
Saguaro N.P.
Hot Springs N.P.
Atlanta

Los Angeles
San Diego

Carlsbad Caverns
Dallas
Guadalupe Mountains N.P.
Big Bend N.P.
Houston
New Orleans

Orlando
Tampa
Dry Tortugas N.P.
Miami
Everglades N.P.

☐ Major tourist centres
● Major concentration of hotels
☐ Major National Parks

Tropic of Cancer

A
Gulf of Campeche
Yucatán Peninsula
Yucatán Channel
Isthmus of Tehuantepec
Greater Antilles
Cuba
Turks & Caicos Is.
Hispaniola
9200
Puerto Rico
Guadeloupe
Dominica
Martinique

NORTH
ATLANTIC
OCEAN

B
Guatemala Trench
G. de Honduras
Coco
L. Nicaragua
Panama Canal
Jamaica
Caribbean Sea
C. Gracias a Dios
Lesser Antilles
St. Lucia
St. Vincent
Barbados
Grenada
Tobago
Trinidad
I. Margarita
C. de la Aguja
5800
Sierra Nevada de Santa Marta

C
Panama Canal
G. of Darién
Gulf of Panamá
Cordillera Occidental
Cordillera Central
Cordillera Oriental
C. de San Francisco
Magdalena
Cord. de Mérida
L. Maracaibo
Llanos
Orinoco
Meta
Guaviare
Guiana Highlands
Mt. Roraima 2810
Sierra Pacaraima
Branco
Sierra Tumucumaque
Curumayá
Essequibo
C. Orange

D
Galapagos Is.
G. of Guayaquil
Pta. Pariñas
Pta. Negra
Cotopaxi 5897
Chimborazo 6267
Caquetá
Napo
Marañón
Ucayali
Putumayo
Japurá
Amazon
Selvas
Juruá
Purus
Madeira
Amazon
Roosevelt
Tapajós
Xingu
Tocantins
Araguaia
Teles Pires
Arinos
Marajó I.
Equator
Parnaíba
São Francisco
Plat. of Borborema
C. de São Roque
Brazilian Highlands
Huascarán 6768

E
PACIFIC
Chile Peru
Chincha Alta
Madre de Dios
L. Titicaca
Bolivian Plateau
Nevada Ancohuma 6580
L. de Poopó
Guaporé
Mamoré
Plateau of Mato Grosso
Paraguay
Paraná
Serra da Mantiqueira
Pico da Bandeira 2890
Serra do Mar
Abrolhos Bank

F
Tropic of Capricorn
San Félix
San Ambrosio
Trench
Atacama Desert
8050
Cerro Ojos del Salado 6863
Salinas Grandes
Andes
Gran Chaco
Pilcomayo
Salado
Paraná
Entre Ríos
Uruguay
Iguaçu Falls
C. Frio
L. dos Patos

G
OCEAN
Arch. de Juan Fernández
Mt. Aconcagua 6962
Sierra de Córdoba
L. Mar Chiquita
Pampas
Colorado
Negro
Bahía Blanca
Río de la Plata
SOUTH
ATLANTIC
OCEAN

H
Chile Rise
Chiloé I.
Chonos Archipelago
Taitao Peninsula
Gulf of Penas
Wellington I.
Madre de Dios I.
Magellan's Str.
Santa Inés I.
Canal Cockburn
Canal Beagle
Tierra del Fuego
Staten I.
C. Horn
Mte. San Valentín 4058
Patagonia
Andes
G. San Matías
Valdés Peninsula 40
Gulf of San Jorge
Argentine Basin
6212
Falkland Is.
West Falkland
East Falkland
South Georgia

ft / m scale:
12000 / 4000
9000 / 3000
6000 / 2000
3000 / 1000
1500 / 500
600 / 200
0 / 0
200 / 600
1000 / 3000
2000 / 6000
4000 / 12000
6000 / 18000
8000 / 24000
m / ft

Projection: Lambert's Azimuthal Equal Area
100 0 200 400 600 800 1000 1200 1400 km
100 0 200 400 600 800 1000 miles
1:28 000 000
60 West from Greenwich 50
COPYRIGHT PHILIP'S

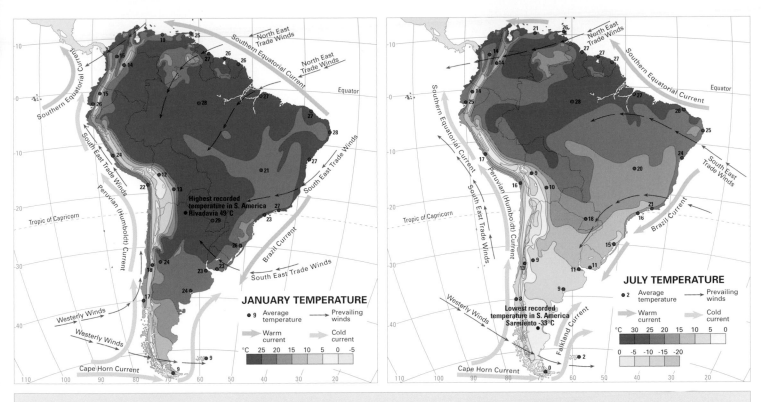

JANUARY TEMPERATURE

- 9 Average temperature
- → Prevailing winds
- ⟶ Warm current
- ⟶ Cold current

°C 25 20 15 10 5 0 -5

North East Trade Winds
Southern Equatorial Current
North East Trade Winds
Southern Equatorial Current
South East Trade Winds
South East Trade Winds
South East Trade Winds
Brazil Current
South Equatorial Current
South East Trade Winds
Peruvian (Humboldt) Current
Westerly Winds
Westerly Winds
Cape Horn Current
Equator
Tropic of Capricorn

Highest recorded temperature in S. America Rivadavia 49°C

JULY TEMPERATURE

- 2 Average temperature
- → Prevailing winds
- ⟶ Warm current
- ⟶ Cold current

°C 30 25 20 15 10 5 0

0 -5 -10 -15 -20

North East Trade Winds
Southern Equatorial Current
South East Trade Winds
Southern Equatorial Current
Peruvian (Humboldt) Current
South East Trade Winds
Brazil Current
Westerly Winds
Falkland Current
Cape Horn Current
Equator
Tropic of Capricorn

Lowest recorded temperature in S. America Sarmiento -33°C

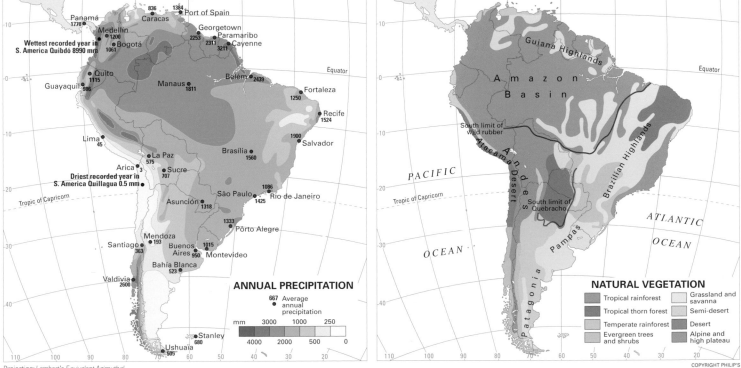

Climate graphs (with Temperature and Precipitation):

- **BOGOTA** — Precipitation 1061mm/42in
- **BRASILIA** — Precipitation 1560mm/61in
- **BUENOS AIRES** — Precipitation 950mm/37in
- **CARACAS** — Precipitation 836mm/33in
- **LIMA** — Precipitation 45mm/2in
- **MANAUS** — Precipitation 1811mm/71in
- **RIO DE JANEIRO** — Precipitation 1086mm/43in
- **SANTIAGO** — Precipitation 363mm/14in
- **STANLEY** — Precipitation 681mm/27in

maximum
Average monthly temperature
minimum
Average annual precipitation
Average monthly precipitation
Months of the year

JFMAMJJASOND

ANNUAL PRECIPITATION

- 667 Average annual precipitation

mm 3000 1000 250
4000 2000 500 0

Panamá 1770
Caracas 836 / Port of Spain 1384
Medellin 1200
Georgetown 2253
Paramaribo 2311
Cayenne 3211
Wettest recorded year in S. America Quibdó 8990 mm
Bogotá 1061
Quito 1115
Guayaquil 986
Belém 2439
Manaus 1811
Fortaleza 1250
Recife 1524
Lima 45
La Paz 575
Salvador 1900
Arica 3
Sucre 707
Brasilia 1560
Driest recorded year in S. America Quillagua 0.5 mm
São Paulo 1425
Rio de Janeiro 1086
Asunción 1318
Pôrto Alegre 1333
Mendoza 193
Santiago 363
Buenos Aires 950
Montevideo 1015
Bahía Blanca 523
Valdivia 2600
Stanley 680
Ushuaia 505
Equator
Tropic of Capricorn

NATURAL VEGETATION

- Tropical rainforest
- Tropical thorn forest
- Temperate rainforest
- Evergreen trees and shrubs
- Grassland and savanna
- Semi-desert
- Desert
- Alpine and high plateau

Guiana Highlands
Amazon Basin
South limit of wild rubber
Andes
Atacama Desert
Brazilian Highlands
South limit of Quebracho
Pampas
Patagonia
PACIFIC OCEAN
ATLANTIC OCEAN
Equator
Tropic of Capricorn

Projection: Lambert's Equivalent Azimuthal

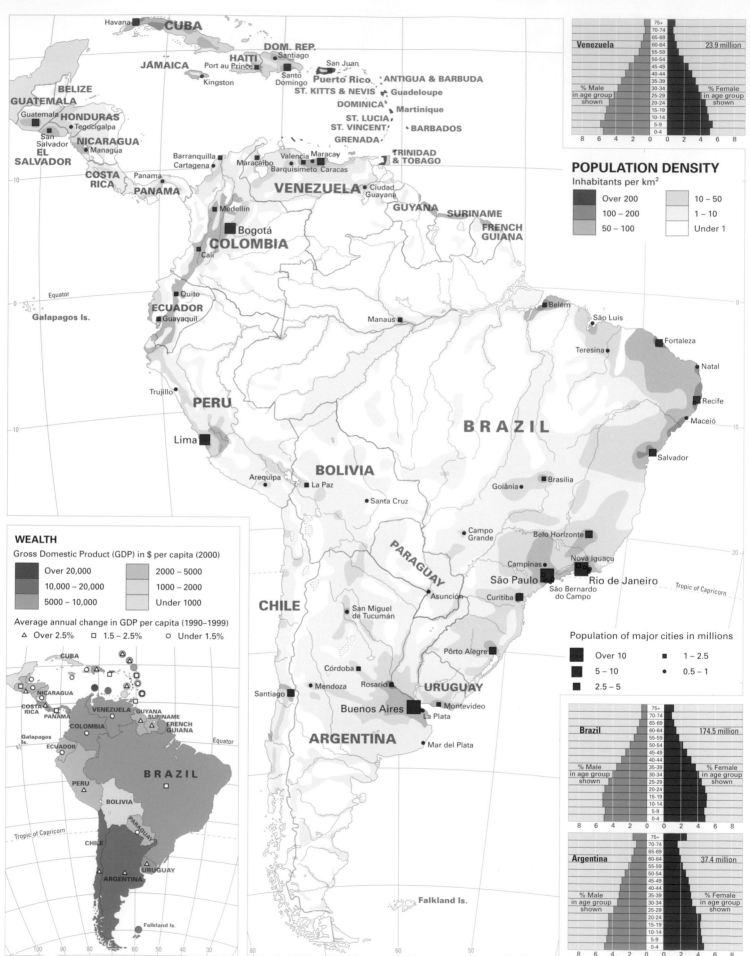

CUBA
Havana
JAMAICA
Kingston
HAITI Port au Prince
Santiago
DOM. REP.
Santo Domingo
San Juan
Puerto Rico
ANTIGUA & BARBUDA
ST. KITTS & NEVIS • Guadeloupe
DOMINICA
BELIZE • Martinique
GUATEMALA **ST. LUCIA**
Guatemala **HONDURAS** **ST. VINCENT** • **BARBADOS**
• Tegucigalpa **GRENADA**
San Salvador **NICARAGUA** **TRINIDAD**
EL SALVADOR Managua **& TOBAGO**
COSTA Panama
RICA Panama
PANAMA
Barranquilla
Cartagena Maracaibo Valencia Maracay
Barquisimeto Caracas
VENEZUELA • Ciudad
Guayana
Medellín **GUYANA** **SURINAME**
Bogotá **FRENCH**
COLOMBIA **GUIANA**
Cali
Equator
Quito
ECUADOR
Galapagos Is. Guayaquil Manaus Belém
São Luís
Fortaleza
Teresina Natal
Trujillo
PERU Recife
B R A Z I L Maceió
Lima
Salvador
BOLIVIA
Arequipa La Paz Goiânia Brasília
Santa Cruz

POPULATION DENSITY
Inhabitants per km²

Over 200	10 – 50
100 – 200	1 – 10
50 – 100	Under 1

Venezuela 23.9 million
% Male in age group shown
% Female in age group shown

Campo Grande Belo Horizonte
Nova Iguaçu
Campinas Rio de Janeiro
São Paulo Tropic of Capricorn
São Bernardo do Campo
PARAGUAY Curitiba

Population of major cities in millions

Over 10	1 – 2.5
5 – 10	0.5 – 1
2.5 – 5	

CHILE San Miguel de Tucumán
Asunción
Pôrto Alegre
URUGUAY
Córdoba
Santiago Mendoza Rosario
Buenos Aires Montevideo
La Plata
ARGENTINA Mar del Plata

WEALTH
Gross Domestic Product (GDP) in $ per capita (2000)

Over 20,000	2000 – 5000
10,000 – 20,000	1000 – 2000
5000 – 10,000	Under 1000

Average annual change in GDP per capita (1990–1999)
△ Over 2.5% ☐ 1.5 – 2.5% ○ Under 1.5%

CUBA
NICARAGUA
COSTA RICA
PANAMA **VENEZUELA** **GUYANA**
SURINAME
COLOMBIA **FRENCH GUIANA**
Galapagos Is. Equator
ECUADOR
PERU
B R A Z I L
BOLIVIA
PARAGUAY
Tropic of Capricorn
CHILE
URUGUAY
ARGENTINA
Falkland Is.

Brazil 174.5 million
% Male in age group shown
% Female in age group shown

Argentina 37.4 million
% Male in age group shown
% Female in age group shown

Falkland Is.

Projection: Lambert's Equivalent Azimuthal

COPYRIGHT PHILIP'S

LAND USE

Arable
Market gardening and plantations
Pasture
Woods and forests
Rough grazing
Non-productive

Main fishing areas

Beef cattle
Dairy cattle
Pigs
Sheep

Maize
Millet and sorghum
Rice
Wheat

Groundnuts
Potatoes
Soya beans

Bananas
Citrus fruit
Fruit and vegetables
Vines

Cacao
Coconut palms
Cotton
Sugar cane
Tobacco
Coffee
Tea

MINERALS
Iron and ferro-alloys

Chrome
Cobalt
Iron ore
Manganese
Molybdenum
Nickel ore

Non-ferrous metals

Aluminium
Bauxite
Copper
Tin

Precious metals & stones

Diamonds
Gold
Silver

Fertilizers

Phosphates

Structure

Pre-Cambrian shield
Palaeozoic folding
Mesozoic folding
Cenozoic folding
Igneous structures

ENERGY

Oil
Natural gas
Coal and lignite
Nuclear power
Hydro-electric power

Energy production per capita (1998)
million tonnes of oil equivalent

Over 15
10 – 15
5 – 10
0.5 – 5
Less than 0.5

Projection: *Lambert's Equivalent Azimuthal*

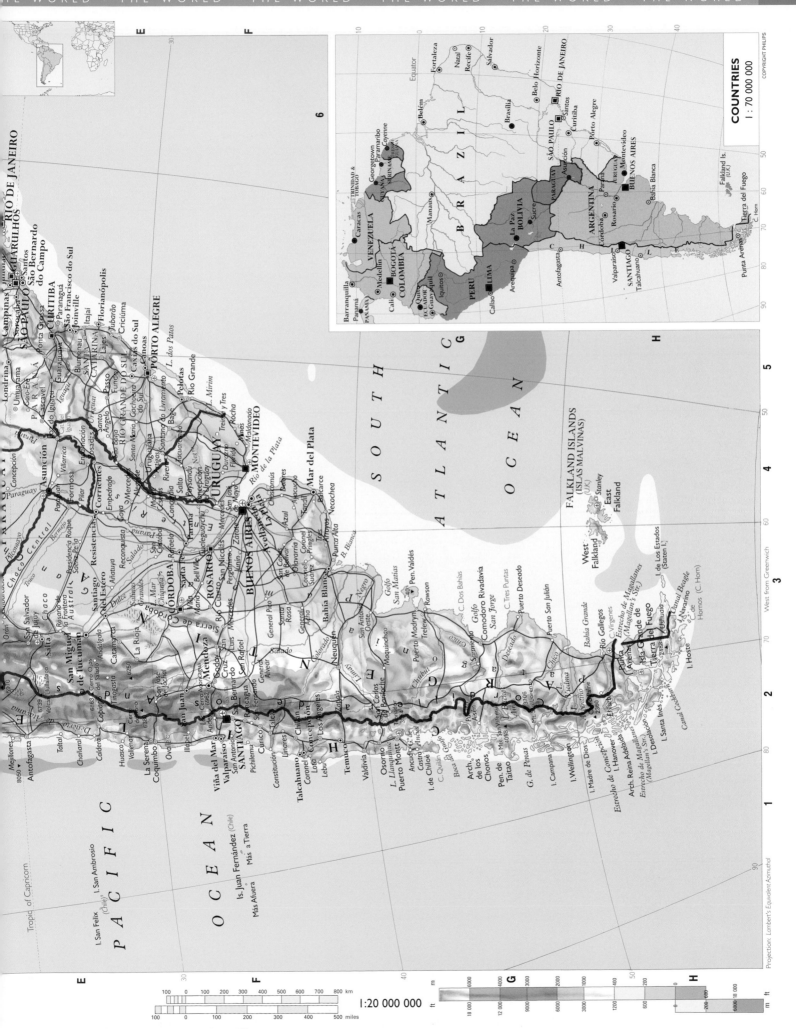

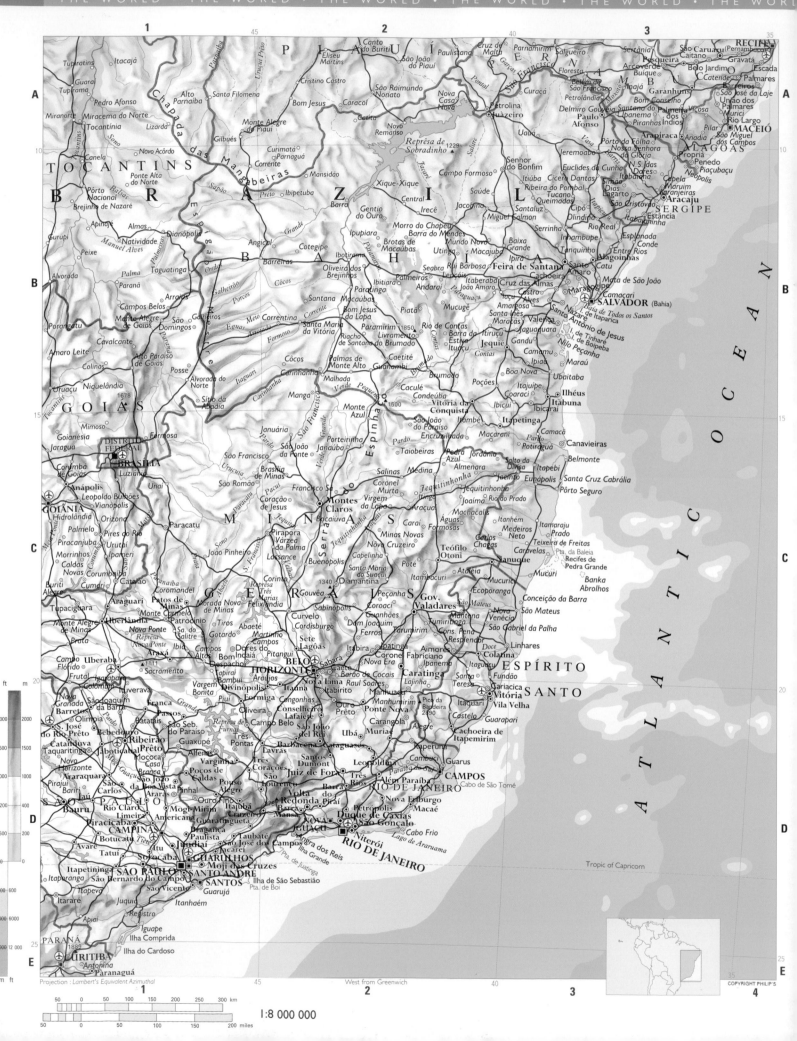

Projection : Lambert's Equivalent Azimuthal

West from Greenwich

1:8 000 000

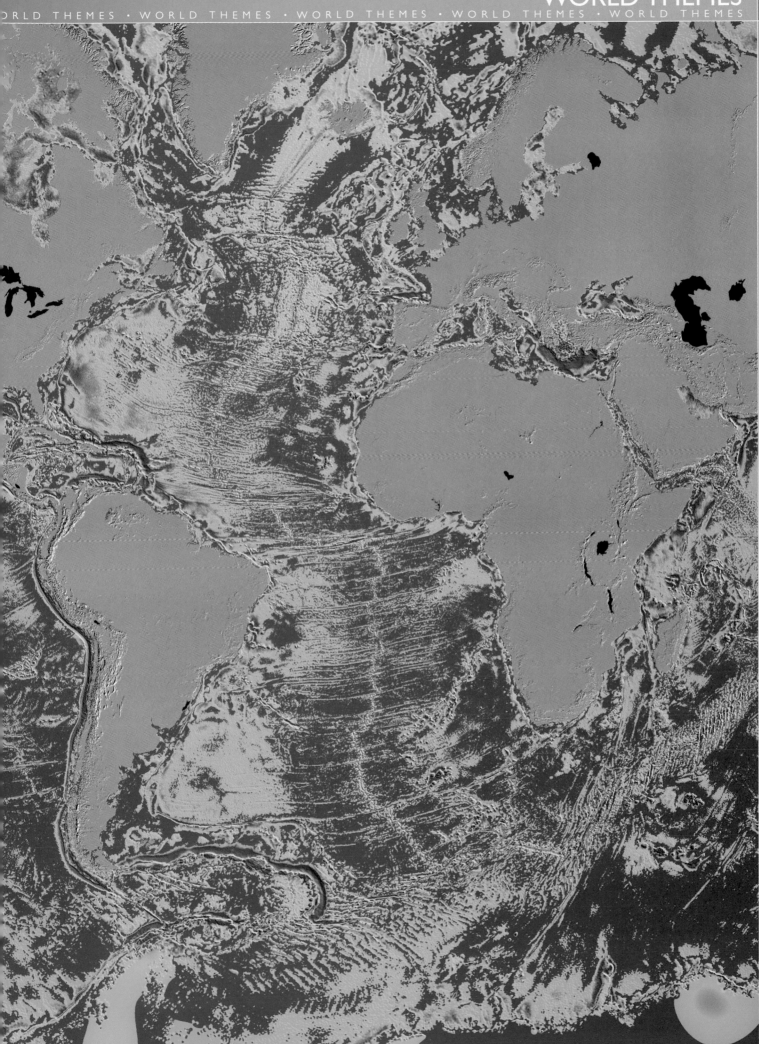

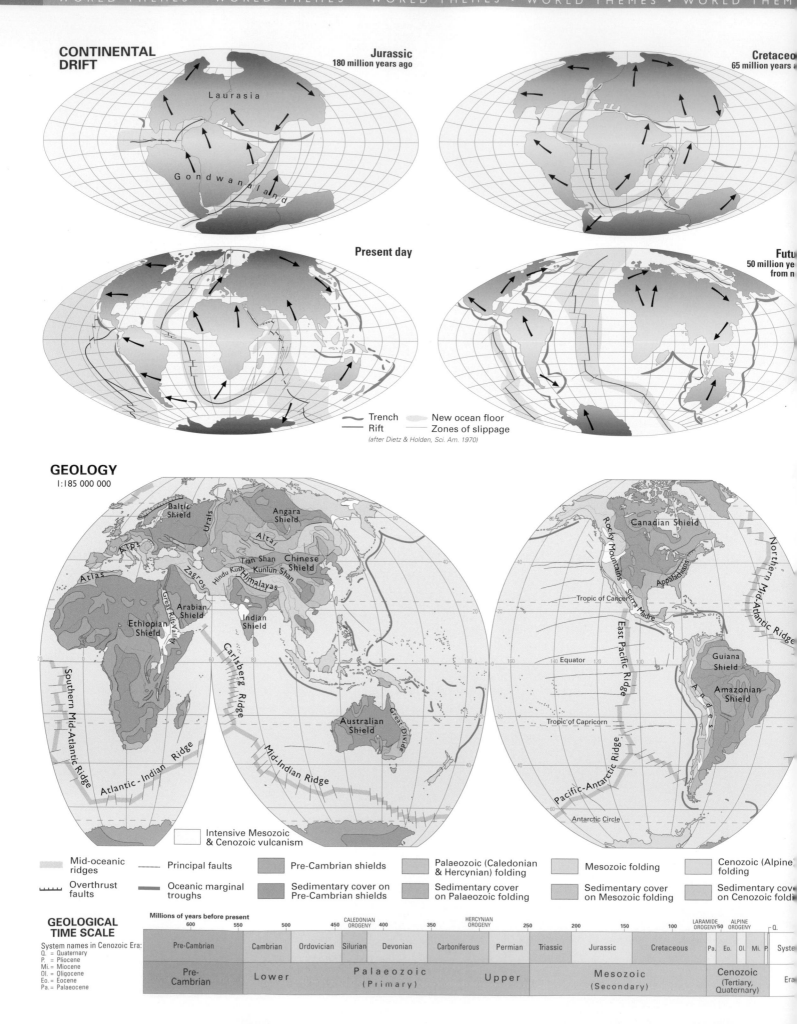

CONTINENTAL DRIFT

Jurassic
180 million years ago

Laurasia

Gondwanaland

Cretaceo
65 million years a

Present day

Futu
50 million ye
from n

Trench — New ocean floor
Rift — Zones of slippage
(after Dietz & Holden, Sci. Am. 1970)

GEOLOGY
1:185 000 000

Baltic Shield
Urals
Angara Shield
Altai
Alps
Tian Shan
Chinese Shield
Kunlun Shan
Atlas
Zagros
Hindu Kush
Himalayas
Great Rift Valley
Arabian Shield
Indian Shield
Ethiopian Shield
Carlsberg Ridge
Southern Mid-Atlantic Ridge
Atlantic-Indian Ridge
Mid-Indian Ridge
Australian Shield
Great Divide
Pacific-Antarctic Ridge

Canadian Shield
Rocky Mountains
Appalachians
Sierra Madre
Tropic of Cancer
Northern Mid-Atlantic Ridge
East Pacific Ridge
Equator
Guiana Shield
Amazonian Shield
Andes
Tropic of Capricorn
Antarctic Circle

Intensive Mesozoic & Cenozoic vulcanism

Mid-oceanic ridges	Principal faults	Pre-Cambrian shields
Overthrust faults	Oceanic marginal troughs	Sedimentary cover on Pre-Cambrian shields

Palaeozoic (Caledonian & Hercynian) folding
Sedimentary cover on Palaeozoic folding
Mesozoic folding
Sedimentary cover on Mesozoic folding
Cenozoic (Alpine folding
Sedimentary cov on Cenozoic foldi

GEOLOGICAL TIME SCALE

System names in Cenozoic Era:
Q. = Quaternary
P. = Pliocene
Mi. = Miocene
Ol. = Oligocene
Eo. = Eocene
Pa. = Palaeocene

Millions of years before present

600	550	500	450	400	350	250	200	150	100	50	Q.	
Pre-Cambrian		Cambrian	Ordovician	Silurian	Devonian	Carboniferous	Permian	Triassic	Jurassic	Cretaceous	Pa. Eo. Ol. Mi. P.	System

CALEDONIAN OROGENY   HERCYNIAN OROGENY   LARAMIDE OROGENY   ALPINE OROGENY

Pre-Cambrian	Lower	Palaeozoic (Primary)	Upper	Mesozoic (Secondary)	Cenozoic (Tertiary, Quaternary)	Era

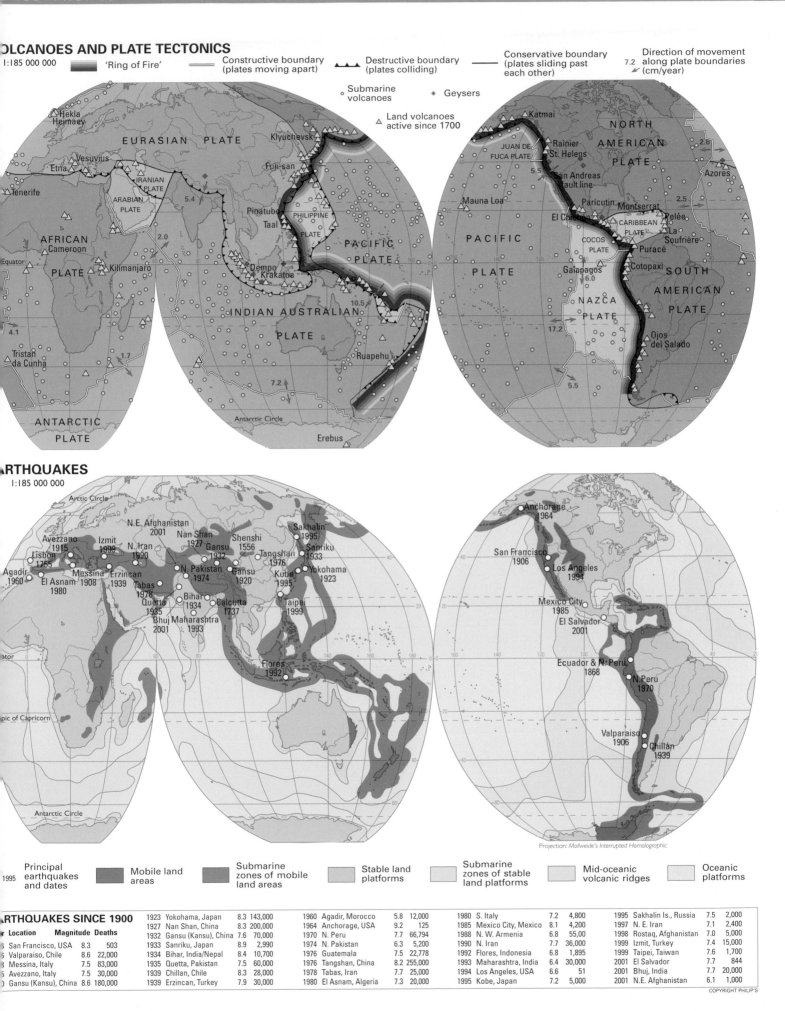

VOLCANOES AND PLATE TECTONICS

1:185 000 000   'Ring of Fire'   Constructive boundary (plates moving apart)   Destructive boundary (plates colliding)   Conservative boundary (plates sliding past each other)   7.2 Direction of movement along plate boundaries (cm/year)

Submarine volcanoes   Geysers   Land volcanoes active since 1700

EARTHQUAKES

1:185 000 000

Projection: Mollweide's Interrupted Homolographic

Principal earthquakes and dates | Mobile land areas | Submarine zones of mobile land areas | Stable land platforms | Submarine zones of stable land platforms | Mid-oceanic volcanic ridges | Oceanic platforms

EARTHQUAKES SINCE 1900

Location	Magnitude	Deaths		Location	Magnitude	Deaths		Location	Magnitude	Deaths		Location	Magnitude	Deaths		Location	Magnitude	Deaths
San Francisco, USA	8.3	503	1923	Yokohama, Japan	8.3	143,000	1960	Agadir, Morocco	5.8	12,000	1980	S. Italy	7.2	4,800	1995	Sakhalin Is., Russia	7.5	2,000
Valparaiso, Chile	8.6	22,000	1927	Nan Shan, China	8.3	200,000	1964	Anchorage, USA	9.2	125	1985	Mexico City, Mexico	8.1	4,200	1997	N. E. Iran	7.1	2,400
Messina, Italy	7.5	83,000	1932	Gansu (Kansu), China	7.6	70,000	1970	N. Peru	7.7	66,794	1988	N. W. Armenia	6.8	55,000	1998	Rostaq, Afghanistan	7.0	5,000
Avezzano, Italy	7.5	30,000	1933	Sanriku, Japan	8.9	2,990	1974	N. Pakistan	6.3	5,200	1990	N. Iran	7.7	36,000	1999	Izmit, Turkey	7.4	15,000
Gansu (Kansu), China	8.6	180,000	1934	Bihar, India/Nepal	8.4	10,700	1976	Guatemala	7.5	22,778	1992	Flores, Indonesia	6.8	1,895	1999	Taipei, Taiwan	7.6	1,700
			1935	Quetta, Pakistan	7.5	60,000	1976	Tangshan, China	8.2	255,000	1993	Maharashtra, India	6.4	30,000	2001	El Salvador	7.7	844
			1939	Chillan, Chile	8.3	28,000	1978	Tabas, Iran	7.7	25,000	1994	Los Angeles, USA	6.6	51	2001	Bhuj, India	7.7	20,000
			1939	Erzincan, Turkey	7.9	30,000	1980	El Asnam, Algeria	7.3	20,000	1995	Kobe, Japan	7.2	5,000	2001	N.E. Afghanistan	6.1	1,000

COPYRIGHT PHILIP'S

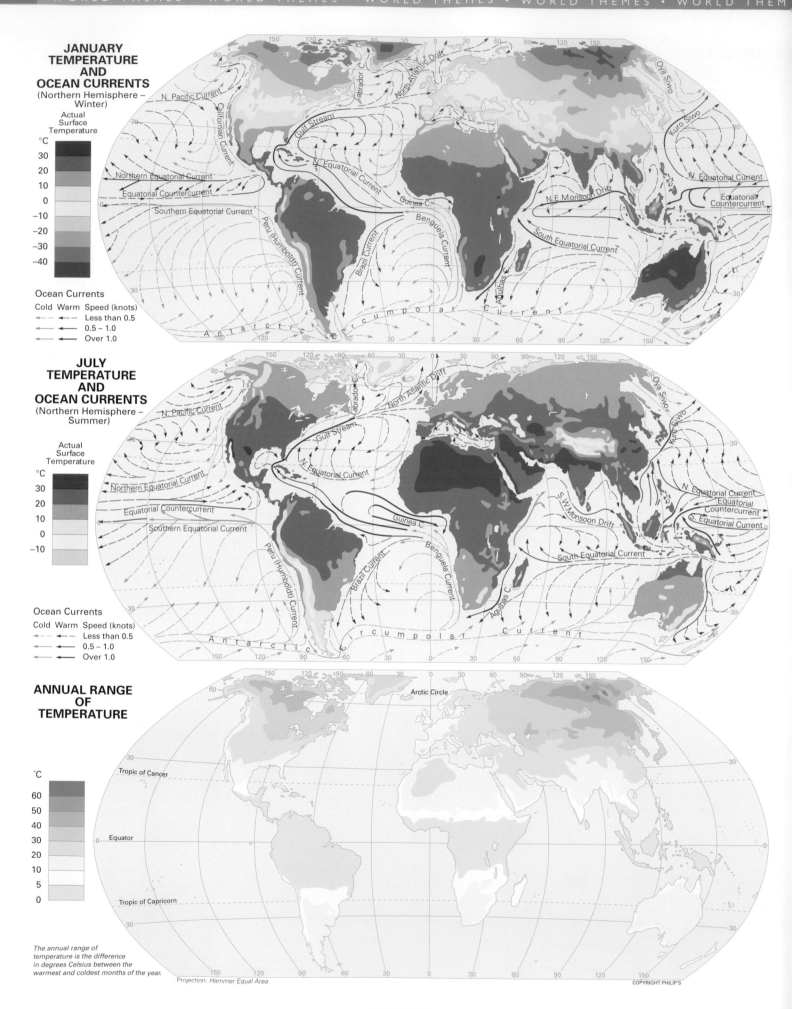

JANUARY TEMPERATURE AND OCEAN CURRENTS
(Northern Hemisphere – Winter)

Actual Surface Temperature

°C
30
20
10
0
−10
−20
−30
−40

Ocean Currents

Cold Warm Speed (knots)
Less than 0.5
0.5 – 1.0
Over 1.0

JULY TEMPERATURE AND OCEAN CURRENTS
(Northern Hemisphere – Summer)

Actual Surface Temperature

°C
30
20
10
0
−10

Ocean Currents

Cold Warm Speed (knots)
Less than 0.5
0.5 – 1.0
Over 1.0

ANNUAL RANGE OF TEMPERATURE

°C
60
50
40
30
20
10
5
0

The annual range of temperature is the difference in degrees Celsius between the warmest and coldest months of the year.

Projection: Hammer Equal Area

COPYRIGHT PHILIP'S

1 : 190 000 000

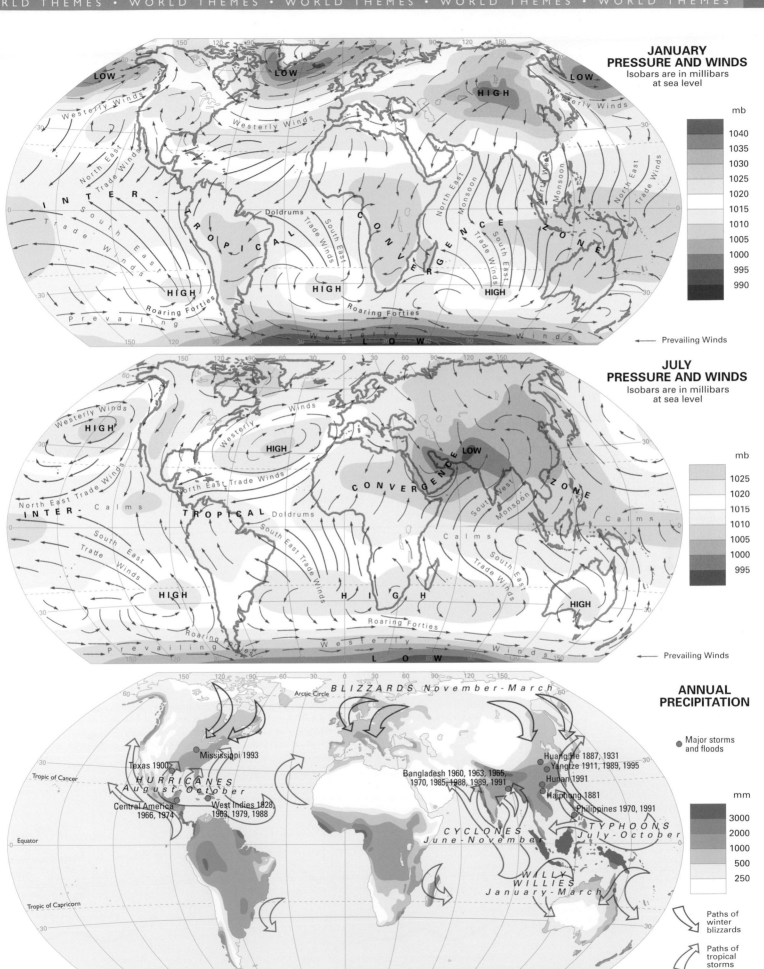

JANUARY PRESSURE AND WINDS
Isobars are in millibars at sea level

mb
1040
1035
1030
1025
1020
1015
1010
1005
1000
995
990

⟵ Prevailing Winds

JULY PRESSURE AND WINDS
Isobars are in millibars at sea level

mb
1025
1020
1015
1010
1005
1000
995

⟵ Prevailing Winds

ANNUAL PRECIPITATION

● Major storms and floods

mm
3000
2000
1000
500
250

⟡ Paths of winter blizzards

⟡ Paths of tropical storms

Projection: Hammer Equal Area

COPYRIGHT PHILIP'S

CLIMATE REGIONS (after Köppen)

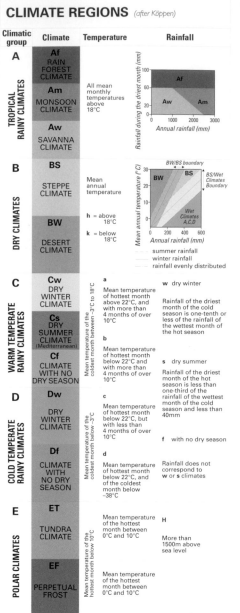

Climatic group	Climate	Temperature	Rainfall
A TROPICAL RAINY CLIMATES	**Af** RAIN FOREST CLIMATE / **Am** MONSOON CLIMATE / **Aw** SAVANNA CLIMATE	All mean monthly temperatures above 18°C	
B DRY CLIMATES	**BS** STEPPE CLIMATE / **BW** DESERT CLIMATE	Mean annual temperature. h = above 18°C, k = below 18°C	summer rainfall / winter rainfall / rainfall evenly distributed
C WARM TEMPERATE RAINY CLIMATES	**Cw** DRY WINTER CLIMATE / **Cs** DRY SUMMER CLIMATE (Mediterranean) / **Cf** CLIMATE WITH NO DRY SEASON	Mean temperature of the coldest month between −3°C to 18°C	a Mean temperature of hottest month above 22°C, and with more than 4 months of over 10°C / b Mean temperature of hottest month below 22°C and with more than 4 months of over 10°C
D COLD TEMPERATE RAINY CLIMATES	**Dw** DRY WINTER CLIMATE / **Df** CLIMATE WITH NO DRY SEASON	Mean temperature of the coldest month below −3°C	c Mean temperature of hottest month below 22°C, but with less than 4 months of over 10°C / d Mean temperature of hottest month below 22°C, and of the coldest month below −38°C
E POLAR CLIMATES	**ET** TUNDRA CLIMATE / **EF** PERPETUAL FROST	Mean temperature of the hottest month between 0°C and 10°C / Mean temperature of the hottest month between 0°C and 10°C	w dry winter: Rainfall of the driest month of the cold season is one-tenth or less of the wettest month of the hot season / s dry summer: Rainfall of the driest month of the hot season is less than one-third of the rainfall of the wettest month of the cold season and less than 40mm / f with no dry season: Rainfall does not correspond to w or s climates / H More than 1500m above sea level

Rainfall during the driest month (mm) — Af chart: Af, Aw, Am; Annual rainfall (mm) 1000 2000 3000

Mean annual temperature (°C): BW/BS boundary; BW, BS; BS/Wet Climates Boundary; Wet Climates A,C,D; Annual rainfall (mm) 200 400 600

CLIMATE RECORDS

Highest recorded temperature: Al Aziziyah, Libya, 58°C, 13 September 1922.

Lowest recorded temperature (outside poles): Verkhoyansk, Siberia, −68°C, 6 February 1933. Verkhoyansk also registered the greatest annual range of temperature: −70°C to 37°C.

Highest barometric pressure: Agata, Siberia, 1,083.8 mb at altitude 262 m, 31 December 1968.

Lowest barometric pressure: Typhoon Tip, 480 km west of Guam, Pacific Ocean, 870 mb, 12 October 1979.

Driest place: Quillagua, N. Chile, 0.5 mm, 1964–2001.

Wettest place (12 months): Cherrapunji, Meghalaya, N.E. India, August 1860 to August 1861. Cherrapunji also holds the record for rainfall in one month: 2930 mm, July 1861.

Highest recorded wind speed: Mt Washington, New Hampshire, USA, 371 km/h, 12 April 1934. This is three times as strong as hurricane force on the Beaufort Scale.

Windiest place: Commonwealth Bay, George V Coast, Antarctica, where gales frequently reach over 320 km/h.

Projection: Interrupted Mollweide's Homolographic

THE MONSOON

In early March, which normally marks the end of the subcontinent's cool season and the start of the hot season, winds blow outwards from the mainland. But as the overhead sun and the ITCZ move northwards, the land is intensely heated, and a low-pressure system develops. The south-east trade winds, which are drawn across the Equator, change direction and are sucked into the interior to become south-westerly winds, bringing heavy rain. By November, the overhead sun and the ITCZ have again moved southwards and the wind directions are again reversed. Cool winds blow from the Asian interior to the sea, losing any moisture on the Himalayas before descending to the coast.

Monthly rainfall
mm 400 200 100 50 25
→ wind direction
▬ ITCZ (intertrop converge zone)

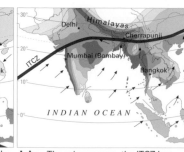
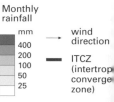

March – Start of the hot, dry season, the ITCZ is over the southern Indian Ocean.

July – The rainy season, the ITCZ has migrated northwards; winds blow onshore.

November – The ITCZ has returned s the offshore winds are cool and dry.

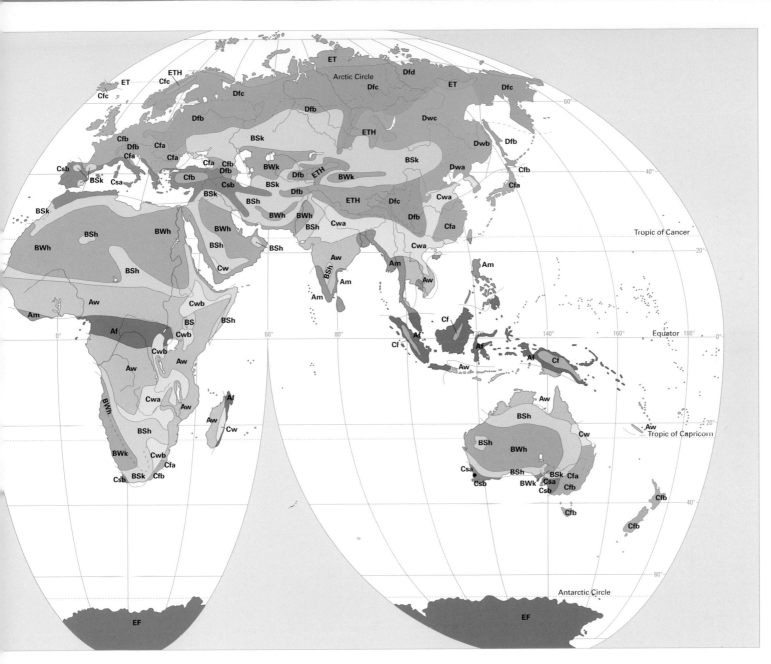

EL NIÑO

In a normal year, south-easterly trade winds drive surface waters westwards off the coast of South America, drawing cold, nutrient-rich water up from below. In an El Niño year (which occurs every 2–7 years), warm water from the west Pacific suppresses up-welling in the east, depriving the region of nutrients. The water is warmed by as much as 7°C, disturbing the tropical atmospheric circulation. During an intense El Niño, the south-east trade winds change direction and become equatorial westerlies, resulting in climatic extremes in many regions of the world, such as drought in parts of Australia and India, and heavy rainfall in south-eastern USA. An intense El Niño occurred in 1997–8, with resultant freak weather conditions across the entire Pacific region.

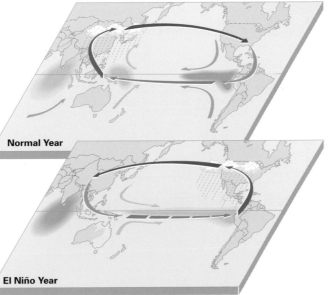

Normal Year

El Niño Year

WINDCHILL FACTOR

In sub-zero weather, even moderate winds significantly reduce effective temperatures. The chart below shows the windchill effect across a range of speeds.

	Wind speed (km/h)				
	16	32	48	64	80
0°C	–8	–14	–17	–19	–20
–5°C	–14	–21	–25	–27	–28
–10°C	–20	–28	–33	–35	–36
–15°C	–26	–36	–40	–43	44
–20°C	–32	–42	–48	–51	–52
–25°C	–38	–49	–56	–59	–60
–30°C	–44	–57	–63	–66	–68
–35°C	–51	–64	–72	–74	–76
–40°C	–57	–71	–78	–82	–84
–45°C	–63	–78	–86	–90	–92
–50°C	–69	–85	–94	–98	–100

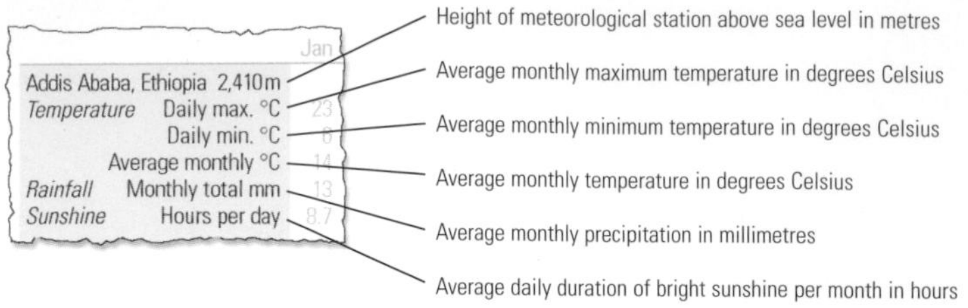
Jan
Addis Ababa, Ethiopia 2,410m
Temperature Daily max. °C 23
Daily min. °C 6
Average monthly °C 14
Rainfall Monthly total mm 13
Sunshine Hours per day 8.7
Height of meteorological station above sea level in metres
Average monthly maximum temperature in degrees Celsius
Average monthly minimum temperature in degrees Celsius
Average monthly temperature in degrees Celsius
Average monthly precipitation in millimetres
Average daily duration of bright sunshine per month in hours

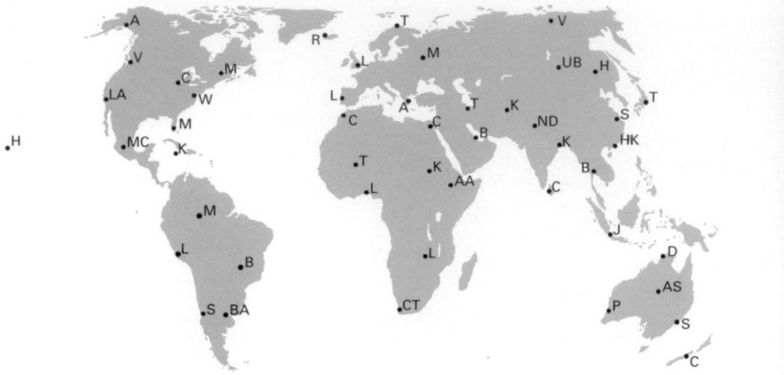
A
V
R
T
M
V
UB
H
LA
C
M
W
L
A
C
T
K
ND
S
T
H
MC
K
M
C
B
K
HK
T
K
AA
L
B
C
M
J
L
B
L
D
AS
CT
P
S
BA
S
C

		Jan	Feb	Mar	Apr	May	June	July	Aug	Sept	Oct	Nov	Dec	Year
Addis Ababa, Ethiopia 2,410m														
Temperature	Daily max. °C	23	24	25	24	25	23	20	20	21	22	23	22	23
	Daily min. °C	6	7	9	10	9	10	11	11	10	7	5	5	8
	Average monthly °C	14	15	17	17	17	16	16	15	15	15	14	14	15
Rainfall	Monthly total mm	13	35	67	91	81	117	247	255	167	29	8	5	1,115
Sunshine	Hours per day	8.7	8.2	7.6	8.1	6.5	4.8	2.8	3.2	5.2	7.6	6.7	7	6.4
Alice Springs, Australia 580m														
Temperature	Daily max. °C	35	35	32	27	23	19	19	23	27	31	33	35	28
	Daily min. °C	21	20	17	12	8	5	4	6	10	15	18	20	13
	Average monthly °C	28	27	25	20	15	12	12	14	18	23	25	27	21
Rainfall	Monthly total mm	44	33	27	10	15	13	7	8	7	18	29	38	249
Sunshine	Hours per day	10.3	10.4	9.3	9.2	8	8	8.9	9.8	10	9.7	10.1	10	9.5
Anchorage, USA 183m														
Temperature	Daily max. °C	−7	−3	0	7	13	18	19	17	13	6	−2	−6	−6
	Daily min. °C	−15	−12	−9	−2	4	8	10	9	5	−2	−9	−14	−2
	Average monthly °C	−11	−7	−4	3	9	13	15	13	9	2	−5	−10	−4
Rainfall	Monthly total mm	20	18	13	11	13	25	47	64	64	47	28	24	374
Sunshine	Hours per day	2.4	4.1	6.6	8.3	8.3	9.2	8.5	6	4.4	3.1	2.6	1.6	5.4
Athens, Greece 107m														
Temperature	Daily max. °C	13	14	16	20	25	30	33	33	29	24	19	15	23
	Daily min. °C	6	7	8	11	16	20	23	23	19	15	12	8	14
	Average monthly °C	10	10	12	16	20	25	28	28	24	20	15	11	18
Rainfall	Monthly total mm	62	37	37	23	23	14	6	7	15	51	56	71	402
Sunshine	Hours per day	3.9	5.2	5.8	7.7	8.9	10.7	11.9	11.5	9.4	6.8	4.8	3.8	7.3
Bahrain City, Bahrain 2m														
Temperature	Daily max. °C	20	21	25	29	33	36	37	38	36	32	27	22	30
	Daily min. °C	14	15	18	22	25	29	31	32	29	25	22	16	23
	Average monthly °C	17	18	21	25	29	32	34	35	32	29	25	19	26
Rainfall	Monthly total mm	18	12	10	9	2	0	0	0	0	0.4	3	16	70
Sunshine	Hours per day	5.9	6.9	7.9	8.8	10.6	13.2	12.1	12	12	10.3	7.7	6.4	9.5
Bangkok, Thailand 10m														
Temperature	Daily max. °C	32	33	34	35	34	33	32	32	32	31	31	31	33
	Daily min. °C	20	23	24	26	25	25	25	24	24	24	23	20	24
	Average monthly °C	26	28	29	30	30	29	28	28	28	28	27	26	28
Rainfall	Monthly total mm	9	30	36	82	165	153	168	183	310	239	55	8	1,438
Sunshine	Hours per day	8.2	8	8	10	7.5	6.1	4.7	5.2	5.2	6.1	7.3	7.8	7
Brasilia, Brazil 910m														
Temperature	Daily max. °C	28	28	28	28	27	27	27	29	30	29	28	27	28
	Daily min. °C	18	18	18	17	15	13	13	14	16	18	18	18	16
	Average monthly °C	23	23	23	22	21	20	20	21	23	24	23	22	22
Rainfall	Monthly total mm	252	204	227	93	17	3	6	3	30	127	255	343	1,560
Sunshine	Hours per day	5.8	5.7	6	7.4	8.7	9.3	9.6	9.8	7.9	6.5	4.8	4.4	7.2
Buenos Aires, Argentina 25m														
Temperature	Daily max. °C	30	29	26	22	18	14	14	16	18	21	25	28	22
	Daily min. °C	17	17	16	12	9	5	6	6	8	10	14	16	11
	Average monthly °C	23	23	21	17	13	10	10	11	13	15	19	22	16
Rainfall	Monthly total mm	79	71	109	89	76	61	56	61	79	86	84	99	950
Sunshine	Hours per day	9.2	8.5	7.5	6.8	4.9	3.5	3.8	5.2	6	6.8	8.1	8.5	6.6
Cairo, Egypt 75m														
Temperature	Daily max. °C	19	21	24	28	32	35	35	35	33	30	26	21	28
	Daily min. °C	9	9	12	14	18	20	22	22	20	18	14	10	16
	Average monthly °C	14	15	18	21	25	28	29	28	26	24	20	16	22
Rainfall	Monthly total mm	4	4	3	1	2	1	0	0	1	1	3	7	27
Sunshine	Hours per day	6.9	8.4	8.7	9.7	10.5	11.9	11.7	11.3	10.4	9.4	8.3	6.4	9.5
Cape Town, South Africa 44m														
Temperature	Daily max. °C	26	26	25	23	20	18	17	18	19	21	24	25	22
	Daily min. °C	15	15	14	11	9	7	7	7	8	10	13	15	11
	Average monthly °C	21	20	20	17	14	13	12	12	14	16	18	20	16
Rainfall	Monthly total mm	12	19	17	42	67	98	68	76	36	45	12	13	505
Sunshine	Hours per day	11.4	10.2	9.4	7.7	6.1	5.7	6.4	6.6	7.6	8.6	10.2	10.9	8.4
Casablanca, Morocco 59m														
Temperature	Daily max. °C	17	18	20	21	22	24	26	26	26	24	21	18	22
	Daily min. °C	8	9	11	12	15	18	19	20	18	15	12	10	14
	Average monthly °C	13	13	15	16	18	21	23	23	22	20	17	14	18
Rainfall	Monthly total mm	78	61	54	37	20	3	0	1	6	28	58	94	440
Sunshine	Hours per day	5.2	6.3	7.3	9	9.4	9.7	10.2	9.7	9.1	7.4	5.9	5.3	7.9

		Jan	Feb	Mar	Apr	May	June	July	Aug	Sept	Oct	Nov	Dec	Year
Chicago, USA 186m														
Temperature	Daily max. °C	1	2	6	14	21	26	29	28	24	17	8	2	15
	Daily min. °C	−7	−6	−2	5	11	16	20	19	14	8	0	−5	−6
	Average monthly °C	−3	−2	2	9	16	21	24	23	19	13	4	−2	4
Rainfall	Monthly total mm	47	41	70	77	96	103	86	80	69	71	56	48	844
Sunshine	Hours per day	4	5	6.6	6.9	8.9	10.2	10	9.2	8.2	6.9	4.5	3.7	7
Christchurch, New Zealand 5m														
Temperature	Daily max. °C	21	21	19	17	13	11	10	11	14	17	19	21	16
	Daily min. °C	12	12	10	7	4	2	1	3	5	7	8	11	7
	Average monthly °C	16	16	15	12	9	6	6	7	9	12	13	16	11
Rainfall	Monthly total mm	56	46	43	46	76	69	61	58	51	51	51	61	669
Sunshine	Hours per day	7	6.5	5.6	4.7	4.3	3.9	4.1	4.7	5.6	6.1	6.9	6.3	5.5
Colombo, Sri Lanka 10m														
Temperature	Daily max. °C	30	31	31	31	30	30	29	29	30	29	29	30	30
	Daily min. °C	22	22	23	24	25	25	25	25	25	24	23	22	24
	Average monthly °C	26	26	27	28	28	27	27	27	27	27	26	26	27
Rainfall	Monthly total mm	101	66	118	230	394	220	140	102	174	348	333	142	2,368
Sunshine	Hours per day	7.9	9	8.1	7.2	6.4	5.4	6.1	6.3	6.2	6.5	6.4	7.8	6.9
Darwin, Australia 30m														
Temperature	Daily max. °C	32	32	33	33	33	31	31	32	33	34	34	33	33
	Daily min. °C	25	25	25	24	23	21	19	21	23	25	26	26	24
	Average monthly °C	29	29	29	29	28	26	25	26	28	29	30	29	28
Rainfall	Monthly total mm	405	309	279	77	8	2	0	1	15	48	108	214	1,466
Sunshine	Hours per day	5.8	5.8	6.6	9.8	9.3	10	9.9	10.4	10.1	9.4	9.6	6.8	8.6
Harbin, China 175m														
Temperature	Daily max. °C	−14	−9	0	12	21	26	29	27	20	12	−1	−11	9
	Daily min. °C	−26	−23	−12	−1	7	14	18	16	8	0	−12	−22	−3
	Average monthly °C	−20	−16	−6	6	14	20	23	22	14	6	−7	−17	3
Rainfall	Monthly total mm	4	6	17	23	44	92	167	119	52	36	12	5	577
Sunshine	Hours per day	6.4	7.8	8	7.8	8.3	8.6	8.6	8.2	7.2	6.9	6.1	5.7	7.5
Hong Kong, China 35m														
Temperature	Daily max. °C	18	18	20	24	28	30	31	31	30	27	24	20	25
	Daily min. °C	13	13	16	19	23	26	26	26	25	23	19	15	20
	Average monthly °C	16	15	18	22	25	28	28	28	27	25	21	17	23
Rainfall	Monthly total mm	30	60	70	133	332	479	286	415	364	33	46	17	2,265
Sunshine	Hours per day	4.7	3.5	3.1	3.8	5	5.4	6.8	6.5	6.6	7	6.2	5.5	5.3
Honolulu, Hawaii 5m														
Temperature	Daily max. °C	26	26	26	27	28	29	29	29	30	29	28	26	28
	Daily min. °C	19	19	19	20	21	22	23	23	23	22	21	20	21
	Average monthly °C	23	22	23	23	24	26	26	26	26	26	24	23	24
Rainfall	Monthly total mm	96	84	73	33	25	8	11	23	25	47	55	76	556
Sunshine	Hours per day	7.3	7.7	8.3	8.6	8.8	9.1	9.4	9.3	9.2	8.3	7.5	6.2	8.3
Jakarta, Indonesia 10m														
Temperature	Daily max. °C	29	29	30	31	31	31	31	31	31	31	30	29	30
	Daily min. °C	23	23	23	24	24	23	23	23	23	23	23	23	23
	Average monthly °C	26	26	27	27	27	27	27	27	27	27	27	26	27
Rainfall	Monthly total mm	300	300	211	147	114	97	64	43	66	112	142	203	1,799
Sunshine	Hours per day	6.1	6.5	7.7	8.5	8.4	8.5	9.1	9.5	9.6	9	7.7	7.1	8.1
Kabul, Afghanistan 1,791m														
Temperature	Daily max. °C	2	4	12	19	26	31	33	33	30	22	17	8	20
	Daily min. °C	−8	−6	1	6	11	13	16	15	11	6	1	−3	5
	Average monthly °C	−3	−1	6	13	18	22	25	24	20	14	9	3	12
Rainfall	Monthly total mm	28	61	72	117	33	1	7	1	0	1	37	14	372
Sunshine	Hours per day	5.9	6	5.7	6.8	10.1	11.5	11.4	11.2	9.8	9.4	7.8	6.1	8.5
Khartoum, Sudan 380m														
Temperature	Daily max. °C	32	33	37	40	42	41	38	36	38	39	35	32	37
	Daily min. °C	16	17	20	23	26	27	26	25	25	25	21	17	22
	Average monthly °C	24	25	28	32	34	34	32	30	32	32	28	25	30
Rainfall	Monthly total mm	0	0	0	1	7	5	56	80	28	2	0	0	179
Sunshine	Hours per day	10.6	11.2	10.4	10.8	10.4	10.1	8.6	8.6	9.6	10.3	10.8	10.6	10.2
Kingston, Jamaica 35m														
Temperature	Daily max. °C	30	30	30	31	31	32	32	32	32	31	31	31	31
	Daily min. °C	20	20	20	21	22	24	23	23	23	23	22	21	22
	Average monthly °C	25	25	25	26	26	28	28	28	27	27	26	26	26
Rainfall	Monthly total mm	23	15	23	31	102	89	38	91	99	180	74	36	801
Sunshine	Hours per day	8.3	8.8	8.7	8.7	8.3	7.8	8.5	8.5	7.6	7.3	8.3	7.7	8.2

		Jan	Feb	Mar	Apr	May	June	July	Aug	Sept	Oct	Nov	Dec	Year
Kolkata (Calcutta), India 5m														
Temperature	Daily max. °C	27	29	34	36	35	34	32	32	32	32	29	26	31
	Daily min. °C	13	15	21	24	25	26	26	26	26	23	18	13	21
	Average monthly °C	20	22	27	30	30	30	29	29	29	28	23	20	26
Rainfall	Monthly total mm	10	30	34	44	140	297	325	332	253	114	20	5	1,604
Sunshine	Hours per day	8.6	8.7	8.9	9	8.7	5.4	4.1	4.1	5.1	6.5	8.3	8.4	7.1
Lagos, Nigeria 40m														
Temperature	Daily max. °C	32	33	33	32	31	29	28	28	29	30	31	32	31
	Daily min. °C	22	23	23	23	23	22	22	21	22	22	23	22	22
	Average monthly °C	27	28	28	28	27	26	25	24	25	26	27	27	26
Rainfall	Monthly total mm	28	41	99	99	203	300	180	56	180	190	63	25	1,464
Sunshine	Hours per day	5.9	6.8	6.3	6.1	5.6	3.8	2.8	3.3	3	5.1	6.6	6.5	5.2
Lima, Peru 120m														
Temperature	Daily max. °C	28	29	29	27	24	20	20	19	20	22	24	26	24
	Daily min. °C	19	20	19	17	16	15	14	14	14	15	16	17	16
	Average monthly °C	24	24	24	22	20	17	17	16	17	18	20	21	20
Rainfall	Monthly total mm	1	1	1	1	5	5	8	8	8	3	3	1	45
Sunshine	Hours per day	6.3	6.8	6.9	6.7	4	1.4	1.1	1	1.1	2.5	4.1	5	3.9
Lisbon, Portugal 77m														
Temperature	Daily max. °C	14	15	17	20	21	25	27	28	26	22	17	15	21
	Daily min. °C	8	8	10	12	13	15	17	17	17	14	11	9	13
	Average monthly °C	11	12	14	16	17	20	22	23	21	18	14	12	17
Rainfall	Monthly total mm	111	76	109	54	44	16	3	4	33	62	93	103	708
Sunshine	Hours per day	4.7	5.9	6	8.3	9.1	10.6	11.4	10.7	8.4	6.7	5.2	4.6	7.7
London (Kew), UK 5m														
Temperature	Daily max. °C	6	7	10	13	17	20	22	21	19	14	10	7	14
	Daily min. °C	2	2	3	6	8	12	14	13	11	8	5	4	7
	Average monthly °C	4	5	7	9	12	16	18	17	15	11	8	5	11
Rainfall	Monthly total mm	54	40	37	37	46	45	57	59	49	57	64	48	593
Sunshine	Hours per day	1.7	2.3	3.5	5.7	6.7	7	6.6	6	5	3.3	1.9	1.4	4.3
Los Angeles, USA 30m														
Temperature	Daily max. °C	18	18	18	19	20	22	24	24	24	23	22	19	21
	Daily min. °C	7	8	9	11	13	15	17	17	16	14	11	9	12
	Average monthly °C	12	13	14	15	17	18	21	21	20	18	16	14	17
Rainfall	Monthly total mm	69	74	46	28	3	3	0	0	5	10	28	61	327
Sunshine	Hours per day	6.9	8.2	8.9	8.8	9.5	10.3	11.7	11	10.1	8.6	8.2	7.6	9.2
Lusaka, Zambia 1,154m														
Temperature	Daily max. °C	26	26	26	27	25	23	23	26	29	31	29	27	27
	Daily min. °C	17	17	16	15	12	10	9	11	15	18	18	17	15
	Average monthly °C	22	22	21	21	18	17	16	19	22	25	23	22	21
Rainfall	Monthly total mm	224	173	90	19	3	1	0	1	1	17	85	196	810
Sunshine	Hours per day	5.1	5.4	6.9	8.9	9	9	9.1	9.6	9.5	9	7	5.5	7.8
Manaus, Brazil 45m														
Temperature	Daily max. °C	31	31	31	31	31	31	32	33	34	34	33	32	32
	Daily min. °C	24	24	24	24	24	24	24	24	24	25	25	24	24
	Average monthly °C	28	28	28	27	28	28	28	29	29	29	29	28	28
Rainfall	Monthly total mm	278	278	300	287	193	99	61	41	62	112	165	220	2,096
Sunshine	Hours per day	3.9	4	3.6	3.9	5.4	6.9	7.9	8.2	7.5	6.6	5.9	4.9	5.7
Mexico City, Mexico 2,309m														
Temperature	Daily max. °C	21	23	26	27	26	25	23	24	23	22	21	21	24
	Daily min. °C	5	6	7	9	10	11	11	11	11	9	6	5	8
	Average monthly °C	13	15	16	18	18	18	17	17	17	16	14	13	16
Rainfall	Monthly total mm	8	4	9	23	57	111	160	149	119	46	16	7	709
Sunshine	Hours per day	7.3	8.1	8.5	8.1	7.8	7	6.2	6.4	5.6	6.3	7	7.3	7.1
Miami, USA 2m														
Temperature	Daily max. °C	24	25	27	28	30	31	32	32	31	29	27	25	28
	Daily min. °C	14	15	16	19	21	23	24	24	24	22	18	15	20
	Average monthly °C	19	20	21	23	25	27	28	28	27	25	22	20	24
Rainfall	Monthly total mm	51	48	58	99	163	188	170	178	241	208	71	43	1,518
Sunshine	Hours per day	7.7	8.3	8.7	9.4	8.9	8.5	8.7	8.4	7.1	6.5	7.5	7.1	8.1
Montreal, Canada 57m														
Temperature	Daily max. °C	–6	–4	2	11	18	23	26	25	20	14	5	–3	11
	Daily min. °C	–13	–11	–5	2	9	14	17	16	11	6	0	–9	3
	Average monthly °C	–9	–8	–2	6	13	19	22	20	16	10	3	–6	7
Rainfall	Monthly total mm	87	76	86	83	81	91	98	87	96	84	89	89	1,047
Sunshine	Hours per day	2.8	3.4	4.5	5.2	6.7	7.7	8.2	7.7	5.6	4.3	2.4	2.2	5.1
Moscow, Russia 156m														
Temperature	Daily max. °C	–6	–4	1	9	18	22	24	22	17	10	1	–5	9
	Daily min. °C	–14	–16	–11	–1	5	9	12	9	4	–2	–6	–12	–2
	Average monthly °C	–10	–10	–5	4	12	15	18	16	10	4	–2	–8	4
Rainfall	Monthly total mm	31	28	33	35	52	67	74	74	58	51	36	36	575
Sunshine	Hours per day	1	1.9	3.7	5.2	7.8	8.3	8.4	7.1	4.4	2.4	1	0.6	4.4
New Delhi, India 220m														
Temperature	Daily max. °C	21	24	29	36	41	39	35	34	34	34	28	23	32
	Daily min. °C	6	10	14	20	26	28	27	26	24	17	11	7	18
	Average monthly °C	14	17	22	28	33	34	31	30	29	26	20	15	25
Rainfall	Monthly total mm	25	21	13	8	13	77	178	184	123	10	2	11	665
Sunshine	Hours per day	7.7	8.2	8.2	8.7	9.2	7.9	6	6.3	6.9	9.4	8.7	8.3	8

		Jan	Feb	Mar	Apr	May	June	July	Aug	Sept	Oct	Nov	Dec	Year
Perth, Australia 60m														
Temperature	Daily max. °C	29	30	27	25	21	18	17	18	19	21	25	27	23
	Daily min. °C	17	18	16	14	12	10	9	9	10	11	14	16	13
	Average monthly °C	23	24	22	19	16	14	13	13	15	16	19	22	18
Rainfall	Monthly total mm	8	13	22	44	128	189	177	145	84	58	19	13	900
Sunshine	Hours per day	10.4	9.8	8.8	7.5	5.7	4.8	5.4	6	7.2	8.1	9.6	10.4	7.8
Reykjavik, Iceland 18m														
Temperature	Daily max. °C	2	3	5	6	10	13	15	14	12	8	5	4	8
	Daily min. °C	–3	–3	–1	1	4	7	9	8	6	3	0	–2	3
	Average monthly °C	0	0	2	4	7	10	12	11	9	5	3	1	5
Rainfall	Monthly total mm	89	64	62	56	42	42	50	56	67	94	78	79	779
Sunshine	Hours per day	0.8	2	3.6	4.5	5.9	6.1	5.8	5.4	3.5	2.3	1.1	0.3	3.7
Santiago, Chile 520m														
Temperature	Daily max. °C	30	29	27	24	19	15	15	17	19	22	26	29	23
	Daily min. °C	12	11	10	7	5	3	3	4	6	7	9	11	7
	Average monthly °C	21	20	18	15	12	9	9	10	12	15	17	20	15
Rainfall	Monthly total mm	3	3	5	13	64	84	76	56	31	15	8	5	363
Sunshine	Hours per day	10.8	8.9	8.5	5.5	3.6	3.3	3.3	3.6	4.8	6.1	8.7	10.1	6.4
Shanghai, China 5m														
Temperature	Daily max. °C	8	8	13	19	24	28	32	32	27	23	17	10	20
	Daily min. °C	–1	0	4	9	14	19	23	23	19	13	7	2	11
	Average monthly °C	3	4	8	14	19	23	27	27	23	18	12	6	15
Rainfall	Monthly total mm	48	59	84	94	94	180	147	142	130	71	51	36	1,136
Sunshine	Hours per day	4	3.7	4.4	4.8	5.4	4.7	6.9	7.5	5.3	5.6	4.7	4.5	5.1
Sydney, Australia 40m														
Temperature	Daily max. °C	26	26	25	22	19	17	17	18	20	22	24	25	22
	Daily min. °C	18	19	17	14	11	9	8	9	11	13	16	17	14
	Average monthly °C	22	22	21	18	15	13	12	13	16	18	20	21	18
Rainfall	Monthly total mm	89	101	127	135	127	117	117	76	74	71	74	74	1,182
Sunshine	Hours per day	7.5	7	6.4	6.1	5.7	5.3	6.1	7	7.3	7.5	7.5	7.5	6.8
Tehran, Iran 1,191m														
Temperature	Daily max. °C	9	11	16	21	29	30	37	36	29	24	16	11	22
	Daily min. °C	–1	1	4	10	16	20	23	23	18	12	6	1	11
	Average monthly °C	4	6	10	15	22	25	30	29	23	18	11	6	17
Rainfall	Monthly total mm	37	23	36	31	14	2	1	1	1	5	29	27	207
Sunshine	Hours per day	5.9	6.7	7.5	7.4	8.6	11.6	11.2	11	10.1	7.6	6.9	6.3	8.4
Timbuktu, Mali 269m														
Temperature	Daily max. °C	31	35	38	41	43	42	38	35	38	40	37	31	37
	Daily min. °C	13	16	18	22	26	27	25	24	24	23	18	14	21
	Average monthly °C	22	25	28	31	34	34	32	30	31	31	28	23	29
Rainfall	Monthly total mm	0	0	0	1	4	20	54	93	31	3	0	0	206
Sunshine	Hours per day	9.1	9.6	9.6	9.7	9.8	9.4	9.6	9	9.3	9.5	9.5	8.9	9.4
Tokyo, Japan 5m														
Temperature	Daily max. °C	9	9	12	18	22	25	29	30	27	20	16	11	19
	Daily min. °C	–1	–1	3	4	13	17	22	23	19	13	7	1	10
	Average monthly °C	4	4	8	11	18	21	25	26	23	17	11	6	14
Rainfall	Monthly total mm	48	73	101	135	131	182	146	147	217	220	101	61	1,562
Sunshine	Hours per day	6	5.9	5.7	6	6.2	5	5.8	6.6	4.5	4.4	4.8	5.4	5.5
Tromsø, Norway 100m														
Temperature	Daily max. °C	–2	–2	0	3	7	12	16	14	10	5	2	0	5
	Daily min. °C	–6	–6	–5	–2	1	6	9	8	5	1	–2	–4	0
	Average monthly °C	–4	–4	–3	0	4	9	13	11	7	3	0	–2	3
Rainfall	Monthly total mm	96	79	91	65	61	59	56	80	109	115	88	95	994
Sunshine	Hours per day	0.1	1.6	2.9	6.1	5.7	6.9	7.9	4.8	3.5	1.7	0.3	0	3.5
Ulan Bator, Mongolia 1,305m														
Temperature	Daily max. °C	–19	–13	–4	7	13	21	22	21	14	6	–6	–16	4
	Daily min. °C	–32	–29	–22	–8	–2	7	11	8	2	–8	–20	–28	–11
	Average monthly °C	–26	–21	–13	–1	6	14	16	14	8	–1	–13	–22	–4
Rainfall	Monthly total mm	1	1	2	5	10	28	76	51	23	5	5	2	209
Sunshine	Hours per day	6.4	7.8	8	7.8	8.3	8.6	8.6	8.2	7.2	6.9	6.1	5.7	7.5
Vancouver, Canada 5m														
Temperature	Daily max. °C	6	7	10	14	17	20	23	22	19	14	9	7	14
	Daily min. °C	0	1	3	5	8	11	13	12	10	7	3	2	6
	Average monthly °C	3	4	6	9	13	16	18	17	14	10	6	4	10
Rainfall	Monthly total mm	214	161	151	90	69	65	39	44	83	172	198	243	1,529
Sunshine	Hours per day	1.6	3	3.8	5.9	7.5	7.4	9.5	8.2	6	3.7	2	1.4	5
Verkhoyansk, Russia 137m														
Temperature	Daily max. °C	–47	–40	–20	–1	11	21	24	21	12	–8	–33	–42	–8
	Daily min. °C	–51	–48	–40	–25	–7	4	6	1	–6	–20	–39	–50	–23
	Average monthly °C	–49	–44	–30	–13	2	12	15	11	3	–14	–36	–46	–16
Rainfall	Monthly total mm	7	5	5	4	5	25	33	30	13	11	10	7	155
Sunshine	Hours per day	0	2.6	6.9	9.6	9.7	10	9.7	7.5	4.1	2.4	0.6	0	5.4
Washington, USA 22m														
Temperature	Daily max. °C	7	8	12	19	25	29	31	30	26	20	14	8	19
	Daily min. °C	–1	–1	2	8	13	18	21	20	16	10	4	–1	9
	Average monthly °C	3	3	7	13	19	24	26	25	21	15	9	4	14
Rainfall	Monthly total mm	84	68	96	85	103	88	108	120	100	78	75	75	1,080
Sunshine	Hours per day	4.4	5.7	6.7	7.4	8.2	8.8	8.6	8.2	7.5	6.5	5.3	4.5	6.8

Tropical Rain Forest

Tall broadleaved evergreen forest, trees 30–50m high with climbers and epiphytes forming continuous canopies. Associated with wet climate 2–3000mm precipitation per year and high temperatures 24–28°C. High diversity of species, typically 100 per ha including lianas, bamboo, palms, rubber, mahogany. Mangrove swamps form in coastal areas.

Subtropical and Temperate Rain Forest

Precipitation which is less than in the Tropical Rain Forest falls in the long wet season interspersed with a season of reduced rainfall and lower temperatures. As a result there are fewer species, a thinner canopy, fewer lianas and denser ground level foliage. Vegetation consists of evergreen oak, laurel, bamboo, magnolia and tree ferns.

Monsoon Woodland and Open Jungle

Mostly deciduous trees because of the long dry season and lower temperatu Trees can reach 30m but are sparser than in the rain forests; there is competition for light and thick jungle vegetation grows at lower levels. H species diversity including lianas, bamboo, teak, sandalwood, sal and ban

Diagram shows the highly stratified nature of the tropical rain forest. Crowns of trees form numerous layers at different heights and the dense shade limits undergrowth.

Temperate Deciduous and Coniferous Forest

A transition zone between broadleaves and conifers. Broadleaves are better suited to the warmer, damper and flatter locations.

Northern Coniferous Forest (Taiga)

Forming a large continuous belt across Northern America and Eurasia with a uniformity in tree species. Characteristically trees are tall, conical with short branches and wax-covered needle-shaped leaves to retain moisture. Cold climate with prolonged harsh winters and cool summers where average temperatures for more than six months of the year are under 0°C. Undergrowth is sparse with mosses and lichens. Tree species include pine, fir, spruce, larch, tamarisk.

Mountainous Forest, mainly Coniferous

Mild winters, high humidity and high levels of rainfall throughout the year provide habitat for dense needle-leaf evergreen forests and the largest trees in the world, up to 100m, including the Douglas fir, redwood and giant sequoia.

High Plateau Steppe and Tundra

Similar to arctic tundra with frozen ground for the majority of the year. Very sparse ground coverage of low, shallow-rooted herbs, small shrubs, mosses, lichens and heather interspersed with bare soil.

Arctic Tundra

Average temperatures are 0°C, precipitation is mainly snowfall and the ground remains frozen for 10 months of the year. Vegetation flourishes when the shallow surface layer melts in the long summer days. Underlying permafrost remains frozen and surface water cannot drain away, making conditions marshy. Consisting of sedges, snow lichen, arctic meadow grass, cotton grasses and dwarf willow.

Polar and Mountainous Ice Desert

Areas of bare rock and ice with patches of rock-strewn lithosols, low in organic matter and low water content. In sheltered patches only a few mosses, lichens and low shrubs can grow, including woolly moss and purple saxifrage.

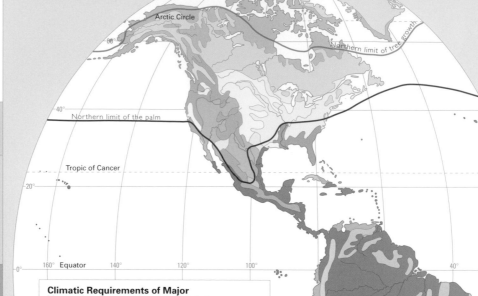

Climatic Requirements of Major Vegetation Types *(After Austin Miller)*

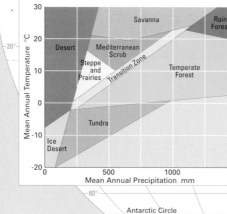

SOIL REGIONS

1:220 000 000

- Tundra soil
- Podzols
- Brown forest soil
- Lightly leached dry forest soil
- Red and yellow subtropical forest soil
- Reddish savanna soil and tropical red earths
- Laterites
- Chernozem
- Degraded chernozem
- Black savanna soil
- Chestnut steppe soil
- Desertic (arid) soil
- Alluvium
- Mountain and high plateau soils
- Oases soil
- Tropical and mangrove swamp

(after Glinka, Stremme, Marbut, and others)

Projection: Interrupted Mollweide's Homolographic

otropical and Temperate Woodland, Scrub and Bush
t clearings with woody shrubs and tall grasses. Trees are fire-resistant and
r deciduous or xerophytic because of long dry periods. Species include
alyptus, acacia, mimosa and euphorbia.

Tropical Savanna with Low Trees and Bush
Tall, coarse grass with enough precipitation to support a scattering of short
deciduous trees and thorn scrub. Vegetation consisting of elephant grass,
acacia, palms and baobob is limited by aridity, grazing animals and periodic
fires; trees have developed thick, woody bark, small leaves or thorns.

Tropical Savanna and Grassland
Areas with a hot climate and long dry season. Extensive areas of tall grasses
often reaching 3.5m with scattered fire and drought resistant bushes, low trees
and thickets of elephant grass. Shrubs include acacia, baobab and palms.

NATURAL VEGETATION
(after Austin Miller)

1:116 000 000

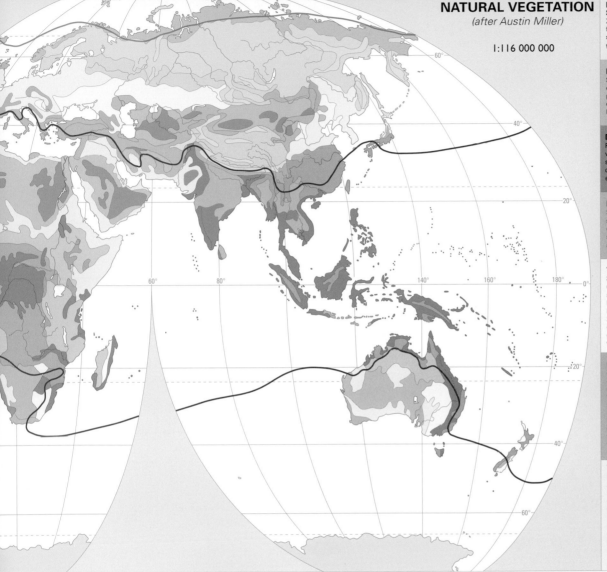

Dry Semi-desert with Shrub and Grass
Xerophytic shrubs with thin grass cover and
few trees, limited by a long dry season and
short, hot, rainy period. Sagebrush, bunch
grass and acacia shrubs are common.

Desert Shrub
Scattered xerophytic plants able to withstand
daytime extremes in temperature and long
periods of drought. There is a large diversity
of desert flora such as cacti, yucca, tamarisk,
hard grass and artemisia.

Desert
Precipitation less than 250mm per year;
vegetation is very sparse, mainly bare rock,
sand dunes and salt flats. Vegetation
comprises a few xerophytic shrubs and
ephemeral flowers.

Dry Steppe and Shrub
Semi-arid with cold, dry winters and hot
summers. Bare soil with sparsely
distributed short grasses and scattered
shrubs and short trees. Species include acacia,
artemisia, saksaul and tamarisk.

Temperate Grasslands, Prairie and Steppe
Continuous, tall, dense and deep-rooted
swards of ancient grasslands, considered to
be natural climax vegetation as determined
by soil and climate. Average precipitation
250–750mm with a long dry season, limiting
growth of trees and shrubs. Includes Stipa
grass, buffalo grass, blue stems and loco
weed.

Mediterranean Hardwood Forest and Scrub
Areas with hot and arid summers. Sparse
evergreen trees are short and twisted
with thick bark, interspersed with areas of
scrub land. Trees have waxy leaves or thorns
and deep root systems to resist drought.
Many of the hardwood forests have been
cleared by man, resulting in extensive scrub
formation – maquis and chaparral. Species
found are evergreen oak, stone pine, cork,
olive and myrtle.

Temperate Deciduous Forest and Meadow
Areas of relatively high, well-distributed
rainfall and temperatures favourable for forest
growth. The tall broadleaved trees form a
canopy in the summer, but shed their leaves
in the winter. The undergrowth is sparse and
poorly developed, but in the spring, herbs
and flowers develop quickly. Diverse species
with up to 20 per ha, including oak, beech,
birch, maple, ash, elm, chestnut and
hornbeam. Many of these forests have been
cleared for urbanization and farming.

OIL DEGRADATION

1:220 000 000

Areas of Concern

Areas of serious concern
Areas of some concern
Stable terrain
Non-vegetated land

Causes of soil Degradation by region)

Grazing practices
Other agricultural practices
Industrialization
Deforestation
Fuelwood collection

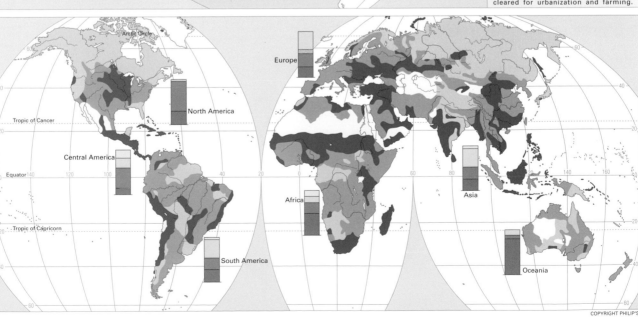

(after Wageningen 1990)

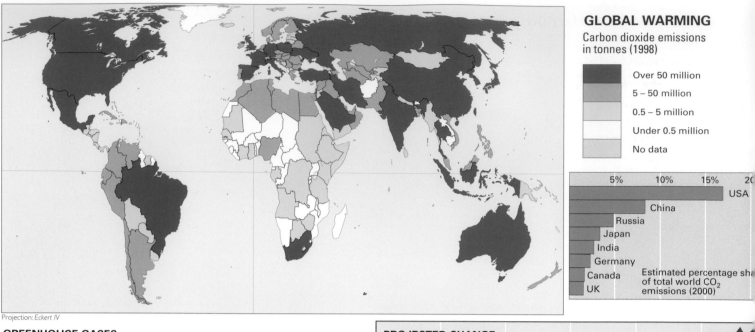

GLOBAL WARMING

Carbon dioxide emissions in tonnes (1998)

- Over 50 million
- 5 – 50 million
- 0.5 – 5 million
- Under 0.5 million
- No data

5%   10%   15%   2(

USA
China
Russia
Japan
India
Germany
Canada
UK

Estimated percentage sha of total world CO_2 emissions (2000)

Projection: *Eckert IV*

GREENHOUSE GASES

There has been a steady increase in the pollution of heat-absorbing greenhouse gases in the atmosphere. With the dangers of ozone depletion caused by CFCs in particular (see below), many countries have banned them and the pie charts show a dramatic drop in emissions.

The global warming potential of each gas is measured in equivalent units of CO_2 warming potential, or teragrams of CO_2 (TgCO$_2$Eq).

1990
Total emissions
23,520 (TgCO$_2$Eq)

Carbon Dioxide 70%
Methane & NO$_2$ 9%
CFCs & HCFCs 21%

1999
Total emissions
25,460 (TgCO$_2$Eq)

Carbon Dioxide 82%
Methane & NO$_2$ 9%
CFCs & HCFCs 9%

PROJECTED CHANGE IN GLOBAL WARMING

C°
+3.0
+2.0
+1.0
0
-0.5

1950   1970   1990   2010   2030   2050

Rise in average temperatures assuming present trends in CO_2 emissions continue

Assuming some cuts are made in emissions

Assuming drastic cuts are made in emissions

THE GREENHOUSE EFFECT

Carbon dioxide is increased by burning fossil fuels and cutting forests

Carbon Dioxide

Rising temperatures would melt snow and ice.

Melting glacial ice could cause oceans to rise.

The carbon dioxide traps the heat being reflected from the Earth, although some heat is lost.

The warming increases water vapour in the air, leading to even greater absorption of heat.

Northern Hemisphere

Southern Hemisphere

THINNING OZONE LAYER

Total atmospheric ozone concentration in the southern and northern hemispheres (Dobson Units, 2000)

In 1985, scientists working in Antarctica discovered a thinning of the ozone layer, comm known as an 'ozone hole'. This caused immediate alarm because the ozone layer abs most of the Sun's dangerous ultraviolet radiation, which is believed to cause an increa skin cancer, cataracts and damage to the immune system. Since 1985, ozone depletion increased and, by 1996, the ozone hole over the South Pole was estimated to be as larg North America. The false colour images, left, show the total atmospheric ozone concentra in the southern hemisphere (in September 2000) and the northern hemisphere (in March 2 with the ozone hole clearly identifiable at the centre. The data is from the Tiros Ozone Ve Sounder, an instrument on the American TIROS weather satellite. The colours represen ozone concentration in Dobson Units (DU). Scientists agree that ozone depletion is cause CFCs, a group of manufactured chemicals used in air conditioning systems and refrigera In a 1987 treaty most industrial nations agreed to phase out CFCs and a complete ban on CFCs was agreed after the end of 1995. However, scientists believe that the chemicals remain in the atmosphere for 50 to 100 years. As a result, ozone depletion will continu many years.

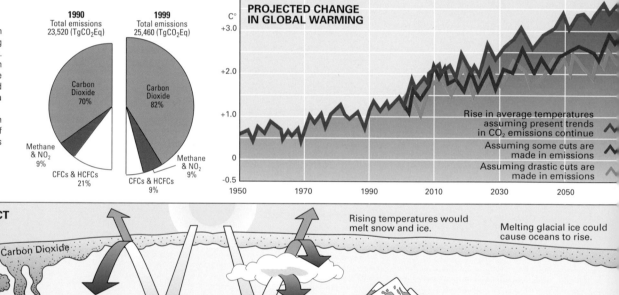

WATER POLLUTION

Severely polluted sea areas and lakes	
Less polluted sea areas and lakes	
Areas of frequent oil pollution by shipping	
Major oil tanker spills	⑨ ◯
Major oil rig blow-outs	▲
Offshore dumpsites for industrial and municipal waste	▼
Severely polluted rivers and estuaries	___

Tanker Name	Tonnes Spilt	Year
① Atlantic Empress	287,000	1979
② ABT Summer	260,000	1991
③ Castillo de Bellver	252,000	1983
④ Amoco Cadiz	223,000	1978
⑤ Haven	144,000	1991
⑥ Odyssey	132,000	1988
⑦ Torrey Canyon	119,000	1967
⑧ Urquiola	100,000	1976
⑨ Hawaiian Patriot	95,000	1977
⑩ Independenta	95,000	1979

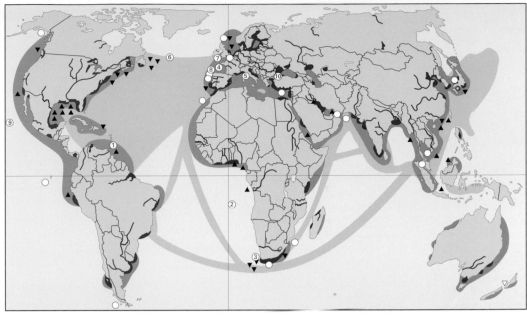

ACID RAIN

Acid rain is caused by high levels of sulphur and nitrogen in the atmosphere. They combine with water vapour and oxygen to form acids (H_2SO_4 and HNO_3) which fall as precipitation.

⠿	Main areas of sulphur and nitrogen emissions (from the burning of fossil fuels)
●	Major cities with levels of air pollution exceeding World Health Organization guidelines

Areas of acid deposition

(pH numbers measure acidity: normal rain is pH 5.6)

	pH less than 4.0 (most acidic)
	pH 4.0 – 4.5
	pH 4.5 – 5.0
⌐ ⌐	Potential problem areas

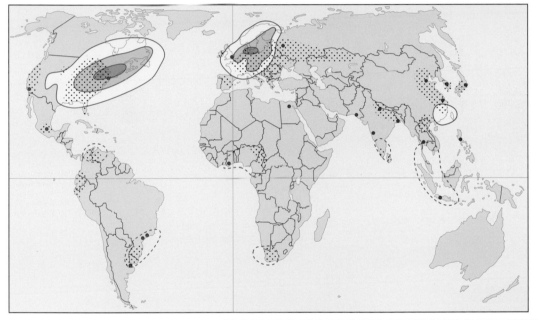

DESERTIFICATION AND DEFORESTATION

Existing deserts	
Areas with a high risk of desertification	
Areas with a moderate risk of desertification	
Former areas of rainforest	
Existing rainforest	
Major famines since 1900 (with dates)	■

Deforestation 1990–2000

	Annual Deforestation (thous. hectares)	Annual Deforestation Rate (%)
Brazil	2,309	0.4
Indonesia	1,312	1.2
Mexico	631	1.1
Congo (Dem. Rep.)	532	0.4
Burma (Myanmar)	517	1.4
Nigeria	398	2.6
Peru	269	1.4

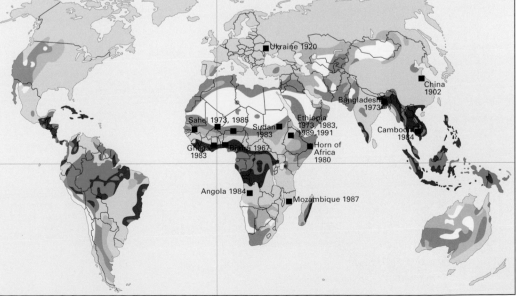
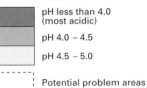

Projection: Modified Hammer Equal Area

COPYRIGHT PHILIP'S

AGRICULTURAL PRODUCTION

Staple Crops

Wheat

China 16.0% | India 11.7% | USA 9.1% | Russia 8.0% | France 5.4%

World total (2001): 582,692,000 tonnes

Rice

China 30.6% | India 22.2% | Indonesia 8.5% | Bangladesh 6.6% | Vietnam 5.4%

World total (2001): 592,831,000 tonnes

Millet

India 32.5% | Nigeria 20.9% | China 8.4% | Niger 8.3% | Russia 4.5%

World total (2001): 29,207,000 tonnes

Rye

Russia 26.4% | Germany 22.7% | Poland 21.7% | Belarus 6.6% | Ukraine 6.6%

World total (2001): 22,718,000 tonnes

Maize

USA 39.6% | China 19.0% | Brazil 6.8% | Mexico 3.1%

World total (2001): 609,182,000 tonnes

Potatoes

China 20.8% | Russia 11.2% | India 8.1% | Poland 6.6% | USA 6.5%

World total (2001): 308,195,000 tonnes

Soybeans

USA 44.5% | Brazil 21.3% | Argentina 15.1% | China 8.7%

World total (2001): 176,639,000 tonnes

Cassava

Nigeria 18.9% | Brazil 13.5% | Thailand 10.2% | Indonesia 9.0% | Dem. Rep. Congo 8.6%

World total (2001): 178,868,000 tonnes

Animal Products

Milk

India 14.4% | USA 12.6% | Russia 5.5% | Germany 4.8% | Pakistan 4.5%

World total (2001): 584,651,000 tonnes

Butter and Ghee

India 30.0% | USA 7.7% | Pakistan 6.2% | France 5.9% | Germany 5.6% | New Zealand 4.7%

World total (2001): 7,503,000 tonnes

Lamb and Mutton

China 19.1% | Australia 8.8% | N. Zealand 7.5% | Turkey 4.2% | Iran 3.7%

World total (2001): 7,532,000 tonnes

Beef and Veal

USA 21.1% | Brazil 11.8% | China 9.1% | Argentina 4.7%

World total (2001): 56,647,000 tonnes

Pigmeat

China 46.9% | USA 9.5% | Germany 4.5%

World total (2001): 91,188,000 tonnes

Sugars

Sugar Cane

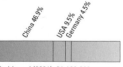

Brazil 27.0% | India 22.8% | China 6.4% | Mexico 3.9%

World total (2001): 1,254,857,000 tonnes

Sugar Beet

France 11.4% | Germany 10.4% | USA 10.0% | Ukraine 6.6% | Russia 6.2% | Turkey 5.2% | Poland 5.5%

World total (2001): 234,245,000 tonnes

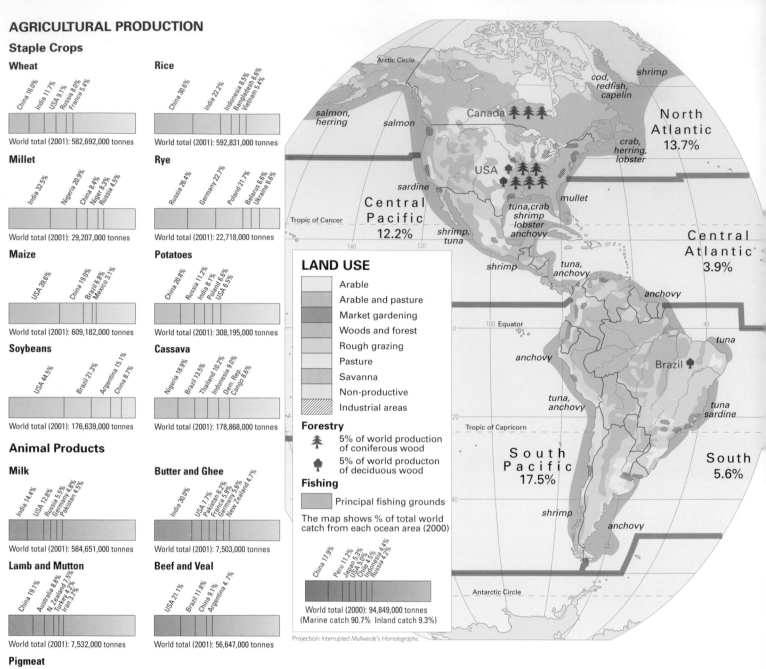

Arctic Circle

shrimp

cod, redfish, capelin

salmon, herring

salmon

Canada

salmon

North Atlantic 13.7%

crab, herring, lobster

USA

sardine

Central Pacific 12.2%

Tropic of Cancer

mullet

tuna, crab shrimp lobster anchovy

shrimp, tuna

Central Atlantic 3.9%

shrimp

tuna, anchovy

anchovy

Equator

anchovy

tuna

Brazil

tuna, anchovy

tuna sardine

Tropic of Capricorn

South Pacific 17.5%

South 5.6%

shrimp

anchovy

Antarctic Circle

LAND USE

- Arable
- Arable and pasture
- Market gardening
- Woods and forest
- Rough grazing
- Pasture
- Savanna
- Non-productive
- Industrial areas

Forestry

🌲 5% of world production of coniferous wood

🌳 5% of world producton of deciduous wood

Fishing

Principal fishing grounds

The map shows % of total world catch from each ocean area (2000)

China 17.9% | Peru 11.2% | Japan 5.3% | USA 5.0% | Chile 4.5% | Indonesia 4.4% | Russia 4.2%

World total (2000): 94,849,000 tonnes
(Marine catch 90.7% Inland catch 9.3%)

Projection: *Interrupted Mollweide's Homolographic*

ARABLE AGRICULTURE

Arable and permanent crops as a % of land area

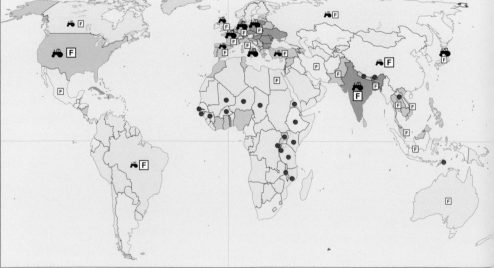

- 40% and over
- 20% – 40%
- 10% – 20%
- Under 10%
- No data

● Over 75% of the total workforce employed in agriculture (2000)

🚜 Over 1 million tractors

🚜 Over 500,000 tractors

F Over 5 million tonnes fertilizer consumed

F Over 1 million tonnes fertilizer consumed

Projection: *Eckert IV*

COPYRIGHT

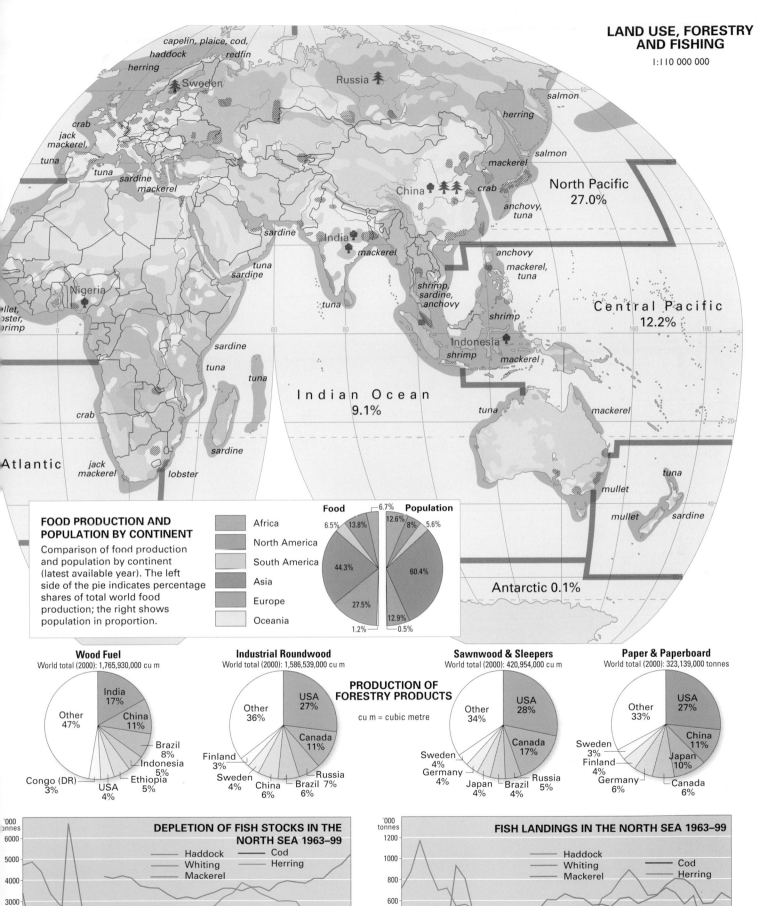

LAND USE, FORESTRY AND FISHING

1:110 000 000

FOOD PRODUCTION AND POPULATION BY CONTINENT

Comparison of food production and population by continent (latest available year). The left side of the pie indicates percentage shares of total world food production; the right shows population in proportion.

- Africa
- North America
- South America
- Asia
- Europe
- Oceania

Food

6.7%
6.5%
13.8%
44.3%
27.5%
1.2%

Population

12.6%
8%
5.6%
60.4%
12.9%
0.5%

PRODUCTION OF FORESTRY PRODUCTS

cu m = cubic metre

Wood Fuel
World total (2000): 1,765,930,000 cu m

- India 17%
- China 11%
- Other 47%
- Brazil 8%
- Indonesia 5%
- Ethiopia 5%
- USA 4%
- Congo (DR) 3%

Industrial Roundwood
World total (2000): 1,586,539,000 cu m

- USA 27%
- Other 36%
- Canada 11%
- Russia 7%
- Brazil 6%
- China 6%
- Sweden 4%
- Finland 3%

Sawnwood & Sleepers
World total (2000): 420,954,000 cu m

- USA 28%
- Other 34%
- Canada 17%
- Russia 5%
- Brazil 4%
- Japan 4%
- Germany 4%
- Sweden 4%

Paper & Paperboard
World total (2000): 323,139,000 tonnes

- USA 27%
- Other 33%
- China 11%
- Japan 10%
- Canada 6%
- Germany 6%
- Finland 4%
- Sweden 3%

DEPLETION OF FISH STOCKS IN THE NORTH SEA 1963–99

'000 tonnes

- Haddock
- Whiting
- Mackerel
- Cod
- Herring

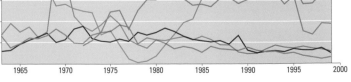

FISH LANDINGS IN THE NORTH SEA 1963–99

'000 tonnes

- Haddock
- Whiting
- Mackerel
- Cod
- Herring

ENERGY PRODUCTION BY REGION
Each square represents 1% of world energy production (2000)

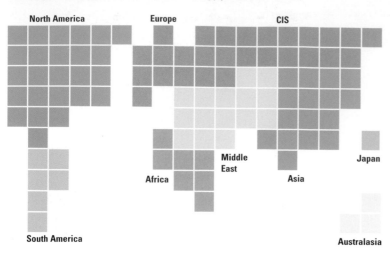

ENERGY CONSUMPTION BY REGION
Each square represents 1% of world energy consumption (2000)

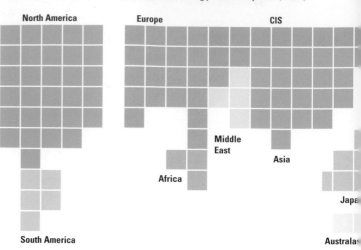

ENERGY BALANCE
Difference between energy production and consumption in millions of tonnes of oil equivalent (MtOe) 2000

↑ Energy surplus in MtOe

Over 35 surplus

1 – 35 surplus

1 deficit – 1 surplus (approx. balance)

1 – 35 deficit

Over 35 deficit

↓ Energy deficit in MtOe

Fossil fuel production

	Principal	Secondary
Oilfields	●	●
Gasfields	▽	▽
Coalfields	▲	▲

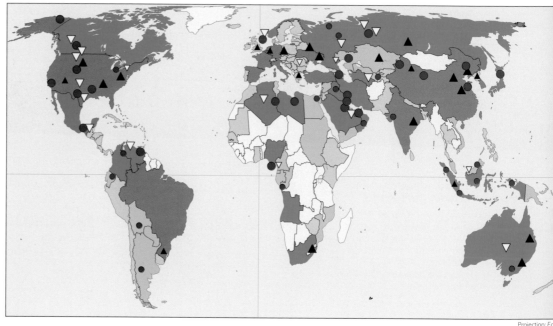

Projection: Ec

OIL RESERVES
World oil reserves by region and country, thousand million tonnes (2001)

Al: Algeria	**Po:** Poland
Br: Brazil	**Qa:** Qatar
Ca: Canada	**Ru:** Russia
Cn: China	**SA:** Saudi Arabia
Iq: Iraq	**S Af:** South Africa
Ka: Kazakhstan	**Tm:** Turkmenistan
Li: Libya	**Uk:** Ukraine
Ma: Malaysia	**UAE:** United Arab Em.
Mx: Mexico	**Ve:** Venezuela
Ni: Nigeria	**Yu:** Yugoslavia

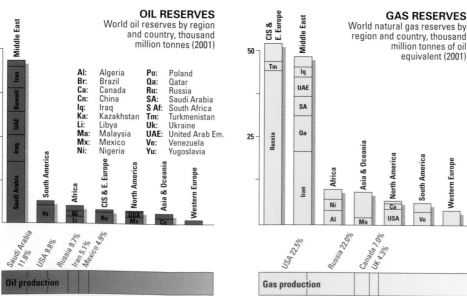

Saudi Arabia 11.8%   USA 9.8%   Russia 9.7%   Iran 5.1%   Mexico 4.9%

Oil production

World total (2001): 3,584,900,000 tonnes

GAS RESERVES
World natural gas reserves by region and country, thousand million tonnes of oil equivalent (2001)

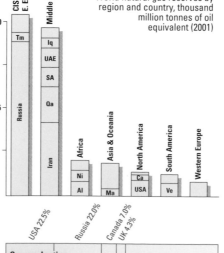

USA 22.5%   Russia 22.0%   Canada 7.0%   UK 4.3%

Gas production

World total (2001): 2,217,700,000 tonnes of oil equivalent

COAL RESERVES
World coal reserves by region and country, thousand million tonnes (2001, including lignite)

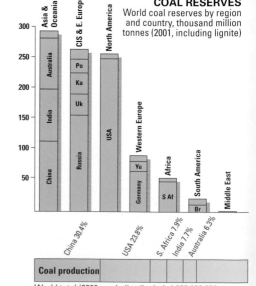

China 30.4%   USA 23.8%   S. Africa 7.9%   India 7.7%   Australia 6.3%

Coal production

World total (2000, excluding lignite): 4,589,200,000 tonnes

ELECTRICITY GENERATION

Percentage of electricity generated by source (1999)

- Over 75% from thermal
- 50 – 75% from thermal
- Over 75% from hydro
- 50 – 75% from hydro
- Over 50% from nuclear
- No dominant source
- No data
- ● elected geothermal plants
- ▲ elected hydroelectric plants

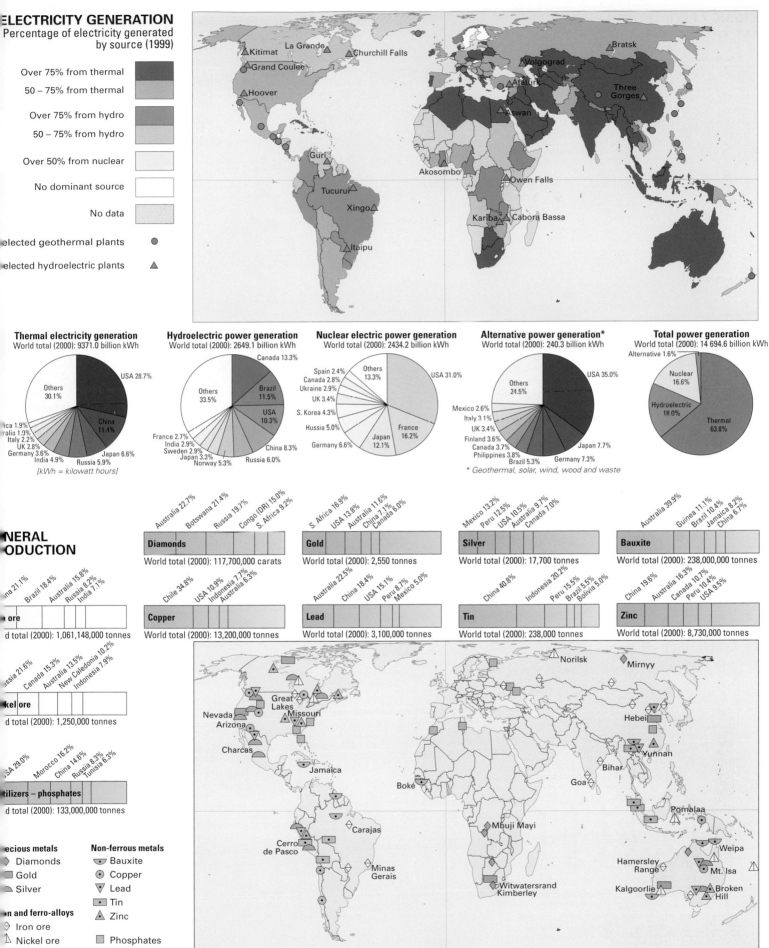

Kitimat, La Grande, Grand Coulee, Churchill Falls, Hoover, Volgograd, Bratsk, Ataturk, Three Gorges, Aswan, Guri, Akosombo, Owen Falls, Tucurui, Xingo, Kariba, Cabora Bassa, Itaipu

Thermal electricity generation
World total (2000): 9371.0 billion kWh

- USA 28.7%
- Others 30.1%
- China 11.4%
- Japan 6.6%
- Russia 5.9%
- India 4.9%
- Germany 3.6%
- UK 2.8%
- Italy 2.2%
- ...alia 1.9%
- ...ica 1.9%

[kWh = kilowatt hours]

Hydroelectric power generation
World total (2000): 2649.1 billion kWh

- Canada 13.3%
- Brazil 11.5%
- USA 10.3%
- China 8.3%
- Russia 6.0%
- Norway 5.3%
- Japan 3.3%
- Sweden 2.9%
- India 2.9%
- France 2.7%
- Others 33.5%

Nuclear electric power generation
World total (2000): 2434.2 billion kWh

- USA 31.0%
- France 16.2%
- Japan 12.1%
- Germany 6.6%
- Russia 5.0%
- S. Korea 4.3%
- UK 3.4%
- Ukraine 2.9%
- Canada 2.8%
- Spain 2.4%
- Others 13.3%

Alternative power generation*
World total (2000): 240.3 billion kWh

- USA 35.0%
- Japan 7.7%
- Germany 7.3%
- Brazil 5.3%
- Philippines 3.8%
- Canada 3.7%
- Finland 3.6%
- UK 3.4%
- Italy 3.1%
- Mexico 2.6%
- Others 24.5%

* Geothermal, solar, wind, wood and waste

Total power generation
World total (2000): 14 694.6 billion kWh

- Alternative 1.6%
- Nuclear 16.6%
- Hydroelectric 18.0%
- Thermal 63.8%

NERAL ODUCTION (MINERAL PRODUCTION)

Diamonds					
Australia 22.7%	Botswana 21.4%	Russia 19.7%	Congo (DR) 15.0%	S. Africa 9.2%	

World total (2000): 117,700,000 carats

Gold					
S. Africa 16.9%	USA 13.8%	Australia 11.6%	China 7.1%	Canada 6.0%	

World total (2000): 2,550 tonnes

Silver					
Mexico 13.2%	Peru 12.5%	USA 10.5%	Australia 9.7%	Canada 7.0%	

World total (2000): 17,700 tonnes

Bauxite					
Australia 39.9%	Guinea 11.1%	Brazil 10.4%	Jamaica 8.2%	China 6.7%	

World total (2000): 238,000,000 tonnes

Copper				
Chile 34.8%	USA 10.9%	Indonesia 7.7%	Australia 6.3%	

World total (2000): 13,200,000 tonnes

Lead				
Australia 22.5%	China 18.4%	USA 15.1%	Peru 8.7%	Mexico 5.0%

World total (2000): 3,100,000 tonnes

Tin				
China 40.8%	Indonesia 20.2%	Peru 15.5%	Brazil 5.5%	Bolivia 5.0%

World total (2000): 238,000 tonnes

Zinc				
China 19.6%	Australia 16.3%	Canada 10.7%	Peru 10.4%	USA 9.5%

World total (2000): 8,730,000 tonnes

...ore (Iron ore)				
...na 21.1%	Brazil 18.4%	Australia 15.8%	Russia 8.2%	India 7.1%

...d total (2000): 1,061,148,000 tonnes

...kel ore (Nickel ore)				
...ssia 21.6%	Canada 15.3%	Australia 13.5%	New Caledonia 10.2%	Indonesia 7.9%

...d total (2000): 1,250,000 tonnes

...tilizers – phosphates				
...SA 29.0%	Morocco 16.2%	China 14.6%	Russia 8.3%	Tunisia 6.3%

...d total (2000): 133,000,000 tonnes

...ecious metals (Precious metals)
- ◆ Diamonds
- ▢ Gold
- ▭ Silver

...n and ferro-alloys (Iron and ferro-alloys)
- ◇ Iron ore
- △ Nickel ore

Non-ferrous metals
- ◓ Bauxite
- ◉ Copper
- ▽ Lead
- ▣ Tin
- △ Zinc
- ▢ Phosphates

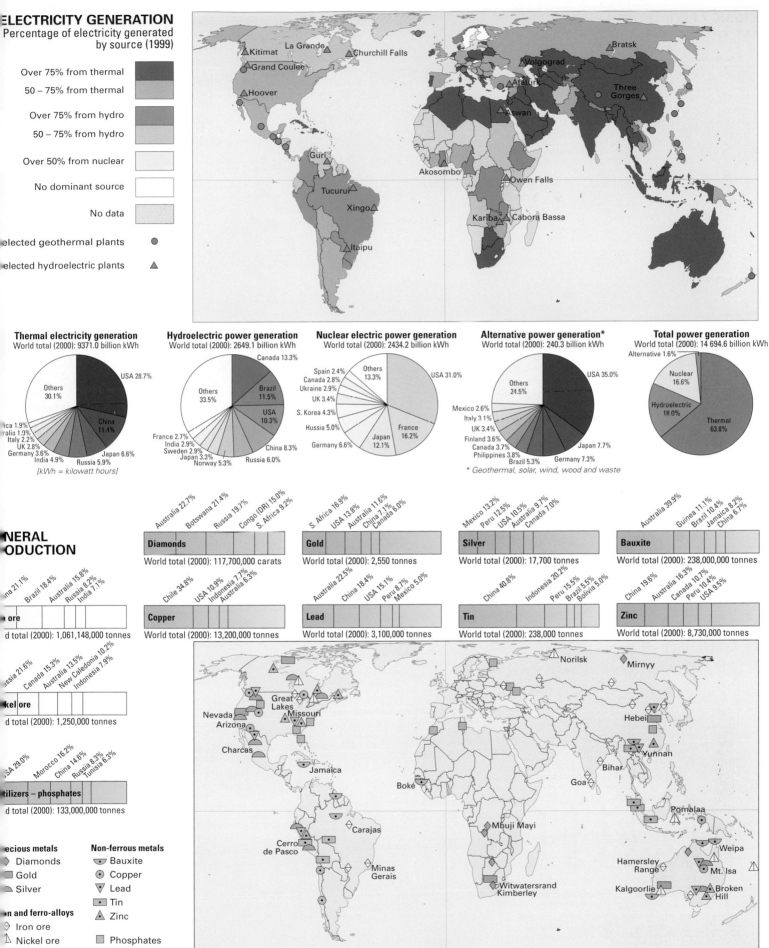

Norilsk, Mirnyy, Great Lakes, Missouri, Hebei, Nevada, Arizona, Yunnan, Charcas, Bihar, Jamaica, Goa, Boké, Carajas, Mbuji Mayi, Pomalaa, Cerro de Pasco, Minas Gerais, Witwatersrand Kimberley, Hamersley Range, Weipa, Mt. Isa, Kalgoorlie, Broken Hill

Projection: Eckert IV

COPYRIGHT PHILIP'S

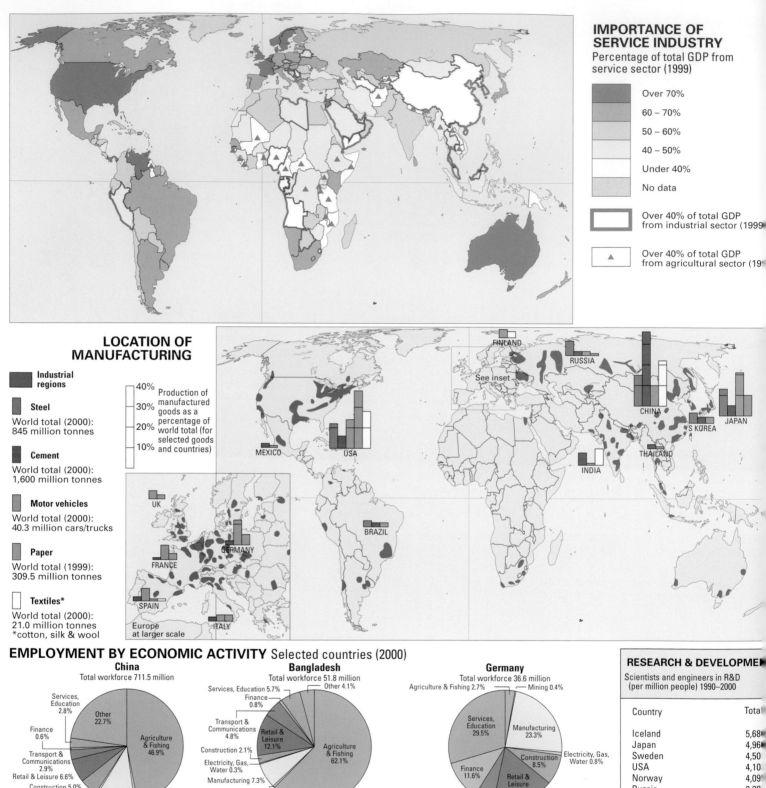

IMPORTANCE OF SERVICE INDUSTRY
Percentage of total GDP from service sector (1999)

- Over 70%
- 60 – 70%
- 50 – 60%
- 40 – 50%
- Under 40%
- No data
- Over 40% of total GDP from industrial sector (1999)
- ▲ Over 40% of total GDP from agricultural sector (19

LOCATION OF MANUFACTURING

- **Industrial regions**

- **Steel**
World total (2000): 845 million tonnes

- **Cement**
World total (2000): 1,600 million tonnes

- **Motor vehicles**
World total (2000): 40.3 million cars/trucks

- **Paper**
World total (1999): 309.5 million tonnes

- **Textiles***
World total (2000): 21.0 million tonnes
*cotton, silk & wool

40% / 30% / 20% / 10% — Production of manufactured goods as a percentage of world total (for selected goods and countries)

Europe at larger scale

EMPLOYMENT BY ECONOMIC ACTIVITY Selected countries (2000)

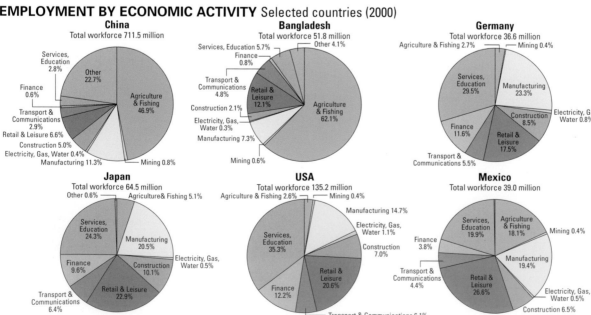

China — Total workforce 711.5 million
- Agriculture & Fishing 46.9%
- Other 22.7%
- Manufacturing 11.3%
- Retail & Leisure 6.6%
- Construction 5.0%
- Transport & Communications 2.9%
- Services, Education 2.8%
- Mining 0.8%
- Finance 0.6%
- Electricity, Gas, Water 0.4%

Bangladesh — Total workforce 51.8 million
- Agriculture & Fishing 62.1%
- Retail & Leisure 12.1%
- Manufacturing 7.3%
- Services, Education 5.7%
- Transport & Communications 4.8%
- Other 4.1%
- Construction 2.1%
- Finance 0.8%
- Mining 0.6%
- Electricity, Gas, Water 0.3%

Germany — Total workforce 36.6 million
- Services, Education 29.5%
- Manufacturing 23.3%
- Retail & Leisure 17.5%
- Finance 11.6%
- Construction 8.5%
- Transport & Communications 5.5%
- Agriculture & Fishing 2.7%
- Electricity, Gas, Water 0.8%
- Mining 0.4%

Japan — Total workforce 64.5 million
- Services, Education 24.3%
- Retail & Leisure 22.9%
- Manufacturing 20.5%
- Construction 10.1%
- Finance 9.6%
- Transport & Communications 6.4%
- Agriculture & Fishing 5.1%
- Other 0.6%
- Electricity, Gas, Water 0.5%

USA — Total workforce 135.2 million
- Services, Education 35.3%
- Retail & Leisure 20.6%
- Manufacturing 14.7%
- Finance 12.2%
- Construction 7.0%
- Transport & Communications 6.1%
- Agriculture & Fishing 2.6%
- Electricity, Gas, Water 1.1%
- Mining 0.4%

Mexico — Total workforce 39.0 million
- Retail & Leisure 26.6%
- Services, Education 19.9%
- Manufacturing 19.4%
- Agriculture & Fishing 18.1%
- Construction 6.5%
- Transport & Communications 4.4%
- Finance 3.8%
- Electricity, Gas, Water 0.5%
- Mining 0.4%

RESEARCH & DEVELOPMEN

Scientists and engineers in R&D (per million people) 1990–2000

Country	Total
Iceland	5,68
Japan	4,96
Sweden	4,50
USA	4,10
Norway	4,09
Russia	3,39
Australia	3,32
Denmark	3,24
Switzerland	3,05
Canada	3,00
Germany	2,87
Azerbaijan	2,73
France	2,68
UK	2,67
Netherlands	2,49
Belgium	2,30
Belarus	2,29
New Zealand	2,19
Singapore	2,18
Estonia	2,16

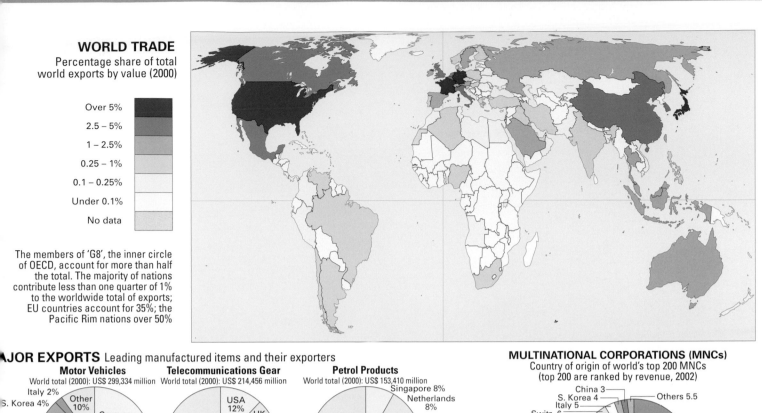

WORLD TRADE
Percentage share of total world exports by value (2000)

- Over 5%
- 2.5 – 5%
- 1 – 2.5%
- 0.25 – 1%
- 0.1 – 0.25%
- Under 0.1%
- No data

The members of 'G8', the inner circle of OECD, account for more than half the total. The majority of nations contribute less than one quarter of 1% to the worldwide total of exports; EU countries account for 35%; the Pacific Rim nations over 50%

MAJOR EXPORTS Leading manufactured items and their exporters

Motor Vehicles
World total (2000): US$ 299,334 million

- Germany 20%
- Japan 19%
- Canada 12%
- Other 10%
- France 7%
- Spain 6%
- Belgium 6%
- Mexico 5%
- USA 5%
- UK 5%
- S. Korea 4%
- Italy 2%

Telecommunications Gear
World total (2000): US$ 214,456 million

- Other 39%
- USA 12%
- Japan 8%
- UK 8%
- Germany 7%
- China 6%
- France 6%
- Sweden 6%
- Canada 5%
- Mexico 5%

Petrol Products
World total (2000): US$ 153,410 million

- Other 45%
- Singapore 8%
- Netherlands 8%
- Russia 7%
- Saudi Arabia 6%
- S. Korea 6%
- USA 5%
- Belgium 5%
- UK 4%
- Kuwait 3%
- Germany 3%

Computers
World total (2000): US$ 182,866 million

- Other 33%
- USA 17%
- Singapore 11%
- Neth. 8%
- UK 8%
- Japan 8%
- China 6%
- Korea 5%
- Mexico 5%

Electrical Components
World total (2000): US$ 274,240 million

- Other 23%
- Thailand 17%
- Hungary 16%
- Portugal 13%
- Ireland 9%
- Japan 6%
- Kuwait 6%
- China 6%
- Germ. 6%

Pharmaceuticals
World total (2000): US$ 107,334 million

- Other 34%
- USA 12%
- Germany 12%
- UK 10%
- Switzerland 10%
- France 10%
- Belgium 6%
- Italy 6%

MULTINATIONAL CORPORATIONS (MNCs)
Country of origin of world's top 200 MNCs (top 200 are ranked by revenue, 2002)

- USA 86
- Japan 32
- Germany 18
- France 16
- UK 13
- Neth. 7.5
- Switz. 6
- Italy 5
- S. Korea 4
- China 3
- Others 5.5

Top ten MNCs by revenue (million US$), 2002

Wal-Mart	Supermarket chain	219,812	USA
Exxon Mobil	Petroleum	191,581	USA
General Motors	Motor vehicles	177,260	USA
BP	Petroleum	174,218	UK
Ford Motor	Motor vehicles	162,412	USA
Enron*	Energy	138,718	USA
DaimlerChrysler	Motor vehicles	136,897	Germany
Royal Dutch/Shell	Petroleum	135,211	Neth/UK
General Electric	Energy and finance	125,913	USA
Toyota Motor	Motor vehicles	120,814	Japan

Enron ceased trading in 2002

INTERNET AND TELECOMMUNICATIONS
Percentage of total population using the Internet (2000)

World total 513.4 million Internet users

- Over 50%
- 10 – 50%
- 5 – 10%
- 1 – 5%
- Under 1%
- No data

Telecommunications
Trade in office machines and telecom equipment, percentage of world total (2001)

- 40%
- 30%
- 20%
- 10%

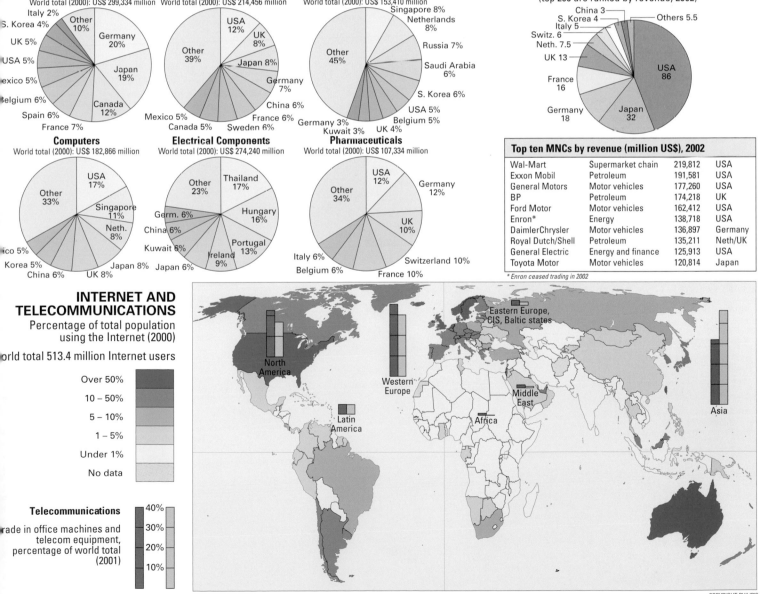

Projection: *Eckert IV*

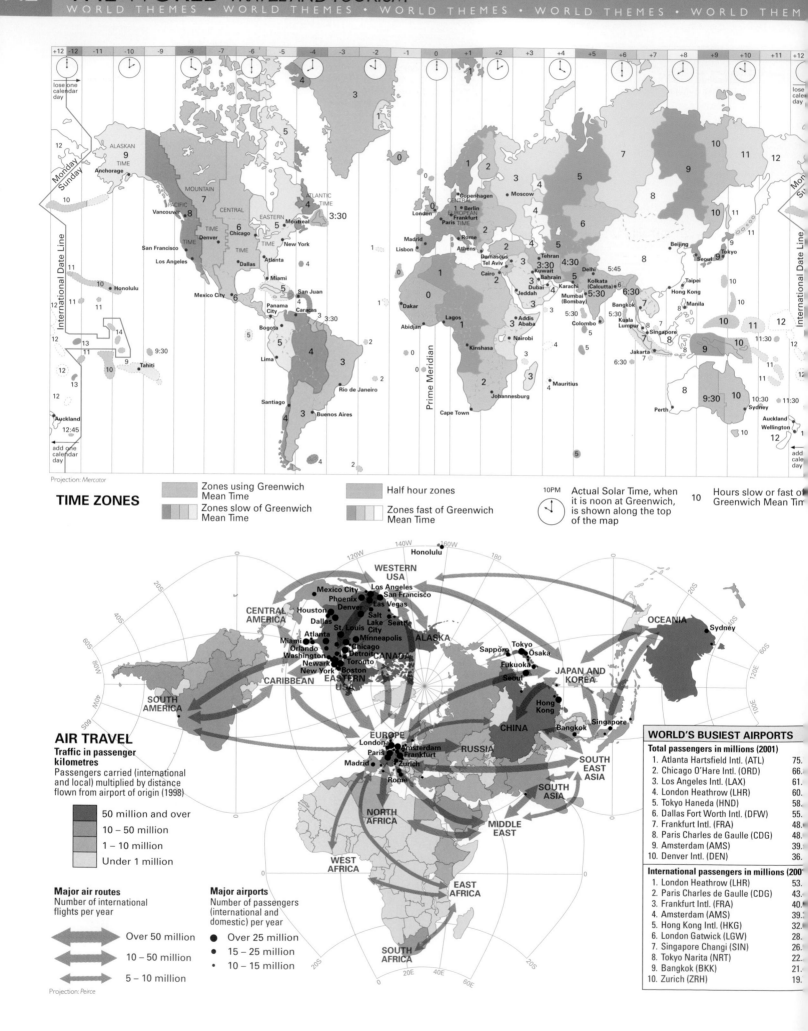

Projection: Mercator

TIME ZONES

	Zones using Greenwich Mean Time		Half hour zones	10PM	Actual Solar Time, when it is noon at Greenwich, is shown along the top of the map		Hours slow or fast of Greenwich Mean Tim
	Zones slow of Greenwich Mean Time		Zones fast of Greenwich Mean Time			10	

AIR TRAVEL

Traffic in passenger kilometres

Passengers carried (international and local) multiplied by distance flown from airport of origin (1998)

- 50 million and over
- 10 – 50 million
- 1 – 10 million
- Under 1 million

Major air routes
Number of international flights per year

- Over 50 million
- 10 – 50 million
- 5 – 10 million

Major airports
Number of passengers (international and domestic) per year

- ● Over 25 million
- • 15 – 25 million
- · 10 – 15 million

Projection: Peirce

WORLD'S BUSIEST AIRPORTS

Total passengers in millions (2001)

1. Atlanta Hartsfield Intl. (ATL)	75.
2. Chicago O'Hare Intl. (ORD)	66.
3. Los Angeles Intl. (LAX)	61.
4. London Heathrow (LHR)	60.
5. Tokyo Haneda (HND)	58.
6. Dallas Fort Worth Intl. (DFW)	55.
7. Frankfurt Intl. (FRA)	48.
8. Paris Charles de Gaulle (CDG)	48.
9. Amsterdam (AMS)	39.
10. Denver Intl. (DEN)	36.

International passengers in millions (200

1. London Heathrow (LHR)	53.
2. Paris Charles de Gaulle (CDG)	43.
3. Frankfurt Intl. (FRA)	40.
4. Amsterdam (AMS)	39.
5. Hong Kong Intl. (HKG)	32.
6. London Gatwick (LGW)	28.
7. Singapore Changi (SIN)	26.
8. Tokyo Narita (NRT)	22.
9. Bangkok (BKK)	21.
10. Zurich (ZRH)	19.

NESCO WORLD HERITAGE SITES 2002

al sites = 730 (563 cultural, 144 natural and 23 mixed)

gion	Natural sites	Cultural sites
ope	21	285
dle East and Turkey	1	31
a and Russia	29	106
ada and USA	18	13
xico and Central America	11	35
th America	19	36
ca	32	57
eania	13	0

Destinations

- ■ Cultural & historical centres
- □ Coastal resorts
- □ Ski resorts
- ▦ Centres of entertainment
- ▦ Places of pilgrimage
- ▦ Places of great natural beauty

- ▦ Other tourist destinations

TOURIST DESTINATIONS
Projection: Peirce

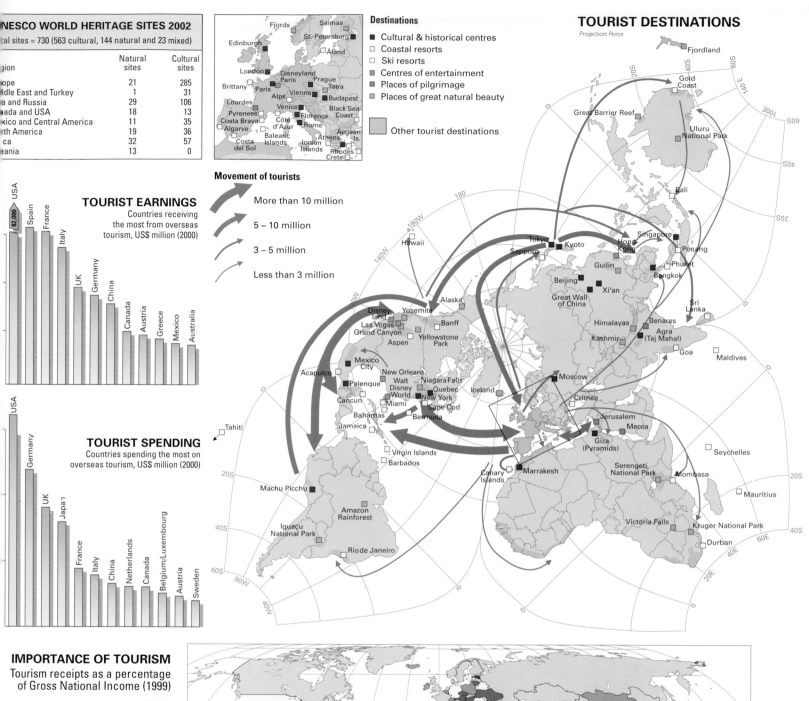

TOURIST EARNINGS
Countries receiving the most from overseas tourism, US$ million (2000)

Movement of tourists

➡ More than 10 million

➡ 5 – 10 million

➡ 3 – 5 million

➜ Less than 3 million

TOURIST SPENDING
Countries spending the most on overseas tourism, US$ million (2000)

IMPORTANCE OF TOURISM
Tourism receipts as a percentage of Gross National Income (1999)

- 10% and over
- 5 – 10%
- 2.5 – 5%
- 1 – 2.5%
- Under 1%
- No data

Arrivals from abroad in millions (2001)

France	75.6
Spain	49.5
USA	45.5
Italy	39.0
China	33.2

(UK = 23.4 million)

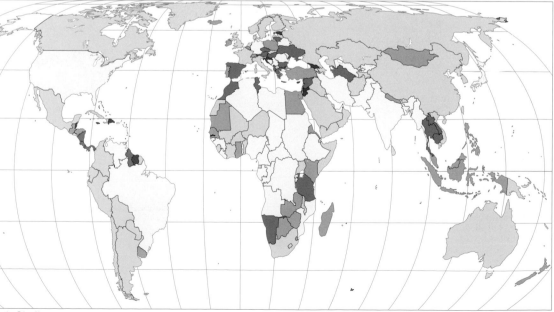

Projection: Eckert IV

COPYRIGHT PHILIP'S

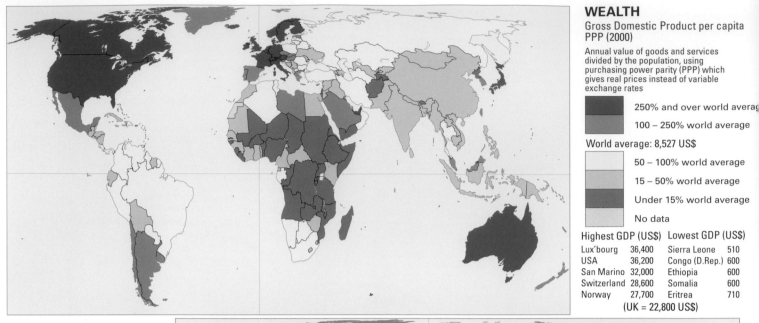

WEALTH

Gross Domestic Product per capita PPP (2000)

Annual value of goods and services divided by the population, using purchasing power parity (PPP) which gives real prices instead of variable exchange rates

- 250% and over world average
- 100 – 250% world average

World average: 8,527 US$

- 50 – 100% world average
- 15 – 50% world average
- Under 15% world average
- No data

Highest GDP (US$)		Lowest GDP (US$)	
Lux'bourg	36,400	Sierra Leone	510
USA	36,200	Congo (D.Rep.)	600
San Marino	32,000	Ethiopia	600
Switzerland	28,600	Somalia	600
Norway	27,700	Eritrea	710

(UK = 22,800 US$)

WATER SUPPLY

Percentage of total population with access to safe drinking water (2000)

- 90% and over
- 75 – 90%
- 60 – 75%
- 45 – 60%
- 30 – 45%
- Under 30%

Least amount of safe drinking water

Afghanistan	13%	Cambodia	30%
Ethiopia	24%	Mauritania	37%
Chad	27%	Angola	38%
Sierra Leone	28%	Oman	39%

Daily consumption per capita

△ Under 80 litres ▲ Over 320 litres

80 litres a day is considered necessary for a reasonable quality of life

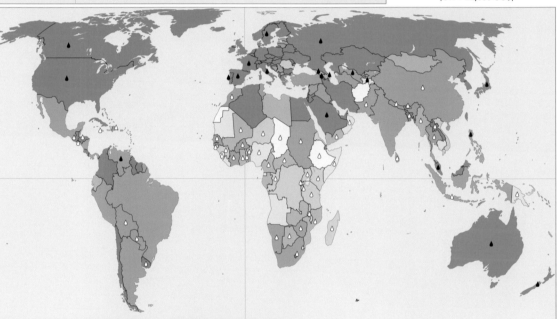

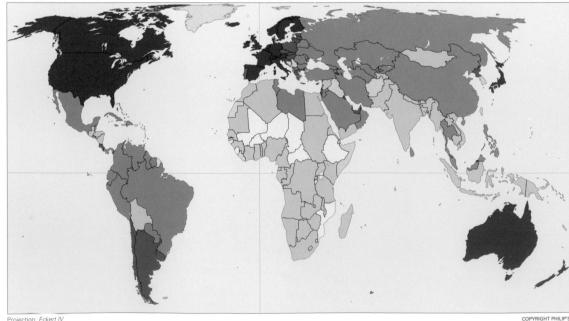

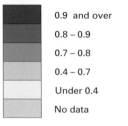

HUMAN DEVELOPMENT INDEX (HDI)

HDI (calculated by the UNDP) gives a value to countries using indicators of life expectancy, education and standards of living in 2000. Higher values show more developed countries

- 0.9 and over
- 0.8 – 0.9
- 0.7 – 0.8
- 0.4 – 0.7
- Under 0.4
- No data

Highest values		Lowest values	
Norway	0.942	Sierra Leone	0.275
Sweden	0.941	Niger	0.277
Canada	0.940	Burundi	0.313
USA	0.939	Mozambique	0.322
Belgium	0.939	Burkina Faso	0.325

(UK = 0.928)

Projection: *Eckert IV*

HEALTH CARE

Number of people per qualified doctor (1999)

Over 15,000	
5,000 – 15,000	
1,000 – 5,000	
500 – 1,000	
Under 500	
No data	

Countries with the most and least people per doctor

Most people		Least people	
Eritrea	33,333	Italy	181
Chad	30,303	Belarus	226
Burkina Faso	29,412	Georgia	229
Niger	28,517	Spain	236
Tanzania	24,390	Russia	238

(UK = 610 people)

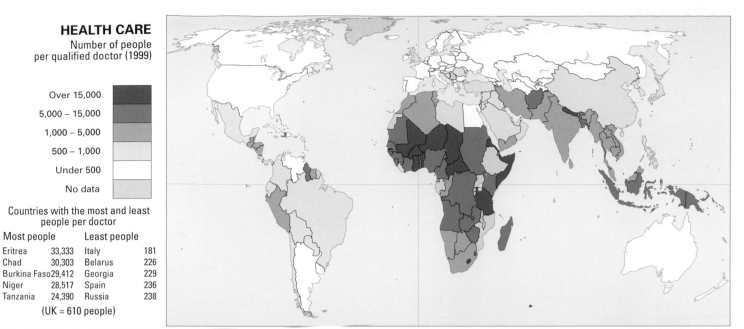

ILLITERACY AND EDUCATION

Percentage of adult population unable to read or write (2000)

60% and over	
40 – 60%	
20 – 40%	
10 – 20%	
Under 10%	
No data	

Countries with the highest and lowest illiteracy rates

Highest (%)		Lowest (%)	
Niger	84	Australia	0
Burkina Faso	76	Denmark	0
Gambia	63	Estonia	0
Afghanistan	63	Finland	0
Senegal	63	Luxembourg	0

(UK = 1%)

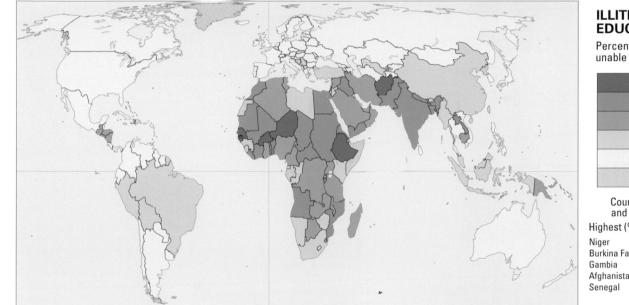
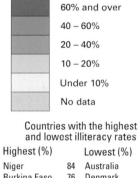

GENDER DEVELOPMENT INDEX (GDI)

GDI shows economic and social differences between men and women by using various UNDP indicators (2002). Countries with higher values of GDI have more equality between men and women

0.8 and over	
0.6 – 0.8	
0.4 – 0.6	
Under 0.4	
No data	

Highest values		Lowest values	
Norway	0.941	Niger	0.263
Australia	0.938	Burundi	0.306
Canada	0.938	Mozambique	0.307
USA	0.937	Burkina Faso	0.312
Sweden	0.936	Ethiopia	0.313

(UK = 0.925)

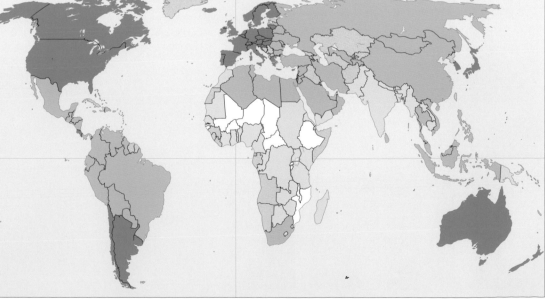

Projection: Eckert IV

AGE DISTRIBUTION PYRAMIDS (2000)

The bars represent the percentage of the total population (males plus females) in each age group. Developed countries such as New Zealand have populations spread evenly across age groups and usually a growing percentage of elderly people. Developing countries such as Kenya have the great majority of their people in the younger age groups, about to enter their most fertile years.

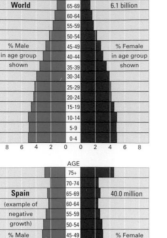

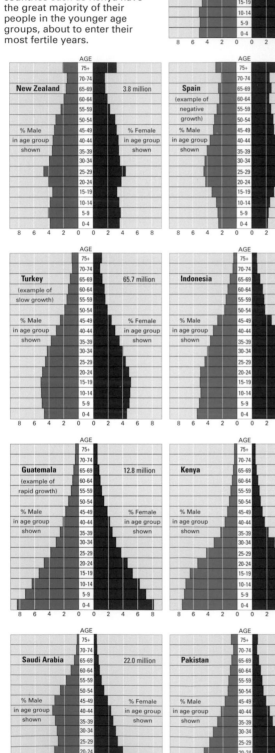

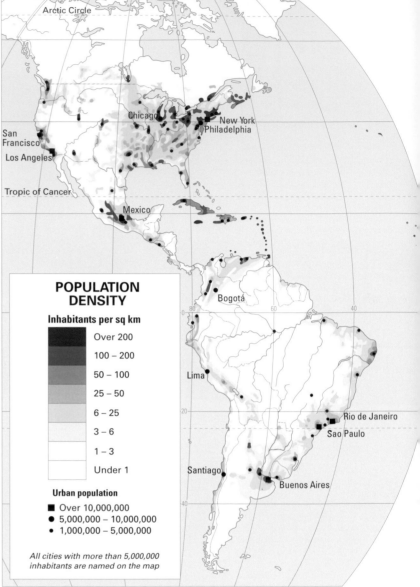

POPULATION DENSITY

Inhabitants per sq km

- Over 200
- 100 – 200
- 50 – 100
- 25 – 50
- 6 – 25
- 3 – 6
- 1 – 3
- Under 1

Urban population

- ■ Over 10,000,000
- ● 5,000,000 – 10,000,000
- • 1,000,000 – 5,000,000

All cities with more than 5,000,000 inhabitants are named on the map

Projection: Interrupted Mollweide's Homolographic

POPULATION CHANGE 1930–2020   Population totals are in millions

Figures in italics represent the percentage average annual increase for the period show

	1930	1930–1960	1960	1960–1990	1990	1990–2020	2020
World	2,013	*1.4%*	3,019	*1.9%*	5,292	*1.4%*	8,062
Africa	155	*2.0%*	281	*2.85*	648	*2.7%*	1,441
North America	135	*1.3%*	199	*1.1%*	276	*0.6%*	327
Latin America*	129	*1.8%*	218	*2.4%*	448	*1.6%*	719
Asia	1,073	*1.5%*	1,669	*2.1%*	3,108	*1.4%*	4,680
Europe	355	*0.6%*	425	*0.55*	498	*0.1%*	514
Oceania	10	*1.4%*	16	*1.75*	27	*1.1%*	37
CIS†	176	*0.7%*	214	*1.0%*	288	*0.6%*	343

* South America plus Central America, Mexico and the West Indies
† Commonwealth of Independent States, formerly the USSR

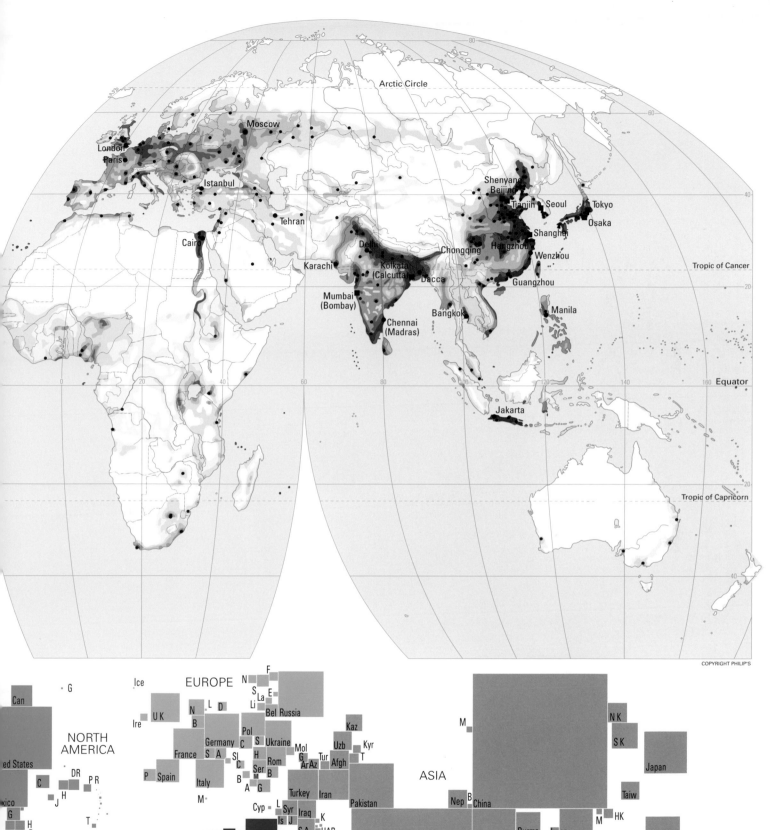

Arctic Circle

Moscow

London
Paris

Istanbul

Tehran

Cairo

Tropic of Cancer

Karachi

Delhi

Kolkata
(Calcutta)

Dacca

Mumbai
(Bombay)

Chennai
(Madras)

Bangkok

Shenyang
Beijing
Tianjin
Seoul
Tokyo
Osaka

Shanghai

Chongqing
Hangzhou

Wenzhou

Guangzhou

Manila

Equator

Jakarta

Tropic of Capricorn

COPYRIGHT PHILIP'S

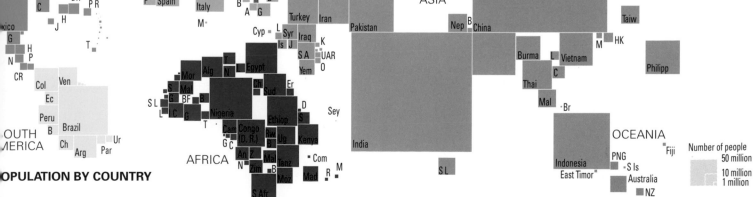

POPULATION BY COUNTRY

EUROPE

ASIA

NORTH
AMERICA

SOUTH
AMERICA

AFRICA

OCEANIA

Number of people
50 million

10 million
1 million

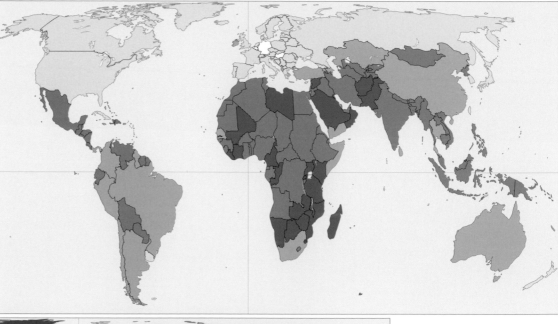

POPULATION DENSITY

Density of people per square kilometre (2001)

- 250 and over
- 100 – 250
- 50 – 100
- 10 – 50
- Under 10
- No data

Most and least densely populated countries

Most		Least	
Singapore	7,049.2	W. Sahara	0.9
Malta	1,234.4	Mongolia	1.7
Maldives	1,036.7	Namibia	2.0
Bangladesh	1,008.5	Australia	2.5
Bahrain	934.8	Mauritania	2.7

(UK = 247.6 people)

POPULATION CHANGE

Change in total population (1990 – 2000)

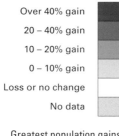

- Over 40% gain
- 20 – 40% gain
- 10 – 20% gain
- 0 – 10% gain
- Loss or no change
- No data

Greatest population gains and losses

Greatest gains (%)		Greatest losses (%)	
Kuwait	75.9	Germany	– 3.2
Namibia	69.4	Tonga	– 3.2
Afghanistan	60.1	Grenada	– 2.4
Mali	55.5	Hungary	– 0.2
Tanzania	54.6	Belgium	– 0.1

(UK = 2% gain)

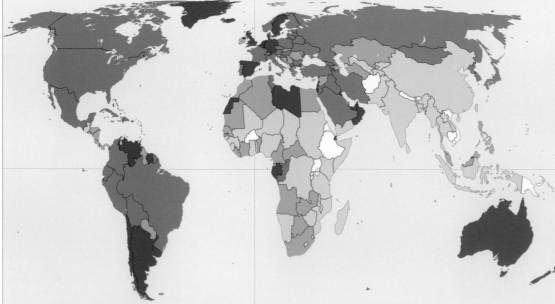

URBAN POPULATION

People living in urban areas as a percentage of total population (2000)

- 80% and over
- 60 – 80%
- 40 – 60%
- 20 – 40%
- Under 20%
- No data

Countries that are the most and least urbanized (%)

Most urbanized		Least urbanized	
Singapore	100	Rwanda	6.4
Nauru	100	Bhutan	7.3
Monaco	100	East Timor	7.4
Vatican City	100	Burundi	9.2
Belgium	97.3	Nepal	10.8

(UK = 89.3%)

Projection: Eckert IV

COPYRIGHT PHILIP'S

CHILD MORTALITY

Deaths of children under 1 year
old per 1000 live births (2001)

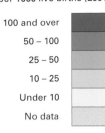

- 100 and over
- 50 – 100
- 25 – 50
- 10 – 25
- Under 10
- No data

Countries with the highest and
lowest child mortality

Highest		Lowest	
Angola	194	Sweden	3
Afghanistan	147	Iceland	4
Sierra Leone	147	Singapore	4
Mozambique	139	Finland	4
Liberia	132	Japan	4

(UK = 6 deaths)

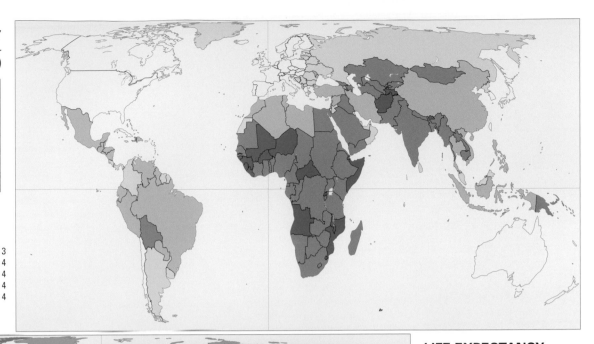

LIFE EXPECTANCY

Life expectancy at birth in years
(2001)

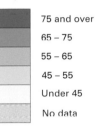

- 75 and over
- 65 – 75
- 55 – 65
- 45 – 55
- Under 45
- No data

Countries with the longest and shortest
life expectancy at birth in years

Longest		Shortest	
Andorra	83.5	Mozambique	36.5
San Marino	81.2	Botswana	37.1
Japan	80.8	Zimbabwe	37.1
Singapore	80.2	Zambia	37.3
Australia	79.9	Trinidad & T.	38.3

(UK = 77.8 years)

FAMILY SIZE

Children born per woman (2001)

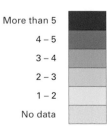

- More than 5
- 4 – 5
- 3 – 4
- 2 – 3
- 1 – 2
- No data

Countries with the largest and
smallest family size

Largest		Smallest	
Somalia	7.1	Bulgaria	1.1
Niger	7.1	Latvia	1.2
Ethiopia	7.0	Spain	1.2
Yemen	7.0	Czech Rep.	1.2
Uganda	7.0	Italy	1.2

(UK = 1.7 children)

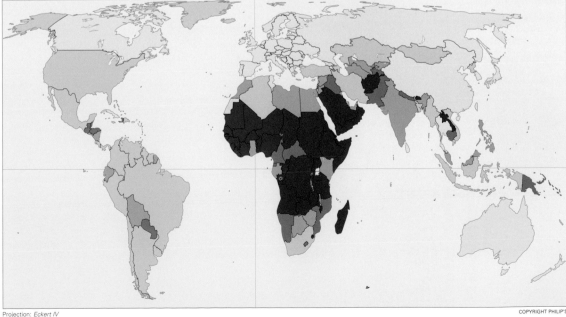

Projection: *Eckert IV*

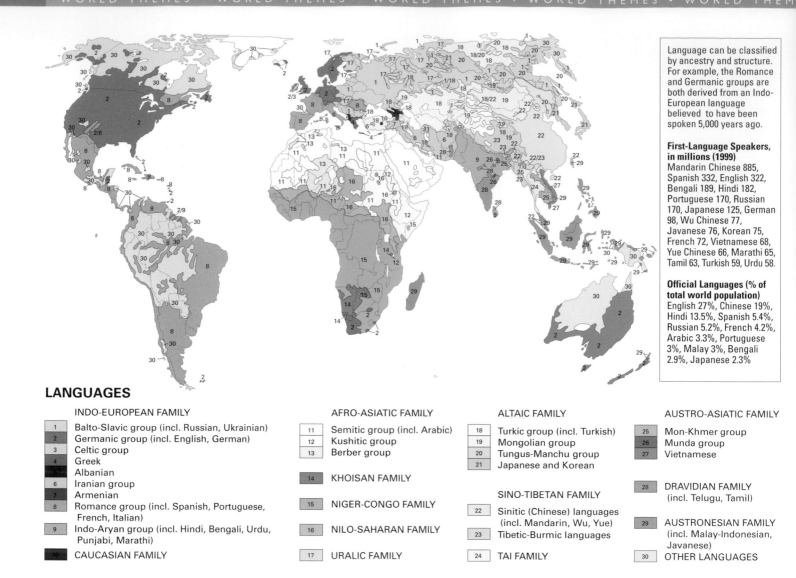

Language can be classified by ancestry and structure. For example, the Romance and Germanic groups are both derived from an Indo-European language believed to have been spoken 5,000 years ago.

First-Language Speakers, in millions (1999)
Mandarin Chinese 885, Spanish 332, English 322, Bengali 189, Hindi 182, Portuguese 170, Russian 170, Japanese 125, German 98, Wu Chinese 77, Javanese 76, Korean 75, French 72, Vietnamese 68, Yue Chinese 66, Marathi 65, Tamil 63, Turkish 59, Urdu 58.

Official Languages (% of total world population)
English 27%, Chinese 19%, Hindi 13.5%, Spanish 5.4%, Russian 5.2%, French 4.2%, Arabic 3.3%, Portuguese 3%, Malay 3%, Bengali 2.9%, Japanese 2.3%

LANGUAGES

INDO-EUROPEAN FAMILY
1 Balto-Slavic group (incl. Russian, Ukrainian)
2 Germanic group (incl. English, German)
3 Celtic group
4 Greek
5 Albanian
6 Iranian group
7 Armenian
8 Romance group (incl. Spanish, Portuguese, French, Italian)
9 Indo-Aryan group (incl. Hindi, Bengali, Urdu, Punjabi, Marathi)
10 CAUCASIAN FAMILY

AFRO-ASIATIC FAMILY
11 Semitic group (incl. Arabic)
12 Kushitic group
13 Berber group

14 KHOISAN FAMILY

15 NIGER-CONGO FAMILY

16 NILO-SAHARAN FAMILY

17 URALIC FAMILY

ALTAIC FAMILY
18 Turkic group (incl. Turkish)
19 Mongolian group
20 Tungus-Manchu group
21 Japanese and Korean

SINO-TIBETAN FAMILY
22 Sinitic (Chinese) languages (incl. Mandarin, Wu, Yue)
23 Tibetic-Burmic languages

24 TAI FAMILY

AUSTRO-ASIATIC FAMILY
25 Mon-Khmer group
26 Munda group
27 Vietnamese

28 DRAVIDIAN FAMILY (incl. Telugu, Tamil)

29 AUSTRONESIAN FAMILY (incl. Malay-Indonesian, Javanese)

30 OTHER LANGUAGES

RELIGIONS

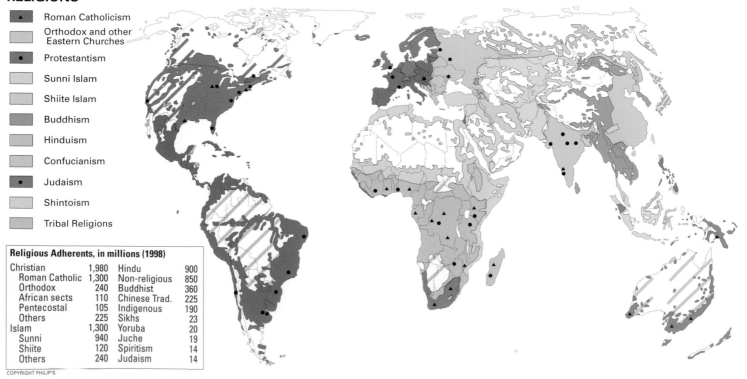

- Roman Catholicism
- Orthodox and other Eastern Churches
- Protestantism
- Sunni Islam
- Shiite Islam
- Buddhism
- Hinduism
- Confucianism
- Judaism
- Shintoism
- Tribal Religions

Religious Adherents, in millions (1998)

Christian	1,980	Hindu	900
Roman Catholic	1,300	Non-religious	850
Orthodox	240	Buddhist	360
African sects	110	Chinese Trad.	225
Pentecostal	105	Indigenous	190
Others	225	Sikhs	23
Islam	1,300	Yoruba	20
Sunni	940	Juche	19
Shiite	120	Spiritism	14
Others	240	Judaism	14

COPYRIGHT PHILIP'S

UNITED NATIONS

Created in 1945 to promote peace and co-operation and based in New York, the United Nations is the world's largest international organization, with 191 members and an annual budget of US $1.3 billion (2002). Each member of the General Assembly has one vote, while the permanent members of the 15-nation Security Council – USA, Russia, China, UK and France – hold a veto. The Secretariat is the UN's principal administrative arm. The 54 members of the Economic and Social Council are responsible for economic, social, cultural, educational, health and related matters. The UN has 16 specialized agencies – based in Canada, France, Switzerland and Italy, as well as the USA – which help members in fields such as education (UNESCO), agriculture (FAO), medicine (WHO) and finance (IFC). By the end of 1994, all the original 11 trust territories of the Trusteeship Council had become independent.

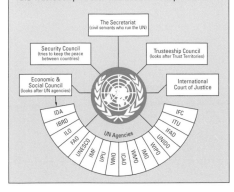

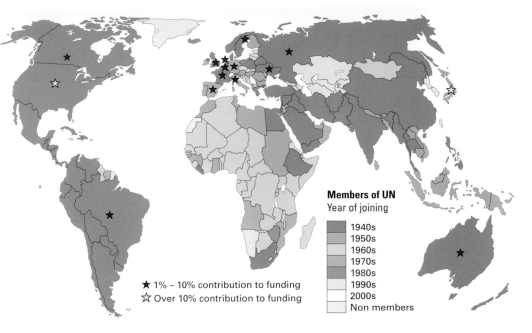

Members of UN
Year of joining

- 1940s
- 1950s
- 1960s
- 1970s
- 1980s
- 1990s
- 2000s
- Non members

★ 1% – 10% contribution to funding
☆ Over 10% contribution to funding

MEMBERSHIP OF THE UN In 1945 there were 51 members; by 2002 membership had increased to 191 following the admission of Switzerland and East Timor. There are 2 independent states which are not members of the UN – Taiwan and the Vatican City. All the successor states of the former USSR had joined by the end of 1992. The official languages of the UN are Chinese, English, French, Russian, Spanish and Arabic.

FUNDING The UN regular budget for 2000 was US $1.3 billion. Contributions are assessed by the members' ability to pay, with the maximum 22% of the total (USA's share), the minimum 0.01%. The 15-country European Union pays over 37% of the budget.

PEACEKEEPING The UN has been involved in 54 peacekeeping operations worldwide since 1948.

INTERNATIONAL ORGANIZATIONS

ACP African-Caribbean-Pacific (formed in 1963). Members have economic ties with the EU.
ARAB LEAGUE (formed in 1945). The League's aim is to promote economic, social, political and military co-operation. There are 21 member nations.
ASEAN Association of South-east Asian Nations (formed in 1967). Cambodia joined in 1999.
CIS The Commonwealth of Independent States (formed in 1991) comprises the countries of the former Soviet Union except for Estonia, Latvia and Lithuania.
COLOMBO PLAN (formed in 1951). Its 25 members aim to promote economic and social development in Asia and the Pacific.
COMMONWEALTH The Commonwealth of Nations evolved from the British Empire; it comprises 16 Queen's realms, 32 republics and 5 indigenous monarchies, giving a total of 53. Nigeria was suspended in 1995, but reinstated in 1999.
EFTA European Free Trade Association (formed in 1960). Portugal left the original 'Seven' in 1989 to join what was then the EC, followed by Austria, Finland and Sweden in 1995. Only 4 members remain: Norway, Iceland, Switzerland and Liechtenstein.
EU European Union (evolved from the European Community in 1993). The 15 members – Austria, Belgium, Denmark, Finland, France, Germany, Greece, Ireland, Italy, Luxembourg, Netherlands, Portugal, Spain, Sweden and the UK – aim to integrate economies, co-ordinate social developments and bring about political union. These members, of what is now the world's biggest market, share agricultural and industrial policies and tariffs on trade. The original body, the European Coal and Steel Community (ECSC), was created in 1951 following the signing of the Treaty of Paris.
LAIA Latin American Integration Association (1980). Its aim is to promote freer regional trade.
NATO North Atlantic Treaty Organization (formed in 1949). It continues after 1991 despite the winding up of the Warsaw Pact. Bulgaria, Romania, Estonia, Latvia, Lithuania, Slovakia and Slovenia are due to become full members in 2004.
OAS Organization of American States (formed in 1948). It aims to promote social and economic co-operation between developed countries of North America and developing nations of Latin America.
OAU Organization of African Unity (formed in 1963). Its 53 members represent over 94% of Africa's population. Arabic, French, Portuguese and English are recognized as working languages.

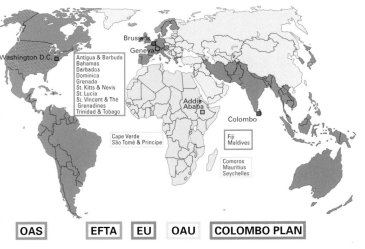

OAS | EFTA | EU | OAU | COLOMBO PLAN

OECD Organization for Economic Co-operation and Development (formed in 1961). It comprises 30 major free-market economies. Poland, Hungary and South Korea joined in 1996. 'G8' is its 'inner group' of leading industrial nations, comprising Canada, France, Germany, Italy, Japan, Russia, UK and USA.
OPEC Organization of Petroleum Exporting Countries (formed in 1960). It controls about three-quarters of the world's oil supply. Gabon left the organization in 1996.

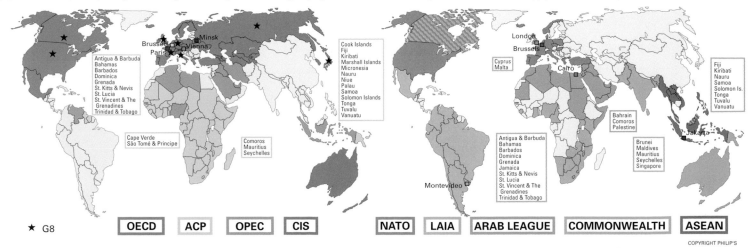

★ G8

OECD | ACP | OPEC | CIS

NATO | LAIA | ARAB LEAGUE | COMMONWEALTH | ASEAN

COPYRIGHT PHILIP'S

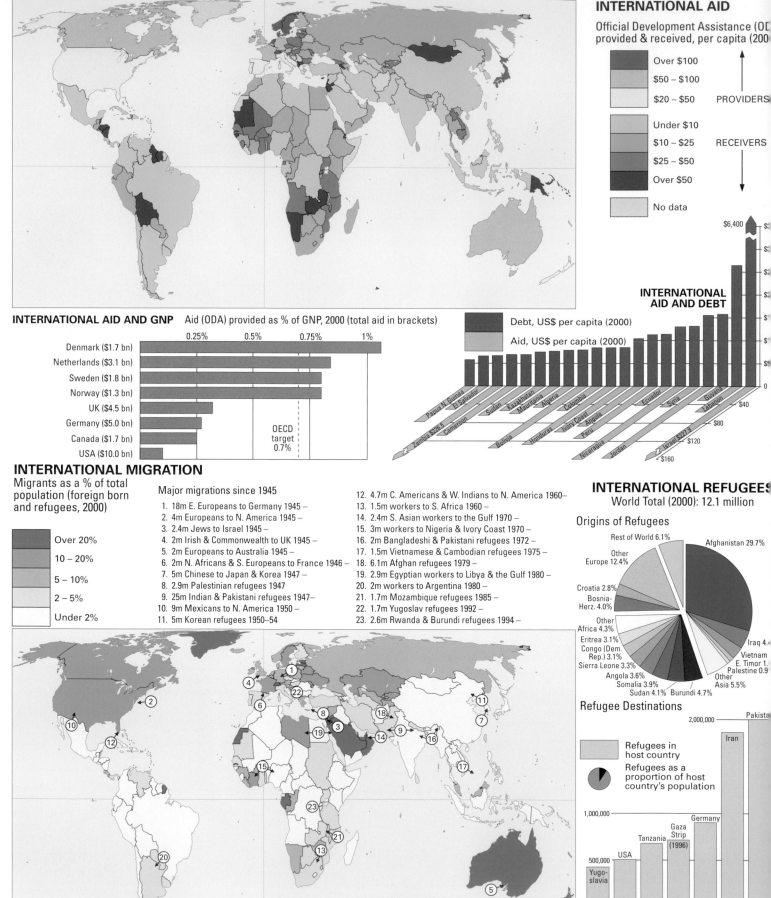

INTERNATIONAL AID

Official Development Assistance (OD
provided & received, per capita (200

- Over $100
- $50 – $100
- $20 – $50   PROVIDERS

- Under $10
- $10 – $25   RECEIVERS
- $25 – $50
- Over $50

- No data

INTERNATIONAL AID AND DEBT

$6,400

- Debt, US$ per capita (2000)
- Aid, US$ per capita (2000)

Papua N. Guinea, El Salvador, Sudan, Kazakhstan, Algeria, Colombia, Ecuador, Syria, Guyana, Lebanon
Zambia $226.5, Cameroon, Bolivia, Honduras, Ivory Coast, Peru, Angola, Nicaragua, Jordan, Israel $271.9

$40, $80, $120, $160

INTERNATIONAL AID AND GNP

Aid (ODA) provided as % of GNP, 2000 (total aid in brackets)

0.25%   0.5%   0.75%   1%

- Denmark ($1.7 bn)
- Netherlands ($3.1 bn)
- Sweden ($1.8 bn)
- Norway ($1.3 bn)
- UK ($4.5 bn)
- Germany ($5.0 bn)
- Canada ($1.7 bn)
- USA ($10.0 bn)

OECD target 0.7%

INTERNATIONAL MIGRATION

Migrants as a % of total population (foreign born and refugees, 2000)

- Over 20%
- 10 – 20%
- 5 – 10%
- 2 – 5%
- Under 2%

Major migrations since 1945

1. 18m E. Europeans to Germany 1945 –
2. 4m Europeans to N. America 1945 –
3. 2.4m Jews to Israel 1945 –
4. 2m Irish & Commonwealth to UK 1945 –
5. 2m Europeans to Australia 1945 –
6. 2m N. Africans & S. Europeans to France 1946 –
7. 5m Chinese to Japan & Korea 1947 –
8. 2.9m Palestinian refugees 1947
9. 25m Indian & Pakistani refugees 1947–
10. 9m Mexicans to N. America 1950 –
11. 5m Korean refugees 1950–54

12. 4.7m C. Americans & W. Indians to N. America 1960–
13. 1.5m workers to S. Africa 1960 –
14. 2.4m S. Asian workers to the Gulf 1970 –
15. 3m workers to Nigeria & Ivory Coast 1970 –
16. 2m Bangladeshi & Pakistani refugees 1972 –
17. 1.5m Vietnamese & Cambodian refugees 1975 –
18. 6.1m Afghan refugees 1979 –
19. 2.9m Egyptian workers to Libya & the Gulf 1980 –
20. 2m workers to Argentina 1980 –
21. 1.7m Mozambique refugees 1985 –
22. 1.7m Yugoslav refugees 1992 –
23. 2.6m Rwanda & Burundi refugees 1994 –

INTERNATIONAL REFUGEES

World Total (2000): 12.1 million

Origins of Refugees

- Afghanistan 29.7%
- Rest of World 6.1%
- Other Europe 12.4%
- Croatia 2.8%
- Bosnia-Herz. 4.0%
- Other Africa 4.3%
- Eritrea 3.1%
- Congo (Dem. Rep.) 3.1%
- Sierra Leone 3.3%
- Angola 3.6%
- Somalia 3.9%
- Sudan 4.1%
- Burundi 4.7%
- Iraq 4.
- Vietnam
- E. Timor 1.
- Palestine 0.9
- Other Asia 5.5%

Refugee Destinations

- Refugees in host country
- Refugees as a proportion of host country's population

2,000,000

Pakista
Iran

1,000,000

Tanzania, Gaza Strip (1996), Germany

500,000

Yugo-slavia, USA

Projection: *Eckert IV*

COPYRIGHT PH

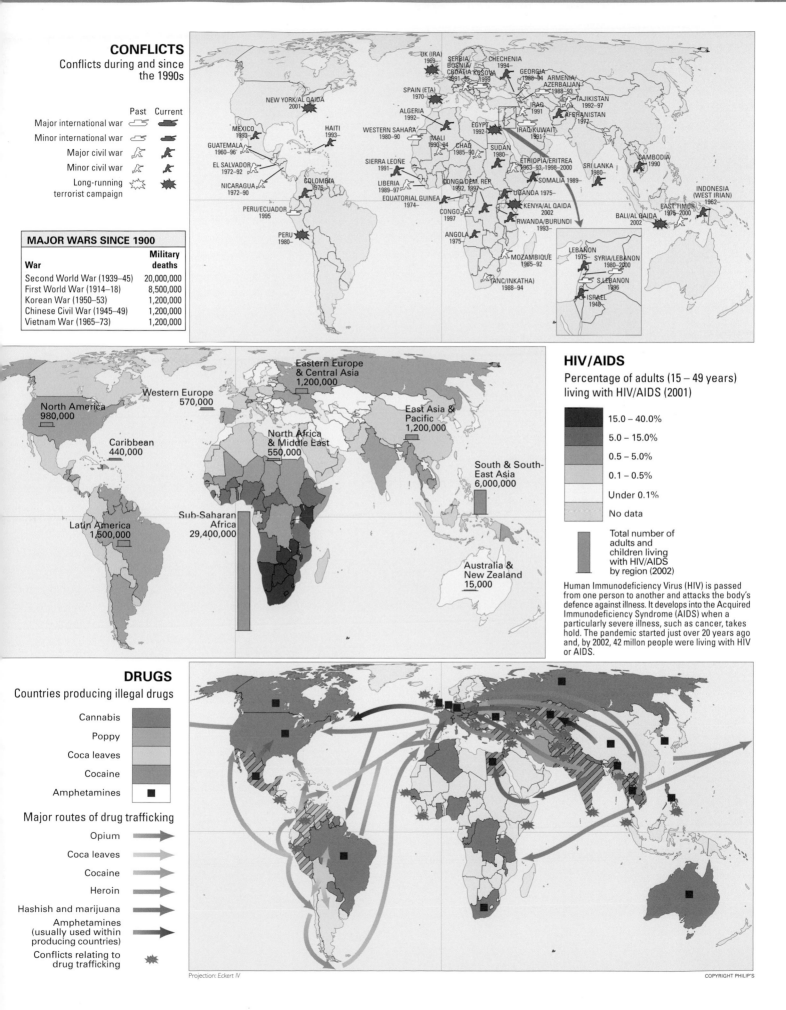

CONFLICTS
Conflicts during and since the 1990s

	Past	Current
Major international war		
Minor international war		
Major civil war		
Minor civil war		
Long-running terrorist campaign		

MAJOR WARS SINCE 1900

War	Military deaths
Second World War (1939–45)	20,000,000
First World War (1914–18)	8,500,000
Korean War (1950–53)	1,200,000
Chinese Civil War (1945–49)	1,200,000
Vietnam War (1965–73)	1,200,000

Conflict labels on map:
UK (IRA) 1969–; SERBIA; BOSNIA; CROATIA 1991–95; KOSOVO 1999; CHECHENIA 1994; GEORGIA 1988–94; ARMENIA/AZERBAIJAN 1988–93; TAJIKISTAN 1992–97; AFGHANISTAN 1977–; NEW YORK/AL QAIDA 2001; SPAIN (ETA) 1970; ALGERIA 1992–; IRAQ 1991; IRAQ/KUWAIT 1991; MEXICO 1993; HAITI 1993; WESTERN SAHARA 1980–90; MALI 1990–94; EGYPT 1992–; GUATEMALA 1960–96; CHAD 1985–90; SUDAN 1980–; ETHIOPIA/ERITREA 1963–93, 1998–2000; SRI LANKA 1980–; CAMBODIA 1990; EL SALVADOR 1972–92; SIERRA LEONE 1991–; LIBERIA 1989–97; CONGO/DEM. REP. 1992, 1997; SOMALIA 1989–; NICARAGUA 1972–90; COLOMBIA 1975–; EQUATORIAL GUINEA 1974–; CONGO 1997; UGANDA 1975–; KENYA/AL QAIDA 2002; INDONESIA (WEST IRIAN) 1962–; EAST TIMOR 1975–2000; PERU/ECUADOR 1995; RWANDA/BURUNDI 1993–; BALI/AL QAIDA 2002; PERU 1980–; ANGOLA 1975–; MOZAMBIQUE 1985–92; (ANC/INKATHA) 1988–94; LEBANON 1975–; SYRIA/LEBANON 1980–2000; S.LEBANON 1996; ISRAEL 1948–

HIV/AIDS
Percentage of adults (15 – 49 years) living with HIV/AIDS (2001)

Shade	Range
	15.0 – 40.0%
	5.0 – 15.0%
	0.5 – 5.0%
	0.1 – 0.5%
	Under 0.1%
	No data

Total number of adults and children living with HIV/AIDS by region (2002)

Human Immunodeficiency Virus (HIV) is passed from one person to another and attacks the body's defence against illness. It develops into the Acquired Immunodeficiency Syndrome (AIDS) when a particularly severe illness, such as cancer, takes hold. The pandemic started just over 20 years ago and, by 2002, 42 millon people were living with HIV or AIDS.

Regional totals on map:
North America 980,000; Western Europe 570,000; Eastern Europe & Central Asia 1,200,000; East Asia & Pacific 1,200,000; Caribbean 440,000; North Africa & Middle East 550,000; South & South-East Asia 6,000,000; Latin America 1,500,000; Sub-Saharan Africa 29,400,000; Australia & New Zealand 15,000

DRUGS
Countries producing illegal drugs

- Cannabis
- Poppy
- Coca leaves
- Cocaine
- Amphetamines ■

Major routes of drug trafficking

- Opium
- Coca leaves
- Cocaine
- Heroin
- Hashish and marijuana
- Amphetamines (usually used within producing countries)
- Conflicts relating to drug trafficking

Projection: Eckert IV

COPYRIGHT PHILIP'S

COUNTRY	POPULATION								LAND AND AGRICULTURE					ENERGY AND TRAD			
	Population total (millions)	Population density (persons per km²)	Life expectancy (years)	Average annual population change (%)	Birth rate (births per thousand)	Death rate (deaths per thousand)	Fertility rate (children born per woman)	Urban population (% of total)	Land area (thousand km²)	Arable & permanent crops (% of land area)	Permanent pasture (% of land area)	Forest (% of land area)	Agricultural workforce (% of total workforce)	Energy produced (tonnes of oil equiv. per capita)	Energy consumed (tonnes of oil equiv. per capita)	Imports (US$ per capita)	Exp (US$ cap
	2001	2001	2001	2002 est.	2001	2001	2001	2001	1999	1999	2000	2000	2000	2000	2000	2000	20
Afghanistan	26.8	41	46	3.4	41	18	5.8	22	625	12	46	2	67	0.01	0.02	6	
Albania	3.5	128	72	1.1	19	7	2.3	42	27	26	16	36	48	0.47	0.56	285	8
Algeria	31.7	13	70	1.7	23	5	2.7	57	2,382	3	14	1	24	4.93	0.98	290	6
Angola	10.4	8	39	2.2	47	25	6.5	34	1,247	3	43	56	72	3.93	0.22	241	75
Argentina	37.4	14	75	1.1	18	8	2.4	88	2,737	10	52	13	10	2.39	1.83	674	70
Armenia	3.3	118	66	–0.2	11	10	1.5	67	28	20	30	12	13	0.31	0.74	274	8
Australia	19.4	3	80	1.0	13	7	1.8	91	7,682	6	53	21	5	12.53	6.35	3,978	3,56
Austria	8.2	99	78	0.2	10	10	1.4	67	83	18	23	47	5	1.76	4.32	8,048	7,75
Azerbaijan	7.8	90	63	0.4	18	10	2.2	52	87	23	29	13	27	2.70	1.72	180	2
Bahamas	0.3	30	70	0.9	19	7	2.3	88	10	1	0	84	4	–	4.71	5,805	1,26
Bahrain	0.6	935	73	1.7	20	4	2.8	92	1	9	6	–	1	17.20	15.61	6,512	8,99
Bangladesh	131.3	1,009	61	1.6	25	9	2.8	25	130	65	5	10	56	0.07	0.10	62	
Barbados	0.3	688	73	0.5	13	9	1.6	50	1	40	5	5	4	0.27	1.67	2,910	94
Belarus	10.4	50	68	–0.1	10	14	1.3	69	207	30	14	45	13	0.21	2.62	802	7
Belgium	10.3	311	78	0.2	11	10	1.6	97	30	25	21	22	2	1.22	6.73	16,181	17,68
Belize	0.3	11	71	2.7	32	5	4.1	48	23	4	2	59	30	–	0.33	1,613	92
Benin	6.6	60	50	2.9	44	15	6.2	42	111	17	5	24	54	0.02	0.05	86	
Bhutan	2.0	44	53	2.2	36	14	5.1	7	47	3	6	64	94	0.25	0.10	131	
Bolivia	8.3	8	64	1.7	27	8	3.5	62	1,084	2	31	49	44	0.66	0.46	224	15
Bosnia-Herzegovina	3.9	77	72	0.8	13	8	1.7	43	51	13	24	45	5	0.20	0.57	625	24
Botswana	1.6	3	37	0.2	29	24	3.7	49	567	1	45	22	45	0.39	0.83	1,387	1,63
Brazil	174.5	21	63	0.9	18	9	2.1	81	8,457	8	22	63	17	0.94	1.31	320	3
Brunei	0.3	65	74	2.1	20	3	2.4	72	5	1	1	84	1	71.70	6.33	3,779	7,4
Bulgaria	7.7	70	71	–1.1	8	15	1.1	67	111	41	15	33	7	1.54	3.06	766	63
Burkina Faso	12.3	45	46	2.6	45	17	6.4	17	274	13	22	26	92	0.01	0.02	50	
Burma (Myanmar)	42.0	64	55	0.6	20	12	2.3	28	658	15	1	52	70	0.09	0.09	60	
Burundi	6.2	242	46	2.4	40	16	6.2	9	26	43	43	4	90	0.01	0.03	18	
Cambodia	12.5	71	57	2.2	33	11	4.7	17	177	22	8	53	70	0.01	0.02	104	
Cameroon	15.8	34	55	2.4	36	12	4.8	49	465	15	4	51	59	0.35	0.13	101	1
Canada	31.6	4	80	1.0	11	7	1.6	79	9,221	5	3	27	2	14.51	10.42	7,540	8,6
Cape Verde Is.	0.4	10	69	0.9	29	7	4.1	62	40	10	6	21	23	–	0.13	617	
Central African Rep.	3.6	6	44	1.8	37	19	4.9	41	623	3	5	37	73	0.01	0.03	43	
Chad	8.7	7	51	3.3	48	15	6.6	24	1,259	3	36	10	75	–	0.01	26	
Chile	15.3	21	76	1.1	17	6	2.2	86	749	3	17	21	16	0.46	1.70	1,109	1,1
China	1,273.1	137	72	0.9	16	7	1.8	36	9,327	15	43	18	67	0.69	0.73	155	
Colombia	40.3	39	71	1.6	22	6	2.7	75	1,039	4	40	48	20	1.93	0.74	307	3
Comoros	0.6	267	60	3.0	40	10	5.3	33	2	53	7	4	74	0.01	0.05	92	
Congo	2.9	9	48	2.2	38	16	5.0	65	342	1	29	65	41	4.88	0.13	301	8
Congo (Dem. Rep.)	53.6	24	49	2.8	46	15	6.8	30	2,267	3	7	60	63	0.05	0.05	12	
Costa Rica	3.8	74	76	1.6	20	4	2.5	59	51	10	46	39	20	0.55	0.97	1,564	1,5
Croatia	4.3	78	74	1.1	13	11	1.9	58	56	28	28	32	8	1.06	2.38	1,800	99
Cuba	11.2	102	76	0.4	12	7	1.6	75	110	41	20	21	14	0.29	0.87	304	1
Cyprus	0.8	83	77	0.6	13	8	1.9	70	9	15	0	13	9	–	3.40	5,245	1,3
Czech Republic	10.3	133	75	–0.1	9	11	1.2	75	77	43	12	34	8	2.55	3.55	3,059	2,7
Denmark	5.4	126	77	0.3	12	11	1.7	85	42	54	8	11	4	5.31	4.13	8,145	9,4
Djibouti	0.5	20	51	2.6	41	15	5.7	84	23	–	56	0	–	–	1.22	954	5
Dominican Republic	8.6	177	73	1.6	25	5	3.0	65	48	32	43	28	17	0.04	0.60	1,119	6
East Timor	0.7	50	–	7.3	–	–	–	7	15	5	10	–	82	–	–	–	
Ecuador	13.2	48	72	2.0	26	5	3.1	63	277	11	18	38	26	1.83	0.67	258	4
Egypt	69.5	70	64	1.7	25	8	3.1	43	995	3	–	0	33	0.96	0.74	244	1
El Salvador	6.2	301	70	1.8	29	6	3.3	60	21	39	38	6	29	0.12	0.46	737	4
Equatorial Guinea	0.5	17	54	2.5	38	13	4.9	48	28	8	4	62	70	16.92	0.14	617	1,7
Eritrea	4.3	43	56	3.8	43	12	5.9	19	121	5	69	16	78	–	0.11	130	
Estonia	1.4	34	70	–0.5	9	13	1.2	69	42	27	7	49	11	0.01	1.62	2,811	2,1
Ethiopia	65.9	66	45	2.6	45	18	7.0	16	1,120	11	20	5	82	0.01	0.02	19	
Fiji	0.8	46	68	1.4	23	6	2.9	49	18	16	10	45	40	0.14	0.55	774	6
Finland	5.2	17	78	0.1	11	10	1.7	59	305	7	0	72	5	2.23	6.30	6,318	8,5
France	59.6	108	79	0.4	12	9	1.8	75	550	35	19	28	3	2.14	4.40	5,374	5,4
Gabon	1.2	5	50	1.0	27	17	3.7	81	258	2	18	85	38	14.92	1.06	819	2,7
Gambia, The	1.4	141	54	3.1	42	12	5.7	31	10	20	46	48	79	–	0.05	144	
Gaza Strip (OPT)*	1.2	3,100	71	4.0	42	4	6.4	–	1	66	–	–	–	–	–	765	20
Georgia	5.0	72	65	–0.6	11	15	1.5	56	70	15	28	43	20	0.34	0.86	180	
Germany	83.0	233	78	0.3	9	11	1.4	88	357	34	14	31	3	1.58	4.24	6,082	6,9
Ghana	19.9	87	57	1.7	29	10	3.8	36	228	23	37	28	57	0.07	0.14	111	
Greece	10.6	82	79	0.2	10	10	1.3	60	129	30	40	28	17	0.97	3.17	3,191	1,4

WEALTH							SOCIAL INDICATORS									COUNTRY
GNI (million US$)	GNI per capita (PPP US$)	GDP per capita (PPP US$)	Average annual growth GDP per capita (%)	Agriculture (% of GDP)	Industry (% of GDP)	Services (% of GDP)	HDI, Human Develop. Index (value)	Food supply (calories per capita per day)	Population per doctor	Adults living with HIV/AIDS (% 15–49 year olds)	GDI, Gender Develop. Index (value)	Female illiteracy (% female adults)	Male illiteracy (% male adults)	Aid donated (−) /received (US$ per capita)	Military spending (US$ per capita)	
1999	1999	2000	1990–99	1999	1999	1999	2000	2000	1999	1999	2000	1999	1999	2000	1999	
–	–	800	–	52	29	19	–	1,539	9,091	–	–	79	49	–	–	Afghanistan
3,146	3,240	3,000	2.8	55	24	21	0.733	2,864	775	0.1	0.729	23	9	91	14	Albania
46,548	4,840	5,500	−0.5	11	37	52	0.697	2,944	1,182	0.1	0.679	44	23	5	63	Algeria
3,276	1,100	1,000	−2.8	7	60	33	0.403	1,903	12,987	3.0	–	72	44	30	94	Angola
276,097	11,940	12,900	3.6	6	32	62	0.844	3,181	373	0.7	0.836	3	3	2	118	Argentina
1,878	2,360	3,000	−3.9	40	25	35	0.754	1,944	316	0.1	0.751	3	1	65	20	Armenia
397,345	23,850	23,200	2.9	3	26	71	0.939	3,176	417	0.2	0.938	1	1	−51	365	Australia
205,743	24,600	25,000	1.4	2	30	68	0.926	3,757	331	0.2	0.921	1	1	−52	210	Austria
3,705	2,450	3,000	−10.7	22	33	45	0.741	2,468	278	0.1	–	–	–	18	15	Azerbaijan
4,526	15,500	15,000	−0.1	3	7	90	0.826	2,443	659	4.1	0.825	4	5	18	67	Bahamas
4,909	12,060	15,900	0.8	1	46	53	0.831	–	1,000	0.2	0.822	18	10	76	530	Bahrain
47,071	1,530	1,570	3.1	30	18	52	0.478	2,103	5,000	0.1	0.468	71	48	9	4	Bangladesh
2,294	14,010	14,500	1.5	4	16	80	0.871	3,022	797	1.2	–	–	–	1	–	Barbados
26,299	6,880	7,500	−2.9	13	46	41	0.788	2,902	226	0.3	0.786	1	1	4	15	Belarus
252,051	25,710	25,300	1.4	1	26	73	0.939	3,701	253	0.2	0.933	1	1	−80	245	Belgium
673	4,750	3,200	0.7	18	24	58	0.784	2,888	1,825	2.0	0.764	7	7	57	85	Belize
2,320	920	1,030	1.8	38	14	48	0.420	2,558	17,544	2.5	0.404	76	45	36	4	Benin
399	1,260	1,100	3.4	38	37	25	0.494	–	6,250	0.1	–	–	–	26	–	Bhutan
8,092	2,300	2,600	1.8	16	31	53	0.653	2,218	770	0.1	0.645	21	8	57	18	Bolivia
4,706	1,210	1,700	32.7	19	23	58	–	2,661	699	0.1	–	–	–	–	–	Bosnia-Herzegovina
5,139	6,540	6,600	1.8	4	46	50	0.572	2,255	4,202	35.8	0.566	21	26	19	41	Botswana
730,424	6,840	6,500	1.5	9	29	62	0.757	2,985	786	0.6	0.751	15	15	2	80	Brazil
7,753	24,620	17,600	−0.5	5	46	49	0.856	2,832	1,179	0.2	0.851	13	6	2	1143	Brunei
11,572	5,070	6,200	−2.1	15	29	56	0.779	2,467	290	0.1	0.778	2	1	40	43	Bulgaria
2,602	960	1,000	1.4	26	27	47	0.325	2,293	29,412	6.4	0.312	87	67	27	6	Burkina Faso
–	–	1,500	5.1	42	17	41	0.552	2,842	3,367	2.0	0.548	20	11	3	1	Burma (Myanmar)
823	570	720	−5.0	50	18	32	0.313	1,605	–	11.3	0.306	61	44	15	9	Burundi
3,023	1,350	1,300	1.9	50	15	35	0.543	2,070	3,367	4.0	0.537	–	20	32	9	Cambodia
8,798	1,490	1,700	−1.5	43	20	37	0.512	2,255	13,514	7.7	0.500	31	19	24	8	Cameroon
614,003	25,440	24,800	1.7	3	31	66	0.940	3,174	436	0.3	0.938	1	1	−55	246	Canada
569	4,450	1,700	3.2	13	19	68	0.715	3,278	5,848	0.2	0.704	35	16	232	10	Cape Verde Is.
1,035	1,150	1,700	−0.3	53	20	27	0.375	1,946	28,571	13.8	0.364	67	41	21	8	Central African Rep.
1,555	840	1,000	−0.9	40	14	46	0.365	2,046	30,303	2.7	0.353	68	50	15	5	Chad
69,602	8,410	10,100	5.6	8	38	54	0.831	2,882	907	0.2	0.824	5	4	3	167	Chile
979,894	3,550	3,600	9.5	15	50	35	0.726	3,029	618	0.1	0.724	25	9	1	10	China
90,007	5,580	6,200	1.4	19	26	55	0.772	2,597	862	0.3	0.767	9	9	5	73	Colombia
189	1,430	720	−3.1	40	4	56	0.511	1,753	13,514	0.1	0.505	48	34	31	–	Comoros
1,571	540	1,100	−3.3	10	48	42	0.512	2,223	3,984	6.4	0.506	27	13	11	38	Congo
4,985	710	600	−8.1	58	17	25	0.431	1,514	14,493	5.1	0.420	51	28	3	5	Congo (Dem. Rep.)
12,828	7,880	6,700	3.0	13	31	56	0.820	2,783	709	0.5	0.814	5	5	3	18	Costa Rica
20,222	7,260	5,800	1.0	10	19	71	0.809	2,483	437	0.1	0.806	3	1	15	122	Croatia
–	–	1,700	–	7	37	56	0.795	2,564	189	0.1	–	–	–	4	–	Cuba
9,086	19,080	13,800	2.8	7	22	71	0.883	3,259	392	0.1	0.879	5	1	71	463	Cyprus
51,623	12,840	12,900	0.9	4	42	54	0.849	3,104	330	0.1	0.846	1	1	43	117	Czech Republic
170,685	25,600	25,500	2.0	3	25	72	0.926	3,396	345	0.2	0.924	1	1	−311	466	Denmark
511	2,120	1,300	−5.1	3	22	75	0.445	2,050	7,143	11.8	–	47	25	155	38	Djibouti
16,130	5,210	5,700	3.9	11	32	57	0.727	2,325	464	2.8	0.718	17	17	7	22	Dominican Republic
–	–	–	–	–	–	–	–	–	–	–	–	–	–	–	–	East Timor
16,841	2,820	2,900	0.0	14	36	50	0.732	2,693	590	0.3	0.718	11	7	11	52	Ecuador
86,544	3,460	3,600	2.4	17	32	51	0.642	3,346	495	0.1	0.628	57	34	19	61	Egypt
11,806	4,260	4,000	2.8	12	28	60	0.706	2,503	934	0.6	0.696	24	19	29	18	El Salvador
516	3,910	2,000	16.3	20	60	20	0.679	–	4,065	0.5	0.669	27	8	44	8	Equatorial Guinea
779	1,040	710	2.2	16	27	57	0.421	1,665	33,333	2.9	0.410	61	34	41	46	Eritrea
4,906	8,190	10,000	−0.3	4	31	65	0.826	3,376	337	0.1	–	1	1	45	50	Estonia
6,524	620	600	2.4	45	12	43	0.327	2,023	–	10.6	0.313	68	57	11	2	Ethiopia
1,848	4,780	7,300	1.2	16	30	54	0.758	2,861	2,101	0.1	0.746	10	5	34	30	Fiji
127,764	22,600	22,900	2.0	4	28	68	0.930	3,227	334	0.1	0.928	1	1	−72	346	Finland
1,453,211	23,020	24,400	1.1	3	26	71	0.928	3,591	330	0.4	0.926	1	1	−69	675	France
3,987	5,280	6,300	0.6	10	60	30	0.637	2,564	–	4.2	–	–	–	10	76	Gabon
415	1,550	1,100	−0.6	21	12	67	0.405	2,474	28,571	2.0	0.397	72	57	35	2	Gambia, The
5,063	1,780	1,000	−0.2	9	28	63	–	–	–	–	–	–	–	–	–	Gaza Strip (OPT)*
3,362	2,540	4,600	–	32	23	45	0.748	2,412	229	0.1	–	–	–	34	4	Georgia
2,103,804	23,510	23,400	1.0	1	31	68	0.925	3,451	286	0.1	0.920	1	1	−61	400	Germany
7,451	1,850	1,900	1.6	36	25	39	0.548	2,699	16,129	3.6	0.544	39	21	31	3	Ghana
127,648	15,800	17,200	1.8	8	28	64	0.885	3,705	255	0.2	0.879	4	2	−21	577	Greece

COUNTRY	POPULATION								LAND AND AGRICULTURE					ENERGY AND TRADE			
	Population total (millions)	Population density (persons per km²)	Life expectancy (years)	Average annual population change (%)	Birth rate (births per thousand)	Death rate (deaths per thousand)	Fertility rate (children born per woman)	Urban population (% of total)	Land area (thousand km²)	Arable & permanent crops (% of land area)	Permanent pasture (% of land area)	Forest (% of land area)	Agricultural workforce (% of total workforce)	Energy produced (tonnes of oil equiv. per capita)	Energy consumed (tonnes of oil equiv. per capita)	Imports (US$ per capita)	Expor (US$ capita
	2001	2001	2001	2002 est.	2001	2001	2001	2001		1999	1999	2000	2000	2000	2000	2000	200
Guatemala	13.0	120	67	2.3	35	7	4.6	40	108	18	24	26	46	0.15	0.30	339	22
Guinea	7.6	31	46	2.2	40	18	5.4	28	246	6	44	28	84	0.01	0.07	83	10
Guinea-Bissau	1.3	47	50	2.2	39	15	5.2	32	28	12	38	78	83	–	0.08	42	6
Guyana	0.7	4	63	0.2	18	9	2.1	36	197	3	6	86	18	0.01	0.77	947	818
Haiti	7.0	253	49	1.4	32	15	4.4	36	28	33	18	3	62	0.01	0.08	172	2
Honduras	6.4	58	69	2.3	32	6	4.2	53	112	16	13	48	32	0.09	0.38	437	31
Hungary	10.1	109	72	–0.3	9	13	1.3	65	92	55	12	20	11	1.13	2.63	2,731	2,49
Iceland	0.3	3	80	0.5	15	7	2.0	92	100	0	23	0	8	7.71	11.33	7,914	7,19
India	1,030.0	346	63	1.5	24	9	3.0	28	2,973	57	4	22	60	0.23	0.31	59	4
Indonesia	227.7	126	68	1.5	22	6	2.6	41	1,812	17	6	58	48	0.85	0.43	177	28
Iran	66.1	41	70	0.8	17	5	2.0	64	1,636	12	27	5	26	3.98	1.80	227	37
Iraq	23.3	53	67	2.8	35	6	4.8	68	437	13	9	2	10	6.08	1.18	591	93
Ireland	3.9	57	77	1.1	15	8	1.9	59	69	16	48	10	10	0.36	3.93	11,898	19,13
Israel	5.9	288	79	1.5	19	6	2.6	92	21	21	7	6	3	0.01	3.35	5,911	5,30
Italy	57.7	196	79	0.1	9	10	1.2	67	294	39	16	34	5	0.60	3.47	4,012	4,18
Ivory Coast	16.4	52	45	2.5	40	17	5.7	44	318	23	41	–	49	0.13	0.17	153	23
Jamaica	2.7	246	75	0.6	18	5	2.1	56	11	25	21	30	21	0.07	1.49	1,125	63
Japan	126.8	348	81	0.2	10	8	1.4	79	375	13	1	64	4	0.86	4.33	2,800	3,550
Jordan	5.2	58	78	2.9	25	3	3.3	79	89	4	9	1	11	0.05	1.08	776	38
Kazakhstan	16.7	6	63	0.1	17	11	2.1	56	2,670	11	68	5	18	4.44	2.70	412	52
Kenya	30.8	54	47	1.2	29	14	3.5	33	569	8	37	30	75	0.03	0.13	98	5
Korea, North	22.0	182	71	1.1	19	7	2.3	60	120	17	0	68	30	2.97	3.22	44	2
Korea, South	47.9	485	75	0.9	15	6	1.7	82	99	19	1	63	10	0.61	4.14	3,350	3,60
Kuwait	2.0	115	76	3.3	22	2	3.2	96	18	0	8	0	1	64.76	12.52	3,722	113,61
Kyrgyzstan	4.8	25	63	1.5	26	9	3.2	34	192	7	48	5	26	0.82	1.16	122	10
Laos	5.6	24	53	2.5	38	13	5.1	19	231	4	4	54	76	0.05	0.05	96	5
Latvia	2.4	38	69	–0.8	8	15	1.2	60	62	30	10	47	12	0.24	1.64	1,342	88
Lebanon	3.6	355	72	1.4	20	6	2.1	90	10	30	2	4	4	0.02	1.69	1,709	19
Lesotho	2.1	72	49	1.3	31	16	4.1	28	30	11	66	0	38	–	0.04	322	8
Liberia	3.2	34	51	1.9	47	16	6.4	45	96	3	21	36	68	–	0.05	53	1
Libya	5.2	3	76	2.4	28	4	3.6	88	1,760	1	8	0	6	15.98	2.79	1,450	2,65
Lithuania	3.6	56	69	–0.3	10	13	1.4	69	65	46	8	31	12	0.74	1.87	1,357	1,02
Luxembourg	0.4	174	77	1.3	12	9	1.7	92	3	–	–	–	2	0.13	12.17	22,573	17,15
Macedonia (FYROM)	2.0	81	74	0.4	14	8	1.8	59	25	25	26	36	13	0.96	1.58	978	68
Madagascar	16.0	28	55	3.0	43	12	5.8	29	582	5	41	20	74	0.01	0.04	43	3
Malawi	10.5	112	37	1.4	38	23	5.2	15	94	21	20	28	83	0.02	0.05	41	3
Malaysia	22.2	68	71	1.9	25	5	3.2	57	329	23	1	59	19	3.64	2.11	3,716	4,40
Mali	11.0	9	47	3.0	49	19	6.8	30	1,220	4	25	11	81	0.01	0.02	52	4
Malta	0.4	1,234	78	0.7	13	8	1.9	91	1	28	–	–	1	–	3.24	6,582	5,06
Mauritania	2.7	3	51	3.0	43	14	6.2	58	1,025	1	38	0	53	0.01	0.45	111	12
Mauritius	1.2	586	71	0.9	17	7	2.0	41	2	52	3	8	12	0.03	0.75	1,933	1,34
Mexico	101.9	53	72	1.5	23	5	2.6	74	1,909	14	42	29	21	2.31	1.53	1,728	1,64
Micronesia, Fed. States	0.1	193	–	–	–	–	–	28	1	51	14	–	–	–	–	1,244	54
Moldova	4.4	135	65	0.1	13	13	1.7	42	33	66	11	10	23	0.02	0.64	172	11
Mongolia	2.7	2	64	1.5	22	7	2.4	57	1,567	1	75	7	24	0.43	0.62	192	17
Morocco	30.6	69	69	1.7	24	6	3.1	55	446	21	47	7	36	0.01	0.35	398	24
Mozambique	19.4	25	36	1.1	37	24	4.8	32	784	4	56	39	81	0.09	0.04	72	2
Namibia	1.8	2	41	1.2	35	21	4.8	31	823	1	46	10	41	–	0.36	890	77
Nepal	25.3	177	58	2.3	33	10	4.6	12	143	21	12	27	93	0.01	0.06	47	1
Netherlands	16.0	472	78	0.5	12	9	1.7	89	34	28	30	11	3	3.93	6.16	12,590	13,15
New Zealand	3.9	14	78	1.1	14	8	1.8	86	268	12	50	30	9	4.25	5.36	3,701	3,77
Nicaragua	4.9	41	69	2.1	28	5	3.2	56	121	23	40	27	20	0.03	0.30	325	12
Niger	10.4	8	42	2.7	51	23	7.1	21	1,267	4	9	1	88	0.01	0.04	31	3
Nigeria	126.6	139	51	2.5	40	14	5.6	44	911	34	43	15	33	1.02	0.17	84	17
Norway	4.5	15	79	0.5	13	10	1.8	75	307	3	1	29	5	57.10	10.05	7,817	13,14
Oman	2.6	12	72	3.4	38	4	6.0	76	212	0	5	0	36	22.91	3.33	1,716	4,23
Pakistan	144.6	188	61	2.1	31	9	4.4	33	771	28	6	3	47	0.21	0.33	66	5
Panama	2.8	38	76	1.3	19	5	2.3	56	74	9	20	39	20	0.32	1.40	2,424	2,00
Papua New Guinea	5.0	11	63	2.4	32	8	4.3	17	453	1	0	68	74	0.78	0.23	198	41
Paraguay	5.7	14	74	2.6	31	5	4.1	56	397	6	55	59	34	2.44	0.52	576	61
Peru	27.5	22	70	1.7	24	6	3.0	73	1,280	3	21	51	30	0.36	0.51	269	25
Philippines	82.8	278	68	2.0	27	6	3.4	59	298	34	4	19	40	0.09	0.37	422	45
Poland	38.6	127	73	–0.1	10	10	1.4	62	304	47	13	31	22	1.99	2.40	1,105	
Portugal	9.4	103	76	0.2	12	10	1.5	64	92	30	16	40	13	0.36	2.89	4,341	2,76
Qatar	0.7	70	73	3.0	16	4	3.2	93	11	2	5	0	1	101.49	23.74	4,941	12,74

WEALTH							SOCIAL INDICATORS									COUNTRY
GNI (million US$)	GNI per capita (PPP US$)	GDP per capita (PPP US$)	Average annual growth GDP per capita (%)	Agriculture (% of GDP)	Industry (% of GDP)	Services (% of GDP)	HDI, Human Develop. Index (value)	Food supply (calories per capita per day)	Population per doctor	Adults living with HIV/AIDS (% 15–49 year olds)	GDI, Gender Develop. Index (value)	Female illiteracy (% female adults)	Male illiteracy (% male adults)	Aid donated (−)/received (US$ per capita)	Military spending (US$ per capita)	
1999	1999	2000	1990–99	1999	1999	1999	2000	2000	1999	1999	2000	1999	1999	2000	1999	
8,625	3,630	3,700	1.5	23	20	57	0.631	2,171	2,020	1.4	0.617	40	24	20	11	Guatemala
3,556	1,870	1,300	1.5	22	35	43	0.414	2,353	7,692	1.5	–	–	–	20	7	Guinea
194	630	850	−1.9	54	15	31	0.349	2,333	6,024	2.5	0.325	82	42	61	7	Guinea-Bissau
651	3,330	4,800	5.2	35	32	33	0.708	2,582	5,525	3.0	0.698	2	1	155	9	Guyana
3,584	1,470	1,800	−3.4	32	20	48	0.471	2,056	11,905	5.2	0.467	53	49	30	–	Haiti
4,829	2,270	2,700	0.3	16	32	52	0.638	2,395	1,202	1.9	0.628	26	26	70	6	Honduras
46,751	11,050	11,200	1.4	5	35	60	0.835	3,458	280	0.1	0.833	1	1	25	82	Hungary
8,197	27,210	24,800	1.8	15	21	64	0.936	3,342	307	0.1	0.934	1	1	–	–	Iceland
1,834	2,230	2,200	4.1	25	24	51	0.577	2,428	2,083	0.7	0.560	56	32	1	13	India
25,043	2,660	2,900	3.0	21	35	44	0.684	2,902	6,250	0.1	0.678	19	9	8	5	Indonesia
3,729	5,520	6,300	1.9	24	28	48	0.721	2,913	1,176	0.1	0.703	31	17	2	84	Iran
–	–	2,500	–	6	13	81	–	2,197	1,818	0.1	–	–	–	–	–	Iraq
30,559	22,460	21,600	6.1	4	38	58	0.925	3,613	457	0.1	0.917	1	1	−61	194	Ireland
99,574	18,070	18,900	2.3	4	37	59	0.896	3,562	260	0.1	0.891	6	2	135	1,475	Israel
62,910	22,000	22,100	1.2	3	30	67	0.913	3,661	181	0.4	0.907	2	1	−24	360	Italy
0,387	1,540	1,600	0.6	32	18	50	0.428	2,590	11,111	10.8	0.411	63	46	21	6	Ivory Coast
6,311	3,390	3,700	−6.0	7	35	58	0.742	2,693	714	0.7	0.739	10	18	4	12	Jamaica
54,545	25,170	24,900	1.1	2	35	63	0.933	2,762	518	0.1	0.927	1	1	−107	339	Japan
7,717	3,880	3,500	1.1	3	25	72	0.717	2,749	602	0.1	0.701	17	6	107	127	Jordan
8,732	4,790	5,000	−4.9	10	30	60	0.750	2,991	283	0.1	–	2	1	11	20	Kazakhstan
0,696	1,010	1,500	−0.3	25	13	62	0.513	1,965	7,576	14.0	0.511	25	12	17	7	Kenya
–	–	1,000	–	30	42	28	0.882	2,185	337	–	–	–	–	–	196	Korea, North
97,910	15,530	16,100	4.7	6	41	53	–	3,093	735	0.1	0.875	4	1	4	259	Korea, South
–	–	15,000	–	0	55	45	0.813	3,132	529	0.1	0.804	21	16	1	1,056	Kuwait
1,465	2,420	2,700	−6.4	39	22	39	0.712	2,871	332	0.1	–	–	–	45	3	Kyrgyzstan
1,476	1,430	1,700	3.8	51	22	27	0.485	2,266	4,115	0.1	0.472	68	37	50	11	Laos
5,913	6,220	7,200	−3.7	5	33	62	0.800	2,855	355	0.1	0.798	1	1	38	25	Latvia
5,796	4,410	5,000	5.7	12	27	61	0.755	3,155	476	0.1	0.739	20	8	54	101	Lebanon
1,158	2,350	2,400	2.1	18	38	44	0.535	2,300	18,519	23.6	0.521	7	28	19	17	Lesotho
–	–	1,100	–	60	10	30	–	2,076	43,478	–	–	33	10	–	–	Liberia
–	–	8,900	–	7	47	46	0.773	3,305	781	0.1	0.753	–	–	3	250	Libya
9751	6,490	7,300	−3.9	10	33	57	0.808	3,040	253	0.1	0.806	–	–	27	49	Lithuania
8,545	41,230	36,400	3.8	1	30	69	0.925	3,701	368	0.2	0.914	1	1	−287	328	Luxembourg
3,348	4,590	4,400	−1.5	12	25	63	0.772	3,006	490	0.1	–	–	–	123	38	Macedonia (FYROM)
3,712	790	800	−1.2	30	14	56	0.469	2,007	9,346	0.2	0.463	41	27	20	2	Madagascar
1,961	570	900	0.9	37	29	34	0.400	2,181	–	16.0	0.389	55	26	42	1	Malawi
76,944	7,640	10,300	4.7	14	44	42	0.782	2,919	1,520	0.4	0.776	17	9	2	78	Malaysia
2,577	740	850	1.1	46	21	33	0.386	2403	21277	2.0	0.739	67	53	33	5	Mali
3,492	14,930	14,300	4.2	3	26	71	0.875	3543	383	0.1	0.378	8	9	54	150	Malta
1,001	1,550	2,000	1.3	25	31	44	0.438	2638	7,246	0.5	0.860	69	48	77	16	Mauritania
4,157	8,950	10,400	3.9	10	29	61	0.772	2985	1,176	0.1	0.429	19	12	17	9	Mauritius
28,877	8,070	9,100	1.0	5	27	68	0.796	3165	536	0.3	0.762	11	7	1	41	Mexico
212	1,830	2,000	−1.8	19	4	77	–	–	1,745	–	0.789	–	–	–	–	Micronesia, Fed. States
1,481	2,100	2,500	−10.8	31	35	34	0.701	3764	286	0.2	0.698	2	1	28	1	Moldova
927	1,610	1,780	−0.6	36	22	42	0.655	1981	411	0.1	0.653	48	27	82	10	Mongolia
33,715	3,320	3,500	0.4	15	33	52	0.602	2964	2,174	0.1	0.585	65	39	14	48	Morocco
3,804	810	1,000	3.8	44	19	37	0.322	1927	–	13.2	0.307	72	41	45	2	Mozambique
3,211	5,580	4,300	0.8	12	25	63	0.610	2649	3,390	19.5	0.604	20	18	84	61	Namibia
5,173	1,280	1,360	2.3	41	22	37	0.490	2436	25,000	0.3	0.470	77	42	15	2	Nepal
97,384	24,410	24,400	2.1	3	27	70	0.935	3,294	398	0.2	0.930	1	1	−196	411	Netherlands
53,299	17,630	17,700	1.8	8	23	69	0.917	3,252	460	0.1	0.914	1	1	−29	239	New Zealand
2,012	2,060	2,700	0.4	31	23	46	0.635	2,227	1,168	0.2	0.629	30	33	114	5	Nicaragua
1,974	740	1,000	−1.0	40	18	42	0.277	2,089	28,571	1.4	0.263	92	77	20	2	Niger
31,600	770	950	−0.5	40	40	20	0.462	2,850	5,405	5.1	0.449	46	29	1	3	Nigeria
49,280	28,140	27,700	3.2	2	25	73	0.942	3,414	242	0.1	0.941	1	1	−281	708	Norway
–	–	7,700	0.3	3	40	57	0.751	–	752	0.1	0.722	40	21	17	960	Oman
62,915	1,860	2,000	1.3	25	25	50	0.499	2,452	1,754	0.1	0.468	70	41	5	18	Pakistan
8,657	5,450	6,000	2.4	7	17	76	0.787	2,488	600	1.5	0.784	9	8	6	46	Panama
3,834	2,260	2,500	2.3	30	35	35	0.535	2,175	13,699	0.2	0.530	44	29	55	9	Papua New Guinea
8,374	4,380	4,750	−0.2	28	21	51	0.740	2,533	911	0.1	0.727	8	6	14	23	Paraguay
53,705	4,480	4,550	3.2	15	42	43	0.747	2,624	107	0.4	0.729	15	6	15	40	Peru
77,967	3,990	3,800	0.9	20	32	48	0.754	2,379	813	0.1	0.751	5	5	7	13	Philippines
57,429	8,390	8,500	4.4	4	36	60	0.833	3,376	424	0.1	0.831	1	1	36	82	Poland
10,175	15,860	15,800	2.3	4	36	60	0.880	3,716	321	0.7	0.876	11	6	−29	246	Portugal
–	–	20,300	–	1	49	50	0.803	–	794	0.1	0.794	17	20	1	1,205	Qatar

COUNTRY	POPULATION								LAND AND AGRICULTURE					ENERGY AND TRADI			
	Population total (millions)	Population density (persons per km²)	Life expectancy (years)	Average annual population change (%)	Birth rate (births per thousand)	Death rate (deaths per thousand)	Fertility rate (children born per woman)	Urban population (% of total)	Land area (thousand km²)	Arable & permanent crops (% of land area)	Permanent pasture (% of land area)	Forest (% of land area)	Agricultural workforce (% of total workforce)	Energy produced (tonnes of oil equiv. per capita)	Energy consumed (tonnes of oil equiv. per capita)	Imports (US$ per capita)	Expo (US$ capit
	2001	2001	2001	2002 est.	2001	2001	2001	2001		1999	1999	2000	2000	2000	2000	2000	200
Romania	22.4	97	70	−0.2	11	12	1.4	55	230	43	21	28	15	1.42	1.79	532	50
Russia	145.5	9	67	−0.3	9	14	1.3	73	16,996	8	5	50	10	7.50	4.86	304	72
Rwanda	7.3	296	39	1.2	34	21	4.9	6	25	45	22	12	90	0.01	0.04	34	
St Lucia	0.2	259	73	1.2	22	5	2.4	38	1	28	3	15	–		0.35	1,958	43
Saudi Arabia	22.8	11	68	3.3	37	6	6.3	86	2,150	2	79	1	10	23.34	5.05	1,323	3,56
Senegal	10.3	53	63	2.9	37	8	5.1	47	193	12	29	32	74	0.01	0.16	126	9
Sierra Leone	5.4	76	46	3.2	45	19	6.0	37	72	16	–	67	–	–	0.06	27	1
Singapore	4.3	7,049	80	3.5	13	4	1.2	100	1	2	–	3	0.1	–	9.87	29,535	31,86
Slovak Republic	5.4	113	74	0.1	10	9	1.3	57	48	33	18	42	9	1.20	3.64	2,364	2,21
Slovenia	1.9	96	75	0.1	9	9	1.3	49	20	10	15	55	2	1.80	3.72	5,130	4,61
Solomon Is.	0.4	17	72	2.9	34	4	4.7	20	28	2	1	91	73	–	0.13	317	34
Somalia	7.5	12	47	3.5	47	18	7.1	27	627	2	69	12	71	–	13.00	42	2
South Africa	43.6	36	48	0.1	21	17	2.4	57	1,221	13	69	7	10	4.17	2.68	633	70
Spain	40.0	77	79	0.1	9	9	1.2	78	499	37	23	29	7	0.79	3.40	4,004	1,33
Sri Lanka	19.4	300	72	0.9	17	9	2.0	23	65	29	7	30	46	0.06	0.24	314	26
Sudan	36.0	15	57	2.7	38	10	5.4	36	2,376	7	46	26	61	0.25	0.05	33	4
Suriname	0.4	3	72	0.6	21	6	2.5	74	156	0	0	90	19	2.34	1.93	1,210	1,02
Swaziland	1.1	64	39	1.6	40	22	5.8	26	17	10	67	30	34	0.21	0.50	841	79
Sweden	8.9	22	80	0.1	10	11	1.5	83	412	7	1	66	3	3.95	6.38	9,014	10,76
Switzerland	7.3	184	80	0.2	10	9	1.5	67	40	11	29	30	4	2.20	4.26	12,577	12,53
Syria	16.7	91	69	2.5	31	5	4.0	51	184	30	45	3	28	2.21	1.24	209	28
Taiwan	22.4	921	77	0.8	14	6	1.8	–	36	–	–	–	67	0.55	4.25	6,259	6,63
Tajikistan	6.6	47	64	2.1	33	8	4.3	28	141	6	25	3	34	0.56	0.93	119	11
Tanzania	36.2	41	52	2.6	40	13	5.4	32	884	5	40	44	80	0.02	0.04	43	10
Thailand	61.8	121	69	0.9	17	8	1.9	20	511	35	2	29	56	0.52	1.04	1,000	1,10
Togo	5.2	95	54	2.5	37	11	5.3	33	54	42	18	9	60	0.01	0.09	88	6
Trinidad & Tobago	1.2	228	69	−0.5	14	8	1.8	74	5	24	2	50	9	16.85	8.78	2,564	2,73
Tunisia	9.7	63	74	1.1	17	5	2.0	66	155	33	25	3	25	0.64	0.76	866	62
Turkey	66.5	86	71	1.2	18	6	2.1	66	770	35	16	13	46	0.38	1.21	838	40
Turkmenistan	4.6	10	61	1.8	29	9	3.6	45	470	4	65	8	33	11.22	2.02	358	52
Uganda	24.0	122	43	2.9	48	18	6.9	14	197	35	9	21	80	0.02	0.03	46	2
Ukraine	48.8	84	66	−0.7	9	16	1.3	68	604	58	14	17	14	1.80	3.34	308	29
United Arab Emirates	2.4	29	74	1.6	18	4	3.2	87	83	2	4	4	5	71.62	18.23	14,125	19,11
United Kingdom	58.8	243	78	0.2	12	10	1.7	89	241	25	47	11	2	4.74	4.18	5,432	4,72
USA	278.1	30	77	0.9	14	9	2.1	77	9,159	20	26	25	2	6.49	8.95	4,398	2,79
Uruguay	3.4	19	75	0.8	17	9	2.4	91	175	7	77	7	13	0.54	1.24	1,012	77
Uzbekistan	25.2	61	64	1.6	26	8	3.1	37	414	12	55	5	28	2.42	1.92	103	11
Venezuela	23.9	27	73	1.5	21	5	2.5	87	882	4	21	56	8	9.42	2.87	615	1.37
Vietnam	79.9	246	70	1.4	21	6	2.5	24	325	23	2	30	67	0.35	0.21	190	17
West Bank (OPT)*	2.1	361	72	3.4	36	4	4.9	–	6	36	4		11	–	–	765	20
Western Sahara	0.3	1	–	–	–	–	–	95	266	–	–	–	–	–	0.25	–	
Yemen	18.1	34	60	3.4	43	10	7.0	25	528	3	4	1	51	1.28	0.19	149	23
Yugoslavia	10.7	105	74	−0.1	13	11	1.8	52	102	37	17	3	20	1.18	1.40	309	14
Zambia	9.8	13	37	1.9	41	22	5.5	40	743	7	43	42	69	0.22	0.25	107	9
Zimbabwe	11.4	29	37	0.1	25	23	3.3	35	387	9	23	49	63	0.32	0.56	114	15

NOTES

OPT*
Occupied Palestinian Territory. Some of the figures for the West Bank and Gaza Strip are combined to summarize the territory as a whole.

PER CAPITA
An amount divided by the total population of a country or the amount per person.

PPP
Purchasing Power Parity (PPP) is a method used to enable real comparisons to be made between countries when measuring wealth. The UN International Comparison Programme gives estimates of the PPP for each country, so it can be used as an indicator of real price levels for goods and services rather than using currency exchange rates (see GNI and GDP per capita).

POPULATION TOTAL
These are estimates of the mid-year total in 2001.

POPULATION DENSITY
The total population divided by the total land area (both are recorded in the table above).

LIFE EXPECTANCY
The average age that a child born today is expected to live to, if mortality levels of today last throughout its lifetime.

AVERAGE ANNUAL CHANGE
These are estimates of the percentage growth or decline of a country's population as a yearly average.

BIRTH/DEATH RATES
These are 2001 estimates from the CIA World Factbook.

FERTILITY RATE
The average number of children that a woman gives birth to in her lifetime.

URBAN POPULATION
The percentage of the total population living in towns and cities (each country will differ with regard to which size or type of town is defined as an urban area).

LAND AREA
The total land area of a country, less the area of major lakes and rivers, in square kilometres.

ARABLE AND PERMANENT CROPS
The percentage of the total land area that is used for crops and fruit (including temporary fallow land or meadows).

PERMANENT PASTURE
The percentage of total land area that has permanent forage crops for cattle or horses, cultivated or wild. Some land may be classified both as permanent pasture or as forest (see Forest), especially areas of scrub or savannah.

FOREST
Natural/planted trees including cleared la that will be reforested in the near future a percentage of the total land area.

AGRICULTURAL WORKFORCE
The population working in agriculture (including hunting and fishing) as a percentage of the total working population.

PRODUCTION AND CONSUMPTIO OF ENERGY
The total amount of commercial energ produced or consumed in a country pe capita (see note). It is expressed in met tonnes of oil equivalent (an energy uni giving the heating value derived from o tonne of oil).

IMPORTS AND EXPORTS
The total value of goods imported into country and exported to other countri given in US dollars ($) per capita.

WEALTH							SOCIAL INDICATORS									COUNTRY
GNI (million US$)	GNI per capita (PPP US$)	GDP per capita (PPP US$)	Average annual growth GDP per capita (%)	Agriculture (% of GDP)	Industry (% of GDP)	Services (% of GDP)	HDI, Human Develop. Index (value)	Food supply (calories per capita per day)	Population per doctor	Adults living with HIV/AIDS (% 15–49 year olds)	GDI, Gender Develop. Index (value)	Female illiteracy (% female adults)	Male illiteracy (% male adults)	Aid donated (–) /received (US$ per capita)	Military spending (US$ per capita)	
1999	1999	2000	1990–99	1999	1999	1999	2000	2000	1999	1999	2000	1999	1999	2000	1999	
3,034	5,970	5,900	–0.5	14	33	53	0.775	3,274	543	0.1	0.773	3	1	19	32	Romania
3,995	6,990	7,700	–5.9	7	34	59	0.781	2,917	238	0.2	0.780	1	1	11	314	Russia
2,041	880	900	–0.3	40	20	40	0.403	2,077	–	11.2	0.398	41	27	44	8	Rwanda
590	5,200	4,500	0.9	11	32	57	0.772	2,838	2,114	–	–	–	–	70	31	St Lucia
9,365	11,050	10,500	–1.1	6	47	47	0.759	2,875	602	0.1	0.731	34	17	1	934	Saudi Arabia
4,685	1,400	1,600	0.6	19	20	61	0.431	2,257	13,333	1.8	0.421	73	54	41	7	Senegal
653	440	510	–7.0	43	26	31	0.275	1,863	13,699	3.0	–	–	–	34	11	Sierra Leone
5,429	22,310	26,500	4.7	0	30	70	0.885	–	615	0.2	0.880	12	4	0	1,282	Singapore
0,318	10,430	10,200	1.6	5	29	66	0.835	3,133	283	0.1	0.833	1	1	21	70	Slovak Republic
9,862	16,050	12,000	2.5	4	35	61	0.879	3,168	439	0.1	0.877	1	1	32	185	Slovenia
320	2,050	2,000	0.3	50	4	46	0.622	2,277	7,143	–	–	–	–	143	–	Solomon Is.
–	–	600	–	60	10	30	–	1,628	25,000	0.1	–	74	50	–	–	Somalia
3,569	8,710	8,500	–0.2	5	30	65	0.695	2,886	1,776	19.9	0.689	16	14	11	47	South Africa
3,082	17,850	18,000	2.0	4	31	65	0.913	3,352	236	0.6	0.906	3	2	–31	150	Spain
5,578	3,230	3,250	4.0	21	19	60	0.741	2,405	2,740	0.1	0.737	11	6	14	38	Sri Lanka
9,435	330	1,000	–	39	17	44	0.499	2,348	11,111	1.0	0.478	55	31	6	18	Sudan
684	3,780	3,400	3.3	13	22	65	0.756	2,652	3,968	1.3	–	–	–	79	21	Suriname
379	4,380	4,000	–0.2	10	46	44	0.577	2,620	6,623	25.3	0.567	22	20	12	21	Swaziland
940	22,150	22,200	1.2	2	28	70	0.941	3,109	322	0.1	0.936	1	1	–203	562	Sweden
3,856	28,760	28,600	–0.1	3	31	66	0.928	3,293	310	0.5	0.923	1	1	–122	431	Switzerland
3,172	3,450	3,100	2.7	29	22	49	0.691	3,038	694	0.1	0.669	41	12	9	58	Syria
–	–	17,400	–	3	33	64	–	–	–	–	–	–	–	–	360	Taiwan
749	280	1,140	–	20	18	62	0.667	1,720	498	0.1	0.664	1	1	22	3	Tajikistan
515	500	710	–0.1	49	17	34	0.440	1,906	24,390	8.1	0.436	34	16	29	1	Tanzania
051	5,950	6,700	3.8	13	40	47	0.762	2,506	4,167	2.2	0.760	7	3	10	29	Thailand
398	1,380	1,500	–0.5	42	21	37	0.493	2,329	13,158	6.0	0.475	60	26	14	6	Togo
142	7,690	9,500	2.0	2	44	54	0.805	2,777	1,269	1.1	0.798	8	5	1	64	Trinidad & Tobago
757	5,700	6,500	2.9	14	32	54	0.722	3,299	1,429	0.1	0.709	41	20	23	38	Tunisia
490	6,440	6,800	2.2	15	29	56	0.742	3,416	826	0.1	0.734	24	7	5	161	Turkey
205	3,340	4,300	–9.6	25	43	32	0.741	2,675	333	0.1	–	–	–	7	20	Turkmenistan
794	1,160	1,100	4.0	43	17	40	0.444	2,359	–	8.3	0.437	45	23	34	4	Uganda
991	3,360	3,850	–10.3	12	26	62	0.748	2,871	334	1.0	0.744	1	1	11	10	Ukraine
673	19,340	22,800	–1.6	3	52	45	0.812	3,192	552	0.2	0.798	22	26	2	615	United Arab Emirates
3,843	22,220	22,800	2.1	2	25	73	0.928	3,334	610	0.1	0.925	1	1	–75	622	United Kingdom
9,500	31,910	36,200	2.0	2	18	80	0.939	3,772	358	0.6	0.937	1	1	–36	987	USA
604	8,750	9,300	3.0	10	28	62	0.831	2,879	270	0.3	0.828	2	3	5	52	Uruguay
613	2,230	2,400	–3.1	28	21	51	0.727	2,371	324	0.1	0.725	16	7	7	8	Uzbekistan
313	5,420	6,200	–0.5	5	24	71	0.770	2,256	423	0.5	0.764	8	7	3	39	Venezuela
733	1,860	1,950	6.2	25	35	40	0.688	2,583	2,083	0.2	0.687	9	5	21	8	Vietnam
063	1,780	1,500	–0.2	9	28	63	–	–	–	–	–	–	–	–	–	West Bank (OPT)*
–	–	–	–	–	–	–	–	–	–	–	–	–	–	–	–	Western Sahara
088	730	820	–0.4	20	42	38	0.479	2,038	4,348	0.1	0.426	76	33	15	24	Yemen
–	–	2,300	–	20	50	30	–	2,570	–	0.1	–	–	–	–	71	Yugoslavia
222	720	880	–2.4	18	27	55	0.433	1,912	14,493	20.0	0.424	30	15	81	8	Zambia
302	2,690	2,500	0.6	28	32	40	0.551	2,117	7,194	25.1	0.545	16	8	16	10	Zimbabwe

ss National Income: this used
e referred to as GNP (Gross
onal Product) and is a good
ation of a country's wealth.
the income in US dollars from
ds and services in a country
ne year, including income from
seas.

PER CAPITA
GNI (see above) divided by the
population by using the PPP
od (see note).

PER CAPITA
ss Domestic Product using PPP
note) in US dollars per capita.
GDP is the value of all goods
services made in a country in
year, but unlike GNI (see above)
es not include income gained from
ad.

AVERAGE ANNUAL GROWTH IN GDP
The Gross Domestic Product growth or decline (decline shown as a negative [–] number) per capita, as an average over the ten years from 1990 to 1999.

AGRICULTURE, INDUSTRY AND SERVICES
The percentage contributions that each of these three sectors makes to a country's GDP (see note).

HDI, HUMAN DEVELOPMENT INDEX
Produced by the UN Development Programme using indicators of life expectancy, knowledge and standards of living to give a value between 0 and 1 for each country. A high value shows a higher human development.

FOOD INTAKE
The amount of food (measured in calories) supplied, divided by the total population. Belgium and Luxembourg are shown as one country.

ADULTS LIVING WITH HIV/AIDS
The percentage of all adults (aged 15–49) who have the Human Immunodeficiency Virus or the Acquired Immunodeficiency Syndrome. The total number of adults and children with HIV/AIDS in 2002 was 42 million.

POPULATION PER DOCTOR
The total population divided by the number of qualified doctors.

GDI, GENDER DEVELOPMENT INDEX
Like the HDI (see note), the GDI uses the same UNDP indicators but gives a value between 0 and 1 to measure the social and economic differences between men and woman. The higher the value, the more equality exists between men and women.

FEMALE/MALE ILLITERACY
The percentage of all adult women or men (over 15 years) who cannot read or write simple sentences.

AID DONATED AND RECEIVED
Aid defined here is Official Development Assistance (ODA) in US dollars per capita. The OECD Development Assistance Committee uses donations from donor countries and redistributes the money in the form of grants or loans to developing countries on their list of aid recipients. Donations are shown in the table with a negative (–) number. The money is given for economic development and welfare and not for military purposes.

MILITARY SPENDING
Government spending on the military or defence in US dollars divided by the total population.

Each topic list is divided into continents and within a continent the items are listed in order of size. The bottom part of many of the lists is selective in order to give examples from as many different countries as possible. The figures are rounded as appropriate.

World, Continents, Oceans

	km^2	miles^2	%
The World	509,450,000	196,672,000	–
Land	149,450,000	57,688,000	29.3
Water	360,000,000	138,984,000	70.7
Asia	44,500,000	17,177,000	29.8
Africa	30,302,000	11,697,000	20.3
North America	24,241,000	9,357,000	16.2
South America	17,793,000	6,868,000	11.9
Antarctica	14,100,000	5,443,000	9.4
Europe	9,957,000	3,843,000	6.7
Australia & Oceania	8,557,000	3,303,000	5.7
Pacific Ocean	179,679,000	69,356,000	49.9
Atlantic Ocean	92,373,000	35,657,000	25.7
Indian Ocean	73,917,000	28,532,000	20.5
Arctic Ocean	14,090,000	5,439,000	3.9

Ocean Depths

Atlantic Ocean	m	ft
Puerto Rico (Milwaukee) Deep	9,220	30,249
Cayman Trench	7,680	25,197
Gulf of Mexico	5,203	17,070
Mediterranean Sea	5,121	16,801
Black Sea	2,211	7,254
North Sea	660	2,165

Indian Ocean	m	ft
Java Trench	7,450	24,442
Red Sea	2,635	8,454

Pacific Ocean	m	ft
Mariana Trench	11,022	36,161
Tonga Trench	10,882	35,702
Japan Trench	10,554	34,626
Kuril Trench	10,542	34,587

Arctic Ocean	m	ft
Molloy Deep	5,608	18,399

Mountains

Europe		m	ft
Elbrus	Russia	5,642	18,510
Mont Blanc	France/Italy	4,807	15,771
Monte Rosa	Italy/Switzerland	4,634	15,203
Dom	Switzerland	4,545	14,911
Liskamm	Switzerland	4,527	14,852
Weisshorn	Switzerland	4,505	14,780
Taschorn	Switzerland	4,490	14,730
Matterhorn/Cervino	Italy/Switzerland	4,478	14,691
Mont Maudit	France/Italy	4,465	14,649
Dent Blanche	Switzerland	4,356	14,291
Nadelhorn	Switzerland	4,327	14,196
Grandes Jorasses	France/Italy	4,208	13,806
Jungfrau	Switzerland	4,158	13,642
Grossglockner	Austria	3,797	12,457
Mulhacén	Spain	3,478	11,411
Zugspitze	Germany	2,962	9,718
Olympus	Greece	2,917	9,570
Triglav	Slovenia	2,863	9,393
Gerlachovka	Slovak Republic	2,655	8,711
Galdhöpiggen	Norway	2,468	8,100
Kebnekaise	Sweden	2,117	6,946
Ben Nevis	UK	1,343	4,406

Asia		m	ft
Everest	China/Nepal	8,850	29,035
K2 (Godwin Austen)	China/Kashmir	8,611	28,251
Kanchenjunga	India/Nepal	8,598	28,208
Lhotse	China/Nepal	8,516	27,939
Makalu	China/Nepal	8,481	27,824
Cho Oyu	China/Nepal	8,201	26,906
Dhaulagiri	Nepal	8,172	26,811
Manaslu	Nepal	8,156	26,758
Nanga Parbat	Kashmir	8,126	26,660
Annapurna	Nepal	8,078	26,502
Gasherbrum	China/Kashmir	8,068	26,469
Broad Peak	China/Kashmir	8,051	26,414
Xixabangma	China	8,012	26,286
Kangbachen	India/Nepal	7,902	25,925
Trivor	Pakistan	7,720	25,328
Pik Kommunizma	Tajikistan	7,495	24,590
Demavend	Iran	5,604	18,386
Ararat	Turkey	5,165	16,945
Gunong Kinabalu	Malaysia (Borneo)	4,101	13,455
Fuji-San	Japan	3,776	12,388

Africa		m	ft
Kilimanjaro	Tanzania	5,895	19,340
Mt Kenya	Kenya	5,199	17,057
Ruwenzori	Uganda/Congo (D.R.)	5,109	16,762
Ras Dashan	Ethiopia	4,620	15,157
Meru	Tanzania	4,565	14,977
Karisimbi	Rwanda/Congo (D.R.)	4,507	14,787
Mt Elgon	Kenya/Uganda	4,321	14,176
Batu	Ethiopia	4,307	14,130
Toubkal	Morocco	4,165	13,665
Mt Cameroon	Cameroon	4,070	13,353

Oceania		m	ft
Puncak Jaya	Indonesia	5,030	16,503
Puncak Trikora	Indonesia	4,750	15,584
Puncak Mandala	Indonesia	4,702	15,427
Mt Wilhelm	Papua New Guinea	4,508	14,790
Mauna Kea	USA (Hawaii)	4,205	13,796
Mauna Loa	USA (Hawaii)	4,170	13,681
Mt Cook (Aoraki)	New Zealand	3,753	12,313
Mt Kosciuszko	Australia	2,237	7,339

North America		m	ft
Mt McKinley (Denali)	USA (Alaska)	6,194	20,321
Mt Logan	Canada	5,959	19,551
Pico de Orizaba	Mexico	5,610	18,405
Mt St Elias	USA/Canada	5,489	18,008
Popocatepetl	Mexico	5,452	17,887
Mt Foraker	USA (Alaska)	5,304	17,401
Ixtaccihuatl	Mexico	5,286	17,342
Lucania	Canada	5,227	17,149
Mt Steele	Canada	5,073	16,644
Mt Bona	USA (Alaska)	5,005	16,420
Mt Whitney	USA	4,418	14,495
Tajumulco	Guatemala	4,220	13,845
Chirripó Grande	Costa Rica	3,837	12,589
Pico Duarte	Dominican Rep.	3,175	10,417

South America		m	ft
Aconcagua	Argentina	6,962	22,841
Bonete	Argentina	6,872	22,546
Ojos del Salado	Argentina/Chile	6,863	22,516
Pissis	Argentina	6,779	22,241
Mercedario	Argentina/Chile	6,770	22,211
Huascaran	Peru	6,768	22,204
Llullaillaco	Argentina/Chile	6,723	22,057
Nudo de Cachi	Argentina	6,720	22,047
Yerupaja	Peru	6,632	21,758
Sajama	Bolivia	6,542	21,463
Chimborazo	Ecuador	6,267	20,561
Pico Colon	Colombia	5,800	19,029
Pico Bolivar	Venezuela	5,007	16,427

Antarctica		m	ft
Vinson Massif		4,897	16,066
Mt Kirkpatrick		4,528	14,855

Rivers

Europe		km	miles
Volga	Caspian Sea	3,700	2,300
Danube	Black Sea	2,850	1,770
Ural	Caspian Sea	2,535	1,575
Dnepr (Dnipro)	Black Sea	2,285	1,420
Kama	Volga	2,030	1,260
Don	Volga	1,990	1,240
Petchora	Arctic Ocean	1,790	1,110
Oka	Volga	1,480	920
Dnister (Dniester)	Black Sea	1,400	870
Vyatka	Kama	1,370	850
Rhine	North Sea	1,320	820
N. Dvina	Arctic Ocean	1,290	800
Elbe	North Sea	1,145	710

Asia		km	miles
Yangtze	Pacific Ocean	6,380	3,960
Yenisey–Angara	Arctic Ocean	5,550	3,445
Huang He	Pacific Ocean	5,464	3,395
Ob–Irtysh	Arctic Ocean	5,410	3,360
Mekong	Pacific Ocean	4,500	2,795
Amur	Pacific Ocean	4,400	2,730
Lena	Arctic Ocean	4,400	2,730
Irtysh	Ob	4,250	2,640
Yenisey	Arctic Ocean	4,090	2,540
Ob	Arctic Ocean	3,680	2,285
Indus	Indian Ocean	3,100	1,925
Brahmaputra	Indian Ocean	2,900	1,800
Syrdarya	Aral Sea	2,860	1,775
Salween	Indian Ocean	2,800	1,740
Euphrates	Indian Ocean	2,700	1,675
Amudarya	Aral Sea	2,540	1,575

Africa		km	miles
Nile	Mediterranean	6,670	4,140
Congo	Atlantic Ocean	4,670	2,900
Niger	Atlantic Ocean	4,180	2,595
Zambezi	Indian Ocean	3,540	2,200
Oubangi/Uele	Congo (Dem. Rep.)	2,250	1,400
Kasai	Congo (Dem. Rep.)	1,950	1,210
Shaballe	Indian Ocean	1,930	1,200
Orange	Atlantic Ocean	1,860	1,155
Cubango	Okavango Delta	1,800	1,120
Limpopo	Indian Ocean	1,600	995
Senegal	Atlantic Ocean	1,600	995

Australia		km	miles
Murray–Darling	Indian Ocean	3,750	2,330
Darling	Murray	3,070	1,905
Murray	Indian Ocean	2,575	1,600
Murrumbidgee	Murray	1,690	1,050

North America		km	miles
Mississippi–Missouri	Gulf of Mexico	6,020	3,740
Mackenzie	Arctic Ocean	4,240	2,630
Mississippi	Gulf of Mexico	3,780	2,350
Missouri	Mississippi	3,780	2,350
Yukon	Pacific Ocean	3,185	1,980
Rio Grande	Gulf of Mexico	3,030	1,880
Arkansas	Mississippi	2,340	1,450
Colorado	Pacific Ocean	2,330	1,445
Red	Mississippi	2,040	1,270
Columbia	Pacific Ocean	1,950	1,210
Saskatchewan	Lake Winnipeg	1,940	1,205

South America		km	miles
Amazon	Atlantic Ocean	6,450	4,010
Paraná–Plate	Atlantic Ocean	4,500	2,800
Purus	Amazon	3,350	2,080
Madeira	Amazon	3,200	1,990
São Francisco	Atlantic Ocean	2,900	1,800
Paraná	Plate	2,800	1,740
Tocantins	Atlantic Ocean	2,750	1,710
Paraguay	Paraná	2,550	1,580
Orinoco	Atlantic Ocean	2,500	1,550
Pilcomayo	Paraná	2,500	1,550
Araguaia	Tocantins	2,250	1,400

Lakes

Europe		km^2	miles^2
Lake Ladoga	Russia	17,700	6,800
Lake Onega	Russia	9,700	3,700
Saimaa system	Finland	8,000	3,100
Vänern	Sweden	5,500	2,100

Asia		km^2	miles^2
Caspian Sea	Asia	371,800	143,550
Lake Baykal	Russia	30,500	11,780
Aral Sea	Kazakhstan/Uzbekistan	28,687	11,086
Tonlé Sap	Cambodia	20,000	7,700
Lake Balqash	Kazakhstan	18,500	7,100

Africa		km^2	miles^2
Lake Victoria	East Africa	68,000	26,000
Lake Tanganyika	Central Africa	33,000	13,000
Lake Malawi/Nyasa	East Africa	29,600	11,430
Lake Chad	Central Africa	25,000	9,700
Lake Turkana	Ethiopia/Kenya	8,500	3,300
Lake Volta	Ghana	8,500	3,300

Australia		km^2	miles^2
Lake Eyre	Australia	8,900	3,400
Lake Torrens	Australia	5,800	2,200
Lake Gairdner	Australia	4,800	1,900

North America		km^2	miles^2
Lake Superior	Canada/USA	82,350	31,800
Lake Huron	Canada/USA	59,600	23,010
Lake Michigan	USA	58,000	22,400
Great Bear Lake	Canada	31,800	12,280
Great Slave Lake	Canada	28,500	11,000
Lake Erie	Canada/USA	25,700	9,900
Lake Winnipeg	Canada	24,400	9,400
Lake Ontario	Canada/USA	19,500	7,500
Lake Nicaragua	Nicaragua	8,200	3,200

South America		km^2	miles^2
Lake Titicaca	Bolivia/Peru	8,300	3,200
Lake Poopo	Peru	2,800	1,100

Islands

Europe		km^2	miles^2
Great Britain	UK	229,880	88,700
Iceland	Atlantic Ocean	103,000	39,800
Ireland	Ireland/UK	84,400	32,600
Novaya Zemlya (N.)	Russia	48,200	18,600
Sicily	Italy	25,500	9,800
Corsica	France	8,700	3,400

Asia		km^2	miles^2
Borneo	South-east Asia	744,360	287,400
Sumatra	Indonesia	473,600	182,860
Honshu	Japan	230,500	88,980
Celebes	Indonesia	189,000	73,000
Java	Indonesia	126,700	48,900
Luzon	Philippines	104,700	40,400
Hokkaido	Japan	78,400	30,300

Africa		km^2	miles^2
Madagascar	Indian Ocean	587,040	226,660
Socotra	Indian Ocean	3,600	1,400
Réunion	Indian Ocean	2,500	965

Oceania		km^2	miles^2
New Guinea	Indonesia/Papua NG	821,030	317,000
New Zealand (S.)	Pacific Ocean	150,500	58,100
New Zealand (N.)	Pacific Ocean	114,700	44,300
Tasmania	Australia	67,800	26,200
Hawaii	Pacific Ocean	10,450	4,000

North America		km^2	miles^2
Greenland	Atlantic Ocean	2,175,600	839,800
Baffin Is.	Canada	508,000	196,100
Victoria Is.	Canada	212,200	81,900
Ellesmere Is.	Canada	212,000	81,800
Cuba	Caribbean Sea	110,860	42,800
Hispaniola	Dominican Rep./Haiti	76,200	29,400
Jamaica	Caribbean Sea	11,400	4,400
Puerto Rico	Atlantic Ocean	8,900	3,400

South America		km^2	miles^2
Tierra del Fuego	Argentina/Chile	47,000	18,100
Falkland Is. (E.)	Atlantic Ocean	6,800	2,600

How to use the Index

The index contains the names of all the principal places and features shown on the maps. Each name is followed by an additional entry in italics giving the country or region within which it is located. The alphabetical order of names composed of two or more words is governed primarily by the first word and then by the second. This is an example of the rule:

Abbeville, *France*	**68 A4**	50 6N	1 49 E
Abbey Town, *U.K.*	**22 C2**	54 51N	3 17W
Abbots Bromley, *U.K.*	**23 G5**	52 50N	1 52W
Abbotsbury, *U.K.*	**24 E3**	50 40N	2 37W

Physical features composed of a proper name (Erie) and a description (Lake) are positioned alphabetically by the proper name. The description is positioned after the proper name and is usually abbreviated:

Erie, L., *N. Amer.* **112 D7** 42 15N 81 0W

Where a description forms part of a settlement or administrative name, however, it is always written in full and put in its true alphabetic position:

Mount Isa, *Australia* .... **98 E6** 20 42S 139 26 E

Names beginning with M' and Mc are indexed as if they were spelled Mac. Names beginning St. are alphabetized under Saint, but Santa and San are spelt in full and are alphabetized accordingly. If the same place name occurs two or more times in the index and all are in the same country, each is followed by the name of the administrative subdivision in which it is located.

The number in bold type which follows each name in the index refers to the number of the map page where that feature or place will be found. This is usually the largest scale at which the place or feature appears.

The letter and figure which are in bold type immediately after the page number give the grid square on the map page, within which the feature is situated. The letter represents the latitude and the figure the longitude. A lower case letter immediately after the page number refers to an inset map on that page.

In some cases the feature itself may fall within the specified square, while the name is outside. This is usually the case only with features which are larger than a grid square.

The geographical co-ordinates which follow the letter-figure references give the latitude and longitude of each place. The first co-ordinate indicates latitude – the distance north or south of the Equator. The second co-ordinate indicates longitude – the distance east or west of the Greenwich Meridian. Both latitude and longitude are measured in degrees and minutes (there are 60 minutes in a degree).

The latitude is followed by N(orth) or S(outh) and the longitude by E(ast) or W(est).

Rivers are indexed to their mouths or confluences, and carry the symbol → after their names. The following symbols are also used in the index: ■ country, ▨ overseas territory or dependency, □ first order administrative area, △ national park.

Abbreviations used in the Index

Afghan. – Afghanistan
Ala. – Alabama
Alta. – Alberta
Amer. – America(n)
Arch. – Archipelago
Ariz. – Arizona
Ark. – Arkansas
Atl. Oc. – Atlantic Ocean
B. – Baie, Bahía, Bay, Bucht, Bugt
B.C. – British Columbia
Bangla. – Bangladesh
C. – Cabo, Cap, Cape, Coast
C.A.R. – Central African Republic
Calif. – California
Cent. – Central
Chan. – Channel
Colo. – Colorado
Conn. – Connecticut
Cord. – Cordillera
Cr. – Creek
D.C. – District of Columbia
Del. – Delaware
Domin. – Dominica
Dom. Rep. – Dominican Republic
E. – East
El Salv. – El Salvador
Eq. Guin. – Equatorial Guinea
Fla. – Florida
Falk. Is. – Falkland Is.
G. – Golfe, Golfo, Gulf
Ga. – Georgia
Hd. – Head
Hts. – Heights
I.(s). – Île, Ilha, Insel, Isla, Island, Isle(s)
Ill. – Illinois
Ind. – Indiana
Ind. Oc. – Indian Ocean
Ivory C. – Ivory Coast
Kans. – Kansas
Ky. – Kentucky
L. – Lac, Lacul, Lago, Lagoa, Lake, Limni, Loch, Lough
La. – Louisiana
Lux. – Luxembourg
Madag. – Madagascar
Man. – Manitoba
Mass. – Massachusetts
Md. – Maryland
Me. – Maine
Mich. – Michigan
Minn. – Minnesota
Miss. – Mississippi
Mo. – Missouri
Mont. – Montana
Mozam. – Mozambique
Mt.(s) – Mont, Monte, Monti, Montaña, Mountain
N. – Nord, Norte, North, Northern,
N.B. – New Brunswick
N.C. – North Carolina
N. Cal. – New Caledonia
N. Dak. – North Dakota
N.H. – New Hampshire
N.J. – New Jersey
N. Mex. – New Mexico
N.S. – Nova Scotia
N.S.W. – New South Wales
N.W.T. – North West Territory
N.Y. – New York
N.Z. – New Zealand
Nebr. – Nebraska
Neths. – Netherlands
Nev. – Nevada
Nfld. – Newfoundland
Nic. – Nicaragua
Okla. – Oklahoma
Ont. – Ontario
Oreg. – Oregon
P.E.I. – Prince Edward Island
Pa. – Pennsylvania
Pac. Oc. – Pacific Ocean
Pen. – Peninsula, Péninsule
Phil. – Philippines
Pk. – Peak
Plat. – Plateau
Prov. – Province, Provincial
Pt. – Point
Pta. – Ponta, Punta
Pte. – Pointe
Qué. – Québec
Queens. – Queensland
R. – Rio, River
R.I. – Rhode Island
Ra.(s) – Range(s)
Reg. – Region
Rep. – Republic
Res. – Reserve, Reservoir
S. – San, South
Si. Arabia – Saudi Arabia
S.C. – South Carolina
S. Dak. – South Dakota
Sa. – Serra, Sierra
Sask. – Saskatchewan
Scot. – Scotland
Sd. – Sound
Sib. – Siberia
St. – Saint, Sankt, Sint
Str. – Strait, Stretto
Switz. – Switzerland
Tas. – Tasmania
Tenn. – Tennessee
Tex. – Texas
U.A.E. – United Arab Emirates
U.K. – United Kingdom
U.S.A. – United States of America
Va. – Virginia
Vic. – Victoria
Vol. – Volcano
Vt. – Vermont
W. – West
W. Va. – West Virginia
Wash. – Washington
Wis. – Wisconsin

A

Aachen, *Germany* **66 C4** 50 45N 6 6 E
Aalst, *Belgium* **65 D4** 50 56N 4 2 E
Aarau, *Switz.* **66 E5** 47 23N 8 4 E
Aare →, *Switz.* **66 E5** 47 33N 8 14 E
Aba, *Nigeria* **94 G7** 5 10N 7 19 E
Ābādān, *Iran* **86 D7** 30 22N 48 20 E
Abakan, *Russia* **79 D11** 53 40N 91 10 E
Abancay, *Peru* **120 D2** 13 35S 72 55W
Abariringa, *Kiribati* **99 A16** 2 50S 171 40W
Abaya, L., *Ethiopia* **88 F2** 6 30N 37 50 E
Abbé, L., *Ethiopia* **88 E3** 11 8N 41 47 E
Abbeville, *France* **68 A4** 50 6N 1 49 E
Abbey Town, *U.K.* **22 C2** 54 51N 3 17W
Abbots Bromley, *U.K.* **23 G5** 52 50N 1 52W
Abbotsbury, *U.K.* **24 E3** 50 40N 2 37W
Abéché, *Chad* **95 F10** 13 50N 20 35 E
Abeokuta, *Nigeria* **94 G6** 7 3N 3 19 E
Aberaeron, *U.K.* **26 C5** 52 15N 4 15W
Aberchirder, *U.K.* **19 G12** 57 34N 2 37W
Aberdare, *U.K.* **24 C2** 51 43N 3 27W
Aberdeen, *U.K.* **19 H13** 57 9N 2 5W
Aberdeen, *S. Dak., U.S.A.* **110 A7** 45 28N 98 29W
Aberdeen, *Wash., U.S.A.* **110 A2** 46 59N 123 50W
Aberdyfi, *U.K.* **26 B5** 52 33N 4 3W
Aberfeldy, *U.K.* **19 J10** 56 37N 3 51W
Aberfoyle, *U.K.* **20 B7** 56 11N 4 23W
Abergavenny, *U.K.* **24 C2** 51 49N 3 1W
Abergele, *U.K.* **26 A6** 53 17N 3 35W
Aberporth, *U.K.* **26 C4** 52 8N 4 33W
Abersoch, *U.K.* **26 B5** 52 49N 4 30W
Abersychan, *U.K.* **24 C2** 51 44N 3 3W
Abert, L., *U.S.A.* **110 B2** 42 38N 120 14W
Abertillery, *U.K.* **24 C2** 51 44N 3 8W
Aberystwyth, *U.K.* **26 C5** 52 25N 4 5W
Abhā, *Si. Arabia* **88 D3** 18 0N 42 34 E
Abidjan, *Ivory C.* **94 G5** 5 26N 3 58W
Abilene, *U.S.A.* **110 D7** 32 28N 99 43W
Abingdon, *U.K.* **24 C6** 51 40N 1 17W
Abitibi, L., *Canada* **109 D12** 48 40N 79 40W
Abkhazia □, *Georgia* **73 F7** 43 12N 41 5 E
Abomey, *Benin* **94 G6** 7 10N 2 5 E
Aboyne, *U.K.* **19 H12** 57 4N 2 47W
Absaroka Range, *U.S.A.* **110 B5** 44 45N 109 50W
Abu Dhabi, *U.A.E.* **87 E8** 24 28N 54 22 E
Abu Hamed, *Sudan* **95 E12** 19 32N 33 13 E
Abuja, *Nigeria* **94 G7** 9 5N 7 32 E
Abunã, *Brazil* **120 C3** 9 40S 65 20W
Abunã →, *Brazil* **120 C3** 9 41S 65 20W
Acaponeta, *Mexico* **114 C3** 22 30N 105 20W
Acapulco, *Mexico* **114 D5** 16 51N 99 56W
Acarai, Serra, *Brazil* **120 B4** 1 50N 57 50W
Accomac, *U.S.A.* **113 G10** 37 43N 75 40W
Accra, *Ghana* **94 G5** 5 35N 0 6W
Accrington, *U.K.* **23 E4** 53 45N 2 22W
Aceh □, *Indonesia* **83 C1** 4 15N 97 30 E
Achill Hd., *Ireland* **28 D1** 53 58N 10 15W
Achill I., *Ireland* **28 D1** 53 58N 10 1W
Acklins I., *Bahamas* **115 C10** 22 30N 74 0W
Acle, *U.K.* **25 A12** 52 39N 1 33 E
Aconcagua, Cerro, *Argentina* **121 F3** 32 39S 70 0W
Acre □, *Brazil* **120 C2** 9 1S 71 0W
Acre →, *Brazil* **120 C3** 8 45S 67 22W
Acton Burnell, *U.K.* **23 G3** 52 37N 2 41W
Ad Dammām, *Si. Arabia* **86 E7** 26 20N 50 5 E
Ad Dīwānīyah, *Iraq* **86 D6** 32 0N 45 0 E
Adair, C., *Canada* **109 A12** 71 30N 71 34W
Adak I., *U.S.A.* **108 C2** 51 45N 176 45W
Adamawa Highlands, *Cameroon* **95 G7** 7 20N 12 20 E
Adam's Bridge, *Sri Lanka* **84 Q11** 9 15N 79 40 E
Adana, *Turkey* **73 G6** 37 0N 35 16 E
Adare, C., *Antarctica* **55 D11** 71 0S 171 0 E
Addis Ababa, *Ethiopia* **88 F2** 9 2N 38 42 E
Adelaide, *Australia* **98 G6** 34 52S 138 30 E
Adelaide I., *Antarctica* **55 C17** 67 15S 68 30W
Adelaide Pen., *Canada* **108 B10** 68 15N 97 30W
Adélie Land, *Antarctica* **55 C10** 68 0S 140 0 E
Aden, *Yemen* **88 E4** 12 45N 45 0 E
Aden, G. of, *Asia* **88 E4** 12 30N 47 30 E
Adigrat, *Ethiopia* **88 E2** 14 20N 39 26 E
Adirondack Mts., *U.S.A.* **113 D10** 44 0N 74 0W
Adjuntas, *Puerto Rico* **115 d** 18 10N 66 43W
Admiralty Is., *Papua N. G.* **102 H6** 2 0S 147 0 E
Adour →, *France* **68 E3** 43 32N 1 32W
Adrar, *Mauritania* **94 D3** 20 30N 7 30 E
Adrar des Iforas, *Algeria* **94 C5** 27 51N 0 11 E
Adrian, *U.S.A.* **112 E5** 41 54N 84 2W
Adriatic Sea, *Medit. S.* **70 C6** 43 0N 16 0 E
Adwick le Street, *U.K.* **23 E6** 53 34N 1 10W
Adygea □, *Russia* **73 F7** 45 0N 40 0 E
Ægean Sea, *Medit. S.* **71 E11** 38 30N 25 0 E
Aerhtai Shan, *Mongolia* **79 E10** 46 40N 92 45 E
Afghanistan ■, *Asia* **84 C4** 33 0N 65 0 E
Africa **90 E6** 10 0N 20 0 E
Afyon, *Turkey* **73 G5** 38 45N 30 33 E
Agadez, *Niger* **94 E7** 16 58N 7 59 E
Agadir, *Morocco* **94 B4** 30 28N 9 55W
Agartala, *India* **85 H17** 23 50N 91 23 E
Agen, *France* **68 D4** 44 12N 0 38 E
Agra, *India* **84 F10** 27 17N 77 58 E
Ağri, *Turkey* **73 G7** 39 44N 43 3 E
Agrigento, *Italy* **70 F5** 37 19N 13 34 E
Agua Prieta, *Mexico* **114 A3** 31 20N 109 32W
Aguadilla, *Puerto Rico* **115 d** 18 26N 67 10W
Aguascalientes, *Mexico* **114 C4** 21 53N 102 12W
Aguila, Punta, *Puerto Rico* **115 d** 17 57N 67 13W
Aguja, C. de la, *Colombia* **116 B3** 11 18N 74 12W
Agujereada, Pta., *Puerto Rico* **115 d** 18 30N 67 8W
Agulhas, C., *S. Africa* **97 L4** 34 52S 20 0 E
Ahmadabad, *India* **84 H8** 23 0N 72 40 E
Ahmadnagar, *India* **84 K9** 19 7N 74 46 E
Ahmadpur, *Pakistan* **84 E7** 29 12N 71 10 E
Ahvāz, *Iran* **86 D7** 31 20N 48 40 E
Ahvenanmaa, *Finland* **63 E8** 60 15N 20 0 E
Aihui, *China* **81 A7** 50 10N 127 30 E
Ailsa Craig, *U.K.* **20 D5** 55 15N 5 6W
Ainsdale, *U.K.* **23 E2** 53 37N 3 2W
Aïr, *Niger* **94 E7** 18 30N 8 0 E
Air Force I., *Canada* **109 B12** 67 58N 74 5W
Airdrie, *Canada* **108 C8** 51 18N 114 2W
Airdrie, *U.K.* **21 C8** 55 52N 3 57W
Aire →, *U.K.* **23 E7** 53 43N 0 55W
Aisgill, *U.K.* **22 D4** 54 23N 2 21W
Aisne →, *France* **68 B5** 49 26N 2 50 E
Aix-en-Provence, *France* **68 E6** 43 32N 5 27 E
Aix-les-Bains, *France* **68 D6** 45 41N 5 53 E
Aizawl, *India* **85 H18** 23 40N 92 44 E
Aizuwakamatsu, *Japan* **82 E6** 37 30N 139 56 E
Ajaccio, *France* **68 F8** 41 55N 8 40 E
Ajaria □, *Georgia* **73 F7** 41 30N 42 0 E
Ajdābiyā, *Libya* **95 B10** 30 54N 20 4 E
'Ajmān, *U.A.E.* **87 E8** 25 25N 55 30 E
Ajmer, *India* **84 F9** 26 28N 74 37 E
Akhisar, *Turkey* **73 G4** 38 56N 27 48 E
Akimiski I., *Canada* **109 C11** 52 50N 81 30W
Akita, *Japan* **82 D7** 39 45N 140 7 E
'Akko, *Israel* **86 C3** 32 55N 35 4 E
Aklavik, *Canada* **108 B6** 68 12N 135 0W
Akola, *India* **84 J10** 20 42N 77 2 E
Akpatok I., *Canada* **109 B13** 60 25N 68 8W
Akranes, *Iceland* **63 B1** 64 19N 22 5W
Akron, *U.S.A.* **112 E7** 41 5N 81 31W
Aksai Chin, *China* **84 B11** 35 15N 79 55 E
Aksaray, *Turkey* **73 G5** 38 25N 34 2 E
Akşehir Gölü, *Turkey* **73 G5** 38 30N 31 25 E
Aksu, *China* **80 B3** 41 5N 80 10 E
Aksum, *Ethiopia* **88 E2** 14 5N 38 40 E
Akure, *Nigeria* **94 G7** 7 15N 5 5 E
Akureyri, *Iceland* **63 A2** 65 40N 18 6W
Al 'Aqabah, *Jordan* **86 D3** 29 31N 35 0 E
Al 'Aramah, *Si. Arabia* **86 E6** 25 30N 46 0 E
Al 'Ayn, *U.A.E.* **87 E8** 24 15N 55 45 E
Al Fāw, *Iraq* **86 D7** 30 0N 48 30 E
Al Ḥillah, *Iraq* **86 C6** 32 30N 44 25 E
Al Hoceïma, *Morocco* **94 A5** 35 8N 3 58W
Al Ḥudaydah, *Yemen* **88 E3** 14 50N 43 0 E
Al Hufūf, *Si. Arabia* **86 E7** 25 25N 49 45 E
Al Jawf, *Libya* **95 D10** 24 10N 23 24 E
Al Jawf, *Si. Arabia* **86 D4** 29 55N 39 40 E
Al Khalīl, *West Bank* **86 D3** 31 32N 35 6 E
Al Khums, *Libya* **95 B8** 32 40N 14 17 E
Al Kufrah, *Libya* **90 D6** 24 17N 23 15 E
Al Kūt, *Iraq* **86 C6** 32 30N 46 0 E
Al Manāmah, *Bahrain* **87 E7** 26 10N 50 30 E
Al Mubarraz, *Si. Arabia* **86 E7** 25 30N 49 40 E
Al Mukallā, *Yemen* **88 E4** 14 33N 49 2 E
Al Musayyib, *Iraq* **86 C6** 32 49N 44 20 E
Al Qāmishlī, *Syria* **86 B5** 37 2N 41 14 E
Al Qaţīf, *Si. Arabia* **86 E7** 26 35N 50 0 E
Alabama □, *U.S.A.* **111 D9** 33 0N 87 0W
Alabama →, *U.S.A.* **111 D9** 31 8N 87 57W
Alagoas □, *Brazil* **122 A3** 9 0S 36 0W
Alagoinhas, *Brazil* **122 B3** 12 7S 38 20W
Alai Range, *Asia* **87 B13** 39 45N 72 0 E
Alamogordo, *U.S.A.* **110 D5** 32 54N 105 57W
Alamosa, *U.S.A.* **110 C5** 37 28N 105 52W
Aland Is. = Ahvenanmaa, *Finland* **63 E8** 60 15N 20 0 E
Alanya, *Turkey* **73 G5** 36 38N 32 0 E
Alaşehir, *Turkey* **73 G4** 38 23N 28 30 E
Alaska □, *U.S.A.* **108 B5** 64 0N 154 0W
Alaska, G. of, *Pac. Oc.* **108 C5** 58 0N 145 0W
Alaska Peninsula, *U.S.A.* **108 C4** 56 0N 159 0W
Alaska Range, *U.S.A.* **108 B4** 62 50N 151 0W
Alba-Iulia, *Romania* **67 E12** 46 8N 23 39 E
Albacete, *Spain* **69 C5** 39 0N 1 50W
Albanel, L., *Canada* **109 C12** 50 55N 73 12W
Albania ■, *Europe* **71 D9** 41 0N 20 0 E
Albany, *Australia* **98 H2** 35 1S 117 58 E
Albany, *Ga., U.S.A.* **111 D10** 31 35N 84 10W
Albany, *N.Y., U.S.A.* **113 D11** 42 39N 73 45W
Albany, *Oreg., U.S.A.* **110 B2** 44 38N 123 6W
Albany →, *Canada* **109 C11** 52 17N 81 31W
Albemarle Sd., *U.S.A.* **111 C11** 36 5N 76 0W
Albert, L., *Africa* **96 D6** 1 30N 31 0 E
Albert Lea, *U.S.A.* **111 B8** 43 39N 93 22W
Albert Nile →, *Uganda* **96 D6** 3 36N 32 2 E
Alberta □, *Canada* **108 C8** 54 40N 115 0W
Albertville, *France* **68 D7** 45 40N 6 22 E
Albi, *France* **68 E5** 43 56N 2 9 E
Albion, *U.S.A.* **112 D5** 42 15N 84 45W
Ålborg, *Denmark* **63 F5** 57 2N 9 54 E
Albrighton, *U.K.* **23 G4** 52 38N 2 16W
Albuquerque, *U.S.A.* **110 C5** 35 5N 106 39W
Albury-Wodonga, *Australia* **98 H8** 36 3S 146 56 E
Alcalá de Henares, *Spain* **69 B4** 40 28N 3 22W
Alcester, *U.K.* **23 H5** 52 14N 1 52W
Alchevsk, *Ukraine* **73 E6** 48 30N 38 45 E
Aldabra Is., *Seychelles* **91 G8** 9 22S 46 28 E
Aldan →, *Russia* **79 C14** 63 28N 129 35 E
Aldborough, *U.K.* **22 D6** 54 5N 1 22W
Aldbourne, *U.K.* **24 D5** 51 29N 1 37W

Aldbrough   **Bacău**

Back   **Bienville, L.**

Big Belt Mts.   **Burns**

Burnside   **Cheviot Hills**

Chew Bahir   **Culm**

Culpeper, *U.S.A.* **112 F9** 38 30N 78 0W
Cumaná, *Venezuela* **120 A3** 10 30N 64 5W
Cumberland, *U.S.A.* **112 F8** 39 39N 78 46W
Cumberland →, *U.S.A.* **111 C9** 36 15N 87 0W
Cumberland Pen., *Canada* **109 B13** 67 0N 64 0W
Cumberland Plateau, *U.S.A.* **111 C10** 36 0N 85 0W
Cumberland Sd., *Canada* **109 B13** 65 30N 66 0W
Cumbernauld, *U.K.* **21 C8** 55 57N 3 58W
Cumbria □, *U.K.* **22 C3** 54 42N 2 52W
Cumbrian Mts., *U.K.* **22 D2** 54 30N 3 0W
Cummertrees, *U.K.* **22 C2** 54 59N 3 20W
Cumnock, *U.K.* **20 D7** 55 28N 4 17W
Cumnor, *U.K.* **24 C6** 51 44N 1 19W
Cumwhinton, *U.K.* **22 C3** 54 52N 2 50W
Cunene →, *Angola* **97 H2** 17 20S 11 50 E
Cúneo, *Italy* **68 D7** 44 23N 7 32 E
Cunnamulla, *Australia* **98 F8** 28 2S 145 38 E
Cupar, *U.K.* **21 B9** 56 19N 3 1W
Curaçao, *Neth. Ant.* **115 E11** 12 10N 69 0W
Curicó, *Chile* **121 F2** 34 55S 71 20W
Curitiba, *Brazil* **122 E1** 25 20S 49 10W
Curry Rivel, *U.K.* **24 D3** 51 1N 2 52W
Curvelo, *Brazil* **122 C2** 18 45S 44 27W
Cuttack, *India* **85 J14** 20 25N 85 57 E
Cuxhaven, *Germany* **66 B5** 53 51N 8 41 E
Cuyahoga Falls, *U.S.A.* **112 E7** 41 8N 81 29W
Cuyuni →, *Guyana* **120 B4** 6 23N 58 41W
Cuzco, *Peru* **120 D2** 13 32S 72 0W
Cwmbran, *U.K.* **24 C2** 51 39N 3 2W
Cyclades, *Greece* **71 F11** 37 0N 24 30 E
Cynthiana, *U.S.A.* **112 F5** 38 23N 84 18W
Cyprus ■, *Asia* **86 C3** 35 0N 33 0 E
Cyrenaica, *Libya* **95 C10** 27 0N 23 0 E
Czech Rep. ■, *Europe* **66 D8** 50 0N 15 0 E
Częstochowa, *Poland* **67 C10** 50 49N 19 7 E

D

Da Hinggan Ling, *China* **81 B7** 48 0N 121 0 E
Da Lat, *Vietnam* **83 B2** 11 56N 108 25 E
Da Nang, *Vietnam* **83 B2** 16 4N 108 13 E
Da Qaidam, *China* **80 C4** 37 50N 95 15 E
Daba Shan, *China* **81 C5** 32 0N 109 0 E
Dadra & Nagar Haveli □, *India* **84 J8** 20 5N 73 0 E
Dadu, *Pakistan* **84 F5** 26 45N 67 45 E
Dagestan □, *Russia* **73 F8** 42 30N 47 0 E
Dagupan, *Phil.* **83 B4** 16 3N 120 20 E
Dahod, *India* **84 H9** 22 50N 74 15 E
Daingean, *Ireland* **28 E7** 53 18N 7 17W
Dajarra, *Australia* **98 E6** 21 42S 139 30 E
Dakar, *Senegal* **94 F2** 14 34N 17 29W
Dakhla, *W. Sahara* **94 D2** 23 50N 15 53W
Dalandzadgad, *Mongolia* **80 B5** 43 27N 104 30 E
Dalap-Uliga-Darrit, *Marshall Is.* **102 G9** 7 7N 171 24 E
Dalbeattie, *U.K.* **21 E8** 54 56N 3 50W
Dalhart, *U.S.A.* **110 C6** 36 4N 102 31W
Dalhousie, *Canada* **113 A14** 48 5N 66 26W
Dali, *China* **80 D5** 25 40N 100 10 E
Dalian, *China* **81 C7** 38 50N 121 40 E
Daliang Shan, *China* **80 D5** 28 0N 102 45 E
Dalkeith, *U.K.* **21 C9** 55 54N 3 4W
Dallas, *U.S.A.* **111 D7** 32 47N 96 49W
Dalmatia, *Croatia* **70 C7** 43 20N 17 0 E
Dalmellington, *U.K.* **20 D7** 55 19N 4 23W
Daloa, *Ivory C.* **94 G4** 7 0N 6 30W
Dalry, *U.K.* **20 C6** 55 42N 4 43W
Dalton, *Dumf. & Gall., U.K.* **22 B2** 55 4N 3 24W
Dalton, *N. Yorks., U.K.* **22 D5** 54 28N 1 32W
Dalton-in-Furness, *U.K.* **22 D2** 54 10N 3 11W
Daly Waters, *Australia* **98 D5** 16 15S 133 24 E
Daman, *India* **84 J8** 20 25N 72 57 E
Damaraland, *Namibia* **97 H2** 20 0S 15 0 E
Damascus, *Syria* **86 C4** 33 30N 36 18 E
Damerham, *U.K.* **24 E5** 50 56N 1 51W
Dampier, *Australia* **98 E2** 20 41S 116 42 E
Danakil Desert, *Ethiopia* **88 E3** 12 45N 41 0 E
Danbury, *U.S.A.* **113 E11** 41 24N 73 28W
Dandong, *China* **81 B7** 40 10N 124 20 E
Danube →, *Europe* **67 F15** 45 20N 29 40 E
Danville, *Ill., U.S.A.* **112 E4** 40 8N 87 37W
Danville, *Ky., U.S.A.* **112 G5** 37 39N 84 46W
Danville, *Va., U.S.A.* **111 C11** 36 36N 79 23W
Dar Banda, *Africa* **90 F6** 8 0N 23 0 E
Dar es Salaam, *Tanzania* **96 F7** 6 50S 39 12 E
Darbhanga, *India* **85 F14** 26 15N 85 55 E
Dardanelles, *Turkey* **71 D12** 40 17N 26 32 E
Darent →, *U.K.* **25 D9** 51 28N 0 14 E
Dârfûr, *Sudan* **95 F10** 13 40N 24 0 E
Darién, G. del, *Colombia* **120 B2** 9 0N 77 0W
Darjiling, *India* **85 F16** 27 3N 88 18 E
Darling →, *Australia* **98 G7** 34 4S 141 54 E
Darling Ra., *Australia* **98 G2** 32 30S 116 0 E
Darlington, *U.K.* **22 C5** 54 32N 1 33W
Darmstadt, *Germany* **66 D5** 49 51N 8 39 E
Darnah, *Libya* **95 B10** 32 45N 22 45 E
Darnley, C., *Antarctica* **55 C6** 68 0S 69 0 E
Darnley B., *Canada* **108 B7** 69 30N 123 30W
Dart →, *U.K.* **27 G6** 50 24N 3 39W
Dartford, *U.K.* **25 D9** 51 26N 0 13 E
Dartington, *U.K.* **27 G6** 50 27N 3 43W
Dartmoor, *U.K.* **27 F6** 50 38N 3 57W
Dartmouth, *Canada* **109 D13** 44 40N 63 30W
Dartmouth, *U.K.* **27 G6** 50 21N 3 36W
Darton, *U.K.* **23 E5** 53 35N 1 31W
Darwen, *U.K.* **23 E4** 53 42N 2 29W
Darwin, *Australia* **98 C5** 12 25S 130 51 E
Dashen, Ras, *Ethiopia* **88 E2** 13 8N 38 26 E
Dashhowuz, *Turkmenistan* **87 A9** 41 49N 59 58 E
Dasht →, *Pakistan* **84 G2** 25 10N 61 40 E
Datong, *China* **81 B6** 40 6N 113 18 E
Daugavpils, *Latvia* **72 C4** 55 53N 26 32 E
Dauphin, *Canada* **108 C9** 51 9N 100 5W
Dauphiné, *France* **68 D6** 45 15N 5 25 E
Davangere, *India* **84 M9** 14 25N 75 55 E
Davao, *Phil.* **83 C4** 7 0N 125 40 E
Davenport, *U.S.A.* **111 B8** 41 32N 90 35W
Daventry, *U.K.* **23 H6** 52 16N 1 10W
Davis Str., *N. Amer.* **109 B14** 65 0N 58 0W
Dawlish, *U.K.* **27 F7** 50 35N 3 28W
Dawna Ra., *Burma* **85 L21** 16 30N 98 30 E
Dawros Hd., *Ireland* **28 B4** 54 50N 8 33W
Dawson, *Canada* **108 B6** 64 10N 139 30W
Dawson Creek, *Canada* **108 C7** 55 45N 120 15W
Dax, *France* **68 E3** 43 44N 1 3W
Daxian, *China* **80 C5** 31 15N 107 23 E
Daxue Shan, *China* **80 C5** 30 30N 101 30 E
Dayr az Zawr, *Syria* **86 C5** 35 20N 40 5 E
Dayton, *U.S.A.* **112 F5** 39 45N 84 12W
Daytona Beach, *U.S.A.* **111 E10** 29 13N 81 1W
De Aar, *S. Africa* **97 L4** 30 39S 24 0 E
De Pere, *U.S.A.* **112 C3** 44 27N 88 4W
De Ridder, *U.S.A.* **111 D8** 30 51N 93 17W
Dead Sea, *Asia* **86 D3** 31 30N 35 30 E
Deal, *U.K.* **25 D11** 51 13N 1 25 E
Dean, Forest of, *U.K.* **24 C3** 51 45N 2 33W
Dearham, *U.K.* **22 C2** 54 44N 3 25W
Dease →, *Canada* **108 C7** 59 56N 128 32W
Dease Lake, *Canada* **108 C6** 58 25N 130 6W
Death Valley, *U.S.A.* **110 C3** 36 15N 116 50W
Deben →, *U.K.* **25 B11** 52 0N 1 25 E
Debenham, *U.K.* **25 B11** 52 14N 1 12 E
Debre Markos, *Ethiopia* **88 E2** 10 20N 37 40 E
Debre Tabor, *Ethiopia* **88 E2** 11 50N 38 26 E
Debrecen, *Hungary* **67 E11** 47 33N 21 42 E
Decatur, *Ala., U.S.A.* **111 D9** 34 36N 86 59W
Decatur, *Ill., U.S.A.* **111 C9** 39 51N 88 57W
Decatur, *Ind., U.S.A.* **112 E5** 40 50N 84 56W
Deccan, *India* **84 L11** 18 0N 79 0 E
Deddington, *U.K.* **24 C6** 51 59N 1 18W
Dee →, *Aberds., U.K.* **19 H13** 57 9N 2 5W
Dee →, *Dumf. & Gall., U.K.* **20 E7** 54 51N 4 3W
Dee →, *Wales, U.K.* **23 F2** 53 22N 3 17W
Deeping Fen, *U.K.* **23 G8** 52 45N 0 15W
Deeping St. Nicholas, *U.K.* **23 G8** 52 44N 0 12W
Deer Lake, *Canada* **109 D14** 49 11N 57 27W
Defiance, *U.S.A.* **112 E5** 41 17N 84 22W
Dehra Dun, *India* **84 D11** 30 20N 78 4 E
Del Rio, *U.S.A.* **110 E6** 29 22N 100 54W
Delabole, *U.K.* **27 F4** 50 37N 4 46W
Delaware, *U.S.A.* **112 E6** 40 18N 83 4W
Delaware □, *U.S.A.* **113 F10** 39 0N 75 20W
Delaware →, *U.S.A.* **113 F10** 39 15N 75 20W
Delaware B., *U.S.A.* **111 C12** 39 0N 75 10W
Delft, *Neths.* **65 B4** 52 1N 4 22 E
Delfzijl, *Neths.* **65 A6** 53 20N 6 55 E
Delgado, C., *Mozam.* **96 G8** 10 45S 40 40 E
Delhi, *India* **84 E10** 28 38N 77 17 E
Delice, *Turkey* **73 G5** 39 54N 34 2 E
Delicias, *Mexico* **114 B3** 28 10N 105 30W
Déline, *Canada* **108 B7** 65 11N 123 25W
Delphos, *U.S.A.* **112 E5** 40 51N 84 21W
Delta Junction, *U.S.A.* **108 B5** 64 2N 145 44W
Demavend, *Iran* **87 C8** 35 56N 52 10 E
Deming, *U.S.A.* **110 D5** 32 16N 107 46W
Demopolis, *U.S.A.* **111 D9** 32 31N 87 50W
Den Helder, *Neths.* **65 B4** 52 57N 4 45 E
Denbigh, *U.K.* **23 F2** 53 12N 3 25W
Denby Dale, *U.K.* **23 E5** 53 34N 1 40W
Denham, Mt., *Jamaica* **114 a** 18 13N 77 32W
Denizli, *Turkey* **73 G4** 37 42N 29 2 E
Denmark ■, *Europe* **63 F6** 55 45N 10 0 E
Denmark Str., *Atl. Oc.* **54 C6** 66 0N 30 0W
Dennery, *St. Lucia* **115 f** 13 55N 60 54W
Denny, *U.K.* **21 B8** 56 1N 3 55W
Denpasar, *Indonesia* **83 D3** 8 39S 115 13 E
Dent, *U.K.* **22 D4** 54 17N 2 27W
Denton, *Gt. Man., U.K.* **23 F4** 53 27N 2 9W
Denton, *Lincs., U.K.* **23 G7** 52 53N 0 43W
Denton, *U.S.A.* **111 D7** 33 13N 97 8W
D'Entrecasteaux Is., *Papua N. G.* **98 B9** 9 0S 151 0 E
Denver, *U.S.A.* **110 C5** 39 44N 104 59W
Deoghar, *India* **85 G15** 24 30N 86 42 E
Deolali, *India* **84 K8** 19 58N 73 50 E
Dera Ghazi Khan, *Pakistan* **84 D7** 30 5N 70 43 E
Dera Ismail Khan, *Pakistan* **84 D7** 31 50N 70 50 E
Derbent, *Russia* **73 F8** 42 5N 48 15 E
Derby, *Australia* **98 D3** 17 18S 123 38 E
Derby, *U.K.* **23 G6** 52 56N 1 28W
Derg →, *U.K.* **28 B7** 54 44N 7 26W
Derg, L., *Ireland* **30 C6** 53 0N 8 20W
Derryveagh Mts., *Ireland* **28 B5** 54 56N 8 11W
Derwent →, *Derby, U.K.* **23 G6** 52 57N 1 28W
Derwent →, *N. Yorks., U.K.* **23 E7** 53 45N 0 58W
Derwent →, *Tyne & W., U.K.* **22 C5** 54 58N 1 41W
Derwent Water, *U.K.* **22 C2** 54 35N 3 9W
Des Moines, *U.S.A.* **111 B8** 41 35N 93 37W
Des Moines →, *U.S.A.* **111 B8** 40 23N 91 25W
Desborough, *U.K.* **23 H7** 52 27N 0 49W
Deschutes →, *U.S.A.* **110 A2** 45 38N 120 55W
Dese, *Ethiopia* **88 E2** 11 5N 39 40 E
Deseado →, *Argentina* **121 G3** 47 45S 65 54W
Desford, *U.K.* **23 G6** 52 37N 1 17W
Desolación, I., *Chile* **121 H2** 53 0S 74 0W
Dessau, *Germany* **66 C7** 51 51N 12 14 E
Detour, Pt., *U.S.A.* **112 C4** 45 40N 86 40W
Detroit, *U.S.A.* **112 D6** 42 20N 83 3W
Deutsche Bucht, *Germany* **66 A5** 54 15N 8 0 E
Deventer, *Neths.* **65 B6** 52 15N 6 10 E
Deveron →, *U.K.* **19 G12** 57 41N 2 32W
Devils Lake, *U.S.A.* **110 A7** 48 7N 98 52W
Devizes, *U.K.* **24 D5** 51 22N 1 58W
Devon □, *U.K.* **24 E1** 50 50N 3 40W
Devon I., *Canada* **54 B3** 75 10N 85 0W
Devonport, *U.K.* **27 G5** 50 22N 4 11W
Dewey, *Puerto Rico* **115 d** 18 18N 65 18W
Dewsbury, *U.K.* **23 E5** 53 42N 1 37W
Dezfūl, *Iran* **86 C7** 32 20N 48 30 E
Dezhneva, C., *Russia* **79 C20** 66 5N 169 40W
Dhahran, *Si. Arabia* **86 E7** 26 10N 50 7 E
Dhaka, *Bangla.* **85 H17** 23 43N 90 26 E
Dhaka □, *Bangla.* **85 G17** 24 25N 90 25 E
Dhamtari, *India* **85 J12** 20 42N 81 35 E
Dhanbad, *India* **85 H15** 23 50N 86 30 E
Dharwad, *India* **84 M9** 15 30N 75 4 E
Dhaulagiri, *Nepal* **85 E13** 28 39N 83 28 E
Dhenkanal, *India* **85 J14** 20 45N 85 35 E
Dhuburi, *India* **85 F16** 26 2N 89 59 E
Dhule, *India* **84 J9** 20 58N 74 50 E
Diamantina, *Brazil* **122 C2** 18 17S 43 40W
Diamantina →, *Australia* **98 F6** 26 45S 139 10 E
Diamantino, *Brazil* **120 D4** 14 30S 56 30W
Dibrugarh, *India* **85 F19** 27 29N 94 55 E
Dickinson, *U.S.A.* **110 A6** 46 53N 102 47W
Didcot, *U.K.* **24 C6** 51 36N 1 14W
Diefenbaker, L., *Canada* **108 C9** 51 0N 106 55W
Diego Garcia, *Ind. Oc.* **53 E13** 7 50S 72 50 E
Dieppe, *France* **68 B4** 49 54N 1 4 E
Digby, *Canada* **109 D13** 44 38N 65 50W
Digne-les-Bains, *France* **68 E7** 44 5N 6 12 E
Dijon, *France* **68 C6** 47 20N 5 3 E
Dili, *E. Timor* **83 D4** 8 39S 125 34 E
Dillingham, *U.S.A.* **108 C4** 59 3N 158 28W
Dimitrovgrad, *Bulgaria* **71 C11** 42 5N 25 35 E
Dimitrovgrad, *Russia* **72 D8** 54 14N 49 39 E
Dinajpur, *Bangla.* **85 G16** 25 33N 88 43 E
Dinan, *France* **68 B2** 48 28N 2 2W
Dinant, *Belgium* **65 D4** 50 16N 4 55 E
Dinaric Alps, *Croatia* **70 C7** 44 0N 16 30 E
Dingle, *Ireland* **30 D2** 52 9N 10 17W
Dingle B., *Ireland* **30 D2** 52 3N 10 20W
Dingwall, *U.K.* **19 G9** 57 36N 4 26W
Dire Dawa, *Ethiopia* **88 F3** 9 35N 41 45 E
Dirranbandi, *Australia* **98 F8** 28 33S 148 17 E
Disappointment, C., *U.S.A.* **110 A2** 46 18N 124 5W
Disappointment, L., *Australia* **98 E3** 23 20S 122 40 E
Diss, *U.K.* **25 B11** 52 23N 1 7 E
Distington, *U.K.* **22 C1** 54 36N 3 32W
Distrito Federal □, *Brazil* **122 C1** 15 45S 47 45W
Ditchingham, *U.K.* **25 B11** 52 28N 1 28 E
Ditchling Beacon, *U.K.* **25 E8** 50 54N 0 6W
Dittisham, *U.K.* **27 G6** 50 22N 3 37W
Ditton Priors, *U.K.* **23 H3** 52 30N 2 34W
Diu, *India* **84 J7** 20 45N 70 58 E
Divinópolis, *Brazil* **122 D2** 20 10S 44 54W
Dixon Entrance, *U.S.A.* **108 C6** 54 30N 132 0W
Diyarbakır, *Turkey* **73 G7** 37 55N 40 18 E
Dizzard Pt., *U.K.* **27 F4** 50 44N 4 40W
Djerba, I. de, *Tunisia* **95 B8** 33 50N 10 48 E
Djerid, Chott, *Tunisia* **94 B7** 33 42N 8 30 E
Djibouti, *Djibouti* **88 E3** 11 30N 43 5 E
Djibouti ■, *Africa* **88 E3** 12 0N 43 0 E
Dnepropetrovsk, *Ukraine* **73 E6** 48 30N 35 0 E
Dnieper →, *Ukraine* **73 E5** 46 30N 32 18 E
Dniester →, *Europe* **67 E16** 46 18N 30 17 E
Dniprodzerzhynsk, *Ukraine* **73 E5** 48 32N 34 37 E
Doba, *Chad* **95 G9** 8 40N 16 50 E
Dobrich, *Bulgaria* **71 C12** 43 37N 27 49 E
Docking, *U.K.* **25 A10** 52 54N 0 38 E
Doddington, *Cambs., U.K.* **23 H9** 52 30N 0 3 E
Doddington, *Northumb., U.K.* **22 A5** 55 33N 1 54W
Dodecanese, *Greece* **71 F12** 36 35N 27 0 E
Dodge City, *U.S.A.* **110 C6** 37 45N 100 1W
Dodman Pt., *U.K.* **27 G4** 50 13N 4 48W
Dodoma, *Tanzania* **96 F7** 6 8S 35 45 E
Doha, *Qatar* **87 E7** 25 15N 51 35 E
Dolbeau-Mistassini, *Canada* **109 D12** 48 53N 72 14W
Dole, *France* **68 C6** 47 7N 5 31 E
Dolgarrog, *U.K.* **26 A6** 53 11N 3 50W
Dolgellau, *U.K.* **24 A1** 52 45N 3 53W
Dolo, *Ethiopia* **88 G3** 4 11N 42 3 E
Dolomites, *Italy* **70 A4** 46 23N 11 51 E
Dolores, *Argentina* **121 F4** 36 20S 57 40W
Dolphin and Union Str., *Canada* **108 B8** 69 5N 114 45W
Dolphinton, *U.K.* **22 A2** 55 42N 3 25W
Dolton, *U.K.* **27 F5** 50 53N 4 2W
Dominica ■, *W. Indies* **115 D12** 15 20N 61 20W
Dominican Rep. ■, *W. Indies* **115 D10** 19 0N 70 30W
Don →, *Russia* **73 E6** 47 4N 39 18 E
Don →, *Aberds., U.K.* **19 H13** 57 11N 2 5W
Don →, *S. Yorks., U.K.* **23 E7** 53 41N 0 52W
Don Figuero Mts., *Jamaica* **114 a** 18 5N 77 36W
Donaghadee, *U.K.* **29 B10** 54 39N 5 33W
Doncaster, *U.K.* **23 E6** 53 32N 1 6W
Dondra Head, *Sri Lanka* **84 S12** 5 55N 80 40 E
Donegal, *Ireland* **28 B5** 54 39N 8 5W
Donegal □, *Ireland* **28 B5** 54 53N 8 0W
Donegal B., *Ireland* **28 B4** 54 31N 8 49W
Donets →, *Russia* **73 E7** 47 33N 40 55 E
Donetsk, *Ukraine* **73 E6** 48 0N 37 45 E
Dong Hoi, *Vietnam* **83 B2** 17 29N 106 36 E
Dongola, *Sudan* **95 E12** 19 9N 30 22 E
Dongting Hu, *China* **81 D6** 29 18N 112 45 E
Donhead, *U.K.* **24 D4** 51 1N 2 7W
Donington, *U.K.* **23 G8** 52 54N 0 12W
Donna Nook, *U.K.* **23 F9** 53 29N 0 8 E
Donostia-San Sebastián, *Spain* **69 A5** 43 17N 1 58W
Doon →, *U.K.* **20 D6** 55 27N 4 39W
Dorchester, *Dorset, U.K.* **24 E4** 50 42N 2 27W
Dorchester, *Oxon., U.K.* **24 C6** 51 39N 1 10W
Dorchester, C., *Canada* **109 B12** 65 27N 77 27W
Dordogne →, *France* **68 D3** 45 2N 0 36W
Dordrecht, *Neths.* **65 C4** 51 48N 4 39 E
Dorking, *U.K.* **25 D8** 51 14N 0 19W
Dornie, *U.K.* **18 H6** 57 17N 5 31W
Dornoch, *U.K.* **19 G9** 57 53N 4 2W
Dornoch Firth, *U.K.* **19 G9** 57 51N 4 4W
Döröö Nuur, *Mongolia* **80 B4** 48 0N 93 0 E
Dorset □, *U.K.* **24 E4** 50 45N 2 26W
Dorstone, *U.K.* **24 B3** 52 3N 2 59W
Dortmund, *Germany* **66 C4** 51 30N 7 28 E
Dos Bahías, C., *Argentina* **121 G3** 44 58S 65 32W
Dothan, *U.S.A.* **111 D9** 31 13N 85 24W
Douai, *France* **68 A5** 50 21N 3 4 E
Douala, *Cameroon* **96 D1** 4 0N 9 45 E
Doubs →, *France* **68 C6** 46 53N 5 1 E
Douglas, *U.K.* **29 C13** 54 10N 4 28W
Douglas, *U.S.A.* **110 D5** 31 21N 109 33W
Dounreay, *U.K.* **19 E10** 58 35N 3 44W
Dourados, *Brazil* **120 E4** 22 9S 54 50W
Douro →, *Europe* **69 B1** 41 8N 8 40W
Dove →, *Derby, U.K.* **23 G5** 52 51N 1 36W
Dove →, *N. Yorks., U.K.* **22 D7** 54 15N 0 55W
Dove Dale, *U.K.* **23 F5** 53 7N 1 46W
Dover, *U.K.* **25 D11** 51 7N 1 19 E
Dover, *Del., U.S.A.* **113 F10** 39 10N 75 32W
Dover, *N.H., U.S.A.* **113 D12** 43 12N 70 56W
Dover, Str. of, *Europe* **64 F7** 51 0N 1 30 E
Dover-Foxcroft, *U.S.A.* **113 C13** 45 11N 69 13W
Doveridge, *U.K.* **23 G5** 52 54N 1 49W
Dovrefjell, *Norway* **63 E5** 62 15N 9 33 E
Down □, *U.K.* **29 C9** 54 23N 6 2W
Downham, *U.K.* **25 B9** 52 26N 0 14 E
Downham Market, *U.K.* **25 A9** 52 37N 0 23 E
Downpatrick, *U.K.* **29 C10** 54 20N 5 43W
Downpatrick Hd., *Ireland* **28 C3** 54 20N 9 21W
Downton, *U.K.* **24 E5** 50 59N 1 44W
Draguignan, *France* **68 E7** 43 32N 6 27 E
Drake Passage, *S. Ocean* **55 B17** 58 0S 68 0W
Drakensberg, *S. Africa* **97 L5** 31 0S 28 0 E
Drammen, *Norway* **63 F6** 59 42N 10 12 E
Drava →, *Croatia* **71 B8** 45 33N 18 55 E
Drenthe □, *Neths.* **65 B6** 52 52N 6 40 E
Dresden, *Germany* **66 C7** 51 3N 13 44 E
Dreux, *France* **68 B4** 48 44N 1 23 E
Driffield, *U.K.* **23 D8** 54 0N 0 26W
Drina →, *Bos.-H.* **71 B8** 44 53N 19 21 E
Drobeta-Turnu Severin, *Romania* **67 F12** 44 39N 22 41 E
Drogheda, *Ireland* **29 D9** 53 43N 6 22W
Drohobych, *Ukraine* **73 E3** 49 20N 23 30 E
Droichead Nua, *Ireland* **31 B9** 53 11N 6 48W
Droitwich, *U.K.* **23 H4** 52 16N 2 8W
Dromore, *U.K.* **28 B7** 54 31N 7 28W
Dromore West, *Ireland* **28 C4** 54 15N 8 52W
Dronfield, *U.K.* **23 F6** 53 19N 1 27W
Drumheller, *Canada* **108 C8** 51 25N 112 40W
Drummond I., *U.S.A.* **112 B5** 46 1N 83 39W
Drummondville, *Canada* **113 C11** 45 55N 72 25W
Druridge B., *U.K.* **22 B5** 55 17N 1 32W
Dry Harbour Mts., *Jamaica* **114 a** 18 19N 77 24W
Dryden, *Canada* **108 D10** 49 47N 92 50W
Drygalski I., *Antarctica* **55 C7** 66 0S 92 0 E
Du Bois, *U.S.A.* **112 E8** 41 8N 78 46W
Dubai, *U.A.E.* **87 E8** 25 18N 55 20 E
Dubawnt →, *Canada* **108 B9** 64 33N 100 6W
Dubawnt L., *Canada* **108 B9** 63 8N 101 28W
Dubbo, *Australia* **98 G8** 32 11S 148 35 E
Dublin, *Ireland* **31 B10** 53 21N 6 15W
Dublin, *U.S.A.* **111 D10** 32 32N 82 54W
Dublin □, *Ireland* **31 B10** 53 24N 6 20W
Dubrovnik, *Croatia* **71 C8** 42 39N 18 6 E
Dubuque, *U.S.A.* **111 B8** 42 30N 90 41W
Ducie I., *Pac. Oc.* **103 K15** 24 40S 124 48W
Duddington, *U.K.* **23 G7** 52 36N 0 32W
Duddon →, *U.K.* **22 D2** 54 12N 3 15W
Dudinka, *Russia* **79 C10** 69 30N 86 13 E
Dudley, *U.K.* **23 G4** 52 31N 2 5W
Duffield, *U.K.* **23 G6** 52 59N 1 29W
Dufftown, *U.K.* **19 H11** 57 27N 3 8W
Duisburg, *Germany* **66 C4** 51 26N 6 45 E
Dukinfield, *U.K.* **23 F4** 53 28N 2 6W
Dulce →, *Argentina* **121 F3** 30 32S 62 33W
Duluth, *U.S.A.* **111 A8** 46 47N 92 6W
Dulverton, *U.K.* **24 D1** 51 2N 3 33W
Dumbarton, *U.K.* **20 C6** 55 57N 4 33W
Dumfries, *U.K.* **21 D8** 55 4N 3 37W
Dumfries & Galloway □, *U.K.* **21 D8** 55 9N 3 58W
Dumyât, *Egypt* **95 B12** 31 24N 31 48 E
Dún Laoghaire, *Ireland* **31 B10** 53 17N 6 8W
Dunbar, *U.K.* **21 B10** 56 0N 2 31W
Dunblane, *U.K.* **21 B8** 56 11N 3 58W
Duncan, *U.S.A.* **110 D7** 34 30N 97 57W
Duncansby Head, *U.K.* **19 E11** 58 38N 3 1W
Dunchurch, *U.K.* **23 H6** 52 21N 1 17W
Dundalk, *Ireland* **29 C9** 54 1N 6 24W
Dundalk Bay, *Ireland* **29 D9** 53 55N 6 15W
Dundee, *U.K.* **21 B10** 56 28N 2 59W
Dundrum, *U.K.* **29 C10** 54 16N 5 52W
Dundrum B., *U.K.* **29 C10** 54 13N 5 47W
Dunedin, *N.Z.* **99 K13** 45 50S 170 33 E
Dunfermline, *U.K.* **21 B9** 56 5N 3 27W
Dungannon, *U.K.* **29 B8** 54 31N 6 46W
Dungarvan, *Ireland* **31 D7** 52 5N 7 37W
Dungarvan Harbour, *Ireland* **31 D7** 52 4N 7 35W
Dungeness, *U.K.* **25 E10** 50 54N 0 59 E
Dunhuang, *China* **80 B4** 40 8N 94 36 E
Dunkeld, *U.K.* **21 A8** 56 34N 3 35W
Dunkerque, *France* **68 A5** 51 2N 2 20 E
Dunkery Beacon, *U.K.* **24 D1** 51 9N 3 36W
Dunkirk, *U.S.A.* **112 D8** 42 29N 79 20W
Dunleer, *Ireland* **29 D9** 53 50N 6 24W
Dunmanway, *Ireland* **30 E4** 51 43N 9 6W
Dunmore, *U.S.A.* **113 E10** 41 25N 75 38W
Dunnet Hd., *U.K.* **19 E11** 58 40N 3 21W
Dunoon, *U.K.* **20 C6** 55 57N 4 56W
Duns, *U.K.* **21 C11** 55 47N 2 20W
Dunsford, *U.K.* **24 E1** 50 41N 3 42W
Dunstable, *U.K.* **25 C7** 51 53N 0 32W
Dunster, *U.K.* **24 D2** 51 11N 3 27W
Dunston, *U.K.* **23 G4** 52 46N 2 7W
Dunvegan, *U.K.* **18 H4** 57 27N 6 35W
Duque de Caxias, *Brazil* **122 D2** 22 45S 43 19W
Durance →, *France* **68 E6** 43 55N 4 45 E
Durango, *Mexico* **114 C4** 24 3N 104 39W
Durango, *U.S.A.* **110 C5** 37 16N 107 53W
Durant, *U.S.A.* **111 D7** 33 59N 96 25W
Durazno, *Uruguay* **121 F4** 33 25S 56 31W
Durban, *S. Africa* **97 K6** 29 49S 31 1 E
Düren, *Germany* **66 C4** 50 48N 6 29 E
Durg, *India* **85 J12** 21 15N 81 22 E
Durgapur, *India* **85 H15** 23 30N 87 20 E
Durham, *U.K.* **22 C5** 54 47N 1 34W
Durham, *U.S.A.* **111 C11** 35 59N 78 54W
Durham □, *U.K.* **22 C5** 54 42N 1 45W
Durlston Hd., *U.K.* **24 E5** 50 36N 1 57W
Durness, *U.K.* **19 E8** 58 34N 4 45W
Durrës, *Albania* **71 D8** 41 19N 19 28 E
Durrington, *U.K.* **24 D5** 51 12N 1 47W
Durrow, *Ireland* **31 C8** 52 51N 7 24W
Dursey I., *Ireland* **30 E2** 51 36N 10 12W
Dursley, *U.K.* **24 C4** 51 40N 2 21W
Dushanbe, *Tajikistan* **79 F8** 38 33N 68 48 E
Düsseldorf, *Germany* **66 C4** 51 14N 6 47 E
Dutch Harbor, *U.S.A.* **108 C3** 53 53N 166 32W
Duyun, *China* **80 D5** 26 18N 107 29 E
Dvina, N. →, *Russia* **72 B7** 64 32N 40 30 E
Dwarka, *India* **84 H6** 22 18N 69 8 E
Dyce, *U.K.* **19 H13** 57 13N 2 12W
Dyer, C., *Canada* **109 B13** 66 37N 61 16W
Dyersburg, *U.S.A.* **111 C9** 36 3N 89 23W
Dyfi →, *U.K.* **26 B5** 52 32N 4 3W
Dymchurch, *U.K.* **25 D11** 51 1N 1 0 E
Dymock, *U.K.* **24 C4** 51 59N 2 26W
Dzerzhinsk, *Russia* **72 C7** 56 14N 43 30 E
Dzhankoy, *Ukraine* **73 E5** 45 40N 34 20 E
Dzhugdzhur Ra., *Russia* **79 D15** 57 30N 138 0 E
Dzuumod, *Mongolia* **80 B5** 47 45N 106 58 E

E

Eagle, *U.S.A.* **108 B5** 64 47N 141 12W
Eagle L., *U.S.A.* **113 B13** 46 20N 69 22W
Eagle Pass, *U.S.A.* **110 E6** 28 43N 100 30W
Eaglesfield, *U.K.* **22 B2** 55 4N 3 12W
Eakring, *U.K.* **23 F7** 53 9N 0 58W
Ealing □, *U.K.* **25 C8** 51 31N 0 20W
Earby, *U.K.* **23 E4** 53 55N 2 7W
Eardisley, *U.K.* **24 B2** 52 8N 3 1W
Earith, *U.K.* **23 H9** 52 22N 0 2 E
Earl Shilton, *U.K.* **23 G6** 52 35N 1 18W
Earl Soham, *U.K.* **25 B11** 52 14N 1 18 E
Earls Barton, *U.K.* **23 H7** 52 16N 0 45W
Earl's Colne, *U.K.* **25 C10** 51 56N 0 43 E
Earlston, *U.K.* **22 A3** 55 39N 2 40W
Earn →, *U.K.* **21 B9** 56 21N 3 18W
Earn, L., *U.K.* **20 B7** 56 23N 4 13W
Earsdon, *U.K.* **22 B6** 55 3N 1 29W
Easebourne, *U.K.* **25 E7** 51 0N 0 43W
Easington, *Durham, U.K.* **22 C6** 54 47N 1 21W
Easington, *E. Riding, U.K.* **23 E9** 53 39N 0 6 E
Easington Colliery, *U.K.* **22 C6** 54 48N 1 19W
Easingwold, *U.K.* **22 D6** 54 8N 1 11W
East Bengal, *Bangla.* **85 H17** 24 0N 90 0 E
East Bergholt, *U.K.* **25 C11** 51 59N 1 3 E
East Beskids, *Europe* **67 D11** 49 20N 22 0 E
East Brent, *U.K.* **24 D3** 51 15N 2 56W
East China Sea, *Asia* **81 D7** 30 0N 126 0 E
East Cowes, *U.K.* **24 E6** 50 45N 1 16W
East Dereham, *U.K.* **25 A10** 52 41N 0 57 E
East Falkland, *Falk. Is.* **121 H4** 51 30S 58 30W
East Fen, *U.K.* **23 F9** 53 4N 0 5 E
East Grinstead, *U.K.* **25 D9** 51 7N 0 0W
East Harling, *U.K.* **25 B10** 52 26N 0 56 E
East Ilsley, *U.K.* **24 C6** 51 31N 1 16W
East Indies, *Asia* **74 K15** 0 0 120 0 E
East Kilbride, *U.K.* **20 C7** 55 47N 4 11W
East Lansing, *U.S.A.* **112 D5** 42 44N 84 29W
East London, *S. Africa* **97 L5** 33 0S 27 55 E
East Markham, *U.K.* **23 F7** 53 15N 0 53W
East Moor, *U.K.* **23 F5** 53 16N 1 34W
East Pacific Ridge, *Pac. Oc.* **103 J17** 15 0S 110 0W
East Pt., *Br. Virgin Is.* **115 e** 18 40N 64 18W
East Pt., *Canada* **113 B17** 46 27N 61 58W
East Sea = Japan, Sea of, *Asia* **82 D4** 40 0N 135 0 E
East Siberian Sea, *Russia* **79 B18** 73 0N 160 0 E
East Sussex □, *U.K.* **25 E9** 50 56N 0 19 E
East Timor ■, *Asia* **83 D4** 8 50S 126 0 E
East Wittering, *U.K.* **25 E7** 50 46N 0 52W
East Woodhay, *U.K.* **24 D6** 51 21N 1 25W
Eastbourne, *U.K.* **25 E9** 50 46N 0 18 E

Eastchurch, U.K. 25 D10 51 24N 0 53 E
Easter I., Chile 103 K17 27 7S 109 23W
Eastern Ghats, India 84 N11 14 0N 78 50 E
Eastern Group, Fiji 99 D15 17 0S 178 30W
Eastleigh, U.K. 24 E6 50 58N 1 21W
Eastmain, Canada 109 C12 52 10N 78 30W
Eastmain →, Canada 109 C12 52 27N 78 26W
Eastnor, U.K. 24 B4 52 2N 2 23W
Easton, Dorset, U.K. 24 E4 50 33N 2 26W
Easton, Northants., U.K. 23 G7 52 37N 0 31W
Easton, Md., U.S.A. 113 F9 38 47N 76 5W
Easton, Pa., U.S.A. 113 E10 40 41N 75 13W
Easton-in-Gordano, U.K. 24 D3 51 28N 2 42W
Eastport, U.S.A. 113 C14 44 56N 67 0W
Eastry, U.K. 25 D11 51 14N 1 19 E
Eastwood, U.K. 23 F6 53 1N 1 18W
Eaton, U.K. 23 G7 52 51N 0 49W
Eaton Socon, U.K. 23 H8 52 14N 0 17W
Eau Claire, U.S.A. 111 B8 44 49N 91 30W
Eau Claire, L. à l', Canada 109 C12 56 10N 74 25W
Ebberston, U.K. 22 D7 54 14N 0 37W
Ebbw Vale, U.K. 24 C2 51 46N 3 12W
Ebetsu, Japan 82 B7 43 7N 141 34 E
Ebro →, Spain 69 B6 40 43N 0 54 E
Ecclefechan, U.K. 22 B2 55 4N 3 16W
Eccleshall, U.K. 23 G4 52 52N 2 15W
Ech Chéliff, Algeria 94 A6 36 10N 1 20 E
Echo Bay, Canada 108 B8 66 5N 117 55W
Eckington, U.K. 23 F6 53 18N 1 22W
Eclipse Sd., Canada 109 A11 72 38N 79 0W
Ecuador ■, S. Amer. 120 C2 2 0S 78 0W
Ed Damazin, Sudan 95 F12 11 46N 34 21 E
Edam, Neths. 65 B5 52 31N 5 3 E
Eday, U.K. 19 D12 59 11N 2 47W
Eddrachillis B., U.K. 18 F7 58 17N 5 14W
Eddystone, U.K. 27 G5 50 11N 4 16W
Eden →, U.K. 22 C2 54 57N 3 1W
Edenbridge, U.K. 25 D9 51 12N 0 5 E
Edenderry, Ireland 29 E7 53 21N 7 4W
Edge Hill, U.K. 24 B6 52 8N 1 26W
Edinburgh, U.K. 21 C9 55 57N 3 13W
Edington, U.K. 24 D4 51 17N 2 5W
Edirne, Turkey 73 F4 41 40N 26 34 E
Edmonton, Canada 108 C8 53 30N 113 30W
Edmundbyers, U.K. 22 C5 54 50N 1 58W
Edmundston, Canada 109 D13 47 23N 68 20W
Edremit, Turkey 86 B1 39 34N 27 0 E
Edson, Canada 108 C8 53 35N 116 28W
Edward, L., Africa 96 E5 0 25S 29 40 E
Edward VII Land, Antarctica 55 E13 80 0S 150 0W
Edwards Plateau, U.S.A. 110 D6 30 45N 101 20W
Effingham, U.S.A. 112 F3 39 7N 88 33W
Eganville, Canada 112 C9 45 32N 77 5W
Eger, Hungary 67 E11 47 53N 20 27 E
Egham, U.K. 25 D7 51 25N 0 32W
Egremont, U.K. 22 D1 54 29N 3 32W
Eğridir, Turkey 73 G5 37 52N 30 51 E
Eğridir Gölü, Turkey 73 G5 37 53N 30 50 E
Egton, U.K. 22 D7 54 28N 0 44W
Egypt ■, Africa 95 C12 28 0N 31 0 E
Eifel, Germany 66 C4 50 15N 6 50 E
Eigg, U.K. 18 J5 56 54N 6 10W
Eil, L., U.K. 18 J7 56 51N 5 16W
Eindhoven, Neths. 65 C5 51 26N 5 28 E
Eire = Ireland ■, Europe 64 E2 53 50N 7 52W
Eivissa, Spain 69 C6 38 54N 1 26 E
El Aaiún, W. Sahara 94 C3 27 9N 13 12W
El 'Alamein, Egypt 95 B11 30 48N 28 58 E
El Centro, U.S.A. 110 D3 32 48N 115 34W
El Dorado, U.S.A. 111 D8 33 12N 92 40W
El Faiyûm, Egypt 95 C12 29 19N 30 50 E
El Fâsher, Sudan 95 F11 13 33N 25 26 E
El Fuerte, Mexico 114 B3 26 30N 108 40W
El Gîza, Egypt 95 C12 30 0N 31 10 E
El Istiwa'iya, Sudan 95 G11 5 0N 28 0 E
El Jadida, Morocco 94 B4 33 11N 8 17W
El Khârga, Egypt 95 C12 25 30N 30 33 E
El Mahalla el Kubra, Egypt 95 B12 31 0N 31 0 E
El Mansûra, Egypt 95 B12 31 0N 31 19 E
El Minyâ, Egypt 95 C12 28 7N 30 33 E
El Obeid, Sudan 95 F12 13 8N 30 10 E
El Oued, Algeria 94 B7 33 20N 6 58 E
El Paso, U.S.A. 110 D5 31 45N 106 29W
El Reno, U.S.A. 110 C7 35 32N 97 57W
El Salvador ■, Cent. Amer. 114 E7 13 50N 89 0W
El Tigre, Venezuela 120 B3 8 44N 64 15W
Elat, Israel 86 D3 29 30N 34 56 E
Elâzığ, Turkey 73 G6 38 37N 39 14 E
Elba, Italy 70 C4 42 46N 10 17 E
Elbasan, Albania 71 D9 41 9N 20 9 E
Elbe →, Europe 66 B5 53 50N 9 0 E
Elbert, Mt., U.S.A. 110 C5 39 7N 106 27W
Elbeuf, France 68 B4 49 17N 1 2 E
Elbląg, Poland 67 A10 54 10N 19 25 E
Elbrus, Asia 73 F7 43 21N 42 30 E
Elburz Mts., Iran 87 B8 36 0N 52 0 E
Elche, Spain 69 C5 38 15N 0 42W
Eldoret, Kenya 96 D7 0 30N 35 17 E
Elektrostal, Russia 72 C6 55 41N 38 32 E
Elephant Butte Reservoir, U.S.A. 110 D5 33 9N 107 11W
Elephant I., Antarctica 55 C18 61 0S 55 0W
Elephants →, Africa 97 J6 24 10S 32 40 E
Eleuthera, Bahamas 115 C9 25 0N 76 20W
Elgin, U.K. 19 G11 57 39N 3 19W
Elgin, U.S.A. 112 D3 42 2N 88 17W
Elgon, Mt., Africa 96 D6 1 10N 34 30 E
Elham, U.K. 25 D11 51 9N 1 8 E
Elishaw, U.K. 22 B4 55 15N 2 14W
Elista, Russia 73 E7 46 16N 44 14 E
Elizabeth, U.S.A. 113 E10 40 40N 74 13W
Elizabeth City, U.S.A. 111 C11 36 18N 76 14W
Elizabethtown, U.S.A. 112 G5 37 42N 85 52W
Elkhart, U.S.A. 112 E5 41 41N 85 58W
Elkins, U.S.A. 112 F8 38 55N 79 51W
Elko, U.S.A. 110 B3 40 50N 115 46W
Elland, U.K. 23 E5 53 41N 1 50W
Ellen →, U.K. 22 C2 54 44N 3 30W
Ellensburg, U.S.A. 110 A2 46 59N 120 34W
Ellerton, Barbados 115 g 13 7N 59 33W
Ellesmere, U.K. 23 G3 52 55N 2 53W
Ellesmere I., Canada 54 B4 79 30N 80 0W
Ellesmere Port, U.K. 23 F3 53 17N 2 54W
Ellington, U.K. 22 B5 55 14N 1 33W
Elliot Lake, Canada 109 D11 46 25N 82 35W
Ellon, U.K. 19 H13 57 22N 2 4W
Ellsworth Land, Antarctica 55 D16 76 0S 89 0W
Elmalı, Turkey 73 G4 36 44N 29 56 E
Elmira, U.S.A. 112 D9 42 6N 76 48W
Elmswell, U.K. 25 B10 52 15N 0 55 E
Eluru, India 85 L12 16 48N 81 8 E
Ely, U.K. 25 B9 52 24N 0 16 E
Ely, U.S.A. 110 C4 39 15N 114 54W
Elyria, U.S.A. 112 E6 41 22N 82 7W
Emāmrūd, Iran 87 B8 36 30N 55 0 E
Embarcación, Argentina 121 E3 23 10S 64 0W
Embleton, U.K. 22 B5 55 29N 1 38W
Emden, Germany 66 B4 53 21N 7 12 E
Emerald, Australia 98 E8 37 56S 145 29 E
Emmeloord, Neths. 65 B5 52 44N 5 46 E
Emmen, Neths. 65 B6 52 48N 6 57 E
Emmonak, U.S.A. 108 B3 62 46N 164 30W
Empalme, Mexico 114 B2 28 1N 110 49W
Empangeni, S. Africa 97 K6 28 50S 31 52 E
Empedrado, Argentina 121 E4 28 0S 58 46W
Emperor Seamount Chain, Pac. Oc. 102 D9 40 0N 170 0 E
Emporia, U.S.A. 111 C7 38 25N 96 11W
Emporium, U.S.A. 112 E8 41 31N 78 14W
Empty Quarter = Rub' al Khālī, Si. Arabia 88 D4 19 0N 48 0 E
Ems →, Germany 66 B4 53 20N 7 12 E
Enard B., U.K. 18 F7 58 5N 5 20W
Encarnación, Paraguay 121 E4 27 15S 55 50W
Encounter B., Australia 98 H6 35 45S 138 45 E
Ende, Indonesia 83 D4 8 45S 121 40 E
Enderbury I., Kiribati 102 H10 3 8S 171 5W
Enderby, U.K. 23 G6 52 36N 1 13W
Enderby Land, Antarctica 55 C5 66 0S 53 0 E
Endicott, U.S.A. 113 D9 42 6N 76 4W
Enewetak Atoll, Marshall Is. 102 F8 11 30N 162 15 E
Enez, Turkey 73 F4 40 45N 26 5 E
Enfer, Pte. d', Martinique 114 c 14 22N 60 54W
Enfield □, U.K. 25 C8 51 38N 0 5W
Engadin, Switz. 66 E6 46 45N 10 10 E
Engels, Russia 73 D8 51 28N 46 6 E
Enggano, Indonesia 83 D2 5 20S 102 40 E
England □, U.K. 64 E6 53 0N 2 0W
English →, Canada 108 C10 49 12N 91 5W
English Channel, Europe 64 F6 50 0N 2 0W
Enid, U.S.A. 110 C7 36 24N 97 53W
Ennadai L., Canada 108 B9 60 58N 101 20W
Ennedi, Chad 95 E10 17 15N 22 0 E
Ennerdale Water, U.K. 22 C2 54 32N 3 24W
Ennis, Ireland 30 C5 52 51N 8 59W
Enniscorthy, Ireland 31 D9 52 30N 6 34W
Enniskillen, U.K. 28 C6 54 21N 7 39W
Ennistimon, Ireland 30 C4 52 57N 9 17W
Enns →, Austria 66 D8 48 14N 14 32 E
Enschede, Neths. 65 B6 52 13N 6 53 E
Ensenada, Mexico 114 A1 31 50N 116 50W
Enstone, U.K. 24 C6 51 55N 1 27W
Entebbe, Uganda 96 D6 0 4N 32 28 E
Entre Rios, Argentina 116 G5 30 30S 58 30W
Enugu, Nigeria 94 G7 6 30N 7 30 E
Épernay, France 68 B5 49 3N 3 56 E
Épinal, France 68 B7 48 10N 6 27 E
Epping, U.K. 25 C9 51 41N 0 7 E
Epping Forest, U.K. 25 C9 51 40N 0 5 E
Epsom, U.K. 25 D8 51 19N 0 16W
Epworth, U.K. 23 E7 53 32N 0 48W
Equatorial Guinea ■, Africa 96 D1 2 0N 8 0 E
Er Rachidia, Morocco 94 B5 31 58N 4 20W
Erciyaş Dağı, Turkey 86 B3 38 30N 35 30 E
Erebus, Mt., Antarctica 55 D11 77 35S 167 0 E
Ereğli, Konya, Turkey 73 G5 37 31N 34 4 E
Ereğli, Zonguldak, Turkey 73 F5 41 15N 31 24 E
Erfurt, Germany 66 C6 50 58N 11 2 E
Eriboll, L., U.K. 19 E8 58 30N 4 42W
Erie, U.S.A. 112 D7 42 8N 80 5W
Erie, L., N. Amer. 112 D7 42 15N 81 0W
Eriskay, U.K. 18 H3 57 4N 7 18W
Eritrea ■, Africa 88 D2 14 0N 38 30 E
Erlangen, Germany 66 D6 49 36N 11 0 E
Ernakulam, India 84 Q10 9 59N 76 22 E
Erne →, Ireland 28 C5 54 30N 8 16W
Erne, Lower L., U.K. 28 C6 54 28N 7 47W
Erne, Upper L., U.K. 28 C6 54 14N 7 32W
Erode, India 84 P10 11 24N 77 45 E
Errigal, Ireland 28 A5 55 2N 8 6W
Erris Hd., Ireland 28 C1 54 19N 10 0W
Erromango, Vanuatu 99 D12 18 45S 169 5 E
Erzgebirge, Germany 66 C7 50 27N 12 55 E
Erzincan, Turkey 73 G6 39 46N 39 30 E
Erzurum, Turkey 73 G7 39 57N 41 15 E
Esbjerg, Denmark 63 F5 55 29N 8 29 E
Escanaba, U.S.A. 112 C4 45 45N 87 4W
Esch-sur-Alzette, Lux. 65 E6 49 32N 6 0 E
Escrick, U.K. 23 E6 53 53N 1 2W
Escuinapa, Mexico 114 C3 22 50N 105 50W
Escuintla, Guatemala 114 E6 14 20N 90 48W
Eşfahān, Iran 87 C7 32 39N 51 43 E
Esha Ness, U.K. 18 B14 60 29N 1 38W
Esk →, Cumb., U.K. 21 E9 54 58N 3 2W
Esk →, Cumb., U.K. 22 D2 54 20N 3 24W
Esk →, N. Yorks., U.K. 22 D7 54 30N 0 37W
Eskdale, U.K. 22 B2 55 12N 3 4W
Esker, Canada 109 C13 53 53N 66 25W
Eskilstuna, Sweden 63 F7 59 22N 16 32 E
Eskişehir, Turkey 73 G5 39 50N 30 30 E
Eslāmābād-e Gharb, Iran 86 C6 34 10N 46 30 E
Esperance, Australia 98 G3 33 45S 121 55 E
Esperance B., St. Lucia 115 f 14 4N 60 55W
Esperanza, Puerto Rico 115 d 18 6N 65 28W
Espinhaço, Serra do, Brazil 122 C2 17 30S 43 30W
Espírito Santo □, Brazil 122 C2 20 0S 40 45W
Espíritu Santo, Vanuatu 99 D12 15 15S 166 50 E
Espoo, Finland 63 E8 60 12N 24 40 E
Essaouira, Morocco 94 B4 31 32N 9 42W
Essen, Germany 66 C4 51 28N 7 2 E
Essequibo →, Guyana 120 B4 6 50N 58 30W
Essex □, U.K. 25 C9 51 54N 0 27 E
Estância, Brazil 122 B3 11 16S 37 26W
Estevan, Canada 108 D9 49 10N 102 59W
Eston, U.K. 22 C6 54 34N 1 8W
Estonia ■, Europe 72 C4 58 30N 25 30 E
Estrela, Serra da, Portugal 69 B2 40 10N 7 45W
Estrondo, Serra do, Brazil 120 C5 7 20S 48 0W
Etawah, India 84 F11 26 48N 79 6 E
Etchingham, U.K. 25 D9 51 0N 0 26 E
Ethiopia ■, Africa 88 F3 8 0N 40 0 E
Ethiopian Highlands, Ethiopia 74 J7 10 0N 37 0 E
Etive, L., U.K. 20 B5 56 29N 5 10W
Etna, Italy 70 F6 37 50N 14 55 E
Eton, U.K. 25 C7 51 30N 0 36W
Etosha Pan, Namibia 97 H3 18 40S 16 30 E
Ettington, U.K. 24 B5 52 8N 1 35W
Ettrick Forest, U.K. 22 A3 55 30N 3 0W
Ettrick Water →, U.K. 21 C10 55 31N 2 55W
Euclid, U.S.A. 112 E7 41 34N 81 32W
Eugene, U.S.A. 110 B2 44 5N 123 4W
Euphrates →, Asia 86 D6 31 0N 47 25 E
Eureka, U.S.A. 110 B2 40 47N 124 9W
Europa, Île, Ind. Oc. 97 J8 22 20S 40 22 E
Europe 56 E10 50 0N 20 0 E
Euxton, U.K. 23 E3 53 41N 2 41W
Evanston, Ill., U.S.A. 112 D4 42 3N 87 41W
Evanston, Wyo., U.S.A. 110 B4 41 16N 110 58W
Evansville, U.S.A. 112 G4 37 58N 87 35W
Evercreech, U.K. 24 D4 51 9N 2 30W
Everest, Mt., Nepal 85 E15 28 5N 86 58 E
Everett, U.S.A. 110 A2 47 59N 122 12W
Everglades, The, U.S.A. 111 E10 25 50N 81 0W
Evesham, U.K. 24 B5 52 6N 1 56W
Évora, Portugal 69 C2 38 33N 7 57W
Évreux, France 68 B4 49 3N 1 8 E
Évvoia, Greece 71 E11 38 30N 24 0 E
Ewe, L., U.K. 18 G6 57 49N 5 38W
Ewell, U.K. 25 D8 51 20N 0 14W
Ewhurst, U.K. 25 D8 51 9N 0 25W
Exe →, U.K. 24 E2 50 41N 3 29W
Exeter, U.K. 24 E1 50 43N 3 31W
Exminster, U.K. 24 E2 50 40N 3 29W
Exmoor, U.K. 24 D1 51 12N 3 45W
Exmouth, U.K. 27 F7 50 37N 3 25W
Exton, U.K. 23 G7 52 42N 0 38W
Extremadura □, Spain 69 C2 39 30N 6 5W
Eyam, U.K. 23 F5 53 17N 1 40W
Eyasi, L., Tanzania 96 E6 3 30S 35 0 E
Eye, Cambs., U.K. 23 G8 52 37N 0 11W
Eye, Suffolk, U.K. 25 B11 52 19N 1 9 E
Eye Pen., U.K. 18 F5 58 13N 6 10W
Eyemouth, U.K. 21 C11 55 52N 2 5W
Eynsham, U.K. 24 C6 51 47N 1 22W
Eyre, L., Australia 98 F6 29 30S 137 26 E
Eyre Pen., Australia 98 G6 33 30S 136 17 E

F

F.Y.R.O.M. = Macedonia ■, Europe 71 D9 41 53N 21 40 E
Fair Hd., U.K. 29 A9 55 14N 6 9W
Fair Isle, U.K. 64 B6 59 30N 1 40W
Fairbanks, U.S.A. 108 B5 64 51N 147 43W
Fairfield, U.S.A. 112 F3 38 23N 88 22W
Fairford, U.K. 24 C5 51 43N 1 46W
Fairlight, U.K. 25 E10 50 52N 0 40 E
Fairmont, U.S.A. 112 F7 39 29N 80 9W
Fairweather, Mt., U.S.A. 108 C6 58 55N 137 32W
Faisalabad, Pakistan 84 D8 31 30N 73 5 E
Faizabad, India 85 F13 26 45N 82 10 E
Fajardo, Puerto Rico 115 d 18 20N 65 39W
Fakenham, U.K. 25 A10 52 51N 0 51 E
Falcon Reservoir, U.S.A. 110 E7 26 34N 99 10W
Faldingworth, U.K. 23 F8 53 21N 0 24W
Falkirk, U.K. 21 C8 56 0N 3 47W
Falkland, U.K. 21 B9 56 16N 3 12W
Falkland Is. ☑, Atl. Oc. 121 H4 51 30S 59 0W
Fall River, U.S.A. 113 E12 41 43N 71 10W
Falmouth, Jamaica 114 a 18 30N 77 40W
Falmouth, U.K. 27 G3 50 9N 5 5W
Falmouth B., U.K. 27 G3 50 6N 5 5W
Falstone, U.K. 22 B4 55 11N 2 26W
Falun, Sweden 63 E7 60 37N 15 37 E
Famagusta, Cyprus 86 C3 35 8N 33 55 E
Fanad Hd., Ireland 28 A6 55 17N 7 38W
Fannich, L., U.K. 19 G8 57 38N 4 59W
Far East, Asia 74 E16 40 0N 130 0 E
Farāh, Afghan. 84 C3 32 20N 62 7 E
Farasan, Si. Arabia 88 D3 16 45N 41 55 E
Fareham, U.K. 24 E6 50 51N 1 11W
Farewell C., Greenland 109 C15 59 48N 43 55W
Fargo, U.S.A. 111 A7 46 53N 96 48W
Faridabad, India 84 E10 28 26N 77 19 E
Faringdon, U.K. 24 C5 51 39N 1 34W
Farmington, U.S.A. 110 C5 36 44N 108 12W
Farmville, U.S.A. 112 G8 37 18N 78 24W
Farnborough, U.K. 25 D7 51 16N 0 45W
Farne Is., U.K. 22 A5 55 38N 1 37W
Farnham, U.K. 25 D7 51 13N 0 47W
Farnworth, U.K. 23 E4 53 34N 2 25W
Faro, Canada 108 B6 62 11N 133 22W
Faroe Is., Atl. Oc. 57 C4 62 0N 7 0W
Fārs □, Iran 87 D8 29 30N 55 0 E
Fāryāb □, Afghan. 87 B11 36 0N 65 0 E
Fataka, Solomon Is. 99 C12 11 55S 170 12 E
Fatehgarh, India 84 F11 27 25N 79 35 E
Fatehpur, Raj., India 84 F9 28 0N 74 40 E
Fatehpur, Ut. P., India 85 G12 25 56N 81 13 E
Faversham, U.K. 25 D10 51 19N 0 56 E
Fawley, U.K. 24 E6 50 50N 1 20W
Fayetteville, Ark., U.S.A. 111 C8 36 4N 94 10W
Fayetteville, N.C., U.S.A. 111 D11 35 3N 78 53W
Fazeley, U.K. 23 G5 52 37N 1 40W
Fazilka, India 84 D9 30 27N 74 2 E
Fdérik, Mauritania 94 D3 22 40N 12 45W
Feale →, Ireland 30 D3 52 27N 9 37W
Fear, C., U.S.A. 111 D11 33 50N 77 58W
Fécamp, France 68 B4 49 45N 0 22 E
Fehmarn, Germany 66 A6 54 27N 11 7 E
Feira de Santana, Brazil 122 B3 12 15S 38 57W
Felipe Carrillo Puerto, Mexico 114 D7 19 38N 88 3W
Felixstowe, U.K. 25 C11 51 58N 1 23 E
Felton, U.K. 22 B5 55 18N 1 42W
Feltwell, U.K. 25 B10 52 30N 0 32 E
Fenny Bentley, U.K. 23 F5 53 3N 1 45W
Fenny Compton, U.K. 24 B6 52 10N 1 23W
Fenny Stratford, U.K. 25 C7 52 0N 0 44W
Fens, The, U.K. 23 G8 52 38N 0 2W
Fenyang, China 81 C6 37 18N 111 48 E
Feodosiya, Ukraine 73 E6 45 2N 35 16 E
Fergus Falls, U.S.A. 111 A7 46 17N 96 4W
Ferkéssédougou, Ivory C. 94 G4 9 35N 5 6W
Fermanagh □, U.K. 28 C6 54 21N 7 40W
Fermont, Canada 109 C13 52 47N 67 5W
Fermoy, Ireland 30 D6 52 9N 8 16W
Fernhurst, U.K. 25 D7 51 3N 0 43W
Ferrara, Italy 70 B4 44 50N 11 35 E
Ferret, C., France 68 D3 44 38N 1 15W
Ferryhill, U.K. 22 C5 54 41N 1 33W
Fès, Morocco 94 B5 34 0N 5 0W
Fethiye, Turkey 73 G4 36 36N 29 6 E
Fetlar, U.K. 18 A16 60 36N 0 52W
Feuilles →, Canada 109 C12 58 47N 70 4W
Feyzābād, Afghan. 87 B12 37 7N 70 33 E
Fezzan, Libya 95 C8 27 0N 13 0 E
Ffestiniog, U.K. 26 B6 52 57N 3 55W
Fianarantsoa, Madag. 97 J9 21 26S 47 5 E
Fife □, U.K. 21 B9 56 16N 3 1W
Fife Ness, U.K. 21 B10 56 17N 2 35W
Figeac, France 68 D5 44 37N 2 2 E
Fiji ■, Pac. Oc. 99 D14 17 20S 179 0 E
Filby, U.K. 25 A12 52 40N 1 39 E
Filey, U.K. 22 D8 54 12N 0 18W
Filey B., U.K. 22 D8 54 12N 0 15W
Filton, U.K. 24 C3 51 30N 2 34W
Fincham, U.K. 25 A9 52 38N 0 30 E
Findhorn →, U.K. 19 G10 57 38N 3 38W
Findlay, U.S.A. 112 E6 41 2N 83 39W
Finedon, U.K. 23 H7 52 21N 0 39W
Finike, Turkey 86 B2 36 21N 30 10 E
Finland ■, Europe 63 E9 63 0N 27 0 E
Finland, G. of, Europe 63 F9 60 0N 26 0 E
Finlay →, Canada 108 C7 57 0N 125 10W
Finn →, Ireland 28 B7 54 51N 7 28W
Firozabad, India 84 F11 27 10N 78 25 E
Firozpur, India 84 D9 30 55N 74 40 E
Fish →, Namibia 97 K3 28 7S 17 10 E
Fishguard, U.K. 26 D4 51 59N 4 58W
Fishtoft, U.K. 23 G9 52 58N 0 1 E
Fisterra, C., Spain 69 A1 42 50N 9 19W
Fitchburg, U.S.A. 113 D12 42 35N 71 48W
Flagstaff, U.S.A. 110 C4 35 12N 111 39W
Flamborough, U.K. 22 D8 54 7N 0 7W
Flamborough Hd., U.K. 22 D8 54 7N 0 5W
Flandre, Europe 65 D2 50 50N 2 30 E
Flathead L., U.S.A. 110 A4 47 51N 114 8W
Flattery, C., U.S.A. 110 A2 48 23N 124 29W
Fleet, U.K. 25 D7 51 17N 0 50W
Fleetwood, U.K. 23 E2 53 55N 3 1W
Flensburg, Germany 66 A5 54 47N 9 27 E
Flers, France 68 B3 48 47N 0 33W
Flimby, U.K. 22 C2 54 42N 3 30W
Flin Flon, Canada 108 C9 54 46N 101 53W
Flinders →, Australia 98 D7 17 36S 140 36 E
Flinders Ranges, Australia 98 G6 31 30S 138 30 E
Flint, U.K. 23 F2 53 15N 3 8W
Flint, U.S.A. 112 D6 43 1N 83 41W
Flint →, U.S.A. 111 D10 30 57N 84 34W
Flint I., Kiribati 103 J12 11 26S 151 48W
Flitwick, U.K. 25 C8 52 0N 0 30W
Flodden, U.K. 22 A4 55 37N 2 8W
Flora, U.S.A. 112 F3 38 40N 88 29W
Florence, Italy 70 C4 43 46N 11 15 E
Florence, U.S.A. 111 D11 34 12N 79 46W
Florencia, Colombia 120 B2 1 36N 75 36W
Flores, Indonesia 83 D4 8 35S 121 0 E
Flores Sea, Indonesia 83 D4 6 30S 120 0 E
Florianópolis, Brazil 121 E5 27 30S 48 30W
Florida, Uruguay 121 F4 34 7S 56 10W
Florida □, U.S.A. 111 E10 28 0N 82 0W
Florida, Straits of, U.S.A. 115 C9 25 0N 80 0W
Florida Keys, U.S.A. 111 F10 24 40N 81 0W
Florø, Norway 63 E5 61 35N 5 1 E
Fly →, Papua N. G. 98 B7 8 25S 143 0 E
Fochabers, U.K. 19 G11 57 37N 3 6W
Focşani, Romania 67 F14 45 41N 27 15 E
Fóggia, Italy 70 D6 41 27N 15 34 E
Foix, France 68 E4 42 58N 1 38 E
Folkestone, U.K. 25 D11 51 5N 1 12 E
Fond-du-Lac, Canada 108 C9 59 19N 107 12W
Fongafale, Tuvalu 99 B14 8 31S 179 13 E
Fontainebleau, France 68 B5 48 24N 2 40 E
Fontenay-le-Comte, France 68 C3 46 28N 0 48W
Fordham, U.K. 25 B9 52 19N 0 23 E
Fordingbridge, U.K. 24 E5 50 56N 1 47W
Forel, Mt., Greenland 54 C6 66 52N 36 55W
Forest Row, U.K. 25 D9 51 5N 0 3 E
Forfar, U.K. 19 J12 56 39N 2 53W
Forlì, Italy 70 B5 44 13N 12 3 E
Formby, U.K. 23 E2 53 34N 3 4W
Formby Pt., U.K. 23 E2 53 33N 3 6W
Formiga, Brazil 122 D1 20 27S 45 25W
Formosa, Argentina 121 E4 26 15S 58 10W
Formosa, Brazil 122 C1 15 32S 47 20W
Forres, U.K. 19 G10 57 37N 3 37W
Forsayth, Australia 98 D7 18 33S 143 34 E
Fort Albany, Canada 109 C11 52 15N 81 35W
Fort Augustus, U.K. 19 H8 57 9N 4 42W
Fort Chipewyan, Canada 108 C8 58 42N 111 8W
Fort Collins, U.S.A. 110 B5 40 35N 105 5W
Fort-Coulonge, Canada 112 C9 45 50N 76 45W
Fort-de-France, Martinique 114 c 14 36N 61 2W
Fort Dodge, U.S.A. 111 B8 42 30N 94 11W
Fort Good Hope, Canada 108 B7 66 14N 128 40W
Fort Kent, U.S.A. 113 B13 47 15N 68 36W
Fort Lauderdale, U.S.A. 111 E10 26 7N 80 8W
Fort Liard, Canada 108 B7 60 14N 123 30W
Fort MacKay, Canada 108 C8 57 12N 111 41W
Fort Macleod, Canada 108 D8 49 45N 113 30W
Fort McMurray, Canada 108 C8 56 44N 111 7W
Fort McPherson, Canada 108 B6 67 30N 134 55W
Fort Morgan, U.S.A. 110 B6 40 15N 103 48W
Fort Myers, U.S.A. 111 E10 26 39N 81 52W
Fort Nelson, Canada 108 C7 58 50N 122 44W
Fort Nelson →, Canada 108 C7 59 32N 124 0W
Fort Peck L., U.S.A. 110 A5 48 0N 106 26W
Fort Providence, Canada 108 B8 61 3N 117 40W
Fort Resolution, Canada 108 B8 61 10N 113 40W
Fort St. John, Canada 108 C7 56 15N 120 50W
Fort Scott, U.S.A. 111 C8 37 50N 94 42W
Fort Shevchenko, Kazakhstan 73 F9 44 35N 50 23 E
Fort Simpson, Canada 108 B7 61 45N 121 15W
Fort Smith, Canada 108 B8 60 0N 111 51W
Fort Smith, U.S.A. 111 C8 35 23N 94 25W
Fort Stockton, U.S.A. 110 D6 30 53N 102 53W
Fort Wayne, U.S.A. 112 E5 41 4N 85 9W
Fort William, U.K. 18 J7 56 49N 5 7W
Fort Worth, U.S.A. 111 D7 32 45N 97 18W
Fort Yukon, U.S.A. 108 B5 66 34N 145 16W
Fortaleza, Brazil 120 C6 3 45S 38 35W
Forth, Firth of, U.K. 21 B10 56 5N 2 55W
Fortrose, U.K. 19 G9 57 35N 4 9W
Foshan, China 81 D6 23 4N 113 5 E
Fostoria, U.S.A. 112 E6 41 10N 83 25W
Fothergill, U.K. 22 C2 54 43N 3 29W
Fotheringhay, U.K. 23 G8 52 32N 0 27W
Fougères, France 68 B3 48 21N 1 14W
Foula, U.K. 64 A5 60 10N 2 5W
Foulness I., U.K. 25 C10 51 36N 0 55 E
Foulness Pt., U.K. 25 C10 51 37N 0 58 E
Foulsham, U.K. 25 A10 52 48N 0 59 E
Foulweather, C., U.S.A. 110 B2 44 50N 124 5W
Fountainhall, U.K. 22 A3 55 44N 2 53W
Fouta Djalon, Guinea 94 F3 11 20N 12 10W
Fovant, U.K. 24 D5 51 4N 2 0W
Fowey, U.K. 27 G4 50 20N 4 39W
Fownhope, U.K. 24 B3 52 0N 2 36W
Foxe Basin, Canada 109 B12 66 0N 77 0W
Foxe Chan., Canada 109 B11 65 0N 80 0W
Foxe Pen., Canada 109 B12 65 0N 76 0W
Foyle, Lough, U.K. 29 A7 55 7N 7 4W
Foynes, Ireland 30 C4 52 37N 9 7W
Foz do Iguaçu, Brazil 121 E4 25 30S 54 30W
Fraddon, U.K. 27 G4 50 23N 4 58W
Framlingham, U.K. 25 B11 52 14N 1 21 E
Franca, Brazil 122 D1 20 33S 47 30W
France ■, Europe 68 C5 47 0N 3 0 E
Franceville, Gabon 96 E2 1 40S 13 32 E
Franche-Comté, France 68 C6 46 50N 5 55 E
Francis Case, L., U.S.A. 110 B7 43 4N 98 34W
Francistown, Botswana 97 J5 21 7S 27 33 E
François L., Canada 108 C7 54 0N 125 30W
Frankfort, Ind., U.S.A. 112 E4 40 17N 86 31W
Frankfort, Ky., U.S.A. 112 F5 38 12N 84 52W
Frankfurt, Brandenburg, Germany 66 B8 52 20N 14 32 E
Frankfurt, Hessen, Germany 66 C5 50 7N 8 41 E
Franklin, N.H., U.S.A. 113 D12 43 27N 71 39W
Franklin, Pa., U.S.A. 112 E8 41 24N 79 50W
Franklin B., Canada 108 B7 69 45N 126 0W
Franklin D. Roosevelt L., U.S.A. 110 A3 48 18N 118 9W
Franklin L., U.S.A. 110 B3 40 25N 115 22W

Hsinchu, Taiwan 81 D7 24 48N 120 58 E
Huacho, Peru 120 D2 11 10S 77 35W
Huai He →, China 81 C6 33 0N 118 30 E
Huainan, China 81 C6 32 38N 116 58 E
Huallaga →, Peru 120 C2 5 15S 75 30W
Huambo, Angola 97 G3 12 42S 15 54 E
Huancavelica, Peru 120 D2 12 50S 75 5W
Huancayo, Peru 120 D2 12 5S 75 12W
Huangshan, China 81 D6 29 42N 118 25 E
Huangshi, China 81 C6 30 10N 115 3 E
Huánuco, Peru 120 C2 9 55S 76 15W
Huaraz, Peru 120 C2 9 30S 77 32W
Huascarán, Peru 120 C2 9 8S 77 36W
Huasco, Chile 121 E2 28 30S 71 15W
Huatabampo, Mexico 114 B3 26 50N 109 50W
Hubei □, China 81 C6 31 0N 112 0 E
Hucknall, U.K. 23 F6 53 3N 1 13W
Huddersfield, U.K. 23 E5 53 39N 1 47W
Hudiksvall, Sweden 63 E7 61 43N 17 10 E
Hudson →, U.S.A. 113 E10 40 42N 74 2W
Hudson Bay, Canada 109 C11 60 0N 86 0W
Hudson Falls, U.S.A. 113 D11 43 18N 73 35W
Hudson Str., Canada 109 B13 62 0N 70 0W
Hue, Vietnam 83 B2 16 30N 107 35 E
Huelva, Spain 69 D2 37 18N 6 57W
Huesca, Spain 69 A5 42 8N 0 25W
Hugh Town, U.K. 27 H1 49 55N 6 19W
Hughenden, Australia 98 E7 20 52S 144 10 E
Hugli →, India 85 J16 21 56N 88 4 E
Huila, Nevado del, Colombia 120 B2 3 0N 76 0W
Huize, China 80 D5 26 24N 103 15 E
Hull = Kingston upon Hull, U.K. 23 E8 53 45N 0 21W
Hull, Canada 109 D12 45 25N 75 44W
Hull →, U.K. 23 E8 53 44N 0 20W
Hullavington, U.K. 24 C4 51 32N 2 8W
Hulme End, U.K. 23 F5 53 8N 1 50W
Hulun Nur, China 81 B6 49 0N 117 30 E
Humacao, Puerto Rico 115 d 18 9N 65 50W
Humaitá, Brazil 120 C3 7 35S 63 1W
Humber →, U.K. 23 E8 53 42N 0 27W
Humber, Mouth of the, U.K. 23 E9 53 32N 0 8 E
Humberside □, U.K. 23 E7 53 48N 0 47W
Humboldt, Canada 108 C9 52 15N 105 9W
Humboldt →, U.S.A. 110 B3 39 59N 118 36W
Humphreys Peak, U.S.A. 110 C4 35 21N 111 41W
Humshaugh, U.K. 22 B4 55 3N 2 8W
Hunan □, China 81 D6 27 30N 112 0 E
Hungary ■, Europe 67 E10 47 20N 19 20 E
Hungary, Plain of, Europe 56 F10 47 0N 20 0 E
Hungerford, U.K. 24 D5 51 25N 1 31W
Hŭngnam, N. Korea 81 C7 39 49N 127 45 E
Hunmanby, U.K. 22 D8 54 10N 0 20W
Hunsrück, Germany 66 D4 49 56N 7 27 E
Hunstanton, U.K. 25 A9 52 56N 0 29 E
Huntingdon, U.K. 23 H8 52 20N 0 11W
Huntington, Ind., U.S.A. 112 E5 40 53N 85 30W
Huntington, W. Va., U.S.A. 112 F6 38 25N 82 27W
Huntly, U.K. 19 H12 57 27N 2 47W
Huntsville, Canada 109 D12 45 20N 79 14W
Huntsville, Ala., U.S.A. 111 D9 34 44N 86 35W
Huntsville, Tex., U.S.A. 111 D7 30 43N 95 33W
Huron, U.S.A. 110 B7 44 22N 98 13W
Huron, L., U.S.A. 112 C6 44 30N 82 40W
Hursley, U.K. 24 D6 51 2N 1 23W
Hurstbourne Tarrant, U.K. 24 D6 51 17N 1 26W
Hurstpierpoint, U.K. 25 E8 50 56N 0 11W
Húsavík, Iceland 63 A2 66 3N 17 21W
Husband's Bosworth, U.K. 23 H6 52 28N 1 4W
Hutchinson, U.S.A. 110 C7 38 5N 97 56W
Huyton, U.K. 23 F3 53 25N 2 51W
Hwang-ho →, China 81 C6 37 55N 118 50 E
Hwange, Zimbabwe 97 H5 18 18S 26 30 E
Hyargas Nuur, Mongolia 80 B4 49 0N 93 0 E
Hyde, U.K. 23 F4 53 27N 2 4W
Hyderabad, India 84 L11 17 22N 78 29 E
Hyderabad, Pakistan 84 G6 25 23N 68 24 E
Hyères, France 68 E7 43 8N 6 9 E
Hyères, Îs. d', France 68 E7 43 0N 6 20 E
Hyndman Peak, U.S.A. 110 B4 43 45N 114 8W
Hythe, U.K. 25 D11 51 4N 1 5 E

I

Ialomiţa →, Romania 67 F14 44 42N 27 51 E
Iaşi, Romania 67 E14 47 10N 27 40 E
Ibadan, Nigeria 94 G6 7 22N 3 58 E
Ibagué, Colombia 120 B2 4 20N 75 20W
Ibarra, Ecuador 120 B2 0 21N 78 7W
Iberian Peninsula, Europe 56 H5 40 0N 5 0W
Ibiá, Brazil 122 C1 19 30S 46 30W
Ibiapaba, Sa. da, Brazil 120 C5 4 0S 41 30W
Ibiza = Eivissa, Spain 69 C6 38 54N 1 26 E
Ibotirama, Brazil 122 B2 12 13S 43 12W
Ibstock, U.K. 23 G6 52 42N 1 24W
Ica, Peru 120 D2 14 0S 75 48W
Iça →, Brazil 120 C3 2 55S 67 58W
Iceland ■, Europe 63 B2 64 45N 19 0W
Ichihara, Japan 82 F7 35 28N 140 5 E
Ichinomiya, Japan 82 F5 35 18N 136 48 E
Idaho □, U.S.A. 110 B4 45 0N 115 0W
Idaho Falls, U.S.A. 110 B4 43 30N 112 2W
Idar-Oberstein, Germany 66 D4 49 43N 7 16 E
Idle →, U.K. 23 F7 53 27N 0 49W
Idlib, Syria 86 C4 35 55N 36 36 E
Idmiston, U.K. 24 D5 51 9N 1 42W
Ieper, Belgium 65 D2 50 51N 2 53 E
Ife, Nigeria 94 G6 7 30N 4 31 E
Igarapava, Brazil 122 D1 20 3S 47 47W
Iglésias, Italy 70 E3 39 19N 8 32 E
Igloolik, Canada 109 B11 69 20N 81 49W
Ignace, Canada 112 A2 49 30N 91 40W
Iguaçu →, Brazil 121 E4 25 36S 54 36W
Iguaçu Falls, Brazil 121 E4 25 41S 54 26W
Iguala, Mexico 114 D5 18 20N 99 40W
Iguatu, Brazil 120 C6 6 20S 39 18W
Iisalmi, Finland 63 E9 63 32N 27 10 E
IJsselmeer, Neths. 65 B5 52 45N 5 20 E
Ikaluktutiak, Canada 108 B9 69 10N 105 0W
Ikeda, Japan 82 F3 34 1N 133 48 E
Ilagan, Phil. 83 B4 17 7N 121 53 E
Īlām, Iran 86 C6 33 36N 46 36 E
Ilchester, U.K. 24 D3 51 0N 2 41W
Île-de-France □, France 68 B5 49 0N 2 20 E
Ilebo, Dem. Rep. of the Congo 96 E4 4 17S 20 55 E
Ilesha, Nigeria 94 G6 7 37N 4 40 E
Ilfracombe, U.K. 27 E5 51 12N 4 8W
Ilhéus, Brazil 122 B3 14 49S 39 2W
Ili →, Kazakhstan 79 E9 45 53N 77 10 E
Iliamna L., U.S.A. 108 C4 59 30N 155 0W
Iligan, Phil. 83 C4 8 12N 124 13 E
Ilkeston, U.K. 23 G6 52 58N 1 19W
Ilkley, U.K. 23 E5 53 56N 1 48W
Illapel, Chile 121 F2 32 0S 71 10W
Iller →, Germany 66 D6 48 23N 9 58 E
Illimani, Nevado, Bolivia 120 D3 16 30S 67 50W
Illinois □, U.S.A. 111 B9 40 15N 89 30W
Illinois →, U.S.A. 111 C8 38 58N 90 28W
Ilmen, L., Russia 72 C5 58 15N 31 10 E
Ilminster, U.K. 24 E3 50 55N 2 55W
Iloilo, Phil. 83 B4 10 45N 122 33 E
Ilorin, Nigeria 94 G6 8 30N 4 35 E
Imabari, Japan 82 F3 34 4N 133 0 E
Imandra, L., Russia 72 A5 67 30N 33 0 E
Immingham, U.K. 23 E8 53 37N 0 13W
Imperatriz, Brazil 120 C5 5 30S 47 29W
Imphal, India 85 G18 24 48N 93 56 E
In Salah, Algeria 94 C6 27 10N 2 32 E
Inari, Finland 63 D9 68 54N 27 5 E
Inarijärvi, Finland 63 D9 69 0N 28 0 E
Ince Burun, Turkey 73 F5 42 7N 34 56 E
Inch'ŏn, S. Korea 81 C7 37 27N 126 40 E
Incomáti →, Mozam. 97 K6 25 46S 32 43 E
Indalsälven →, Sweden 63 E7 62 36N 17 30 E
India ■, Asia 84 K11 20 0N 78 0 E
Indian Ocean, None 53 E13 5 0S 75 0 E
Indiana, U.S.A. 112 E8 40 37N 79 9W
Indiana □, U.S.A. 112 E4 40 0N 86 0W
Indianapolis, U.S.A. 112 F4 39 46N 86 9W
Indigirka →, Russia 79 B16 70 48N 148 54 E
Indira Gandhi Canal, India 84 F8 28 0N 72 0 E
Indo-China, Asia 74 H14 15 0N 102 0 E
Indonesia ■, Asia 83 D3 5 0S 115 0 E
Indore, India 84 H9 22 42N 75 53 E
Indre →, France 68 C4 47 16N 0 11 E
Indus →, Pakistan 84 G5 24 20N 67 47 E
İnebolu, Turkey 73 F5 41 55N 33 40 E
Ingatestone, U.K. 25 C9 51 40N 0 24 E
Ingleborough, U.K. 22 D4 54 10N 2 22W
Ingleton, U.K. 22 D4 54 10N 2 27W
Ingoldmells Pt., U.K. 23 F9 53 11N 0 21 E
Ingolstadt, Germany 66 D6 48 46N 11 26 E
Ingraj Bazar, India 85 G16 24 58N 88 10 E
Ingushetia □, Russia 73 F8 43 20N 44 50 E
Inishbofin, Ireland 28 D1 53 37N 10 13W
Inisheer, Ireland 30 B3 53 3N 9 32W
Inishfree B., Ireland 28 A5 55 4N 8 23W
Inishkea North, Ireland 28 C1 54 9N 10 11W
Inishkea South, Ireland 28 C1 54 7N 10 12W
Inishmaan, Ireland 30 B3 53 5N 9 35W
Inishmore, Ireland 30 B3 53 8N 9 45W
Inishowen Pen., Ireland 29 A7 55 14N 7 15W
Inishshark, Ireland 28 D1 53 37N 10 16W
Inishturk, Ireland 28 D1 53 42N 10 7W
Inishvickillane, Ireland 30 D1 52 3N 10 37W
Inkberrow, U.K. 23 H5 52 13N 1 58W
Inland Sea, Japan 82 F3 34 20N 133 30 E
Inn →, Austria 66 D7 48 35N 13 28 E
Inner Hebrides, U.K. 18 J4 57 0N 6 30W
Inner Mongolia, China 81 B6 42 0N 112 0 E
Inner Sound, U.K. 18 H6 57 30N 5 55W
Innerleithen, U.K. 22 A2 55 37N 3 4W
Innsbruck, Austria 66 E6 47 16N 11 23 E
Inowrocław, Poland 67 B10 52 50N 18 12 E
Insein, Burma 85 L20 16 50N 96 5 E
Inta, Russia 72 A11 66 5N 60 8 E
Interlaken, Switz. 66 E4 46 41N 7 50 E
Inukjuak, Canada 109 C12 58 25N 78 15W
Inuvik, Canada 108 B6 68 16N 133 40W
Inveraray, U.K. 20 B5 56 14N 5 5W
Inverbervie, U.K. 19 J13 56 51N 2 17W
Invercargill, N.Z. 99 K12 46 24S 168 24 E
Invergordon, U.K. 19 G9 57 41N 4 10W
Inverness, U.K. 19 H9 57 29N 4 13W
Inverurie, U.K. 19 H13 57 17N 2 23W
Iona, U.K. 20 B3 56 20N 6 25W
Ionia, U.S.A. 112 D5 42 59N 85 4W
Ionian Is., Greece 71 E9 38 40N 20 0 E
Ionian Sea, Medit. S. 71 E7 37 30N 17 30 E
Iowa □, U.S.A. 111 B8 42 18N 93 30W
Iowa City, U.S.A. 111 B8 41 40N 91 32W
Ipameri, Brazil 122 C1 17 44S 48 9W
Ipatinga, Brazil 122 C2 19 32S 42 30W
Ipoh, Malaysia 83 C2 4 35N 101 5 E
Ipswich, Australia 98 F9 27 35S 152 40 E
Ipswich, U.K. 25 B11 52 4N 1 10 E
Iqaluit, Canada 109 B13 63 44N 68 31W
Iquique, Chile 120 E2 20 19S 70 5W
Iquitos, Peru 120 C2 3 45S 73 10W
Iráklion, Greece 71 G11 35 20N 25 12 E
Iran ■, Asia 87 C8 33 0N 53 0 E
Iran, Plateau of, Asia 74 F9 32 0N 55 0 E
Irapuato, Mexico 114 C4 20 40N 101 30W
Iraq ■, Asia 86 C5 33 0N 44 0 E
Irbil, Iraq 86 B6 36 15N 44 5 E
Irchester, U.K. 23 H7 52 18N 0 39W
Ireland ■, Europe 64 E2 53 50N 7 52W
Iringa, Tanzania 96 F7 7 48S 35 43 E
Irish Sea, U.K. 64 E4 53 38N 4 48W
Irkutsk, Russia 79 D12 52 18N 104 20 E
Irlam, U.K. 23 F4 53 26N 2 26W
Iron Gate, Europe 67 F12 44 44N 22 30 E
Iron Mountain, U.S.A. 112 C3 45 49N 88 4W
Ironbridge, U.K. 23 G3 52 38N 2 30W
Ironton, U.S.A. 112 F6 38 32N 82 41W
Ironwood, U.S.A. 111 A8 46 27N 90 9W
Irrawaddy →, Burma 85 M19 15 50N 95 6 E
Irt →, U.K. 22 D2 54 23N 3 26W
Irthlingborough, U.K. 23 H7 52 20N 0 37W
Irtysh →, Russia 79 C8 61 4N 68 52 E
Irvine, U.K. 20 C6 55 37N 4 41W
Irvinestown, U.K. 28 C6 54 28N 7 39W
Isabela, Puerto Rico 115 d 18 30N 67 2W
Ísafjörður, Iceland 63 A1 66 5N 23 9W
Isar →, Germany 66 D7 48 48N 12 57 E
Isère →, France 68 D6 44 59N 4 51 E
Ishinomaki, Japan 82 D7 38 32N 141 20 E
Ishpeming, U.S.A. 112 B4 46 29N 87 40W
İskenderun, Turkey 73 G6 36 32N 36 10 E
Isla →, U.K. 21 A9 56 32N 3 20W
Islamabad, Pakistan 84 C8 33 40N 73 10 E
Island L., Canada 108 C10 53 47N 94 25W
Island Pond, U.S.A. 113 C12 44 49N 71 53W
Islay, U.K. 20 C3 55 46N 6 10W
Isleham, U.K. 25 B9 52 21N 0 25 E
Islip, U.K. 24 C6 51 50N 1 12W
Ismâ'ilîya, Egypt 95 B12 30 37N 32 18 E
Isparta, Turkey 73 G5 37 47N 30 30 E
Israel ■, Asia 86 C3 32 0N 34 50 E
Issoire, France 68 D5 45 32N 3 15 E
İstanbul, Turkey 71 D13 41 0N 29 0 E
Istra, Croatia 66 F7 45 10N 14 0 E
Istres, France 68 E6 43 31N 4 59 E
Itaberaba, Brazil 122 B2 12 32S 40 18W
Itabira, Brazil 122 C2 19 37S 43 13W
Itabuna, Brazil 122 B3 14 48S 39 16W
Itacoatiara, Brazil 120 C4 3 8S 58 25W
Itajaí, Brazil 121 E5 27 50S 48 39W
Itajubá, Brazil 122 D1 22 24S 45 30W
Italy ■, Europe 70 C5 42 0N 13 0 E
Itaperuna, Brazil 122 D2 21 10S 41 54W
Itapetinga, Brazil 122 C2 15 15S 40 15W
Itapetininga, Brazil 122 D1 23 36S 48 7W
Itapicuru →, Brazil 122 B3 11 47S 37 32W
Itararé, Brazil 122 D1 24 6S 49 23W
Itaúna, Brazil 122 D2 20 4S 44 34W
Itchen →, U.K. 24 E6 50 55N 1 22W
Ithaca, U.S.A. 112 D9 42 27N 76 30W
Ivanava, Belarus 67 B13 52 7N 25 29 E
Ivano-Frankivsk, Ukraine 67 D13 48 40N 24 40 E
Ivanovo, Russia 72 C7 57 5N 41 0 E
Ivinghoe, U.K. 25 C7 51 50N 0 37W
Ivory Coast ■, Africa 94 G4 7 30N 5 0W
Ivujivik, Canada 109 B12 62 24N 77 55W
Ivybridge, U.K. 27 G6 50 23N 3 56W
Iwaki, Japan 82 E7 37 3N 140 55 E
Iwakuni, Japan 82 F3 34 15N 132 8 E
Iwo, Nigeria 94 G6 7 39N 4 9 E
Ixworth, U.K. 25 B10 52 18N 0 51 E
Issyk Kul, Kyrgyzstan 74 E11 42 25N 77 15 E
Izhevsk, Russia 72 C9 56 51N 53 14 E
Izmayil, Ukraine 73 E4 45 22N 28 46 E
İzmir, Turkey 71 E12 38 25N 27 8 E
İznik Gölü, Turkey 73 F4 40 27N 29 30 E
Izumi-Sano, Japan 82 F4 34 23N 135 18 E

J

Jabalpur, India 84 H11 23 9N 79 58 E
Jaboatão, Brazil 120 C6 8 7S 35 1W
Jaboticabal, Brazil 122 D1 21 15S 48 17W
Jackson, Barbados 115 g 13 7N 59 36W
Jackson, Ky., U.S.A. 112 G6 37 33N 83 23W
Jackson, Mich., U.S.A. 112 D5 42 15N 84 24W
Jackson, Miss., U.S.A. 111 D8 32 18N 90 12W
Jackson, Tenn., U.S.A. 111 C9 35 37N 88 49W
Jacksonville, U.S.A. 111 D10 30 20N 81 39W
Jacmel, Haiti 115 D10 18 14N 72 32W
Jacobabad, Pakistan 84 E6 28 20N 68 29 E
Jacobina, Brazil 122 B2 11 11S 40 30W
Jaén, Spain 69 D4 37 44N 3 43W
Jaffna, Sri Lanka 84 Q12 9 45N 80 2 E
Jahrom, Iran 87 D8 28 30N 53 31 E
Jaipur, India 84 F9 27 0N 75 50 E
Jakarta, Indonesia 83 D2 6 9S 106 49 E
Jalālābād, Afghan. 84 B7 34 30N 70 29 E
Jalgaon, India 84 J9 21 0N 75 42 E
Jalna, India 84 K9 19 48N 75 38 E
Jalpaiguri, India 85 F16 26 32N 88 46 E
Jaluit I., Marshall Is. 102 G8 6 0N 169 30 E
Jamaica ■, W. Indies 114 a 18 10N 77 30W
Jamalpur, Bangla. 85 G16 24 52N 89 56 E
Jamalpur, India 85 G15 25 18N 86 28 E
Jambi, Indonesia 83 D2 1 38S 103 30 E
James →, U.S.A. 111 B7 42 52N 97 18W
James B., Canada 109 C11 54 0N 80 0W
Jamestown, N. Dak., U.S.A. 110 A7 46 54N 98 42W
Jamestown, N.Y., U.S.A. 112 D8 42 6N 79 14W
Jammu, India 84 C9 32 43N 74 54 E
Jammu & Kashmir □, India 84 B10 34 25N 77 0 E
Jamnagar, India 84 H7 22 30N 70 6 E
Jamshedpur, India 85 H15 22 44N 86 12 E
Jan Mayen, Arctic 54 B7 71 0N 9 0W
Janaúba, Brazil 122 C2 15 48S 43 19W
Janesville, U.S.A. 111 B9 42 41N 89 1W
Januária, Brazil 122 C2 15 25S 44 25W
Jaora, India 84 H9 23 40N 75 10 E
Japan ■, Asia 82 F5 36 0N 136 0 E
Japan, Sea of, Asia 82 D4 40 0N 135 0 E
Japan Trench, Pac. Oc. 102 D6 32 0N 142 0 E
Japurá →, Brazil 120 C3 3 8S 65 46W
Jari →, Brazil 120 C4 1 9S 51 54W
Jarrow, U.K. 22 C6 54 59N 1 28W
Jarvis I., Pac. Oc. 103 H12 0 15S 160 5W
Jāsk, Iran 87 E9 25 38N 57 45 E
Jasper, Canada 108 C8 52 55N 118 5W
Jauja, Peru 120 D2 11 45S 75 15W
Jaunpur, India 85 G13 25 46N 82 44 E
Java, Indonesia 83 D3 7 0S 110 0 E
Java Sea, Indonesia 83 D2 4 35S 107 15 E
Java Trench, Ind. Oc. 83 D2 9 0S 105 0 E
Jaya, Puncak, Indonesia 83 D5 3 57S 137 17 E
Jebel, Bahr el →, Sudan 95 G12 9 30N 30 25 E
Jedburgh, U.K. 21 D10 55 29N 2 33W
Jedda, Si. Arabia 86 F4 21 29N 39 10 E
Jeffersonville, U.S.A. 112 F5 38 17N 85 44W
Jelenia Góra, Poland 66 C8 50 50N 15 45 E
Jelgava, Latvia 72 C3 56 41N 23 49 E
Jena, Germany 66 C6 50 54N 11 35 E
Jequié, Brazil 122 B2 13 51S 40 5W
Jequitinhonha, Brazil 122 C2 16 30S 41 0W
Jequitinhonha →, Brazil 122 C3 15 51S 38 53W
Jérémie, Haiti 115 D10 18 40N 74 10W
Jerez de la Frontera, Spain 69 D2 36 41N 6 7W
Jersey, U.K. 27 J9 49 11N 2 7W
Jersey City, U.S.A. 113 E10 40 44N 74 4W
Jerusalem, Israel 86 D3 31 47N 35 10 E
Jervaulx, U.K. 22 D5 54 16N 1 43W
Jessore, Bangla. 85 H16 23 10N 89 10 E
Jhang Maghiana, Pakistan 84 D8 31 15N 72 22 E
Jhansi, India 84 G11 25 30N 78 36 E
Jharkhand □, India 85 H14 24 0N 85 50 E
Jhelum, Pakistan 84 C8 33 0N 73 45 E
Jhelum →, Pakistan 84 D8 31 20N 72 10 E
Jiamusi, China 81 B8 46 40N 130 26 E
Ji'an, China 81 D6 27 6N 114 59 E
Jiangmen, China 81 D6 22 32N 113 0 E
Jiangsu □, China 81 C7 33 0N 120 0 E
Jiangxi □, China 81 D6 27 30N 116 0 E
Jiaxing, China 81 C7 30 49N 120 45 E
Jihlava →, Czech Rep. 67 D9 48 55N 16 36 E
Jilin, China 81 B7 43 44N 126 30 E
Jilin □, China 81 B7 44 0N 127 0 E
Jima, Ethiopia 88 F2 7 40N 36 47 E
Jiménez, Mexico 114 B4 27 10N 104 54W
Jinan, China 81 C6 36 38N 117 1 E
Jincheng, China 80 C5 38 30N 102 10 E
Jingdezhen, China 81 D6 29 20N 117 11 E
Jinggu, China 80 D5 23 35N 100 41 E
Jinhua, China 81 D6 29 8N 119 38 E
Jining, Nei Monggol Zizhiqu, China 81 B6 41 5N 113 0 E
Jining, Shandong, China 81 C6 35 22N 116 34 E
Jinja, Uganda 96 D6 0 25N 33 12 E
Jinzhou, China 81 B7 41 5N 121 3 E
Jiujiang, China 81 D6 29 42N 115 58 E
Jixi, China 81 B8 45 20N 130 50 E
Jizzakh, Uzbekistan 87 A11 40 6N 67 50 E
João Pessoa, Brazil 120 C6 7 10S 34 52W
Jodhpur, India 84 F8 26 23N 73 8 E
Johannesburg, S. Africa 97 K5 26 10S 28 2 E
John Crow Mts., Jamaica 114 a 18 5N 76 25W
John Day →, U.S.A. 110 A2 45 44N 120 39W
John o' Groats, U.K. 19 E11 58 38N 3 4W
Johnson City, N.Y., U.S.A. 113 D10 42 7N 75 58W
Johnson City, Tenn., U.S.A. 111 C10 36 19N 82 21W
Johnston I., Pac. Oc. 103 F11 17 10N 169 8W
Johnstown, U.S.A. 112 E8 40 20N 78 55W
Johor Baharu, Malaysia 83 C2 1 28N 103 46 E
Joinville, Brazil 121 E5 26 15S 48 55W
Joliet, U.S.A. 112 E3 41 32N 88 5W
Joliette, Canada 109 D12 46 3N 73 24W
Jolo, Phil. 83 C4 6 0N 121 0 E
Jonesboro, U.S.A. 111 C8 35 50N 90 42W
Jönköping, Sweden 63 F6 57 45N 14 8 E
Jonquière, Canada 109 D12 48 27N 71 14W
Joplin, U.S.A. 111 C8 37 6N 94 31W
Jordan ■, Asia 86 D4 31 0N 36 0 E
Jordan →, Asia 86 D3 31 48N 35 32 E
Jos, Nigeria 94 G7 9 53N 8 51 E
Joseph Bonaparte G., Australia 98 C4 14 35S 128 50 E
Jost Van Dyke, Br. Virgin Is. 115 e 18 29N 64 47W
Jotunheimen, Norway 63 E5 61 35N 8 25 E
Jowzjān □, Afghan. 87 B11 36 10N 66 0 E
Juan de Fuca Str., Canada 110 A2 48 15N 124 0W
Juan Fernández, Arch. de, Pac. Oc. 103 L20 33 50S 80 0W
Juàzeiro, Brazil 122 A2 9 30S 40 30W
Juàzeiro do Norte, Brazil 120 C6 7 10S 39 18W
Juba, Somali Rep. 88 G3 1 30N 42 35 E
Juba, Sudan 95 H12 4 50N 31 35 E
Juchitán, Mexico 114 D5 16 27N 95 5W
Juiz de Fora, Brazil 122 D2 21 43S 43 19W
Juliaca, Peru 120 D2 15 25S 70 10W
Julianatop, Suriname 120 B4 3 40N 56 30W
Jullundur, India 84 D9 31 20N 75 40 E
Junagadh, India 84 J7 21 30N 70 30 E
Jundiaí, Brazil 122 D1 24 30S 47 0W
Juneau, U.S.A. 108 C6 58 18N 134 25W
Junggar Pendi, China 80 B3 44 30N 86 0 E
Junín, Argentina 121 F3 34 33S 60 57W
Jupiter →, Canada 113 A16 49 29N 63 37W
Jura, Europe 66 E4 46 40N 6 5 E
Jura, U.K. 20 C4 56 0N 5 50W
Jura, Sd. of, U.K. 20 C4 55 57N 5 45W
Juruá →, Brazil 120 C3 2 37S 65 44W
Juruena →, Brazil 120 C4 7 20S 58 3W
Jutland, Denmark 63 F5 56 25N 9 30 E
Juventud, I. de la, Cuba 115 C8 21 40N 82 40W
Jyväskylä, Finland 63 E9 62 14N 25 50 E

K

K2, Pakistan 84 B10 35 58N 76 32 E
Kabardino-Balkaria □, Russia 73 F7 43 30N 43 30 E
Kābul, Afghan. 84 B6 34 28N 69 11 E
Kabwe, Zambia 97 G5 14 30S 28 29 E
Kachchh, Gulf of, India 84 H6 22 50N 69 15 E
Kachchh, Rann of, India 84 H7 24 0N 70 0 E
Kachin □, Burma 85 G20 26 0N 97 30 E
Kaçkar, Turkey 73 F7 40 45N 41 10 E
Kadavu, Fiji 99 E14 19 0S 178 15 E
Kadoma, Zimbabwe 97 H5 18 20S 29 52 E
Kaduna, Nigeria 94 F7 10 30N 7 21 E
Kaesŏng, N. Korea 81 C7 37 58N 126 35 E
Kafue →, Zambia 97 H5 15 30S 29 0 E
Kaga Bandoro, C.A.R. 96 C3 7 0N 19 10 E
Kagoshima, Japan 82 H2 31 35N 130 33 E
Kahoolawe, U.S.A. 110 H16 20 33N 156 37W
Kahramanmaraş, Turkey 73 G6 37 37N 36 53 E
Kai, Kepulauan, Indonesia 83 D5 5 55S 132 45 E
Kaieteur Falls, Guyana 120 B4 5 1N 59 10W
Kaifeng, China 81 C6 34 48N 114 21 E
Kailua Kona, U.S.A. 110 J17 19 39N 155 59W
Kainji Res., Nigeria 94 F6 10 1N 4 40 E
Kairouan, Tunisia 95 A8 35 45N 10 5 E
Kaiserslautern, Germany 66 D4 49 26N 7 45 E
Kaitaia, N.Z. 99 H13 35 8S 173 17 E
Kajaani, Finland 63 E9 64 17N 27 46 E
Kajabbi, Australia 98 E7 20 0S 140 1 E
Kakamega, Kenya 96 D6 0 20N 34 46 E
Kakinada, India 85 L13 16 57N 82 11 E
Kalaallit Nunaat = Greenland ☒, N. Amer. 54 C5 66 0N 45 0W
Kalahari, Africa 97 J4 24 0S 21 30 E
Kalamazoo, U.S.A. 112 D5 42 17N 85 35W
Kalamazoo →, U.S.A. 112 D4 42 40N 86 10W
Kalemie, Dem. Rep. of the Congo 96 F5 5 55S 29 9 E
Kalgoorlie-Boulder, Australia 98 G3 30 40S 121 22 E
Kalimantan, Indonesia 83 D3 0 0 114 0 E
Kaliningrad, Russia 72 D3 54 42N 20 32 E
Kalispell, U.S.A. 110 A4 48 12N 114 19W
Kalisz, Poland 67 C10 51 45N 18 8 E
Kalkaska, U.S.A. 112 C5 44 44N 85 11W
Kalmar, Sweden 63 F7 56 40N 16 20 E
Kalmykia □, Russia 73 E8 46 5N 46 1 E
Kaluga, Russia 72 D6 54 35N 36 10 E
Kalutara, Sri Lanka 84 R12 6 35N 80 0 E
Kalyan, India 84 K8 19 15N 73 9 E
Kama →, Russia 72 C9 55 45N 52 0 E
Kamchatka Pen., Russia 79 D18 57 0N 160 0 E
Kamina, Dem. Rep. of the Congo 96 F5 8 45S 25 0 E
Kamloops, Canada 108 C7 50 40N 120 20W
Kampala, Uganda 96 D6 0 20N 32 30 E
Kampong Saom, Cambodia 83 B2 10 38N 103 30 E
Kamyanets-Podilskyy, Ukraine 67 D14 48 45N 26 40 E
Kamyshin, Russia 73 D8 50 10N 45 24 E
Kanaaupscow, Canada 109 C12 53 39N 77 9W
Kananga, Dem. Rep. of the Congo 96 F4 5 55S 22 18 E
Kanash, Russia 72 C8 55 30N 47 32 E
Kanawha →, U.S.A. 112 F6 38 50N 82 9W
Kanazawa, Japan 82 E5 36 30N 136 38 E
Kanchenjunga, Nepal 85 F16 27 50N 88 10 E
Kanchipuram, India 84 N11 12 52N 79 45 E
Kandalaksha, Russia 72 A5 67 9N 32 30 E
Kandanghaur, Indonesia 83 D2 6 21S 108 6 E
Kandi, Benin 94 F6 11 7N 2 55 E
Kandy, Sri Lanka 84 R12 7 18N 80 43 E
Kane, U.S.A. 112 E8 41 40N 78 49W
Kaneohe, U.S.A. 110 H16 21 25N 157 48W
Kangaroo I., Australia 98 H6 35 45S 137 0 E
Kangiqsualujjuaq, Canada 109 C13 58 30N 65 59W
Kangiqsujuaq, Canada 109 B12 61 30N 72 0W
Kangirsuk, Canada 109 B13 60 0N 70 0W
Kanin Pen., Russia 72 A8 68 0N 45 0 E
Kankakee, U.S.A. 112 E4 41 7N 87 52W
Kankakee →, U.S.A. 112 E3 41 23N 88 15W
Kankan, Guinea 94 F4 10 23N 9 15W
Kano, Nigeria 94 F7 12 2N 8 30 E
Kanpur, India 84 F12 26 28N 80 20 E
Kansas □, U.S.A. 110 C7 38 30N 99 0W
Kansas →, U.S.A. 111 C8 39 7N 94 37W
Kansas City, U.S.A. 111 C8 39 6N 94 35W
Kanturk, Ireland 30 D5 52 11N 8 54W

Kaohsiung, *Taiwan* **81 D7** 22 35N 120 16 E
Kaolack, *Senegal* **94 F2** 14 5N 16 8W
Kapaa, *U.S.A.* **110 G15** 22 5N 159 19W
Kapiri Mposhi, *Zambia* **97 G5** 13 59S 28 43 E
Kāpīsā □, *Afghan.* **87 C12** 35 0N 69 20 E
Kaposvár, *Hungary* **67 E9** 46 25N 17 47 E
Kaptai L., *Bangla.* **85 H18** 22 40N 92 20 E
Kapuas →, *Indonesia* **83 D2** 0 25S 109 20 E
Kapuskasing, *Canada* **112 A6** 49 25N 82 30W
Kara Bogaz Gol, *Turkmenistan* **73 F9** 41 0N 53 30 E
Kara Kum, *Turkmenistan* **87 B9** 39 30N 60 0 E
Kara Sea, *Russia* **79 B8** 75 0N 70 0 E
Karabük, *Turkey* **73 F5** 41 12N 32 37 E
Karachey-Cherkessia □, *Russia* **73 F7** 43 40N 41 30 E
Karachi, *Pakistan* **84 G5** 24 53N 67 0 E
Karaganda, *Kazakhstan* **79 E9** 49 50N 73 10 E
Karagiye Depression, *Kazakhstan* **73 F9** 43 27N 51 45 E
Karakalpakstan □, *Uzbekistan* **87 A9** 43 0N 58 0 E
Karakoram, *Pakistan* **84 B10** 35 30N 77 0 E
Karaman, *Turkey* **73 G5** 37 14N 33 13 E
Karamay, *China* **80 B3** 45 30N 84 58 E
Karawang, *Indonesia* **83 D2** 6 30S 107 15 E
Karayazı, *Turkey* **73 G7** 39 41N 42 9 E
Karbalā', *Iraq* **86 C6** 32 36N 44 3 E
Karelia □, *Russia* **72 A5** 65 30N 32 30 E
Kariba, L., *Zimbabwe* **97 H5** 16 40S 28 25 E
Kariba Dam, *Zimbabwe* **97 H5** 16 30S 28 35 E
Karimata, Str. of, *Indonesia* **83 D2** 2 0S 108 40 E
Karlskrona, *Sweden* **63 F7** 56 10N 15 35 E
Karlsruhe, *Germany* **66 D5** 49 0N 8 23 E
Karlstad, *Sweden* **63 F6** 59 23N 13 30 E
Karnak, *Egypt* **95 C12** 25 43N 32 39 E
Karnal, *India* **84 E10** 29 42N 77 2 E
Karnataka □, *India* **84 N10** 13 15N 77 0 E
Kärnten □, *Austria* **66 E8** 46 52N 13 30 E
Kars, *Turkey* **73 F7** 40 40N 43 5 E
Karwar, *India* **84 M9** 14 55N 74 13 E
Kasai →, *Dem. Rep. of the Congo* **96 E3** 3 30S 16 10 E
Kasaragod, *India* **84 N9** 12 30N 74 58 E
Kasba L., *Canada* **108 B9** 60 20N 102 10W
Kāshān, *Iran* **87 C7** 34 5N 51 30 E
Kashi, *China* **80 C2** 39 30N 76 2 E
Kasongo, *Dem. Rep. of the Congo* **96 E5** 4 30S 26 33 E
Kassalâ, *Sudan* **95 E13** 15 30N 36 0 E
Kassel, *Germany* **66 C5** 51 18N 9 26 E
Kastamonu, *Turkey* **73 F5** 41 25N 33 43 E
Kasur, *Pakistan* **84 D9** 31 5N 74 25 E
Katanga □, *Dem. Rep. of the Congo* **96 F4** 8 0S 25 0 E
Katherine →, *Australia* **98 C5** 14 40S 131 42 E
Katihar, *India* **85 G15** 25 34N 87 36 E
Katima Mulilo, *Zambia* **97 H4** 17 28S 24 13 E
Katmandu, *Nepal* **85 F14** 27 45N 85 20 E
Katowice, *Poland* **67 C10** 50 17N 19 5 E
Katrine, L., *U.K.* **20 B7** 56 15N 4 30W
Katsina, *Nigeria* **94 F7** 13 0N 7 32 E
Kattegat, *Denmark* **63 F6** 56 40N 11 20 E
Kauai, *U.S.A.* **110 H15** 22 3N 159 30W
Kauai Channel, *U.S.A.* **110 H15** 21 45N 158 50W
Kaukauna, *U.S.A.* **112 C3** 44 17N 88 17W
Kaunakakai, *U.S.A.* **110 H16** 21 6N 157 1W
Kaunas, *Lithuania* **72 D3** 54 54N 23 54 E
Kaválla, *Greece* **71 D11** 40 57N 24 28 E
Kavieng, *Papua N. G.* **98 A9** 2 36S 150 51 E
Kavīr, Dasht-e, *Iran* **87 C8** 34 30N 55 0 E
Kawagoe, *Japan* **82 F6** 35 55N 139 29 E
Kawaguchi, *Japan* **82 F6** 35 52N 139 45 E
Kawardha, *India* **85 J12** 22 0N 81 17 E
Kawasaki, *Japan* **82 F6** 35 31N 139 43 E
Kayah □, *Burma* **85 K20** 19 15N 97 15 E
Kayes, *Mali* **94 F3** 14 25N 11 30W
Kayin □, *Burma* **85 L20** 18 0N 97 30 E
Kayseri, *Turkey* **73 G6** 38 45N 35 30 E
Kazakhstan ■, *Asia* **79 E9** 50 0N 70 0 E
Kazan, *Russia* **72 C8** 55 50N 49 10 E
Kazan-Rettō, *Pac. Oc.* **102 E6** 25 0N 141 0 E
Kea, *U.K.* **27 G3** 50 14N 5 6W
Keady, *U.K.* **29 C8** 54 15N 6 42W
Kearney, *U.S.A.* **110 B7** 40 42N 99 5W
Keban, *Turkey* **73 G6** 38 50N 38 50 E
Keban Barajı, *Turkey* **73 G6** 38 41N 38 33 E
Kebnekaise, *Sweden* **63 D7** 67 53N 18 33 E
Kebri Dehar, *Ethiopia* **88 F3** 6 45N 44 17 E
Kebumen, *Indonesia* **83 D2** 7 42S 109 40 E
Kecskemét, *Hungary* **67 E10** 46 57N 19 42 E
Kediri, *Indonesia* **83 D3** 7 51S 112 1 E
Keelby, *U.K.* **23 E8** 53 35N 0 16W
Keele, *U.K.* **23 F4** 53 0N 2 17W
Keene, *U.S.A.* **113 D11** 42 56N 72 17W
Keeper Hill, *Ireland* **30 C6** 52 45N 8 16W
Keetmanshoop, *Namibia* **97 K3** 26 35S 18 8 E
Kefallinía, *Greece* **71 E9** 38 15N 20 30 E
Keflavík, *Iceland* **63 B1** 64 2N 22 35W
Kegworth, *U.K.* **23 G6** 52 50N 1 17W
Keighley, *U.K.* **23 E5** 53 52N 1 54W
Keith, *U.K.* **19 G12** 57 32N 2 57W
Kelang, *Malaysia* **83 C2** 3 2N 101 26 E
Keld, *U.K.* **22 D4** 54 24N 2 10W
Kelkit →, *Turkey* **73 F6** 40 45N 36 32 E
Kellogg, *U.S.A.* **110 A3** 47 32N 116 7W
Kells, Rhinns of, *U.K.* **29 A13** 55 7N 4 19W
Kelowna, *Canada* **108 D8** 49 50N 119 25W
Kelsale, *U.K.* **25 B12** 52 14N 1 31 E
Kelsall, *U.K.* **23 F3** 53 13N 2 43W
Kelso, *U.K.* **21 C11** 55 36N 2 26W
Keluang, *Malaysia* **83 C2** 2 3N 103 18 E
Kelvedon, *U.K.* **25 C10** 51 50N 0 43 E
Kem, *Russia* **72 B5** 65 0N 34 38 E
Kemble, *U.K.* **24 C5** 51 40N 1 59W
Kemerovo, *Russia* **79 D10** 55 20N 86 5 E
Kemi, *Finland* **63 D8** 65 44N 24 34 E
Kemijoki →, *Finland* **63 D8** 65 47N 24 32 E
Kemp Land, *Antarctica* **55 C5** 69 0S 55 0 E
Kempsey, *U.K.* **24 B4** 52 8N 2 12W
Kempston, *U.K.* **25 B7** 52 7N 0 30W
Kenai, *U.S.A.* **108 B4** 60 33N 151 16W
Kendal, *U.K.* **22 D3** 54 20N 2 44W
Kendari, *Indonesia* **83 D4** 3 50S 122 30 E
Kenilworth, *U.K.* **23 H5** 52 21N 1 34W
Kenitra, *Morocco* **94 B4** 34 15N 6 40W
Kenmare, *Ireland* **30 E3** 51 53N 9 36W
Kenmare River, *Ireland* **30 E3** 51 48N 9 51W
Kennet →, *U.K.* **25 D7** 51 27N 0 57W
Kennewick, *U.S.A.* **110 A3** 46 12N 119 7W
Kenninghall, *U.K.* **25 B11** 52 26N 1 0 E
Kenogami →, *Canada* **109 C11** 51 6N 84 28W
Kenora, *Canada* **108 D10** 49 47N 94 29W
Kenosha, *U.S.A.* **112 D4** 42 35N 87 49W
Kent, *U.S.A.* **112 E7** 41 9N 81 22W
Kent □, *U.K.* **25 D10** 51 12N 0 40 E
Kent Pen., *Canada* **108 B9** 68 30N 107 0W
Kentisbeare, *U.K.* **24 E2** 50 51N 3 20W
Kenton, *U.S.A.* **112 E6** 40 39N 83 37W
Kentucky □, *U.S.A.* **112 G5** 37 0N 84 0W
Kentucky →, *U.S.A.* **112 F5** 38 41N 85 11W
Kentville, *Canada* **109 D13** 45 6N 64 29W
Kenya ■, *Africa* **96 D7** 1 0N 38 0 E
Kenya, Mt., *Kenya* **96 E7** 0 10S 37 18 E
Kerala □, *India* **84 P10** 11 0N 76 15 E
Kerch, *Ukraine* **73 E6** 45 20N 36 20 E
Kerguelen, *Ind. Oc.* **53 G13** 49 15S 69 10 E
Kericho, *Kenya* **96 E7** 0 22S 35 15 E
Kerinci, *Indonesia* **83 D2** 1 40S 101 15 E
Kermadec Is., *Pac. Oc.* **99 G15** 30 0S 178 15W
Kermadec Trench, *Pac. Oc.* **99 G15** 30 30S 176 0W
Kermān, *Iran* **87 D9** 30 15N 57 1 E
Kerrera, *U.K.* **20 B4** 56 24N 5 33W
Kerrobert, *Canada* **108 C9** 51 56N 109 8W
Kerry □, *Ireland* **30 D3** 52 7N 9 35W
Kerry Hd., *Ireland* **30 D3** 52 25N 9 56W
Kerulen →, *Asia* **81 B6** 48 48N 117 0 E
Kessingland, *U.K.* **25 B12** 52 26N 1 43 E
Keswick, *U.K.* **22 C2** 54 36N 3 8W
Ketchikan, *U.S.A.* **108 C6** 55 21N 131 39W
Kettering, *U.K.* **23 H7** 52 24N 0 43W
Kettle Ness, *U.K.* **22 C7** 54 33N 0 42W
Kettlewell, *U.K.* **22 D4** 54 9N 2 3W
Kewaunee, *U.S.A.* **112 C4** 44 27N 87 31W
Keweenaw B., *U.S.A.* **112 B3** 47 0N 88 15W
Keweenaw Pen., *U.S.A.* **112 B3** 47 30N 88 0W
Keweenaw Pt., *U.S.A.* **112 B4** 47 25N 87 43W
Kexby, *U.K.* **23 F7** 53 22N 0 42W
Key West, *U.S.A.* **111 F10** 24 33N 81 48W
Keyingham, *U.K.* **23 E8** 53 43N 0 7W
Keymer, *U.K.* **25 E8** 50 55N 0 7W
Keynsham, *U.K.* **24 D4** 51 24N 2 29W
Keyser, *U.S.A.* **112 F8** 39 26N 78 59W
Keyworth, *U.K.* **23 G6** 52 52N 1 5W
Khabarovsk, *Russia* **79 E15** 48 30N 135 5 E
Khairpur, *Pakistan* **84 F6** 27 32N 68 49 E
Khambhat, *India* **84 H8** 22 23N 72 33 E
Khambhat, G. of, *India* **84 J8** 20 45N 72 30 E
Khanewal, *Pakistan* **84 D7** 30 20N 71 55 E
Khaniá, *Greece* **71 G11** 35 30N 24 4 E
Kharagpur, *India* **85 H15** 22 20N 87 25 E
Kharg, *Iran* **86 D7** 29 15N 50 28 E
Kharkov, *Ukraine* **73 E6** 49 58N 36 20 E
Khartoum, *Sudan* **95 E12** 15 31N 32 35 E
Khaskovo, *Bulgaria* **71 D11** 41 56N 25 30 E
Khayelitsha, *S. Africa* **97 L3** 34 5S 18 42 E
Khemisset, *Morocco* **94 B4** 33 50N 6 1W
Kherson, *Ukraine* **73 E5** 46 35N 32 35 E
Khmelnytskyy, *Ukraine* **67 D14** 49 23N 27 0 E
Khojak Pass, *Afghan.* **84 D5** 30 51N 66 34 E
Kholm, *Afghan.* **87 B11** 36 45N 67 40 E
Khon Kaen, *Thailand* **83 B2** 16 30N 102 47 E
Khorāsān □, *Iran* **87 C9** 34 0N 58 0 E
Khorramābād, *Iran* **86 C7** 33 30N 48 25 E
Khorrāmshahr, *Iran* **86 D7** 30 29N 48 15 E
Khouribga, *Morocco* **94 B4** 32 58N 6 57W
Khudzhand, *Tajikistan* **87 B12** 40 17N 69 37 E
Khulna, *Bangla.* **85 H16** 22 45N 89 34 E
Khulna □, *Bangla.* **85 H16** 22 25N 89 35 E
Khushab, *Pakistan* **84 C8** 32 20N 72 20 E
Khuzdar, *Pakistan* **84 F5** 27 52N 66 30 E
Khvoy, *Iran* **86 B6** 38 35N 45 0 E
Khyber Pass, *Afghan.* **84 B7** 34 10N 71 8 E
Kibworth Beauchamp, *U.K.* **23 G7** 52 33N 0 59W
Kicking Horse Pass, *Canada* **108 C8** 51 28N 116 16W
Kidderminster, *U.K.* **23 H4** 52 24N 2 15W
Kidlington, *U.K.* **24 C6** 51 50N 1 15W
Kidsgrove, *U.K.* **23 F4** 53 5N 2 14W
Kidstones, *U.K.* **22 D4** 54 13N 2 2W
Kidwelly, *U.K.* **26 D5** 51 44N 4 18W
Kiel, *Germany* **66 A6** 54 19N 10 8 E
Kiel Canal = Nord-Ostsee-Kanal, *Germany* **66 A5** 54 12N 9 32 E
Kielce, *Poland* **67 C11** 50 52N 20 42 E
Kielder, *U.K.* **22 B3** 55 14N 2 35W
Kieler Bucht, *Germany* **66 A6** 54 35N 10 25 E
Kiev, *Ukraine* **67 C16** 50 30N 30 28 E
Kigali, *Rwanda* **96 E6** 1 59S 30 4 E
Kigoma-Ujiji, *Tanzania* **96 E5** 4 55S 29 36 E
Kihei, *U.S.A.* **110 H16** 20 47N 156 28W
Kikwit, *Dem. Rep. of the Congo* **96 E3** 5 0S 18 45 E
Kilauea Crater, *U.S.A.* **110 J17** 19 25N 155 17W
Kilbrannan Sd., *U.K.* **20 C5** 55 37N 5 26W
Kildare, *Ireland* **31 B9** 53 9N 6 55W
Kildare □, *Ireland* **31 B9** 53 10N 6 50W
Kilfinnane, *Ireland* **30 D6** 52 21N 8 28W
Kilham, *U.K.* **22 D8** 54 4N 0 23W
Kilimanjaro, *Tanzania* **96 E7** 3 7S 37 20 E
Kilkee, *Ireland* **30 C3** 52 41N 9 39W
Kilkeel, *U.K.* **29 C10** 54 4N 6 0W
Kilkenny, *Ireland* **31 C8** 52 39N 7 15W
Kilkenny □, *Ireland* **31 C8** 52 35N 7 15W
Kilkhampton, *U.K.* **27 F4** 50 52N 4 31W
Kilkieran B., *Ireland* **28 E2** 53 20N 9 41W
Killala, *Ireland* **28 C3** 54 13N 9 12W
Killala B., *Ireland* **28 C3** 54 16N 9 8W
Killaloe, *Ireland* **30 C6** 52 48N 8 28W
Killarney, *Ireland* **30 D4** 52 4N 9 30W
Killarney Nat. Park △, *Ireland* **30 E3** 52 0N 9 33W
Killary Harbour, *Ireland* **28 D2** 53 38N 9 52W
Killeen, *U.S.A.* **110 D7** 31 7N 97 44W
Killin, *U.K.* **20 B7** 56 28N 4 19W
Killinghall, *U.K.* **22 D5** 54 2N 1 33W
Killorglin, *Ireland* **30 D3** 52 6N 9 47W
Killybegs, *Ireland* **28 B5** 54 38N 8 26W
Kilmarnock, *U.K.* **20 C7** 55 37N 4 29W
Kilrush, *Ireland* **30 C4** 52 38N 9 29W
Kilsby, *U.K.* **23 H6** 52 20N 1 10W
Kilwinning, *U.K.* **20 C6** 55 39N 4 43W
Kimberley, *Australia* **98 D4** 16 20S 127 0 E
Kimberley, *S. Africa* **97 K4** 28 43S 24 46 E
Kimbolton, *U.K.* **23 H8** 52 18N 0 24W
Kimmirut, *Canada* **109 B13** 62 50N 69 50W
Kinabalu, Gunong, *Malaysia* **83 C3** 6 3N 116 14 E
Kincardine, *Canada* **112 C7** 44 10N 81 40W
Kinder Scout, *U.K.* **23 F5** 53 24N 1 52W
Kindersley, *Canada* **108 C9** 51 30N 109 10W
Kindia, *Guinea* **94 F3** 10 0N 12 52W
Kindu, *Dem. Rep. of the Congo* **96 E5** 2 55S 25 50 E
Kineshma, *Russia* **72 C7** 57 30N 42 5 E
Kineton, *U.K.* **24 B5** 52 10N 1 31W
King George I., *Antarctica* **55 C18** 60 0S 60 0W
King George Is., *Canada* **109 C11** 57 20N 80 30W
King I., *Australia* **98 H7** 39 50S 144 0 E
King William I., *Canada* **108 B10** 69 10N 97 25W
Kingman, *U.S.A.* **110 C4** 35 12N 114 4W
King's Lynn, *U.K.* **23 G9** 52 45N 0 24 E
King's Sutton, *U.K.* **24 B6** 52 2N 1 15W
King's Worthy, *U.K.* **24 D6** 51 6N 1 17W
Kingsbridge, *U.K.* **27 G6** 50 17N 3 47W
Kingsbury, *U.K.* **23 G5** 52 34N 1 40W
Kingscourt, *Ireland* **29 D8** 53 55N 6 48W
Kingskerswell, *U.K.* **27 G6** 50 29N 3 35W
Kingsland, *U.K.* **23 H3** 52 15N 2 48W
Kingsteignton, *U.K.* **27 F6** 50 33N 3 36W
Kingston, *Canada* **109 D12** 44 14N 76 30W
Kingston, *Jamaica* **114 a** 18 0N 76 50W
Kingston, *N.Y., U.S.A.* **113 E10** 41 56N 73 59W
Kingston, *Pa., U.S.A.* **113 E10** 41 16N 75 54W
Kingston upon Hull, *U.K.* **23 E8** 53 45N 0 21W
Kingston-upon-Thames □, *U.K.* **25 D8** 51 24N 0 17W
Kingstown, *St. Vincent* **115 E12** 13 10N 61 10W
Kingsville, *U.S.A.* **110 E7** 27 31N 97 52W
Kingswear, *U.K.* **27 G6** 50 21N 3 35W
Kingswood, *U.K.* **24 D3** 51 27N 2 31W
Kington, *U.K.* **23 H2** 52 13N 3 1W
Kingussie, *U.K.* **19 H9** 57 6N 4 2W
Kinlochleven, *U.K.* **18 J6** 56 43N 5 0W
Kinnairds Hd., *U.K.* **19 G13** 57 43N 2 1W
Kinross, *U.K.* **21 B9** 56 13N 3 25W
Kinsale, *Ireland* **30 E5** 51 42N 8 31W
Kinsale, Old Hd. of, *Ireland* **30 E5** 51 37N 8 33W
Kinshasa, *Dem. Rep. of the Congo* **96 E3** 4 20S 15 15 E
Kintore, *U.K.* **19 H13** 57 14N 2 20W
Kintyre, *U.K.* **20 D4** 55 30N 5 35W
Kintyre, Mull of, *U.K.* **20 D4** 55 17N 5 47W
Kippure, *Ireland* **31 B10** 53 11N 6 21W
Kirensk, *Russia* **79 D12** 57 50N 107 55 E
Kirghizia = Kyrgyzstan ■, *Asia* **79 E9** 42 0N 75 0 E
Kirgiz Steppe, *Eurasia* **73 E10** 50 0N 55 0 E
Kiribati ■, *Pac. Oc.* **102 H10** 5 0S 180 0 E
Kırıkkale, *Turkey* **73 G5** 39 51N 33 32 E
Kiritimati, *Kiribati* **103 G12** 1 58N 157 27W
Kirkbean, *U.K.* **22 C1** 54 55N 3 36W
Kirkbride, *U.K.* **22 C2** 54 54N 3 12W
Kirkburton, *U.K.* **23 E5** 53 37N 1 42W
Kirkby, *U.K.* **23 F3** 53 30N 2 54W
Kirkby-in-Ashfield, *U.K.* **23 F6** 53 6N 1 14W
Kirkby Lonsdale, *U.K.* **22 D3** 54 12N 2 36W
Kirkby Malzeard, *U.K.* **22 D5** 54 10N 1 37W
Kirkby Stephen, *U.K.* **22 D4** 54 29N 2 21W
Kirkby Thore, *U.K.* **22 C3** 54 37N 2 32W
Kirkbymoorside, *U.K.* **22 D7** 54 17N 0 56W
Kirkcaldy, *U.K.* **21 B9** 56 7N 3 9W
Kirkcudbright, *U.K.* **20 E7** 54 50N 4 2W
Kirkham, *U.K.* **23 E3** 53 47N 2 53W
Kirkintilloch, *U.K.* **20 C7** 55 56N 4 8W
Kirkland Lake, *Canada* **109 D11** 48 9N 80 2W
Kırklareli, *Turkey* **86 A1** 41 44N 27 15 E
Kirkoswald, *U.K.* **22 C3** 54 46N 2 41W
Kirksville, *U.S.A.* **111 B8** 40 12N 92 35W
Kirkūk, *Iraq* **86 C6** 35 30N 44 21 E
Kirkwall, *U.K.* **19 E12** 58 59N 2 58W
Kirkwhelpington, *U.K.* **22 B5** 55 9N 1 59W
Kirov, *Russia* **72 C8** 58 35N 49 40 E
Kirovohrad, *Ukraine* **73 E5** 48 35N 32 20 E
Kirriemuir, *U.K.* **19 J11** 56 41N 3 1W
Kırşehir, *Turkey* **73 G5** 39 14N 34 5 E
Kirtling, *U.K.* **25 B9** 52 12N 0 28 E
Kirtlington, *U.K.* **24 C6** 51 53N 1 15W
Kirton, *U.K.* **23 G8** 52 56N 0 3W
Kirton in Lindsey, *U.K.* **23 F7** 53 29N 0 34W
Kiruna, *Sweden* **63 D8** 67 52N 20 15 E
Kiryū, *Japan* **82 E6** 36 24N 139 20 E
Kisangani, *Dem. Rep. of the Congo* **96 D5** 0 35N 25 15 E
Kishanganj, *India* **85 F16** 26 3N 88 14 E
Kishinev, *Moldova* **67 E15** 47 2N 28 50 E
Kisii, *Kenya* **96 E6** 0 40S 34 45 E
Kislovodsk, *Russia* **73 F7** 43 50N 42 45 E
Kismayu, *Somali Rep.* **91 G8** 0 22S 42 32 E
Kisumu, *Kenya* **96 E6** 0 3S 34 45 E
Kitakyūshū, *Japan* **82 G2** 33 50N 130 50 E
Kitale, *Kenya* **96 D7** 1 0N 35 0 E
Kitami, *Japan* **82 B8** 43 48N 143 54 E
Kitchener, *Canada* **109 D11** 43 27N 80 29W
Kíthira, *Greece* **71 F10** 36 8N 23 0 E
Kitimat, *Canada* **108 C7** 54 3N 128 38W
Kittanning, *U.S.A.* **112 E8** 40 49N 79 31W
Kitwe, *Zambia* **97 G5** 12 54S 28 13 E
Kivu, L., *Dem. Rep. of the Congo* **96 E5** 1 48S 29 0 E
Kızıl Irmak →, *Turkey* **73 F6** 41 44N 35 58 E
Kizlyar, *Russia* **73 F8** 43 51N 46 40 E
Kladno, *Czech Rep.* **66 C8** 50 10N 14 7 E
Klagenfurt, *Austria* **66 E8** 46 38N 14 20 E
Klaipėda, *Lithuania* **72 C3** 55 43N 21 10 E
Klamath →, *U.S.A.* **110 B2** 41 33N 124 5W
Klamath Falls, *U.S.A.* **110 B2** 42 13N 121 46W
Klarälven →, *Sweden* **63 F6** 59 23N 13 32 E
Klerksdorp, *S. Africa* **97 K5** 26 53S 26 38 E
Kluane L., *Canada* **108 B6** 61 15N 138 40W
Klyuchevskaya, *Russia* **79 D18** 55 50N 160 30 E
Knaresborough, *U.K.* **23 D6** 54 1N 1 28W
Knebworth, *U.K.* **25 C8** 51 52N 0 11W
Knighton, *U.K.* **23 H2** 52 21N 3 3W
Knock, *Ireland* **28 D4** 53 48N 8 55W
Knockmealdown Mts., *Ireland* **30 D7** 52 14N 7 56W
Knossós, *Greece* **71 G11** 35 16N 25 10 E
Knottingley, *U.K.* **23 E6** 53 43N 1 16W
Knowle, *U.K.* **23 H5** 52 24N 1 44W
Knoxville, *U.S.A.* **111 C10** 35 58N 83 55W
Knutsford, *U.K.* **23 F4** 53 18N 2 21W
Kōbe, *Japan* **82 F4** 34 45N 135 10 E
Koblenz, *Germany* **66 C4** 50 21N 7 36 E
Kocaeli, *Turkey* **73 F4** 40 45N 29 50 E
Koch Bihar, *India* **85 F16** 26 22N 89 29 E
Kōchi, *Japan* **82 G3** 33 30N 133 35 E
Kodiak, *U.S.A.* **108 C4** 57 47N 152 24W
Kodiak I., *U.S.A.* **108 C4** 57 30N 152 45W
Koforidua, *Ghana* **94 G5** 6 3N 0 17W
Kōfu, *Japan* **82 F6** 35 40N 138 30 E
Kohat, *Pakistan* **84 C7** 33 40N 71 29 E
Kohima, *India* **85 G19** 25 35N 94 10 E
Kohtla-Järve, *Estonia* **72 C4** 59 20N 27 20 E
Kokkola, *Finland* **63 E8** 63 50N 23 8 E
Koko Kyunzu, *Burma* **85 M18** 14 10N 93 25 E
Kokomo, *U.S.A.* **112 E4** 40 29N 86 8W
Kökshetaū, *Kazakhstan* **79 D8** 53 20N 69 25 E
Koksoak →, *Canada* **109 C13** 58 30N 68 10W
Kola Pen., *Russia* **72 A6** 67 30N 38 0 E
Kolar Gold Fields, *India* **84 N11** 12 58N 78 16 E
Kolguyev, *Russia* **72 A8** 69 20N 48 30 E
Kolhapur, *India* **84 L9** 16 43N 74 15 E
Kolkata, *India* **85 H16** 22 36N 88 24 E
Kolomna, *Russia* **72 C6** 55 8N 38 45 E
Kolomyya, *Ukraine* **73 E4** 48 31N 25 2 E
Kolpino, *Russia* **72 C5** 59 44N 30 39 E
Kolwezi, *Dem. Rep. of the Congo* **96 G5** 10 40S 25 25 E
Kolyma →, *Russia* **79 C18** 69 30N 161 0 E
Kolyma Ra., *Russia* **79 C17** 63 0N 157 0 E
Komandorskiye Is., *Russia* **79 D18** 55 0N 167 0 E
Komatsu, *Japan* **82 E5** 36 25N 136 30 E
Komi □, *Russia* **72 B10** 64 0N 55 0 E
Kompong Cham, *Cambodia* **83 B2** 12 0N 105 30 E
Komsomolsk, *Russia* **79 D15** 50 30N 137 0 E
Konarhā □, *Afghan.* **87 C12** 34 30N 71 3 E
Kong Frederik VI Kyst, *Greenland* **109 B15** 63 0N 43 0W
Konin, *Poland* **67 B10** 52 12N 18 15 E
Konosha, *Russia* **72 B7** 61 0N 40 5 E
Konotop, *Ukraine* **73 D5** 51 12N 33 7 E
Konya, *Turkey* **73 G5** 37 52N 32 35 E
Kootenay L., *Canada* **108 D8** 49 45N 116 50W
Kopet Dagh, *Asia* **87 B9** 38 0N 58 0 E
Korçë, *Albania* **71 D9** 40 37N 20 50 E
Kordestān □, *Iran* **86 C6** 36 0N 47 0 E
Kordofân, *Sudan* **95 F11** 13 0N 29 0 E
Korea, North ■, *Asia* **81 C7** 40 0N 127 0 E
Korea, South ■, *Asia* **81 C7** 36 0N 128 0 E
Korea Bay, *Korea* **81 C7** 39 0N 124 0 E
Korea Strait, *Asia* **81 C7** 34 0N 129 30 E
Korhogo, *Ivory C.* **94 G4** 9 29N 5 28W
Kōriyama, *Japan* **82 E7** 37 24N 140 23 E
Koror, *Palau* **102 G5** 7 20N 134 28 E
Körös →, *Hungary* **67 E11** 46 43N 20 12 E
Korosten, *Ukraine* **73 D4** 50 54N 28 36 E
Kortrijk, *Belgium* **65 D3** 50 50N 3 17 E
Kos, *Greece* **71 F12** 36 50N 27 15 E
Kosciuszko, Mt., *Australia* **98 H8** 36 27S 148 16 E
Košice, *Slovak Rep.* **67 D11** 48 42N 21 15 E
Kosovo □, *Yugoslavia* **71 C9** 42 30N 21 0 E
Kôstî, *Sudan* **95 F12** 13 8N 32 43 E
Kostroma, *Russia* **72 C7** 57 50N 40 58 E
Koszalin, *Poland* **66 A9** 54 11N 16 8 E
Kota, *India* **84 G9** 25 14N 75 49 E
Kota Baharu, *Malaysia* **83 C2** 6 7N 102 14 E
Kota Kinabalu, *Malaysia* **83 C3** 6 0N 116 4 E
Kotabumi, *Indonesia* **83 D2** 4 49S 104 54 E
Kotelnich, *Russia* **72 C8** 58 22N 48 24 E
Kotka, *Finland* **63 E9** 60 28N 26 58 E
Kotlas, *Russia* **72 B8** 61 17N 46 43 E
Kotri, *Pakistan* **84 G6** 25 22N 68 22 E
Kotuy →, *Russia* **79 B12** 71 54N 102 6 E
Kotzebue, *U.S.A.* **108 B3** 66 53N 162 39W
Kovel, *Ukraine* **72 D3** 51 11N 24 38 E
Kovrov, *Russia* **72 C7** 56 25N 41 25 E
Kra, Isthmus of, *Thailand* **83 B1** 10 15N 99 30 E
Kragujevac, *Serbia, Yug.* **71 B9** 44 2N 20 56 E
Krajina, *Bos.-H.* **70 B7** 44 45N 16 35 E
Krakatau, *Indonesia* **83 D2** 6 10S 105 20 E
Kraków, *Poland* **67 C10** 50 4N 19 57 E
Kramatorsk, *Ukraine* **73 E6** 48 50N 37 30 E
Krasnodar, *Russia* **73 E6** 45 5N 39 0 E
Krasnokamsk, *Russia* **72 C10** 58 4N 55 48 E
Krasnoturinsk, *Russia* **72 C11** 59 46N 60 12 E
Krasnoyarsk, *Russia* **79 D11** 56 8N 93 0 E
Krasnýy Luch, *Ukraine* **73 E6** 48 13N 39 0 E
Krefeld, *Germany* **66 C4** 51 20N 6 33 E
Kremenchuk, *Ukraine* **73 E5** 49 5N 33 25 E
Krishna →, *India* **85 M12** 15 57N 80 59 E
Kristiansand, *Norway* **63 F5** 58 8N 8 1 E
Kristiansund, *Norway* **63 E5** 63 7N 7 45 E
Krivoy Rog, *Ukraine* **73 E5** 47 51N 33 20 E
Kronshtadt, *Russia* **72 B4** 59 57N 29 51 E
Kroonstad, *S. Africa* **97 K5** 27 43S 27 19 E
Kropotkin, *Russia* **73 E7** 45 28N 40 28 E
Krosno, *Poland* **67 D11** 49 42N 21 46 E
Kruševac, *Serbia, Yug.* **71 C9** 43 35N 21 28 E
Ksar el Kebir, *Morocco* **94 B4** 35 0N 6 0W
Kuala Belait, *Malaysia* **83 C3** 4 35N 114 11 E
Kuala Lumpur, *Malaysia* **83 C2** 3 9N 101 41 E
Kuala Terengganu, *Malaysia* **83 C2** 5 20N 103 8 E
Kuantan, *Malaysia* **83 C2** 3 49N 103 20 E
Kuching, *Malaysia* **83 C3** 1 33N 110 25 E
Kudymkar, *Russia* **72 C9** 59 1N 54 39 E
Kugluktuk, *Canada* **108 B8** 67 50N 115 5W
Kŭlob, *Tajikistan* **87 B12** 37 55N 69 50 E
Kulsary, *Kazakhstan* **73 E9** 46 59N 54 1 E
Kuma →, *Russia* **73 F8** 44 55N 47 0 E
Kumagaya, *Japan* **82 E6** 36 9N 139 22 E
Kumamoto, *Japan* **82 G2** 32 45N 130 45 E
Kumanovo, *Macedonia* **71 C9** 42 9N 21 42 E
Kumasi, *Ghana* **94 G5** 6 41N 1 38W
Kumbakonam, *India* **84 P11** 10 58N 79 25 E
Kumertau, *Russia* **72 D10** 52 45N 55 57 E
Kungur, *Russia* **72 C10** 57 25N 56 57 E
Kunlun Shan, *Asia* **80 C3** 36 0N 86 30 E
Kunming, *China* **80 D5** 25 1N 102 41 E
Kuopio, *Finland* **63 E9** 62 53N 27 35 E
Kupang, *Indonesia* **83 E4** 10 19S 123 39 E
Kuqa, *China* **80 B3** 41 35N 82 30 E
Kür →, *Azerbaijan* **73 G8** 39 29N 49 15 E
Kurdistan, *Asia* **86 B5** 37 20N 43 30 E
Kure, *Japan* **82 F3** 34 14N 132 32 E
Kurgan, *Russia* **79 D8** 55 26N 65 18 E
Kuril Is., *Russia* **79 E17** 45 0N 150 0 E
Kuril Trench, *Pac. Oc.* **102 C7** 44 0N 153 0 E
Kurnool, *India* **84 M11** 15 45N 78 0 E
Kursk, *Russia* **72 D6** 51 42N 36 11 E
Kuruktag, *China* **80 B3** 41 0N 89 0 E
Kurume, *Japan* **82 G2** 33 15N 130 30 E
Kushiro, *Japan* **82 B9** 43 0N 144 25 E
Kushtia, *Bangla.* **85 H16** 23 55N 89 5 E
Kuskokwim B., *U.S.A.* **108 C3** 59 45N 162 25W
Kütahya, *Turkey* **73 G5** 39 30N 30 2 E
Kutaisi, *Georgia* **73 F7** 42 19N 42 40 E
Kuujjuaq, *Canada* **109 C13** 58 6N 68 15W
Kuujjuarapik, *Canada* **109 C12** 55 20N 77 35W
Kuwait, *Kuwait* **86 D7** 29 30N 48 0 E
Kuwait ■, *Asia* **86 D6** 29 30N 47 30 E
Kuybyshev Res., *Russia* **72 C8** 55 2N 49 30 E
Kuznetsk, *Russia* **72 D8** 53 12N 46 40 E
Kuzomen, *Russia* **72 A6** 66 22N 36 50 E
KwaMashu, *S. Africa* **97 K6** 29 45S 30 58 E
Kwangju, *S. Korea* **81 C7** 35 9N 126 54 E
Kwango →, *Dem. Rep. of the Congo* **96 E3** 3 14S 17 22 E
KwaZulu Natal □, *S. Africa* **97 K6** 29 0S 30 0 E
Kwekwe, *Zimbabwe* **97 H5** 18 58S 29 48 E
Kyle of Lochalsh, *U.K.* **18 H6** 57 17N 5 44W
Kyoga, L., *Uganda* **96 D6** 1 35N 33 0 E
Kyōto, *Japan* **82 F4** 35 0N 135 45 E
Kyrenia, *Cyprus* **86 C3** 35 20N 33 20 E
Kyrgyzstan ■, *Asia* **79 E9** 42 0N 75 0 E
Kyūshū, *Japan* **82 G2** 33 0N 131 0 E
Kyzyl Kum, *Uzbekistan* **87 A10** 42 30N 65 0 E
Kyzyl-Orda, *Kazakhstan* **79 E8** 44 48N 65 28 E

L

La Ceiba, *Honduras* **114 D7** 15 40N 86 50W
La Coruña, *Spain* **69 A1** 43 20N 8 25W
La Crosse, *U.S.A.* **111 B8** 43 48N 91 15W
La Désirade, *Guadeloupe* **114 b** 16 18N 61 3W
La Grande, *U.S.A.* **110 A3** 45 20N 118 5W
La Grande →, *Canada* **109 C12** 53 50N 79 0W
La Grange, *U.S.A.* **111 D10** 33 2N 85 2W
La Junta, *U.S.A.* **110 C6** 37 59N 103 33W
La Loche, *Canada* **108 C9** 56 29N 109 26W
La Louvière, *Belgium* **65 D4** 50 27N 4 10 E
La Mancha, *Spain* **69 C4** 39 10N 2 54W
La Oroya, *Peru* **120 D2** 11 32S 75 54W
La Palma, *Canary Is.* **94 C2** 28 40N 17 50W
La Paz, *Bolivia* **120 D3** 16 20S 68 10W

La Paz   **Luing**

Lule älv   **Mendip Hills**

Mendlesham   **Nasik**

Nasirabad, *India* **84 F9** 26 15N 74 45 E
Nassau, *Bahamas* **115 B9** 25 5N 77 20W
Nasser, L., *Egypt* **95 D12** 23 0N 32 30 E
Natal, *Brazil* **120 C6** 5 47S 35 13W
Natashquan, *Canada* **109 C13** 50 14N 61 46W
Natashquan →, *Canada* **109 C13** 50 7N 61 50W
Natchez, *U.S.A.* **111 D8** 31 34N 91 24W
Natchitoches, *U.S.A.* **111 D8** 31 46N 93 5W
Nathdwara, *India* **84 G8** 24 55N 73 50 E
Natitingou, *Benin* **94 F6** 10 20N 1 26 E
Natron, L., *Tanzania* **96 E7** 2 20S 36 0 E
Natuna Besar, Kepulauan, *Indonesia* **83 C2** 4 0N 108 15 E
Nauru ■, *Pac. Oc.* **102 H8** 1 0S 166 0 E
Navarino, I., *Chile* **121 H3** 55 0S 67 40W
Navarra □, *Spain* **69 A5** 42 40N 1 40W
Navenby, *U.K.* **23 F7** 53 6N 0 31W
Naver →, *U.K.* **19 E9** 58 32N 4 14W
Navojoa, *Mexico* **114 B3** 27 0N 109 30W
Navsari, *India* **84 J8** 20 57N 72 59 E
Nawabshah, *Pakistan* **84 F6** 26 15N 68 25 E
Naxçıvan □, *Azerbaijan* **73 G8** 39 25N 45 26 E
Náxos, *Greece* **71 F11** 37 8N 25 25 E
Nazaré, *Brazil* **122 B3** 13 2S 39 0W
Nazas →, *Mexico* **114 B4** 25 35N 103 25W
Nazca, *Peru* **120 D2** 14 50S 74 57W
Naze, The, *U.K.* **25 C11** 51 53N 1 18 E
Ndjamena, *Chad* **95 F8** 12 10N 14 59 E
Ndola, *Zambia* **97 G5** 13 0S 28 34 E
Neagh, Lough, *U.K.* **29 B9** 54 37N 6 25W
Near Is., *U.S.A.* **108 C1** 52 30N 174 0 E
Neath, *U.K.* **24 C1** 51 39N 3 48W
Nebitdag, *Turkmenistan* **87 B8** 39 30N 54 22 E
Nebraska □, *U.S.A.* **110 B7** 41 30N 99 30W
Neckar →, *Germany* **66 D5** 49 27N 8 29 E
Necochea, *Argentina* **121 F4** 38 30S 58 50W
Needham Market, *U.K.* **25 B11** 52 9N 1 4 E
Needles, The, *U.K.* **24 E5** 50 39N 1 35W
Neenah, *U.S.A.* **112 C3** 44 11N 88 28W
Neepawa, *Canada* **108 C10** 50 15N 99 30W
Neftekumsk, *Russia* **73 F7** 44 46N 44 50 E
Negaunee, *U.S.A.* **112 B4** 46 30N 87 36W
Negele, *Ethiopia* **88 F2** 5 20N 39 36 E
Negombo, *Sri Lanka* **84 R11** 7 12N 79 50 E
Negra, Pta., *Peru* **116 D2** 6 6S 81 10W
Negril, *Jamaica* **114 a** 18 22N 78 20W
Negro →, *Argentina* **121 G3** 41 2S 62 47W
Negro →, *Brazil* **120 C3** 3 0S 60 0W
Negros, *Phil.* **83 C4** 9 30N 122 40 E
Neijiang, *China* **80 D5** 29 35N 104 55 E
Neisse →, *Europe* **66 B8** 52 4N 14 46 E
Neiva, *Colombia* **120 B2** 2 56N 75 18W
Nellore, *India* **84 M11** 14 27N 79 59 E
Nelson, *Canada* **108 D8** 49 30N 117 20W
Nelson, *N.Z.* **99 J13** 41 18S 173 16 E
Nelson, *U.K.* **23 E4** 53 50N 2 13W
Nelson →, *Canada* **108 C10** 54 33N 98 2W
Neman →, *Lithuania* **72 C3** 55 25N 21 10 E
Nenagh, *Ireland* **30 C6** 52 52N 8 11W
Nene →, *U.K.* **23 G9** 52 49N 0 11 E
Nenjiang, *China* **81 B7** 49 10N 125 10 E
Neosho →, *U.S.A.* **111 C7** 36 48N 95 18W
Nepal ■, *Asia* **85 F14** 28 0N 84 30 E
Nephi, *U.S.A.* **110 C4** 39 43N 111 50W
Nephin, *Ireland* **28 C3** 54 1N 9 22W
Neryungri, *Russia* **79 D14** 57 38N 124 28 E
Ness, L., *U.K.* **19 H8** 57 15N 4 32W
Neston, *U.K.* **23 F2** 53 17N 3 4W
Netherbury, *U.K.* **24 E3** 50 46N 2 45W
Netherlands ■, *Europe* **65 C5** 52 0N 5 30 E
Netherlands Antilles ⊠, *W. Indies* **115 E11** 12 15N 69 0W
Netley, *U.K.* **24 E6** 50 52N 1 20W
Nettilling L., *Canada* **109 B12** 66 30N 71 0W
Nettlebed, *U.K.* **25 C7** 51 34N 0 59W
Nettleham, *U.K.* **23 F8** 53 16N 0 29W
Neuchâtel, *Switz.* **66 E4** 47 0N 6 55 E
Neuchâtel, Lac de, *Switz.* **66 E4** 46 53N 6 50 E
Neuquén, *Argentina* **121 F3** 38 55S 68 0W
Neusiedler See, *Austria* **67 E9** 47 50N 16 47 E
Neva →, *Russia* **72 C5** 59 50N 30 30 E
Nevada □, *U.S.A.* **110 C3** 39 0N 117 0W
Nevers, *France* **68 C5** 47 0N 3 9 E
Nevinnomyssk, *Russia* **73 F7** 44 40N 42 0 E
New Abbey, *U.K.* **22 C1** 54 59N 3 37W
New Alresford, *U.K.* **24 D6** 51 5N 1 8W
New Amsterdam, *Guyana* **120 B4** 6 15N 57 36W
New Bedford, *U.S.A.* **113 E12** 41 38N 70 56W
New Britain, *Papua N. G.* **98 B9** 5 50S 150 20 E
New Britain, *U.S.A.* **113 E11** 41 40N 72 47W
New Brunswick, *U.S.A.* **113 E10** 40 30N 74 27W
New Brunswick □, *Canada* **109 D13** 46 50N 66 30W
New Caledonia ⊠, *Pac. Oc.* **99 E12** 21 0S 165 0 E
New Castle, *Ind., U.S.A.* **112 F5** 39 55N 85 22W
New Castle, *Pa., U.S.A.* **112 E7** 41 0N 80 21W
New Delhi, *India* **84 E10** 28 37N 77 13 E
New England, *U.S.A.* **111 B12** 46 32N 102 52W
New Forest, *U.K.* **24 E5** 50 53N 1 34W
New Galloway, *U.K.* **20 D7** 55 5N 4 9W
New Georgia Is., *Solomon Is.* **99 B10** 8 15S 157 30 E
New Glasgow, *Canada* **109 D13** 45 35N 62 36W
New Guinea, *Oceania* **98 B7** 4 0S 136 0 E
New Hampshire □, *U.S.A.* **113 D12** 44 0N 71 30W
New Haven, *U.S.A.* **113 E11** 41 18N 72 55W
New Hebrides = Vanuatu ■, *Pac. Oc.* **99 D12** 15 0S 168 0 E
New Holland, *U.K.* **23 E8** 53 42N 0 21W
New Iberia, *U.S.A.* **111 D8** 30 1N 91 49W
New Ireland, *Papua N. G.* **98 A9** 3 20S 151 50 E
New Jersey □, *U.S.A.* **113 E10** 40 0N 74 30W
New Lexington, *U.S.A.* **112 F6** 39 43N 82 13W
New Liskeard, *Canada* **109 D12** 47 31N 79 41W
New London, *U.S.A.* **113 E11** 41 22N 72 6W
New Mexico □, *U.S.A.* **110 D5** 34 30N 106 0W
New Mills, *U.K.* **23 F5** 53 23N 2 0W
New Milton, *U.K.* **24 E5** 50 45N 1 40W
New Orleans, *U.S.A.* **111 E8** 29 58N 90 4W
New Philadelphia, *U.S.A.* **112 E7** 40 30N 81 27W
New Plymouth, *N.Z.* **99 H13** 39 4S 174 5 E
New Providence I., *Bahamas* **115 B9** 25 25N 78 35W
New Quay, *U.K.* **26 C5** 52 13N 4 21W
New Radnor, *U.K.* **23 H2** 52 15N 3 9W
New Romney, *U.K.* **25 E10** 50 59N 0 57 E
New Ross, *Ireland* **31 D9** 52 23N 6 57W
New Rossington, *U.K.* **23 F6** 53 29N 1 4W
New Siberian Is., *Russia* **79 B15** 75 0N 142 0 E
New South Wales □, *Australia* **98 G8** 33 0S 146 0 E
New York, *U.S.A.* **113 E11** 40 45N 74 0W
New York □, *U.S.A.* **113 D9** 43 0N 75 0W
New Zealand ■, *Oceania* **99 J14** 40 0S 176 0 E
Newark, *Del., U.S.A.* **113 F10** 39 41N 75 46W
Newark, *N.J., U.S.A.* **113 E10** 40 44N 74 10W
Newark, *N.Y., U.S.A.* **112 D9** 43 3N 77 6W
Newark, *Ohio, U.S.A.* **112 E6** 40 3N 82 24W
Newark-on-Trent, *U.K.* **23 F7** 53 5N 0 48W
Newberry, *U.S.A.* **112 B5** 46 21N 85 30W
Newbiggin-by-the-Sea, *U.K.* **22 B5** 55 11N 1 31W
Newbigging, *U.K.* **22 A1** 55 42N 3 34W
Newburgh, *U.S.A.* **113 E10** 41 30N 74 1W
Newburn, *U.K.* **22 C5** 54 59N 1 43W
Newbury, *U.K.* **24 D6** 51 24N 1 20W
Newburyport, *U.S.A.* **113 D12** 42 49N 70 53W
Newby Bridge, *U.K.* **22 D3** 54 17N 2 57W
Newcastle, *Australia* **98 G9** 33 0S 151 46 E
Newcastle, *Canada* **113 B15** 47 1N 65 38W
Newcastle, *U.K.* **29 C10** 54 13N 5 54W
Newcastle Emlyn, *U.K.* **26 C5** 52 2N 4 28W
Newcastle-under-Lyme, *U.K.* **23 F4** 53 1N 2 14W
Newcastle-upon-Tyne, *U.K.* **22 C5** 54 58N 1 36W
Newcastle West, *Ireland* **30 D4** 52 27N 9 3W
Newcastleton, *U.K.* **22 B3** 55 11N 2 49W
Newent, *U.K.* **24 C4** 51 56N 2 24W
Newfoundland □, *Canada* **109 C14** 53 0N 58 0W
Newham □, *U.K.* **25 C9** 51 31N 0 3 E
Newhaven, *U.K.* **25 E9** 50 47N 0 3 E
Newington, *Kent, U.K.* **25 D11** 51 6N 1 7 E
Newington, *Kent, U.K.* **25 D10** 51 21N 0 41 E
Newlyn, *U.K.* **27 G2** 50 6N 5 34W
Newlyn East, *U.K.* **27 G3** 50 22N 5 5W
Newman, *Australia* **98 E2** 23 18S 119 45 E
Newmarket, *Ireland* **30 D5** 52 13N 9 0W
Newmarket, *U.K.* **25 B9** 52 15N 0 25 E
Newnham, *U.K.* **24 C4** 51 48N 2 27W
Newport, *Ireland* **28 D2** 53 53N 9 33W
Newport, *Essex, U.K.* **25 C9** 51 59N 0 14 E
Newport, *I. of W., U.K.* **24 E6** 50 42N 1 17W
Newport, *Newp., U.K.* **24 C3** 51 35N 3 0W
Newport, *Pembs., U.K.* **26 C4** 52 1N 4 51W
Newport, *Telford & Wrekin, U.K.* **23 G4** 52 46N 2 22W
Newport, *Ark., U.S.A.* **111 C8** 35 37N 91 16W
Newport, *Ky., U.S.A.* **112 F5** 39 5N 84 30W
Newport, *R.I., U.S.A.* **113 E12** 41 29N 71 19W
Newport, *Vt., U.S.A.* **113 C11** 44 56N 72 13W
Newport News, *U.S.A.* **111 C11** 36 59N 76 25W
Newport Pagnell, *U.K.* **25 B7** 52 5N 0 43W
Newquay, *U.K.* **27 G3** 50 25N 5 6W
Newry, *U.K.* **29 C9** 54 11N 6 21W
Newton Abbot, *U.K.* **27 F6** 50 32N 3 37W
Newton Arlosh, *U.K.* **22 C2** 54 53N 3 14W
Newton Aycliffe, *U.K.* **22 C5** 54 37N 1 34W
Newton Ferrers, *U.K.* **27 G5** 50 19N 4 3W
Newton le Willows, *U.K.* **23 F3** 53 28N 2 38W
Newton St. Cyres, *U.K.* **24 E1** 50 46N 3 36W
Newton Stewart, *U.K.* **20 E6** 54 57N 4 30W
Newtonmore, *U.K.* **19 H9** 57 4N 4 8W
Newtown, *U.K.* **23 G2** 52 31N 3 19W
Newtown St. Boswells, *U.K.* **22 A3** 55 34N 2 39W
Newtownabbey, *U.K.* **29 B10** 54 40N 5 56W
Newtownards, *U.K.* **29 B10** 54 36N 5 42W
Newtownstewart, *U.K.* **28 B7** 54 43N 7 23W
Neyshābūr, *Iran* **87 B9** 36 10N 58 50 E
Ngaoundéré, *Cameroon* **96 C2** 7 15N 13 35 E
Ngoring Hu, *China* **80 C4** 34 55N 97 5 E
Nha Trang, *Vietnam* **83 B2** 12 16N 109 10 E
Nhamundá →, *Brazil* **120 C4** 2 12S 56 41W
Niagara Falls, *Canada* **109 D12** 43 7N 79 5W
Niagara Falls, *U.S.A.* **112 D8** 43 5N 79 4W
Niamey, *Niger* **94 F6** 13 27N 2 6 E
Nias, *Indonesia* **83 C1** 1 0N 97 30 E
Nicaragua ■, *Cent. Amer.* **114 E7** 11 40N 85 30W
Nicaragua, L. de, *Nic.* **114 E7** 12 0N 85 30W
Nice, *France* **68 E7** 43 42N 7 14 E
Nicholasville, *U.S.A.* **112 G5** 37 53N 84 34W
Nicobar Is., *Ind. Oc.* **83 C1** 8 0N 93 30 E
Nicosia, *Cyprus* **86 C3** 35 10N 33 25 E
Nicoya, Pen. de, *Costa Rica* **114 F7** 9 45N 85 40W
Nidd →, *U.K.* **23 E6** 53 59N 1 23W
Nidderdale, *U.K.* **22 D5** 54 5N 1 46W
Niedersachsen □, *Germany* **66 B5** 52 50N 9 0 E
Nieuw Nickerie, *Suriname* **120 B4** 6 0N 56 59W
Niğde, *Turkey* **86 B3** 37 58N 34 40 E
Niger ■, *W. Afr.* **94 E7** 17 30N 10 0 E
Niger →, *W. Afr.* **94 G7** 5 33N 6 33 E
Nigeria ■, *W. Afr.* **94 G7** 8 30N 8 0 E
Niigata, *Japan* **82 E6** 37 58N 139 0 E
Niihau, *U.S.A.* **110 H14** 21 54N 160 9W
Nijmegen, *Neths.* **65 C5** 51 50N 5 52 E
Nikolayev, *Ukraine* **73 E5** 46 58N 32 0 E
Nikolayevsk-na-Amur, *Russia* **79 D16** 53 8N 140 44 E
Nikopol, *Ukraine* **73 E5** 47 35N 34 25 E
Nile, *Africa* **95 B12** 30 10N 31 6 E
Nimach, *India* **84 G9** 24 30N 74 56 E
Nîmes, *France* **68 E6** 43 50N 4 23 E
Nīmrūz □, *Afghan.* **87 D10** 30 0N 62 0 E
Nīnawá, *Iraq* **86 B5** 36 25N 43 10 E
Ninfield, *U.K.* **25 E9** 50 53N 0 26 E
Ningbo, *China* **81 D7** 29 51N 121 28 E
Ningxia Hui □, *China* **80 C5** 38 0N 106 0 E
Niobrara →, *U.S.A.* **110 B7** 42 46N 98 3W
Niort, *France* **68 C3** 46 19N 0 29W
Nipawin, *Canada* **108 C9** 53 20N 104 0W
Nipigon, *Canada* **112 A3** 49 0N 88 17W
Nipigon, L., *Canada* **109 D11** 49 50N 88 30W
Nipissing, L., *Canada* **109 D12** 46 20N 80 0W
Niquelândia, *Brazil* **122 B1** 14 33S 48 23W
Niš, *Serbia, Yug.* **71 C9** 43 19N 21 58 E
Niterói, *Brazil* **122 D2** 22 52S 43 0W
Nith →, *U.K.* **21 D8** 55 14N 3 33W
Niton, *U.K.* **24 E6** 50 35N 1 17W
Nitra, *Slovak Rep.* **67 D10** 48 19N 18 4 E
Nitra →, *Slovak Rep.* **67 E10** 47 46N 18 10 E
Niuafo'ou, *Tonga* **99 D15** 15 30S 175 58W
Niue, *Cook Is.* **99 D17** 19 2S 169 54W
Nivernais, *France* **68 C5** 47 15N 3 30 E
Nizamabad, *India* **84 K11** 18 45N 78 7 E
Nizhnekamsk, *Russia* **72 C9** 55 38N 51 49 E
Nizhnevartovsk, *Russia* **79 C9** 60 56N 76 38 E
Nizhniy Novgorod, *Russia* **72 C7** 56 20N 44 0 E
Nizhniy Tagil, *Russia* **72 C10** 57 55N 59 57 E
Nizhyn, *Ukraine* **73 D5** 51 5N 31 55 E
Nkongsamba, *Cameroon* **96 D1** 4 55N 9 55 E
Nobeoka, *Japan* **82 G2** 32 36N 131 41 E
Noblesville, *U.S.A.* **112 E5** 40 3N 86 1W
Nogales, *Mexico* **114 A2** 31 20N 110 56W
Nogales, *U.S.A.* **110 D4** 31 20N 110 56W
Noirmoutier, Î. de, *France* **68 C2** 46 58N 2 10W
Nola, *C.A.R.* **96 D3** 3 35N 16 4 E
Nome, *U.S.A.* **108 B3** 64 30N 165 25W
Nord-Ostsee-Kanal, *Germany* **66 A5** 54 12N 9 32 E
Nordelph, *U.K.* **23 G9** 52 35N 0 17 E
Nordfriesische Inseln, *Germany* **66 A5** 54 40N 8 20 E
Nordkapp, *Norway* **63 C9** 71 10N 25 50 E
Nordrhein-Westfalen □, *Germany* **66 C4** 51 45N 7 30 E
Nore →, *Ireland* **31 D9** 52 25N 6 58W
Norfolk, *Nebr., U.S.A.* **111 B7** 42 2N 97 25W
Norfolk, *Va., U.S.A.* **111 C11** 36 51N 76 17W
Norfolk □, *U.K.* **25 A10** 52 39N 0 54 E
Norfolk I., *Pac. Oc.* **99 F12** 28 58S 168 3 E
Norham, *U.K.* **22 A4** 55 43N 2 9W
Norilsk, *Russia* **79 C10** 69 20N 88 6 E
Norman, *U.S.A.* **110 C7** 35 13N 97 26W
Norman Wells, *Canada* **108 B7** 65 17N 126 51W
Normandie, *France* **68 B4** 48 45N 0 10 E
Normanton, *Australia* **98 D7** 17 40S 141 10 E
Normanton, *U.K.* **23 E6** 53 42N 1 24W
Norristown, *U.S.A.* **113 E10** 40 7N 75 21W
Norrköping, *Sweden* **63 F7** 58 37N 16 11 E
Norrland, *Sweden* **63 E7** 62 15N 15 45 E
Norseman, *Australia* **98 G3** 32 8S 121 43 E
Norte, Serra do, *Brazil* **120 D4** 11 20S 59 0W
North, C., *Canada* **109 D13** 47 2N 60 20W
North Battleford, *Canada* **108 C9** 52 50N 108 17W
North Bay, *Canada* **109 D12** 46 20N 79 30W
North Berwick, *U.K.* **21 B10** 56 4N 2 42W
North C., *Canada* **113 B15** 47 5N 64 0W
North C., *N.Z.* **99 G13** 34 23S 173 4 E
North Canadian →, *U.S.A.* **110 C7** 35 16N 95 31W
North Carolina □, *U.S.A.* **111 C11** 35 30N 80 0W
North Cerney, *U.K.* **24 C5** 51 45N 1 57W
North Channel, *Canada* **112 B6** 46 0N 83 0W
North Channel, *U.K.* **20 D4** 55 13N 5 52W
North Dakota □, *U.S.A.* **110 A7** 47 30N 100 15W
North Dorset Downs, *U.K.* **24 E4** 50 51N 2 30W
North Downs, *U.K.* **25 D9** 51 19N 0 21 E
North Esk →, *U.K.* **19 J13** 56 46N 2 24W
North European Plain, *Europe* **56 E10** 55 0N 25 0 E
North Foreland, *U.K.* **25 D11** 51 22N 1 28 E
North Hill, *U.K.* **27 F5** 50 33N 4 27W
North Hykeham, *U.K.* **23 F7** 53 11N 0 35W
North I., *N.Z.* **99 H14** 38 0S 175 0 E
North Korea ■, *Asia* **81 C7** 40 0N 127 0 E
North Magnetic Pole, *Canada* **54 A2** 88 30N 107 0W
North Minch, *U.K.* **18 F6** 58 5N 5 55W
North Molton, *U.K.* **24 D1** 51 3N 3 49W
North Ossetia □, *Russia* **73 F7** 43 30N 44 30 E
North Petherton, *U.K.* **24 D2** 51 5N 3 1W
North Platte, *U.S.A.* **110 B6** 41 8N 100 46W
North Platte →, *U.S.A.* **110 B6** 41 7N 100 42W
North Pole, *Arctic* **54 A** 90 0N 0 0W
North Pt., *Barbados* **115 g** 13 20N 59 37W
North Ronaldsay, *U.K.* **19 D13** 59 22N 2 26W
North Saskatchewan →, *Canada* **108 C9** 53 15N 105 5W
North Sea, *Europe* **64 C7** 56 0N 4 0 E
North Sea Canal = Nord-Ostsee-Kanal, *Germany* **66 A5** 54 12N 9 32 E
North Somercotes, *U.K.* **23 F9** 53 27N 0 8 E
North Sunderland, *U.K.* **22 A5** 55 34N 1 40W
North Tawton, *U.K.* **27 F6** 50 48N 3 54W
North Thompson →, *Canada* **108 C7** 50 40N 120 20W
North Thoresby, *U.K.* **23 F8** 53 28N 0 4W
North Tidworth, *U.K.* **24 D5** 51 15N 1 40W
North Tyne →, *U.K.* **22 C4** 55 0N 2 8W
North Uist, *U.K.* **18 G3** 57 40N 7 15W
North Vernon, *U.S.A.* **112 F5** 39 0N 85 38W
North Walsham, *U.K.* **25 A11** 52 50N 1 22 E
North West C., *Australia* **98 E1** 21 45S 114 9 E
North West Christmas I. Ridge, *Pac. Oc.* **103 G11** 6 30N 165 0W
North West Frontier □, *Pakistan* **84 C7** 34 0N 72 0 E
North West Highlands, *U.K.* **19 G8** 57 33N 4 58W
North West River, *Canada* **109 C13** 53 30N 60 10W
North York Moors, *U.K.* **22 D7** 54 23N 0 53W
North Yorkshire □, *U.K.* **22 D6** 54 15N 1 25W
Northallerton, *U.K.* **22 D6** 54 20N 1 26W
Northam, *Australia* **98 G2** 31 35S 116 42 E
Northam, *U.K.* **27 E5** 51 2N 4 13W
Northampton, *U.K.* **23 H7** 52 15N 0 53W
Northampton, *U.S.A.* **113 D11** 42 19N 72 38W
Northamptonshire □, *U.K.* **23 H7** 52 16N 0 55W
Northern Areas □, *Pakistan* **84 B9** 36 30N 73 0 E
Northern Circars, *India* **85 L13** 17 30N 82 30 E
Northern Ireland □, *U.K.* **29 B8** 54 45N 7 0W
Northern Marianas ⊠, *Pac. Oc.* **102 F6** 17 0N 145 0 E
Northern Territory □, *Australia* **98 E5** 20 0S 133 0 E
Northfleet, *U.K.* **25 D9** 51 26N 0 20 E
Northiam, *U.K.* **25 E10** 50 59N 0 36 E
Northleach, *U.K.* **24 C5** 51 49N 1 50W
Northrepps, *U.K.* **25 A11** 52 54N 1 21 E
Northumberland □, *U.K.* **22 B4** 55 12N 2 0W
Northumberland Str., *Canada* **109 D13** 46 20N 64 0W
Northwest Territories □, *Canada* **108 B9** 63 0N 118 0W
Northwich, *U.K.* **23 F3** 53 15N 2 31W
Northwold, *U.K.* **25 A10** 52 33N 0 36 E
Norton, *N. Yorks., U.K.* **22 D7** 54 8N 0 47W
Norton, *Suffolk, U.K.* **25 B10** 52 16N 0 52 E
Norton Fitzwarren, *U.K.* **24 D2** 51 1N 3 8W
Norton Sd., *U.S.A.* **108 B3** 63 50N 164 0W
Norwalk, *U.S.A.* **112 E6** 41 15N 82 37W
Norway ■, *Europe* **63 E6** 63 0N 11 0 E
Norway House, *Canada* **108 C10** 53 59N 97 50W
Norwegian Sea, *Atl. Oc.* **54 C8** 66 0N 1 0 E
Norwich, *U.K.* **25 A11** 52 38N 1 18 E
Norwich, *U.S.A.* **113 D10** 42 32N 75 32W
Noss Hd., *U.K.* **19 F11** 58 28N 3 3W
Nossob →, *S. Africa* **97 K4** 26 55S 20 45 E
Notre Dame B., *Canada* **109 D14** 49 45N 55 30W
Nottaway →, *Canada* **109 C12** 51 22N 78 55W
Nottingham, *U.K.* **23 G6** 52 58N 1 10W
Nottingham I., *Canada* **109 B12** 63 20N 77 55W
Nottinghamshire □, *U.K.* **23 F6** 53 10N 1 3W
Nouâdhibou, *Mauritania* **94 D2** 20 54N 17 0W
Nouâdhibou, Ras, *Mauritania* **94 D2** 20 50N 17 0W
Nouakchott, *Mauritania* **94 E2** 18 9N 15 58W
Nouméa, *N. Cal.* **99 E12** 22 17S 166 30 E
Nova Casa Nova, *Brazil* **122 A2** 9 25S 41 5W
Nova Friburgo, *Brazil* **122 D2** 22 16S 42 30W
Nova Iguaçu, *Brazil* **122 D2** 22 45S 43 28W
Nova Lima, *Brazil* **122 D2** 19 59S 43 51W
Nova Scotia □, *Canada* **109 D13** 45 10N 63 0W
Nova Venécia, *Brazil* **122 C2** 18 45S 40 24W
Novara, *Italy* **68 D8** 45 28N 8 38 E
Novaya Zemlya, *Russia* **79 B7** 75 0N 56 0 E
Novgorod, *Russia* **72 C5** 58 30N 31 25 E
Novi Sad, *Serbia, Yug.* **71 B8** 45 18N 19 52 E
Novo Remanso, *Brazil* **122 A2** 9 41S 42 4W
Novocherkassk, *Russia* **73 E7** 47 27N 40 15 E
Novokuybyshevsk, *Russia* **72 D8** 53 7N 49 58 E
Novokuznetsk, *Russia* **79 D10** 53 45N 87 10 E
Novomoskovsk, *Russia* **72 D6** 54 5N 38 15 E
Novorossiysk, *Russia* **73 F6** 44 43N 37 46 E
Novoshakhtinsk, *Russia* **73 E6** 47 46N 39 58 E
Novosibirsk, *Russia* **79 D10** 55 0N 83 5 E
Novotroitsk, *Russia* **72 D10** 51 10N 58 15 E
Nowy Sącz, *Poland* **67 D11** 49 40N 20 41 E
Nubia, *Africa* **90 D7** 21 0N 32 0 E
Nubian Desert, *Sudan* **95 D12** 21 30N 33 30 E
Nueces →, *U.S.A.* **110 E7** 27 51N 97 30W
Nueltin L., *Canada* **108 B10** 60 30N 99 30W
Nueva Rosita, *Mexico* **114 B4** 28 0N 101 11W
Nuevitas, *Cuba* **115 C9** 21 30N 77 20W
Nuevo Laredo, *Mexico* **114 B5** 27 30N 99 30W
Nuku'alofa, *Tonga* **99 E16** 21 10S 174 0W
Nukulaelae, *Tuvalu* **99 B14** 9 23S 179 52 E
Nukus, *Uzbekistan* **87 A9** 42 27N 59 41 E
Nullarbor Plain, *Australia* **98 G4** 31 10S 129 0 E
Numazu, *Japan* **82 F6** 35 7N 138 51 E
Nunavut □, *Canada* **109 D8** 66 0N 85 0W
Nuneaton, *U.K.* **23 G6** 52 32N 1 27W
Nunivak I., *U.S.A.* **108 B3** 60 10N 166 30W
Nunney, *U.K.* **24 D4** 51 12N 2 22W
Nuremberg, *Germany* **66 D6** 49 27N 11 3 E
Nusaybin, *Turkey* **73 G7** 37 3N 41 10 E
Nuuk, *Greenland* **109 B14** 64 10N 51 35W
Nyahururu, *Kenya* **96 D7** 0 2N 36 27 E
Nyainqentanglha Shan, *China* **80 D4** 30 0N 90 0 E
Nyâlâ, *Sudan* **95 F10** 12 2N 24 58 E
Nyasa, L., *Africa* **97 G6** 12 30S 34 30 E
Nyíregyháza, *Hungary* **67 E11** 47 58N 21 47 E
Nysa, *Poland* **67 C9** 50 30N 17 22 E

O

Oa, Mull of, *U.K.* **20 C3** 55 35N 6 20W
Oadby, *U.K.* **23 G6** 52 36N 1 5W
Oahe, L., *U.S.A.* **110 A6** 44 27N 100 24W
Oahu, *U.S.A.* **110 H16** 21 28N 157 58W
Oak Hill, *U.S.A.* **112 G7** 37 59N 81 9W
Oak Ridge, *U.S.A.* **111 C10** 36 1N 84 16W
Oakengates, *U.K.* **23 G4** 52 41N 2 26W
Oakham, *U.K.* **23 G7** 52 40N 0 43W
Oakland, *U.S.A.* **110 C2** 37 49N 122 16W
Oates Land, *Antarctica* **55 C11** 69 0S 160 0 E
Oaxaca, *Mexico* **114 D5** 17 2N 96 40W
Ob →, *Russia* **79 C8** 66 45N 69 30 E
Ob, G. of, *Russia* **79 C9** 69 0N 73 0 E
Oba, *Canada* **109 D11** 49 4N 84 7W
Oban, *U.K.* **20 B5** 56 25N 5 29W
Oberhausen, *Germany* **66 C4** 51 28N 6 51 E
Obi, *Indonesia* **83 D4** 1 23S 127 45 E
Óbidos, *Brazil* **120 C4** 1 50S 55 30W
Obihiro, *Japan* **82 B8** 42 56N 143 12 E
Obozerskiy, *Russia* **72 B7** 63 34N 40 21 E
Obshchi Syrt, *Russia* **56 E16** 52 0N 53 0 E
Ocala, *U.S.A.* **111 E10** 29 11N 82 8W
Occidental, Cordillera, *Colombia* **116 C3** 5 0N 76 0W
Ocean City, *U.S.A.* **113 F10** 39 17N 74 35W
Oceanside, *U.S.A.* **110 D3** 33 12N 117 23W
Ochil Hills, *U.K.* **21 B8** 56 14N 3 40W
Ocho Rios, *Jamaica* **114 a** 18 24N 77 6W
Oconto, *U.S.A.* **112 C4** 44 53N 87 52W
Odawara, *Japan* **82 F6** 35 20N 139 6 E
Odense, *Denmark* **63 F6** 55 22N 10 23 E
Oder →, *Europe* **66 B8** 53 33N 14 38 E
Odessa, *Ukraine* **73 E5** 46 30N 30 45 E
Odessa, *U.S.A.* **110 D6** 31 52N 102 23W
Odiham, *U.K.* **25 D7** 51 15N 0 55W
Odintsovo, *Russia* **72 C6** 55 39N 37 15 E
Offa, *Nigeria* **94 G6** 8 13N 4 42 E
Offaly □, *Ireland* **31 B8** 53 15N 7 30W
Offenbach, *Germany* **66 C5** 50 6N 8 44 E
Ogaden, *Ethiopia* **88 F3** 7 30N 45 30 E
Ōgaki, *Japan* **82 F5** 35 21N 136 37 E
Ogasawara Gunto, *Pac. Oc.* **102 E6** 27 0N 142 0 E
Ogbomosho, *Nigeria* **94 G6** 8 1N 4 11 E
Ogden, *U.S.A.* **110 B4** 41 13N 111 58W
Ogdensburg, *U.S.A.* **113 C10** 44 42N 75 30W
Ogooué →, *Gabon* **96 E1** 1 0S 9 0 E
Ohio □, *U.S.A.* **112 E5** 40 15N 82 45W
Ohio →, *U.S.A.* **111 C9** 36 59N 89 8W
Ohře →, *Czech Rep.* **66 C8** 50 30N 14 10 E
Ohrid, L., *Macedonia* **71 D9** 41 8N 20 52 E
Oil City, *U.S.A.* **112 E8** 41 26N 79 42W
Oise →, *France* **68 B5** 49 0N 2 4 E
Oistins, *Barbados* **115 g** 13 4N 59 33W
Oistins B., *Barbados* **115 g** 13 4N 59 33W
Ōita, *Japan* **82 G2** 33 14N 131 36 E
Ojos del Salado, Cerro, *Argentina* **121 E3** 27 0S 68 40W
Oka →, *Russia* **72 C7** 56 20N 43 59 E
Okara, *Pakistan* **84 D8** 30 50N 73 31 E
Okavango Delta, *Botswana* **97 H4** 18 45S 22 45 E
Okayama, *Japan* **82 F3** 34 40N 133 54 E
Okazaki, *Japan* **82 F5** 34 57N 137 10 E
Okeechobee, L., *U.S.A.* **111 E10** 27 0N 80 50W
Okehampton, *U.K.* **27 F5** 50 44N 4 0W
Okhotsk, *Russia* **79 D16** 59 20N 143 10 E
Okhotsk, Sea of, *Asia* **79 D16** 55 0N 145 0 E
Oki-Shotō, *Japan* **82 E3** 36 5N 133 15 E
Okinawa-Jima, *Japan* **81 D7** 26 32N 128 0 E
Oklahoma □, *U.S.A.* **110 C7** 35 20N 97 30W
Oklahoma City, *U.S.A.* **110 C7** 35 30N 97 30W
Oktyabrsk, *Kazakhstan* **73 E10** 49 28N 57 25 E
Oktyabrskiy, *Russia* **72 D9** 54 28N 53 28 E
Öland, *Sweden* **63 F7** 56 45N 16 38 E
Olavarría, *Argentina* **121 F3** 36 55S 60 20W
Old Basing, *U.K.* **24 D6** 51 16N 1 3W
Old Crow, *Canada* **108 B6** 67 30N 139 55W
Old Fletton, *U.K.* **23 G8** 52 33N 0 14W
Old Leake, *U.K.* **23 F9** 53 2N 0 5 E
Old Town, *U.S.A.* **113 C13** 44 56N 68 39W
Oldbury, *U.K.* **24 C3** 51 38N 2 33W
Oldcastle, *Ireland* **29 D7** 53 46N 7 10W
Oldenburg, *Germany* **66 B5** 53 9N 8 13 E
Oldham, *U.K.* **23 E4** 53 33N 2 7W
Oldmeldrum, *U.K.* **19 H13** 57 20N 2 19W
Olean, *U.S.A.* **112 D8** 42 5N 78 26W
Olekminsk, *Russia* **79 C14** 60 25N 120 30 E
Olenek →, *Russia* **79 B14** 73 0N 120 10 E
Oléron, Î. d', *France* **68 D3** 45 55N 1 15W
Oliveira, *Brazil* **122 D2** 20 39S 44 50W
Ollagüe, *Chile* **120 E3** 21 15S 68 10W
Ollerton, *U.K.* **23 F6** 53 12N 1 1W
Olney, *U.K.* **25 B7** 52 10N 0 41W
Olney, *U.S.A.* **112 F3** 38 44N 88 5W
Olomouc, *Czech Rep.* **67 D9** 49 38N 17 12 E
Olsztyn, *Poland* **67 B11** 53 48N 20 29 E
Olt →, *Romania* **67 G13** 43 43N 24 51 E
Olympia, *U.S.A.* **110 A2** 47 3N 122 53W
Olympus, Mt., *Greece* **71 D10** 40 6N 22 23 E
Olympus, Mt., *U.S.A.* **110 A2** 47 48N 123 43W
Omagh, *U.K.* **28 B7** 54 36N 7 19W
Omaha, *U.S.A.* **111 B7** 41 17N 95 58W
Oman ■, *Asia* **88 C6** 23 0N 58 0 E
Oman, G. of, *Asia* **87 E9** 24 30N 58 30 E
Ombersley, *U.K.* **23 H4** 52 16N 2 13W
Omdurmân, *Sudan* **95 E12** 15 40N 32 28 E
Ometepec, *Mexico* **114 D5** 16 39N 98 23W
Omsk, *Russia* **79 D9** 55 0N 73 12 E
Ōmuta, *Japan* **82 G2** 33 5N 130 26 E
Ondangwa, *Namibia* **97 H3** 17 57S 16 4 E
Onega →, *Russia* **72 B6** 63 58N 38 2 E
Onega, G. of, *Russia* **72 B6** 64 24N 36 38 E
Onega, L., *Russia* **72 B6** 61 44N 35 22 E
Oneida, *U.S.A.* **113 D10** 43 6N 75 39W
O'Neill, *U.S.A.* **110 B7** 42 27N 98 39W
Oneonta, *U.S.A.* **113 D10** 42 27N 75 4W
Onitsha, *Nigeria* **94 G7** 6 6N 6 42 E
Onny →, *U.K.* **23 H3** 52 24N 2 47W

Onslow B.   **Podgorica**

Podolsk　　　　　　　　　　　　　　　　　　　　　　　　　　　　　　　**Riccall**

Richards Bay ... ... **San Juan**

S

San Juan

Skull